RECOLLECTIONS OF THREE REIGNS

E·P·DUTTON & CO. INC.
1852 1952
CELEBRATING 100 YEARS OF PUBLISHING

QUEEN VICTORIA.

KING EDWARD VII.

KING GEORGE V.

Recollections of Three Reigns

By

Sir Frederick Ponsonby
first Lord Sysonby

Prepared for press with
notes and an introductory memoir by
COLIN WELCH

New York

E. P. DUTTON & CO., INC.

1952

Library of Congress Catalog Card Number: 52-8262

CONTENTS

5

CONTENTS

BOOK II

6

CONTENTS

7

CONTENTS

8

MEMOIR AND INTRODUCTION

AT THE TIME of his death in October 1935, Lord Sysonby, longer and better known as Sir Frederick Ponsonby, had been Keeper of His Majesty's Privy Purse for twenty-one years. He had spent in all more than forty years in service at Court; his experience was unique, and his passing was comparable to that of an institution.

Born on September 16, 1867, he was a son of General Sir Henry Ponsonby, for many years Private Secretary to Queen Victoria. He was one of three brothers, one older and one younger than himself. They were and remained a devoted trio, despite political differences in later life. All three were to achieve distinction; the eldest, who survives his brothers, is now Major-General Sir John Ponsonby, and the youngest, Arthur, later became Lord Ponsonby of Shulbrede.

Frederick Ponsonby was educated at Eton. He received a commission in the Duke of Cornwall's Light Infantry, later transferring to the Grenadier Guards. He acted as aide-de-camp to the Viceroy of India in 1893-4, and then became Equerry, Assistant Keeper of the Privy Purse and Assistant Private Secretary to Queen Victoria. He served in the South African War in 1901-2.

Returning home after the end of hostilities, he occupied his former position at the Court till the death of King Edward VII, when he became Equerry and Assistant Private Secretary to his successor, King George V. He received the K.C.V.O. in 1910, the G.C.V.O. in 1921, and the G.C.B. in 1926. He was appointed a Privy Councillor in 1914.

On the outbreak of war in 1914, he was released from his Court duties and rejoined his regiment. After a short time spent as a permanent president of courts martial, he went to the front and was mentioned in despatches, an episode characteristically ignored in his recollections. In October 1914, he was recalled; the death of Sir William Carington created the vacancy as Keeper of the Privy Purse which he was to fill with great ability till his own death.

During and after the War his duties became increasingly onerous,

9

especially when he was appointed Treasurer as well as Keeper of the Privy Purse in 1920. As the officer entrusted with all the money granted for the personal use of the King, he had to handle very considerable sums, including a large number of charitable contributions. He was also responsible, at the King's wish, for drastic reforms in the economy of the Royal Household.

In 1928, he became Deputy-Constable and Lieutenant-Governor of Windsor Castle, and he was raised to the Peerage as Lord Sysonby in 1935.

He married Victoria (Ria), daughter of Colonel Hegan Kennard, in 1899 and was succeeded as Lord Sysonby by his only surviving son, the Hon. Edward Gaspard Ponsonby.

* * * * *

In his personal memoir, *King George V,* Mr. John Gore wrote of Sir Frederick: 'If his character was contradictory, his gifts were great. On all social problems and matters of etiquette he was the court of first instance and the court of final appeal. His knowledge of Germany was invaluable. His resource, his conversational gifts, his wit, his faultless manners, adorned and sweetened life in the royal circle.'

A man of good appearance and presence, Sir Frederick was a courtier to his finger-tips. He took great pride in his profession and had no patience with those who dismissed it with a sneer or regarded it as mere sycophancy. His own life was far from an idle or empty one, and he performed all his duties with efficiency and despatch. His methods were not always orthodox or business-like; he knew little of finance or book-keeping, and never kept a copy of a letter. But a saving common sense always came to his rescue.

His devotion to the Royal Family was profound and absolutely genuine. It sprang partly from his long-standing friendship with many of its members and partly from his respect, or even veneration, for the monarchy as an institution. Though he accepted implicitly the present limitation of the royal prerogative, he regarded the King's role constitutionally as one of supreme importance. The monarch was to him not only the fountain of honour, but a repository of hereditary *savoir-faire* and political instinct: any minister who did not consider his sovereign's advice was guilty of grave neglect. While ministries rose and fell, the monarch always remained, above and yet part of politics; he alone, in Sir Frederick's eyes, had long and continuous experience of public affairs and would be at all times likely to take the long view.

Sir Frederick himself always emphasized in his papers that one of the courtier's most important tasks was to keep the sovereign in touch with public opinion and events. Indeed, at a very early age he was told by Queen Victoria that he was far too outspoken and should learn not to express views which no one wished to hear. In later life, however, his advice was sought and usually followed.

But it was in ceremonial matters that Sir Frederick was absolutely in his element. His knowledge of what was done and not done, worn or not worn, said or left unsaid, was exact and comprehensive; no minor slip in etiquette or uniform escaped his notice. Anyone guilty of a breach of convention he would speak of disdainfully as *'the fellow'*! He was an excellent linguist and his knowledge of foreign customs, though not profound, was wide and practical. In conversation, he was polite and inscrutable; even those who knew him well could not always tell whether or not a remark had pleased him.

Yet no man could have been less inhuman. He was the master of convention, never its slave. No one appreciated pomp and circumstance more than he; no one could be more delighted when all was 'well done'. Yet he never mistook the outward form for the real thing. This is well illustrated by the letter he wrote to his solicitor before he died: 'While it is a charming idea that a man's relatives and friends should attend a memorial service and, so to speak, say "Goodbye" to him as he passes on, it so often happens that his nearest relations and most intimate friends are away or unable to attend. Therefore, the service is attended by those who come as a duty and those who are representing someone. It is for this reason that . . . I should prefer that only my wife, my son and my daughter, if they happen to be in London, should attend my funeral, and that there should be no memorial service.'

11

He was personally modest, expecting only the deference due to his rank and position. He had many friends and was always the best of company; like Bismarck, he had little regard for those who had not drunk and gambled a little in their youth. He always lived well, usually to the limits of an income which was never large and which he sometimes thought of augmenting in the most improbable ways; at one time he nursed a project for writing film scripts, and he was always interested in the possibility of raising King John's treasure from the Wash. To his powers as a raconteur, to his vivacity and zest for life, to his charm and sense of fun, the following pages are the best witness.

*   *   *   *   *

In July 1933, Sir Frederick wrote to Mr. S. F. Markham: 'You will be amused to hear that I have embarked on my memoirs, though of course I am keeping this dark. I have merely written down things I remember and the result is like a patchwork quilt. Of course, these cannot be published for many years,[1] but I am doing them now as my memory is still pretty good.' He then asked Mr. Markham if he would look through and criticize the memoirs as they took shape, 'noting "omit", "shorten", "add details about. . . ."' in the margin. This Mr. Markham agreed to do.

Mr. Markham was an old friend and collaborator of Sir Frederick's. On the death of Sir Sydney Lee, he had been entrusted with the completion of the *Life of King Edward VII;* he had consulted Sir Frederick on all the doubtful points as they arose, and he told me that without Sir Frederick's help the second volume, for which he was responsible, could not have achieved the success it did. Again, when Sir Frederick decided to publish the Empress Frederick's letters,[2] Mr. Markham's historical and literary experience was invaluable to him in presenting them to the public. It is, however, worth emphasizing that the present recollections are entirely Sir Frederick's own. Mr. Markham confined himself to advising the author on the presen-

---

[1] He himself stipulated that they should not be published till after the death of all Queen Victoria's children.

[2] The story of how these letters came into Sir Frederick's hands and of the adventures which attended their publication, will be found on pp. 164 *et seq.*

tation of the matter that was laid before him, and was never allowed even to examine the material on which it was based.

This material was described by Sir Frederick in the rough notes which he prepared for a preface (never finished) to *Recollections of Three Reigns*. 'As I have never been able to keep a diary longer than a month, I had no records to work on when I decided to try and put on paper my recollections. Like most people who attempt to write, I found the lack of material an almost insuperable obstacle : incidents and amusing stories were crowded in my memory, but where to begin and how to arrange them in chronological order was altogether beyond me. It was only when I found that my wife had kept my letters to her that I decided to make a start by putting them in order and then making notes of interesting incidents that I remembered to fill in the gaps. If only I could even have kept a record of my engagements, it would have facilitated my efforts and helped me to date incidents accurately.'

Nevertheless, the recollections are quite comprehensive for the latter years of Queen Victoria's reign and for the whole reign of King Edward VII. Sir Frederick felt that political issues had on the whole been sufficiently discussed elsewhere, and he passes lightly over them except where he can throw fresh light on the participants or their motives. But the record of social and ceremonial life, of manners and morals, is complete and satisfying, garnished with the best stories from Sir Frederick's after-dinner repertoire.

The material for the reign of King George V is unfortunately less adequate. Sir Frederick found it increasingly difficult to write about those with whom he was in constant contact. Nevertheless, before he died, he had assembled and put in order some of his letters dealing with the period and had even started to link them together with passages drawn from memory. Some of this material, together with his estimates of many leading figures of the day, was subsequently lost. Book III consists of what remains; it is fragmentary and incomplete, but well worth preserving.

In Books I and II, Sir Frederick summed up Queen Victoria and King Edward VII as he saw them, analysed their characters fairly and sympathetically and described faithfully the qualities which made them loved and respected by their subjects in general and by himself in particular. He would doubtless have wished to do likewise with King George V, but the opportunity was denied him. This omission each reader must repair for himself, bearing in mind the fact that the portrait presented here of a most lovable man and monarch consists of little more than the first brush-strokes on the canvas.

*　　*　　*　　*　　*

My own task has been a simple one. A number of repetitive passages have been suppressed; also a very few which might have caused pain to living people, though on the whole the author's claim in a letter to have 'refrained from ill-natured criticism' is abundantly justified. In Book III I have added some explanatory matter (in italics) which may sometimes help to place the fragments in their true perspective; no attempt, however, has been made to reduce them to a continuous narrative.

Some may feel that there are too many footnotes for a work of this kind. I can only justify my industry by pointing to the sad plight of Herr von Pfyffer, Queen Victoria's German Secretary, mentioned on page 108. Few readers will find themselves as ill-informed as he, who knew not of Mr. Gladstone; but perhaps the memory of his ignorance will make the learned tolerant.

For any errors which have crept into the editorial part of this book, I must accept full responsibility; but I have to acknowledge much assistance in my task. I have to thank Mr. Douglas Jerrold and Sir Charles Petrie for their excellent advice nad criticism and Mr. John Gore for his good wishes and kind permission to quote from his invaluable memoir of King George V. I also owe a debt of gratitude to Mr. Daniel Macmillan for some most valuable information and to my wife for many helpful suggestions. The part played by Mr. S. F. Markham in the initial preparation of the book, and his subsequent assistance to me, could perhaps best be characterized by saying that it might well have been acknowledged on the title page.

C.W.

14

RECOLLECTIONS OF THREE REIGNS

BOOK I

CHAPTER I

Youth — Grenadiers — Days in the field — India

THE EARLY LIVES of great men are tiresome enough in all con-
science, but the adolescence of a mere chronicler of interesting
events would be quite unreadable. The intimate details of my early
life must be assumed because they differed in no way from those
of the rest of my generation. Nor do I intend to weary the reader
with any account of my ancestors, although many writers of auto-
biographies seem to think that details about their ancestry must be
of absorbing interest.

Suffice it to say that my youth was no more idiotic than that of
most of my contemporaries; it was merely uneventful and uninteresting. *'Dans ma plus bête jeunesse'*, as Marcel Prévost puts it, I
always followed the line of least resistance and took a great deal
of trouble to be as like the other boys as possible, avoiding the
things 'that were not done'. At the age of ten I went to Hawtrey's
school at Slough, where I had rather a meteoric career; after three
terms I found myself in the second division and, what I thought
more important, in the second cricket game. Mr. Baldwin was there
with me. When he in after life became Prime Minister I told the
King that he had been at Eton because I was under the impression
that all the boys at Hawtrey's went on to Eton. Baldwin was
furious when the King mentioned this and explained he was at
Harrow.

At the age of twelve I went to Cornish's House at Eton at the
same time as my brother John.[1]

Occasionally as a boy I was brought into contact with statesmen
like Gladstone, Disraeli, Salisbury, Harcourt,[2] and others, who

[1] Later Major-General Sir John Ponsonby.
[2] Sir William Harcourt (1827–1904) ; Chancellor of the Exchequer, 1886 and
1892–5 (revolutionized death duties in Budget of 1894) ; leader of Liberal Party,
1896–8.

17

came to visit my father [3] (who was for many years Private Secretary to Queen Victoria). But as naturally they seldom spoke to me, and as I was singularly unobservant, I remember little worth recording, and that little to my own discomfiture.

Once Gladstone at luncheon was indulging in a scathing attack on the rising generation, pouring scorn on their lack of all knowledge of the classics; and in order to illustrate his point and show the lamentable ignorance that now prevailed, he suddenly turned on me. I was thirteen and at Eton, but my knowledge of the classics was nil. He asked me what the quantity was of some syllable in a quotation from Horace. I had never heard of the quotation and had no idea whether it was long or short, but as I was clearly expected to say something I said 'long'. He thumped the table and cried triumphantly, 'That is what everyone says', and I felt like a man who has backed a winner by mistake. Then in his grand manner he continued, 'But that is wrong, quite wrong; it is short, not long', and after giving very conclusive reasons for this he proceeded: 'Next time you are doing Horace's Odes you will stand up and ask the master whether it is short or long, and when he replies, as he undoubtedly will, that it is long, you will say "No, sir, you are wrong", and you will repeat the reasons I have just given.' I could see myself a pallid youth of thirteen, standing up and laying a trap for the classical master, and then making a muck of the explanation. I could also foresee the quite inevitable result, which would be a sound flogging for impertinence; I never carried out the suggestion.

I remember walking with my two brothers behind Lord Beaconsfield and my father to Whippingham Church; my father was stopped by someone on the road for a few minutes, and we three boys walked on with the sphinxlike Prime Minister. He suddenly asked us where some island in the East was, and of course we didn't know. He murmured, 'My boys, you will probably never get on because you don't know where this island is, but no one expects the British Prime Minister to know where it is.' He then relapsed into silence until my father caught us up.

After Eton had done its best to educate me and I, according to

[3] General the Rt. Hon. Sir Henry Ponsonby.

18

the fashion of the day, had brought to a fine art the practice of doing the minimum amount of work that would suffice to keep me from getting into trouble, I had to go up for the examination for Sandhurst, but a difficulty arose because this took place a week before Henley Regatta. I was at that time rowing in the Eton eight, and Mr. Donaldson, who was coaching us, pointed out that it was impossible for me to do the examination and continue training for the race at Henley. He therefore asked me to choose which I would do, and I at once chose Henley. Unfortunately the point was referred to my father who, not being an old Etonian, knew nothing of the glories of being in the Eton eight, and, perhaps not unnaturally, considered the examination for Sandhurst more important. So without further argument I was eliminated from the eight. I failed in my examination and so missed both opportunities; but, as I was only a few places below the last successful candidate, I was allowed to remain on at Eton for another half and then passed easily into Sandhurst.

When I left Sandhurst there was no prospect of a vacancy in the Grenadiers. As my father, an old Grenadier, would not hear of my going into any other regiment permanently, there was no alternative but to join some other regiment temporarily and be transferred as soon as there was a vacancy.

I was gazetted to the 46th Regiment of Foot (Duke of Cornwall's Light Infantry) and joined them at the Citadel at Plymouth. It was an ideal regiment. It had practically no men. There was an officers' mess, a band, some charming officers, a certain number of excellent N.C.O.s and a sprinkling of old soldiers, but otherwise nothing but recruits. It was what Lord Wolseley described as a 'squeezed lemon'. As soon as a recruit was sufficiently trained, he was packed off to India to feed the other Battalion. Of course, I had to do the goose-step and spend the first few months doing recruits' drill, but after that I had a wonderful time and was away practically every day, merely attending a parade on Saturdays.

It was the custom for all officers off duty to go for a walk round Plymouth every afternoon and have a drink at every opportunity. I used to go with the youngest lot; we had a drink on the pier, then went to the Grand Hotel for a second drink, then to another hotel for a third, then to the Bodega for oysters and Chablis, and finally back to the officers' mess where we had a sherry and bitters. Quite apart from the fact that it was an unwholesome way of spending the afternoon, and that it generally resulted in one's being in a semi-inebriated condition by dinner, there was the daily frittering away of money, which really came to a good deal in the month. I therefore hired a hunter and went out for a ride instead of walking in the town, and once a week I went out hunting with the Dartmoor hounds.

When I joined the Grenadiers I was humiliatingly treated as a raw recruit. I pleaded that I was a trained officer, but was made to begin with the goose-step and recruits' drill. Once I was a fully-fledged subaltern there appeared to be little for me to do. The parades took place in Hyde Park, but, as the Adjutant took the Battalion there, the officers were not expected to join in until the Battalion reached Hyde Park. We all arrived at the last moment in hansom cabs, which, however, were not allowed in the Park itself, and therefore in estimating the exact time it took one to get there, one had to take into consideration the walk from the nearest gate to the parade ground near the Magazine.

When the Battalion went to Windsor I was appointed Whip to the Draghounds, not because I was any use, but because I was likely to be a regular attendant. Harry White was Master, but after the first month he was generally away. I happened by chance to find quite a fast horse, which had been among selling-platers and whose speed as a fox-catcher was unknown. The drag generally developed into a steeplechase, and my usual procedure was to shout authoritatively 'Hold hard! Give the hounds a chance!' and then dig in both spurs and go as hard as I could. This enabled me always to be among the first at the end of the line.

The following year while I was looking out for a good horse I happened to come across one of the most extraordinary horses that ever was foaled. It belonged to Mr. Ernest Pretyman, M.P., and his brother, who was in the Grenadiers, told me it was a good fencer, very fast, and likely to win a point-to-point. I might get it for £100 as it was unknown. Accordingly I went to Tattersalls to bid for it and, to my surprise, got it for £25. This should have warned me that there was something wrong, as it was a big upstanding horse and perfectly sound. The number of people who tried to ride that horse, and the experiences they had, were quite remarkable and would fill a book. Having the horse in London, I lent it to an indifferent rider who did not dare reveal his experiences, but an account in the newspaper of a rider in Rotten Row who had knocked over a pony-cart was generally supposed to describe my friend's adventures. Quite unconscious that there was anything wrong, I lent the animal to my brother John to ride in the Row. The horse went perfectly for about half an hour, when suddenly it took the bit between its teeth, bucked, and bolted just at the end of the Row. It caught an old gentleman broadside, and knocked him and his horse over. After which it bolted nearly the whole length of the Row. A paragraph then appeared in the agony column of *The Times*: 'The galloping cad who knocked an old officer over in Rotten Row yesterday may be glad to learn that there were no bones broken.'

So it was named the Galloping Cad. I determined to try it and accordingly rode it in the Park, but as by then it was getting an evil reputation, I took it up to the top of the Park near Marble Arch. I trotted it and cantered it, sitting very tight and watching every movement, but I found it perfect. After half an hour I pulled up and walked along, slowly pondering whether I should not take it among the other horses in the lower part of the Park. I was completely taken off my guard. Without the slightest warning the animal bucked me off, and I went sprawling. It was most humiliating, especially when Lord Coventry, a fine old sportsman, caught the horse, which had again become like a lamb. I tried to explain matters, but I saw by his face that he thought me a very bad rider.

As my Battalion was going to Pirbright for musketry, I determined to take the horse with me as there would be plenty of room there to tame a wild animal. I had some terrible rides on it. Once it tried to rub me off against a tree, and it constantly bolted and bucked. Drumlanrig, in the Coldstream, who was a good rider, asked me to lend it to him as he wanted to ride out and see his

21

aunt, who lived about six miles off. I told him of its peculiarities and warned him that it was generally coming home that it behaved like a lunatic. The animal went perfectly to start with, and he enjoyed his ride very much, but, on passing through the lodge gates of the house he was visiting, something upset the horse and he arrived at the house at full gallop. Quickly realizing that there was no way through the grounds and that it would be dangerous to gallop back through the lodge gates on to the high-road, Drumlanrig turned the horse on to the lawn and went round and round about thirty times before he could pull up. By that time the beautifully mown lawn was like a ploughed field. He didn't dare go to the house, and thought it best to write afterwards and explain what had happened.

Curiously enough a few days later Edward Tighe in the Grenadiers, who was also quite a good rider, wanted to visit some relations in the neighbourhood, and asked to borrow the horse. I told him of Drumlanrig's adventures, but Tighe said he weighed fourteen stone and no horse would bolt far with him. This time the horse behaved quite well and Tighe visited his relation without mishap. On his return he was congratulating himself on having concealed the fact that he was going home by taking a circuitous route, when the horse bolted and he came back to the stables at full gallop. I happened to be near the stables when I heard the thud of galloping and saw a cloud of dust. I knew at once it was my horse. It pulled up at the stables, and Tighe, in an exhausted condition, said he would never ride it again.

Willy Fox-Pitt, another very fine rider, who understood horses perfectly, said he would like to have a ride on it as he had heard all these terrible stories. He made one stipulation, and that was that he would use a special bit of his own. He mounted the horse at the stables and rode round to make friends with the horse, who, however, didn't like the bit at all. Suddenly, without any warning, the horse put his head down and bolted. The awkward part was that he chose the road or track that led to the rifle-ranges. Away he thundered and we all suddenly realized that the recruits were firing that afternoon. Mercifully, someone saw him coming across the ranges and blew the 'Cease Fire'. Fox-Pitt went right away and took the horse up a steep hill. He laid into the animal and wouldn't let him stop. Eventually he returned with a perfectly tame horse, but admitted that the bit was not a success.

The horse, having proved a failure as a hack, might, I thought, possibly make a good drag horse. At the first meet of the drag, therefore, I rode him. Wilfred Ricardo in the Blues was Master. The horse behaved perfectly at the meet and then jumped beautifully. He seemed to be fairly fast and I finished in the first line among the first few. Then my troubles began. We had to wait about ten minutes to let the stragglers and those who had taken tosses come up. The horse began by being impatient and then became almost unmanageable, rearing, bucking, kicking, and even trying to savage the hounds. I shouted to Ricardo imploring him to get on to the second line, and seeing my difficulties, he decided to do so. But I was all over the place, and had the greatest difficulty in getting to the start of the second line. When we all got away I thought it would be all right, but the horse was thoroughly upset. The first fence we came to was a stout post-and-rail, not a very big jump, but the animal charged it like a bull, and made no attempt to jump at all. I went end over end into the next field, but was not hurt, and the horse went careering all over the country. After an hour I succeeded in capturing him, and then and there I determined to sell him. He went up to Tattersalls, and whenever I heard of any friend thinking of buying him, I told them all about his tricks. Suddenly I heard that Arthur Bigge,[4] who was then Assistant Private Secretary to Queen Victoria, contemplated buying him. I at once went to see him and tried to dissuade him from doing so, but he argued that it would amuse him to try and manage the horse, who was really a fine-looking animal.

There was, of course, no reserve, and Arthur Bigge bought him for £25. After a few days I received a letter from him to say that never had he ridden a more perfect animal. He could not imagine why there had been all these difficulties with him. I thought that

[4] Later 1st Lord Stamfordham. Groom-in-waiting to Queen Victoria, 1880; Assistant Private Secretary, 1880; Equerry-in-Ordinary, 1881; Private Secretary to Queen Victoria, 1895–1901; to Prince of Wales, 1901–10; Private Secretary to King George V from 1910; died 1931.

at last the horse had found its master, but a few days later I read in the newspapers, 'Serious accident out hunting to Colonel Bigge'. It appeared that the horse had bolted and tried to get free of him by taking him amongst trees. He had been finally knocked off by a bough. Arthur Bigge's friends insisted on his selling it, and again it went to Tattersalls, where it was sold for £25. We never heard any more, whether the purchaser was killed or not, or whether the animal recovered. Experts thought there was something the matter with its teeth, and that this accounted for its mad moments.

At this time I had to make a difficult decision, which was whether I should try and become Adjutant or go to India as A.D.C. to the Viceroy. Although I had been Assistant Adjutant for two years and it was generally assumed in the Battalion that I should be the next Adjutant, it was by no means certain that I should be appointed. There was the possibility of my falling between two stools. My finances were at a very low ebb, as I had not only had a racing disaster, but had also got into severe trouble through gambling.

It was the usual custom in those days to gamble very heavily during Ascot week, and the Commanding Officer, Bully Oliphant, a noted gambler himself, had given orders that there were to be no I.O.U.s; everybody would have to play for ready money. This really was a very effective way of preventing people losing more than they could afford to pay. I was away at Hythe at the time, but managed to get away on the Friday and go to the races. That evening I dined in mess and afterwards was made to play whist in the General's rubber for very small points. The General went to bed about 11.30, and I went about looking for a gamble. Eventually I went to the billiard-room, where I found baccarat in full swing. The first opportunity that occurred I bought the bank and had a run of luck. By two o'clock in the morning I had won all the money there was about. Quite unconscious that I was disobeying any rules I said, 'Don't bother about the ready, write I.O.U.s'. At once everyone began gambling in real earnest and while I had been playing with chicken's food before, I was now taking on fairly large amounts. Apparently all the others thought that, as I was an officer of the Battalion quartered at Windsor, I was authorized by the authorities to allow this. The consequence was that by 4 A.M. I had lost all I had won and £500 more. We decided then to go to bed, and the next day I was faced with the problem of how to raise this money. Unfortunately the story got about and was repeated by all the people staying in houses near Windsor, and so of course it reached the ears of the Major-General. The first I knew of this was a letter from the Brigade-Major, Joe Maude, later General Sir Stanley Maude, saying that it had come to the notice of the Major-General that I had gambled at Windsor Barracks and lost a large sum. I was therefore (a) to state the sum I had lost, (b) to describe the circumstances under which I had lost it, (c) to give the names of all the players. I replied that no-one regretted more than I did that I had played baccarat and lost £500. With regard to the last item, however, while I was of course prepared to undergo any censure or punishment which it would be necessary to inflict on me, I did not feel called upon to reveal who the other players were. I received a second letter saying that I had obviously not understood that the first letter was an order from the Major-General, and that in refusing to reveal the names of the other players I was guilty of refusing to obey an order. I replied a second time that this was an order which I could not obey. Bully Oliphant, who had been away, returned, and on hearing the story exploded with rage. He had thought he had made such a thing impossible, and he cursed me roundly. I made it clear that I had not heard of his new rule about playing for ready money, and explained the circumstances under which I had joined the game. Having abused me roundly, he then asked to see the letters I had received, and to my surprise he said I was quite right in refusing to give the names of the other players, and added that he would go to London and see the General about it.

This was where a big man would act in quite a different way from a small-minded man. He was known to be a gambler and everyone would say it was his fault. Instead, however, of throwing me to the wolves and riding off scot-free, here he was taking up my case and prepared to argue with the General about it. The result of his representations to the General was that I was sent for to London and properly wigged, but the point about my refusing to give away the others was dropped.

So my finances were still very low, and after insuring my life and borrowing the money, it seemed to me that the prospect of being able to live in India on my pay offered the surest method of getting straight. There was also the consideration that the General would refuse to allow me to be appointed Adjutant. So I chose India.

I went out with the Elgins,[5] who relieved the Lansdownes in India. The Viceregal staff consisted of Colonel Durant (Military Secretary), Babington Smith [6] (Private Secretary), Pollen, Adam, Baker, Car, Fuller, Bentinck, and myself (A.D.C.s), and Franklyn, the doctor.

My first night in Bombay was a revelation to me. The East was so different from anything I had seen. The noises, the smells, the mysterious behaviour of the gorgeously apparelled servants, the magnificence of the Governor of Bombay's palace, all fascinated me.

The life of an A.D.C. in India was an ideal one for a poor man. Living on my pay, I could afford to keep two polo-ponies, a pony-cart, and two Indian servants, which in England would have been out of the question. Each A.D.C. was given a particular department to supervise, but most of the real work was done by the Private and Military Secretaries.

I always hoped that if there was fighting on the North-West Frontier I might have a good chance of getting there on somebody's staff. I therefore at once began to learn Hindustani. My Munshi [7] came to me every morning at 7 A.M., after I had been out riding. He was a placid old man with a long beard and seemed quite content to sit in the verandah gazing into space. One morning I was very late, having been to a ball the night before and stayed very late. I apologized and gave the reason for being late. He merely remarked, 'This night revelling will make you weak'.

In December 1894 (or whatever date it was) I suddenly re-

[5] Victor Alexander Bruce, 9th Earl of Elgin; Viceroy of India, 1894–99.
[6] Later Sir Henry Babington Smith.
[7] Teacher.

ceived a telegram from Queen Victoria herself offering me the post of Equerry, but I was not at all anxious to return home. I had been very happy in India and, as I had taken the trouble to pass the lower standard and was about to go up for the higher standard in Hindustani, I thought there might be some chance of my seeing active service on the North-West Frontier, all of which would be impossible if I went home. I was, however, given permission to remain out for another three months, and went on a tour round the North-West Frontier with the Viceroy, up the Khyber Pass and to all the principal places in that part of India.

CHAPTER II

Equerry to Queen Victoria — Osborne — Windsor
— Balmoral

WHEN MAJOR-GENERAL Sir Henry Ewart was appointed Crown
Equerry in 1894, that is, the official in charge of the stables, it
created a vacancy among Queen Victoria's Equerries.

In Charles II's reign, the Groom-in-Waiting was the man who
made all the arrangements for the King's journeys and for all the
private ceremonies that were not managed by one of the great
officers of State. He was the only official who attended the King
when he went in the Royal Barge. This post continued to be the
pivot of the Royal Household until Queen Victoria's reign when,
in order that Her Majesty should be attended by adherents of the
Government in office, all grooms were made Parliamentary
grooms, that is to say, they were members of Parliament. As this
entailed their coming in and going out with the Government, it
was obviously impossible to make them responsible for arrangements of any description, and so the Equerries took their places
while the Grooms became purely ceremonial officers.

Whenever a vacancy occurred in the Household all sorts of suggestions were invariably put forward by members of the Royal
Family, but Queen Victoria had definite ideas of her own. On this
occasion she determined to do what she thought would please my
father, Sir Henry Ponsonby, who had been her Private Secretary
for a great many years, and appoint me as a surprise for him.
She therefore telegraphed direct to me in India without telling
him, and the first he heard of it was a telegram from me asking
if I could refuse. He might have thought I was too young at the
age of twenty-seven for such a post. He, however, replied that I
could not well refuse and so I accepted. Later I heard there were

29

two subsidiary reasons for Queen Victoria's deciding to offer me the appointment. I had acted in a French play at Osborne and she thought I should be useful to her in France as I spoke French well. Secondly, there were questions relating to her Indian attendants which she thought that I, fresh from India, would be able to deal with.

As my duties as Equerry to Queen only occupied four months in the year, I had to serve as a soldier for the remaining eight. In those days this presented no real difficulty, but, despite the fact that most of my four months' duty as Equerry had to come out of my leave, I soon incurred the wrath of my commanding officer on account of my absences from the battalion. He suddenly became very democratic, and said that it was monstrous that I should count as an ordinary officer in the battalion when I was so often away. But as my position was laid down in regulations, he could do no more than make caustic remarks on the subject.

When I was gazetted Equerry it shocked the military mind, and the chronicler in the *Guards' Magazine* pointed out that this was a solitary instance of a Lieutenant succeeding a Major-General.

The secret of the unique position Queen Victoria held in this country was that she was the personification of the virtues that were most admired at that time. She was, so to speak, the Mother of Europe, and her influence was felt in most European countries. To have discussed political problems with Prime Ministers and statesmen of every party during her long reign alone gave her an immense advantage in her later years, to say nothing of the fact that, while Governments went in and out, she remained at the head of affairs and insisted on being kept fully informed not only on all domestic affairs, but also about everything connected with foreign affairs and the Dominions.

Sir Henry Campbell-Bannerman [1] told me that once, when he was trying to persuade her to withdraw her opposition to some measure proposed by the Liberal Government, she said to him, 'I

---

[1] (1836–1908) ; Secretary for War, 1886 and 1892–5, when allegations that the War Office was insufficiently supplied with cordite led to the fall of the Rosebery Government; became leader of Liberal Party in 1899 and later Prime Minister, 1905–8.

remember Lord Melbourne using the same arguments many years ago, but it was not true then and it is not true now'. He said he felt like a little boy talking to his grandmother.

I was always struck with the facility with which she expressed herself on paper. She never seemed to want for a word and there is no doubt that very few women of her time would have been able to write the letters and telegrams she did. Her grasp of foreign politics was quite remarkable, but in this she had been well schooled from her youth, first by 'Uncle Leopold', the King of the Belgians, and later by the Prince Consort.

I remember Lord Esher [2] telling me that when he and Arthur Benson had been asked by King Edward to publish her letters,[3] they at first decided to publish only those letters which had been written up to the death of the Prince Consort, as they were under the impression that he had inspired her writings and that after his death the letters would deteriorate. When, however, they looked at the later letters, they found to their surprise that, so far from deteriorating, they became even more interesting. Although possibly they lost in literary style, they gained in interest as they were far more forcibly expressed and full of character.

In 1894 I did my first month's waiting as Equerry. Although I had known a great many people in the Royal Household in my youth, I was quite ignorant of how things were done; nor did I know how the ordinary routine work was distributed. Although I was at an age when I thought I knew everything, I was mercifully shy, and therefore probably not bumptious. My first waiting began at Osborne, where I found Lord Bridport,[4] Lord-in-Waiting, aged eighty, General Sir Michael Biddulph, Groom-in-Wait-

[2] Reginald Baliol Brett, 2nd Viscount Esher. No mere recital of offices held does justice to this remarkable man. On the one hand, he was an intimate friend of Queen Victoria, King Edward VII and King George V; on the other, he was closely in touch with Lord Rosebery, Mr. Balfour and Sir Henry Campbell-Bannerman. His advice was greatly valued by both sides. In other fields, his most important work was connected with army reform, in which he was a strong supporter of Lord Haldane.

[3] *Selections from the Correspondence of Queen Victoria,* edited by Viscount Esher and A. C. Benson, was published in 1907.

[4] Alexander Nelson Hood, 1st Viscount Bridport; grandson of 1st Earl Nelson (Horatio Nelson's brother).

ing, aged seventy, General Sir Lyndoch Gardiner, aged eighty, and my father, Sir Henry Ponsonby, the Queen's Private Secretary, who was over seventy. They must have disliked a young man of twenty-seven being thrust on them, but they never showed it and all were kindness itself.

I soon found that the duties of the Junior Equerry were nil. He had to ride by the Queen's carriage if two Equerries were wanted, or if the Senior Equerry were unable to do so, but otherwise he was not expected to take any part in the routine work. I therefore contented myself with making copies of all the orders issued by the Senior Equerry and picking up as much as I could of the way the machine worked.

The Queen kept very much aloof from the Household generally and everything had to be written to her. Even Sir Arthur Bigge did his work this way. There was, of course, the advantage of having the Queen's decisions on paper, but it gave quite an unnecessary amount of work. The ladies of the Household naturally saw more of the Queen than the men, but as regards myself, I never saw her except when I was invited to dinner. It was a great crime to meet her in the grounds when she was out in her pony chair, and of course we all took very good care that this should never happen. If by any unlucky chance we did come across her, we hid behind bushes. Sir William Harcourt, walking one day with my father, looked up and saw the Queen coming down the path. There was only one small shrub near, and Harcourt asked whether he was expected to hide behind that, but as he was six feet four inches high, my father suggested that the wisest thing to do was simply to turn back.

Unfortunately I had displeased the Queen when I had first been appointed, and it took several years before I was forgiven. She had before I joined the Household a Khitmagar named Abdul Karim, whom she had promoted to be Munshi. There was nothing wrong about this because he was a Mohammedan, and a Munshi, or teacher, is not very high up in the Indian world. Abdul Karim, however, gave himself great airs on his promotion and alleged that his father was a Surgeon-General in the Indian Army. The

Queen thereupon telegraphed to me while I was still in India and instructed me to go and see the father at Agra. I stayed with General Morton there and of course took steps to obey the Queen's commands; I found that the man was not a Surgeon-General but only the apothecary at the jail. I saw him and we had a conversation in Hindustani, but as my knowledge of the language only enabled me to talk platitudes about the weather and the beauties of India, it was not a very inspiring conversation.

When I returned home and took up my appointment the Queen asked whether I had seen Abdul Karim's father and I replied I had done so, but that I had found he was only the apothecary at the jail at Agra. She stoutly denied this and thought I must have seen the wrong man, but I maintained that I was right.

I was under the impression at first that I had merely cleared up some point under discussion, but I soon found that it had been a singularly inopportune moment to have blurted out this undoubtedly true statement of fact.

The Queen had begun to show the Munshi letters and despatches from India and it was found that he had an undesirable friend who was in touch with the disorderly elements in India. Quite obviously this might have led to trouble and therefore Sir Arthur Bigge, Sir Fleetwood Edwards,[5] Sir James Reid,[6] and Colonel Davidson [7] thought it their duty to protest. The result was that the Queen was very angry and did not hesitate to show her displeasure by never speaking to any of them. It was then that I came on the scene and, quite unconscious of the delicacy of the situation, told her that the Munshi's father was not a General but apothecary at the Agra jail. The Queen very much resented this

[5] Sir Fleetwood Isham Edwards. Assistant Keeper of the Privy Purse and Assistant Private Secretary to Queen Victoria, 1878–95; Groom-in-Waiting, 1880–95; Keeper of the Privy Purse to Queen Victoria, 1895–1901; Extra Equerry to Queen Victoria and King Edward VII, 1888–1910. Died 1910.

[6] Sir James Reid, 1st Bart. Resident Physician to Queen Victoria and Physician-in-Ordinary to King Edward VII and King George V. Died 1923.

[7] Later Colonel Sir Arthur Davidson. Groom-in-Waiting to Queen Victoria and later Equerry-in-Waiting, 1895–1901; Equerry, Assistant Keeper of the Privy Purse and Assistant Private Secretary to King Edward VII, 1901–1910; Extra Equerry to King George V and Equerry to Queen Alexandra, from 1910. Died 1922.

proof of the Munshi's untrustworthiness being brought forward at such a moment and was therefore particularly vexed with me.

She asked Prince Louis of Battenberg [8] to come to Osborne and put things right, and no better man could have been chosen. At first he entirely took the Queen's side and maintained that she had a perfect right to show what letters she chose to the Munshi, but when he learnt the other side of the question, and saw the letter from Lord George Hamilton,[9] the Secretary of State for India, to the effect that it would be impossible for him to send highly confiidential papers in future to the Queen if she showed them to the Munshi, he saw that what seemed a trivial matter might have very dangerous consequences. He told her frankly that in India the Hindus would very much resent a Mohammedan being placed in the position of adviser, and that the Indian Princess would not be able to understand a Munshi being placed in such a responsible position.

The result of all this was that the Queen abandoned the idea of letting the Munshi see confidential papers, but in order to show her complete confidence in him she said in future he was to be called her Indian Secretary.

To mark her displeasure towards me, the Queen did not ask me to dinner for a year, I spent a month with her at Cimiez, where there were only Sir Arthur Bigge, Sir James Reid and Sir William Carington,[10] besides myself, to ring the changes on, and yet I was never once invited to dinner, nor did I speak to her during the visit. The day she left for England it was my duty to stand on the reverse side of the carriage in case some unauthorized person should attempt to approach, and there I stood in a tall hat and frock-coat. Just before she got out of the carriage she turned to me and said, 'What a pity it is to leave Nice in such beautiful weather!'

This attitude lasted for a whole year and then, although I was by no means forgiven, I was invited to dinner occasionally.

[8] Later 1st Marquess of Milford Haven. First Sea Lord, 1912–14.
[9] Son of 1st Duke of Abercorn.
[10] Sir William H. P. Carington. Groom-in-Waiting and later Equerry to Queen Victoria, 1880–1901; Comptroller to the Prince of Wales, 1901–10; Keeper of the Privy Purse to King George V from 1910. Died 1914.

Back at Osborne I found life very peaceful, especially in the winter. The Queen spent July and August there, and also December and January. Her Majesty went out in a pony-chair in the morning accompanied by the Lady-in-Waiting or a Maid of Honour, and in the afternoon drove out in a carriage and pair, with an outrider in front. Grey horses were always used: grey ponies they were called in the Equerries' language, but what the origin of this erroneous description of them was I was never able to discover. They were sixteen hands high, and so the word 'pony' was obviously wrong. An Equerry was only required when the Queen drove through Cowes or through Newport or Ryde. Anything in the nature of a function of any sort necessitated two Equerries riding. The Household was expected to be indoors when the Queen was in, but could go out when she did.

Osborne House was mid-Victorian in decoration and some of the rooms were quite startling in their ugliness. Lord Rosebery once said that he thought the drawing-room was the ugliest room in the world, until he saw the drawing-room at Balmoral.

Everyone came down to breakfast and then we all went to our work. This was not easy in my case as I had nothing to do, but I went to the Equerry's room where I had a writing-table, and having read the newspapers, wrote private letters. At noon the Queen went out and the members of the Household all went for a walk, but it was like a lunatic asylum as everybody went alone in different directions. At two o'clock we all assembled for luncheon, where the Master of the Household carved at one end of the table and the Equerry at the other. I had never done much of this and at first my slices of meat were only fit for the workhouse, but by degrees I gained a certain proficiency in the art. These luncheons were always very amusing as there was much wit among the older men. At three the Queen went out driving and again all the members of the Household went walking by themselves. At five the ladies had a big tea, but the men had tea in their several rooms. There was little or nothing to be done till dinner, when we all dressed up in knee-breeches and stockings. All the old men wore breeches which came down to the ankle and were buttoned there. It was supposed to give the same impression as stockings. In most cases they fitted so badly that they resembled the more ancient peg-topped trousers. Lord Salisbury, who as Prime Minister constantly came down to dine and sleep, had such ill-fitting breeches that they looked like ordinary trousers.

The silence in the house was almost oppressive at dinner-time, and those who were asked to dine with the Queen solemnly walked down the corridor with mosaic floors and statues talking almost in a whisper. Sometimes the men were wanted to join the Queen's dinner-party, but if they were not they adjourned to the billiard-room where smoking was allowed.

All this seemed to suit the members of the Household who were over seventy, but I soon found it didn't suit me. In summer I took to bathing before breakfast and swam from a bathing barge where the Royal children were taught to swim later in the day. In the afternoons I rode about the grounds, which were, however, ill-suited for riding as there was little grass. The Household had luncheon separately, but a certain number always dined with the Queen. One of the footmen, who was noted for his cockney accent and lack of good manners, conveyed the Queen's wishes with regard to dinner by putting his head in at the door of the Ladies-in-Waiting drawing-room and saying, 'All what's 'ere dines with the Queen'.

The Queen had a rooted objection to smoking and even disliked reading letters written by anyone who had smoked when writing. Once I received a message from her asking me not to smoke when deciphering telegrams because the official box in which I sent her the decoded telegram smelt strongly of tobacco.

No one was allowed to smoke in any part of Osborne House where the smell might possibly reach the Royal nostrils; this was odd because all her family smoked like chimneys. Originally a smoking-room had been built outside in the garden, a most inconvenient arrangement, as it was unconnected with the house and smokers when it was wet had to walk in the rain to get to it. Later smoking was allowed in the billiard-room, but of course, not in the Household dining-room.

Smoking at Windsor necessitated a very long walk for the guests, as the billiard-room, which was the only room in which smoking was allowed, was a long way off. In conceding the billiard-room to smokers the Queen thought she was really doing all that was necessary. If any gentleman wished to indulge in the disgusting habit of smoking he should go as far away as possible. Many years earlier the Queen had to tackle the difficult problem of smoking. It was when Prince and Princess Christian [11] were married and he came to Balmoral. The Queen heard to her horror that he smoked. It was not so bad as if he drank, but still it was a distinct blemish on his otherwise impeccable character. The Queen, however, decided to be broad-minded and actually to give him a room where he could indulge in this habit. A small room was found near the servants' quarters which could only be reached by crossing the open kitchen courtyard, and in this bare room was placed a wooden chair and table. She looked upon this room as a sort of opium-den. Later when Prince Henry of Battenberg married Princess Beatrice [12] he induced the Queen to alter this barbarous smoking-room, and although she insisted on its being more or less in the servants' quarters, it could be reached without going out of doors, and it was suitably furnished with armchairs, sofas, and writing-tables.

At Windsor the Queen remained in the drawing-room till about eleven and then the guests were allowed to retire to the billiard-room to smoke. A procession was formed and after a long walk the guests reached the smoking-room. A page had to sit up to conduct them to their bedrooms, but often his services were dispensed with when the guests had been at Windsor before.

One night Baron D'Estournelles de Constant,[13] who was later known as 'L'Ange de la Paix', came to dine and sleep. He said he knew his way and therefore would not require the services of the page. He remained up till one o'clock having an interesting discussion with someone whose bedroom happened to be in quite another part of the Castle. The two said 'Goodnight' and D'Estournelles went off to his bedroom. He started well and went up the

---

[11] Prince Christian of Schleswig-Holstein married Princess Helena Victoria, Queen Victoria's third daughter.
[12] Fifth daughter of Queen Victoria.
[13] A prolific writer on peace and member of the two Hague conferences.

stone staircase flanked on each side by armoured figures both on foot and on wooden horses, and he found his way quite correctly into St. George's Hall, a long gallery nearly three hundred feet in length. In those days the castle was lighted at night by little oil lamps with a circular glass shade, placed in niches in the wall. According to modern standards they gave a miserable light, sufficient to anyone who knew his way, but D'Estournelles didn't. At the end of St. George's Hall there were two doors on each side of the throne and, although no real attempt was made to disguise the doors, the woodwork was made to look like the panelling in the rest of the hall. He should have tried the right-hand door, but it happened to be closed and so he went through the left-hand door which was open. After trying different doors he found himself in the chapel and then in the vestry, which was clearly wrong. So he returned and tried other exits from St. George's Hall, always to find himself, like *Alice through the looking glass,* back again eventually in St. George's Hall. After a long perambulation he decided to return to the billiard-room and start again, but he never succeeded in finding the right door from St. George's Hall, and curiously enough never came across any of the night watchmen. When two o'clock came he abandoned the search, collected some rugs and mats, and made himself as comfortable as he could on one of the sofas in the State gallery adjoining the Waterloo gallery. There he slept till the next morning when one of the housemaids came across him, and feeling sure he had been drunk the night before, went off and brought a policeman. He explained the whole thing, but he could see by their faces that neither the policeman nor the housemaid believed a word of his story.

Another case of nocturnal perambulations occurred at Buckingham Palace when Colonel John Clerk, Equerry to Princess Beatrice, was temporarily given one of the bedrooms usually reserved for visitors. It was during the visit of some foreign monarch, and the suite being numerous, the Master of the Household had found some difficulty in providing accommodation for them. It had, however, all been satisfactorily arranged, but when they all arrived the announcement was made that still another lady was arriving later in the evening. The Master of the Household, Lord

Edward Pelham-Clinton,[14] was at his wit's end to know where to put her when he suddenly remembered that Colonel Clerk was occupying one of the guests' bedrooms. The obvious solution occurred to him of asking Clerk to go to a smaller bedroom for a few days to make way for this foreign lady, but he was told that Clerk had gone away for the day and taken his evening clothes with him, which meant that he would not be back till late. He therefore gave instructions for Clerk's things to be moved to another room, wrote a note explaining the matter to Clerk and told the night porter it was to be handed to Clerk on his return.

Clerk having gone to the country and stayed for dinner, sauntered in about one o'clock and was let in by a night porter who quite forgot to hand him the letter. So up in the lift he went, and on arriving at what he thought was still his bedroom he switched on the electric light and walked in. Still unconscious that it was occupied he took off his top-hat and put it on the bed. What he really did was to put it on the lady's stomach, and she woke with a piercing yell. Clerk gazed at her in bed with astonishment and then fled from the room, where he remained outside trying to elucidate the mystery of this furious female in his bed; his thoughts were interrupted by the door of the bedroom being cautiously opened and his top-hat being hurled from the room. He then realized that this most compromising evidence had been left behind. But the question where he was expected to lay his weary head still remained unsolved and so down the lift he went in search of the night porter. He found him in his place at the door, and on asking where his bedroom was, the letter of explanation was handed to him.

The Equerries lived at Barton Manor, a farm-house about a mile from Osborne House. It was quite comfortable, but it necessitated a brougham being ordered to take them to dinner and bring them back to bed. It would have been difficult to walk in knee-breeches and stockings, especially on a wet night. The house was filled with oil paintings, which were really first-rate and which later proved to be valuable. Apparently the Prince Consort had bought the whole collection of pictures from some house when

[14] Later Groom-in-Waiting to King Edward VII.

everything was sold. Osborne House itself was filled with pictures and statues, good, bad, and indifferent. One night Harry Legge [15] and I were waiting in the hall for the clarence that was to take us down to Barton, and I wanted to show him how statues were usually on a pivot to enable you to turn them any way you fancied. I went to the marble statue of Psyche about five foot high on a pedestal and gave it a twist. Apparently it was not on a pivot but it had a circular base which had the same effect. Instead of turning round it fell slowly forward on the top of me and I put my hands up and tried to push it upright again. Harry Legge, who was no weakling, came to help me and we tried till we were purple in the face to save it from falling. I had no idea that a statue was such a heavy thing, but all we were able to do was to prevent it crashing down and being broken into a thousand pieces. I strained my back in my efforts and bruised my head, while Harry Legge hurt his hand and arm before finally letting it down gently on to the floor. We then found that although we had managed to prevent it being smashed, one of the wings of Psyche was chipped. Obviously the thing to do was to get it back on its pedestal before anyone noticed the wing was chipped. We rang and eventually got two footmen, both of them powerful big men, but in powdered hair and red livery which was not intended for manual labour. We tried to raise the statue but all we could manage was to get it two or three feet off the ground. As for getting it back on its pedestal, it was clearly out of the question, so having turned the lights out and told the footmen to report the matter early next morning, we drove off to Barton and so to bed. The next morning a mass of men came and managed to get the statue upright, but they said they could not get it back on its pedestal without a small crane which was generally used for this purpose. All idea, therefore, of hushing up this unfortunate accident was at an end, and I had to see Princess Beatrice and ask her to tell the Queen. I felt like a housemaid confessing to a broken teacup.

I was in disgrace the following day and the Queen wished to

[15] Later Sir Harry Legge. Equerry-in-Waiting to Queen Victoria, King Edward VII and King George V, 1893–1915; Paymaster to the King's Household, 1915–20. Died 1924.

show that she did not at all approve of my breaking statues. Princess Beatrice told me after dinner that the Queen had quite understood it was an accident, but intended to send a message to all the Household that 'they must not touch the statues and certainly not play with them'. This message was duly conveyed to all the ladies and gentlemen, but Lady Lytton,[16] who had not heard about my accident, was mystified at receiving a message that in future she was not to touch the statues and certainly not to play with them, and could make nothing of it.

When the Empress Frederick [17] came to Osborne in 1896 it so happened that the senior Equerry, Sir John M'Neill,[18] had been sent by the Queen to London, and I was doing the Equerry's work. I was making the usual arrangements for the arrival when I was told that a German gentleman had sent in his card and was very anxious to see me. A tall man with spectacles was ushered in and in broken English explained that he was anxious to see the Empress immediately on her arrival. I replied that as soon as Her Majesty arrived I would give his card to Count Seckendorff,[19] who would no doubt arrange an interview. He thanked me but explained that this was not enough as he wished to see the Empress the moment she stepped ashore, and this meant he would have to go to Trinity Pier and receive her, but I told him firmly that I could arrange nothing until I had seen Count Seckendorff. He had such a wild look that I began to fear he was either an anarchist or an escaped lunatic with designs on the Empress's life. I had visions of bomb-throwing and everyone saying that I had not taken obvious precautions. I rang the bell and had him shown out. I then sent a message to Mr. Fraser, the detective from Scotland Yard who was always at the gate, and told him that a German would pass by in a few minutes and that I wished him to be shadowed. One of the plain-clothes police followed the man and

[16] Widow of 1st Earl of Lytton and daughter-in-law of novelist. Sister of Lady Ampthill.

[17] The Empress Frederick (of Germany) was Queen Victoria's eldest daughter, and mother of the Emperor William II.

[18] Major-General Sir John M'Neill, V.C. Later Equerry to King Edward VII. Died 1904.

[19] Head of the Empress Frederick's Household.

reported that he seemed a quiet respectable man, although somewhat eccentric in his habits, and that he was staying at the Medina Hotel. This seemed all right, but in order to take no risks I gave orders that this police officer was to stand near him when the Empress arrived and keep him watched.

The next day I drove down with Princess Beatrice and Miss Minnie Cochrane to Trinity Pier to receive the Empress, and, as soon as we arrived the officer in charge of the pier asked if there was any harm in allowing a German friend of the Empress to come and welcome her. Of course this was my German lunatic, and I said that on no account must he be allowed on the pier.

While we waited Princess Beatrice came to me and said, 'There is a friend of the Empress here. Do you see any objection to his being allowed on the pier?' There was no doubt that the lunatic was a tryer, and I told Princess Beatrice the whole story. She was horrified and seemed quite convinced that the man was an anarchist and a lunatic. I told her of the precautions I had taken, but she was not reassured, and thought I should have taken stronger measures and had the man locked up. But while we were discussing this, the Empress arrived and there was no time to do any more. Her Majesty got into a carriage with Princess Beatrice and drove off. I confess I was nervous and walked to the archway where I could see the crowd. I was astonished to see the Empress wave and kiss her hand to the man as she passed. He turned out to be an eminent sculptor from Berlin and an intimate friend of the Empress. She had told him she would see him the instant she set foot in England and he had taken this literally. Princess Beatrice told her of my precautions and she laughed immoderately, but, although I felt a fool, I comforted myself in the reflection that, had he been mad, I should have rightly been blamed if I had taken no precautions. A very thin line divides genius from lunacy.

At Balmoral the Queen had only a small Household—just enough to do the ordinary work. The Lord-in-Waiting never went there and the Groom-in-Waiting went rarely. The Equerry-in-Waiting did the work of the Master of the Household and generally superintended everything.

When I went to Balmoral as Equerry I was naturally anxious

that everything should go smoothly and I found little difficulty in doing whatever there was to do. The 'Court Circular' was at first rather difficult as it had a language of its own, but after a time I found this quite easy. I was told confidentially by Princess Beatrice that the Queen had remarked how little trouble it gave her when I wrote the 'Court Circular'. It appeared that General Sir Michael Biddulph had made very heavy weather over it, and, in order to make sure he was rightly chronicling the Queen's movements, placed alternatives and synonyms in the margin. 'The Queen went out,' he would write, and in the margin he would add every conceivable alternative for Her Majesty to choose from—proceeded, drove, went for a drive, etc. etc. The Queen found this quite insufferable and therefore when I sent in a plain statement written in 'Court Circular' language, which she could approve of or alter, she found life easier.

Like so many great people the Queen sometimes interested herself in domestic details which she often did not understand. When the King of Portugal came up to stay at Balmoral I experienced some difficulty in finding sufficient room for all the Portuguese suite. The Housekeeper assured me that there really was not sufficient room unless the Queen's own suite was reduced, and suggested as a solution that the Maid of Honour, Miss Lambart, should be told to come the following week.

This seemed to me the only solution and accordingly I wrote a letter to the Queen putting forward this suggestion. If anyone had to write to the Queen it had to be a proper letter beginning '——presents his humble duty to Your Majesty' and the letter placed in an envelope addressed simply 'The Queen'. All such letters had to be sealed with an official seal and not licked. The Private Secretary and Keeper of the Privy Purse always placed their letters in an official box, but humble individuals like me had to use envelopes. My letter was duly returned to me and on it was written 'The Queen has yet to learn that Capt. Ponsonby has anything to do with the Maids of Honour'.

This snub was probably well deserved, but it did not solve the difficulty and I had to invoke the aid of Lady Ampthill, the Lady-in-Waiting, but she was no more successful than I had been, for when she put forward the problem the Queen merely said, 'No room? Then we must double up, that's all'. I did not grasp whether the Queen intended to take part in this unpleasant manœuvre, but I again saw the Housekeeper. To my surprise she told me that the Queen had spoken to her and had said it was all nonsense about there being no room, and that she did not like to contradict Her Majesty, and had said she would be able to find sufficient rooms. She did so eventually, and I felt very small.

There were always two dinners at Balmoral, but usually all the ladies dined with the Queen and the second dinner was merely men. Precisely the same dinner was served in both dining-rooms. It amused me therefore to read in Lord Beaconsfield's biography that in a letter to Mrs. Disraeli dated September 1868, in which he described his visit to Balmoral, he said that after dining one night with the Queen he dined the next with the Household 'and between ourselves I was struck as I have been before by the contrast between the Queen's somewhat simple, but sufficient, dinner, and the banquet of our humbler friends'.[20]

The Queen's dinners at Balmoral were necessarily not large as there were not many people to ask. The conversation was supposed to be general, but the custom was to talk to one's neighbour in very low tones, and those on the right and left of Her Majesty were the only ones who spoke up. A great deal therefore depended on what mood the Queen was in: when she was rather preoccupied and silent the dinner was a dismal affair, but when she was inclined to talk and interpose with witty remarks it went with a swing. Once an earnest clergyman described what he had seen in the East End of London, and by way of showing how overcrowded the houses were, said that in one house he visited he found that seven people slept in one bed. The Queen dryly remarked, 'Had I been one of them I would have slept on the floor'.

Alec Yorke,[21] the Groom-in-Waiting, told me that at dinner he talked to his neighbour about Queen Mary, daughter of Henry VIII, and Her Majesty heard the word Queen and asked which

[20] Buckle's *Life of Disraeli* (John Murray, 1920), v. 53.
[21] The Hon. Alexander Grantham Yorke.

Queen he was talking about. When he told her she replied, 'Oh! my bloody ancestor'.

The Gillies' Ball at Balmoral in those days was bacchanalian, but the hard drinking was supposed to take place late so that if anyone was the worse for drink no one should know of it. But as it began at seven and the Queen's dinner was usually about nine, those who had to wait at table had already been dancing for two hours. On one occasion it was a warm evening and, no doubt without being in the least drunk, some of the servants who waited were in rather a hilarious mood. The piper did not seem to mind whether he made a good shot at the glass when he poured out the wine, and some of the footmen were rather slap-dash in their methods. The piper only made one or two really bad shots, but there were loud crashes when someone outside dropped the plates and dishes. Two old pages eventually ran the dinner and firmly eliminated all those who could not be trusted in the dining-room. The Queen had been brought up to think that everything was excusable on the night of a Gillies' Ball, and that it was up to her to keep the conversation going so that no one would remark anything. She was most amusing and told stories which were really quite funny. She went back to the earlier part of the century and described how badly things were done in those days.

When I went to Windsor I found that the whole system on which meals in the Castle were arranged was very curious. The Queen and the Royal Family had breakfast, luncheon, and dinner in the oak dining-room in the centre of the corridor, but if there was a dinner-party they dined with the Household in the big dining-room. Although no member of the Household ever joined the Royal luncheon, a certain number were asked to dinner. Some members of the Royal Family took advantage of every opportunity to exclude all members of the Household, and I always thought how right they were. A family luncheon is one thing, but once one of the Household came it cramped the conversation. One curious custom, which I was told dated back to the Middle Ages, was that the Lord-in-Waiting not only invariably dined with the Queen and Royal Family, but ran the whole thing and told people where to sit. One would naturally suppose the Master of the

Household would do this. On one occasion Lord Harris was the Lord-in-Waiting. He had just returned from India, where he had been Governor of Bombay, and although he had never had to tell people where to sit at his own dinner, he was a practical man and found no difficulty in this, to him, new duty of the sitting list, which was prepared by the Master of the Household. In an absent moment, however, he placed the French Ambassador, M. Cambon,[22] who was the senior, on the Queen's left, and the Italian Ambassador, who was the junior, on the right. At that time the Queen's eyesight was very bad, but she had passed the sitting list and was naturally under the impression that the senior Ambassador would be on her right. The Queen made a habit of talking to the least interesting neighbour first, so that she could devote the rest of dinner to her most interesting guest, which in this case was M. Cambon. So she turned to the man on her left, thinking it was the Italian Ambassador, and said, "Where is your King now?" Most representatives of a republican country would have been puzzled as to how to answer such a question, but Cambon had already grasped that a mistake had been made and that the Queen thought he was an Italian. He never hesitated a moment and replied as if the Queen had asked him where the King of Italy was. He said that he believed His Majesty was on his yacht and then went on to describe the last interview he had had with the King of Italy, as if it was quite a natural question for the Queen to ask. The Queen at once saw the mistake and carried on the conversation quite naturally. Afterwards she was much put out and hauled the wretched Harris over the coals.

For the purposes of the Household the breakfasts and luncheons were divided into two. In the big dining-room there was breakfast and luncheon for the Ladies-in-Waiting, Women of the Bedchamber, Maids of Honour and any guests, but the only male member of the Household who was allowed to attend these meals was the Lord-in-Waiting. All the other gentlemen of the Household had breakfast and luncheon downstairs in a room adjoining the Equerry's room. There was, however, only one Household dinner, and to this all members of the Household who were not

[22] Paul Cambon, French Ambassador to Court of St. James's, 1898–1920.

invited to dine with the Queen came. Occasionally all the Household were asked to go to the White Drawing-room after dinner and stand there for an hour, but the usual routine was that those who were not wanted by the Queen remained in the Red Drawing-room until a page came in and announced in sepulchral tones that the Queen had gone to bed. Sometimes whist would be played, and candles had to be sent for. After much trouble a card table with candles and cards was prepared. Usually the pack was one card short. As no one had the least knowledge of whist I cannot say it was amusing. Lord Strafford,[23] who was an Equerry, had always been told that the danger of card-playing was that unscrupulous people looked over one's hand, and therefore held his cards so tightly under his chin that it took him nearly two whole minutes to find a card. Of course no smoking was allowed and therefore I looked forward to the page's arrival when the men retired to the billiard-room where they could smoke.

Originally there had been still another dining-room used, but this was before my time. The Doctor, the German Secretary, and the Librarian had their meals separately as the Queen did not include them in the Household, nor were they allowed to wear the Windsor coat. I don't know the exact date, but it must have been quite late in the Queen's reign when these three were considered members of the Household and were allowed to have their meals, not with the Ladies-inWaiting, but with the male members of the Household. Sir James Reid, the Queen's physician, a man of infinite humour, was much amused to see a note from the Queen to the Master of the Household: 'The gentlemen and Sir James Reid are to come this evening to the Drawing-room.'

When any big dinner took place the band of either the Life Guards or the Foot Guards was ordered to play on the Terrace outside the windows of the large dining-room. This small bit of Terrace, or rather part of the battlements, was sufficiently large for a full brass band, and an awning was erected there in case of wet weather; but it had one disadvantage, which was that the band had to go through the dining-room to get there. There was no other means of access.

[23] Sir Henry Byng, 4th Earl of Strafford.

In 1896 I was in waiting with General Sir Lyndoch Gardiner, who as Senior Equerry did everything. As he was over eighty his memory was failing and he was in constant dread of forgetting something and being thought too old for the post of Equerry, although he very much resented anyone reminding him of his duties. He thought this a reflection on his age, and I soon found that any attempt on my part as Junior Equerry to make sure that all the orders had been given was resented and brought forth a snub. So I never attempted to interfere or make sure that nothing had been forgotten.

One day the Queen had a big dinner with several members of the Royal Family and illustrious guests of all sorts. Of course the band was required, but General Gardiner had clean forgotten to order it. It was about five o'clock in the afternoon when he came to me and said he was afraid he would have to resign as he had forgotten all about the band. He nearly broke down and seemed so helpless and miserable that I determined to try and attempt the impossible. The difficulty was that owing to the drains at the Cavalry Barracks being reconstructed the 2nd Life Guards were encamped in Windsor Great Park. In those days there were no telephones or motors: otherwise it would have been easy. I told him to leave it to me and I would see that the band was there.

I at once sent for a groom from the stables and also for the Superintendent of the Stables, Captain Hickey, and I wrote a letter to the Officer Commanding the regiment saying the band was wanted at 8.45, and marked it 'Urgent, to be opened at once'. Having dispatched this by the groom, who was told to gallop all the way, I enquired from the Superintendent how the band usually came, and he told me that a job-master in Windsor usually supplied three large wagonettes or brakes. I told him to order these at once, but he objected as he said they were ordered by the Life Guards. I told him that this time they must be ordered by him and that the Officer Commanding the Life Guards would confirm the order later. Every minute was important. I received a letter from the Adjutant in reply to mine saying he would do his best, but many of the bandsmen were out in Windsor and there might be some difficulty in securing the conveyances. He had,

48

however, sent off to Windsor to try and catch the missing bandsmen there.

There seemed no more to be done, when it suddenly struck me that if the band arrived when we were at dinner there would be no means of getting them on to the terrace. I therefore went off to see the head of the Castle fire brigade and asked him what ladders he had in case of fire. I explained the whole situation to him and he promised to have four ladders ready on the North Terrace so that the band could scale up them and get in their places. I had a man posted at the door at which the band would arrive to tell them to go round by the terrace if they came after 8.45.

The Queen was a few minutes late for dinner, but only a few, and I had hoped she might be very late. She went slowly in to dinner on the arm of her Indian attendant, and the distinguished company followed. When I came in last there was no band and therefore no National Anthem. I thought I had failed, and the despondent look on poor General Gardiner's face made me wretched. But as I sat down I saw through the window dark figures climbing on to the small terrace, and before the Queen had had a mouthful of soup the band struck up an overture. So all was well. But of course the Queen noticed the absence of the National Anthem— she always noticed everything. The next day old Gardiner received a note saying that the band should be warned always to play the National Anthem when she came in to dinner. Gardiner replied that it was his fault and not the band's, but he would see that in the future her wishes were obeyed.

I once nearly got into trouble through dining in barracks without leave. I wanted to go and see the Windsor Strollers act in Windsor Theatre, and when I received an invitation to dine in barracks at 7.30 and afterwards go to the theatre, it seemed an opportunity not to be missed. I waited till after luncheon when the Queen's dinner was all arranged, and as I was not on the list I saw no reason why I should not dine in barracks. I consulted Lord Edward Pelham-Clinton and he said that as I was not to dine with the Queen, he could see no objection to my dining out, but he warned me that occasionally names were added to the dinner list at the last moment. He, however, gave instructions to his clerk to let me or my servant know the minute my name was added to the list.

Having taken the precaution to impress on my servant that he was to keep in constant touch with the clerk and fetch me if I was wanted, I dressed and walked down to barracks feeling I had been over-cautious. On my way down the Castle Hill I chanced to meet the Queen's piper. He naturally noticed my evening clothes and concluded I was dining in Windsor.

Now I had a short time before had occasion to report the piper. It happened in this way. One night after dinner Princess Beatrice found she had left her fan behind in the dining-room and asked me to go back and retrieve it for her. On entering the dining-room I found the band and the servants eating up the fruit and drinking up the wine, but what struck me most was the piper pouring out the Queen's port and handing it to the Band-Sergeant. On my return to the drawing-room I told Lord Edward Pelham-Clinton what I had seen and remarked that, however old this custom might be, it was surely bad for the morals of the band. He was very angry and the next morning had up the head servants and gave them a lecture, whereupon they all stoutly denied there was any truth in my statements, assuring him that I must have been mistaken: the band merely walked round the table on their way through the dining-room, admiring the decorations. Lord Edward explained to me that although he was convinced that all I said was true, it seemed difficult to prove anything with so many witnesses on the other side. As soon as I heard this I went off to barracks at once and asked the Adjutant of the Scots Guards to send for the Sergeant of the band and the two senior bandsmen. I explained to these men that no blame attached to them, but I wanted a clear statement of what exactly had taken place. Then the whole story came out and the Adjutant took everything down and asked them to sign their respective statements. These I took back to Lord Edward, who again sent for the head servants. He read out slowly the dispositions of the bandsmen and the defence collapsed at once. The upper servants confessed everything and only pleaded that it had always been the custom. They were severely spoken to and steps were taken to ensure that this did not happen again.

The piper, therefore, on seeing me going out to dinner, thought this a heaven-sent opportunity of paying off old scores. I learnt afterwards that he hurried off to one of the Queen's dressers and told her to tell the Queen that I was dining out somewhere in Windsor. Apparently the Queen determined to nip this irregularity in the bud, and promptly added my name to her dinner list. It was about a quarter-past eight that this message was sent to the Master of the Household, and, as dinner was at a quarter to nine, there was not much time to spare but the complicated machinery I had devised worked perfectly. The Master of the Household's clerk at once told my servant, who ran down the hill, hailed a cab and galloped to barracks. I had just lighted a cigar and was enjoying my coffee and brandy when the Mess-Sergeant blew into the room and announced that I was wanted at once.

I raced back to the Castle with the old horse gallantly attempting to gallop up the hill. I dashed up to my room and changed into a Windsor coat, breeches, and stockings. Punctually at a quarter to nine I reached the corridor, much to the amusement of Lord Edward. Instead of the reverential hungry frame of mind adopted by the others, I was in roaring spirits and in an after-dinner mood, making jokes to people who had not got a laugh in them and who received my hilarity in stony silence. I made a point of partaking of every dish, but really only toyed with the food. I was conscious of the Queen's eye being fixed on me, but, of course, nothing could be said as I was there.

In 1895, when the Home Rule split took place [24] and the Government was formed of Conservatives and Liberal Unionists, great pains were taken to keep the outgoing and the incoming Governments apart and prevent their meeting. It was felt that those Liberals who had crossed the floor of the House might find it rather awkward if they met their former colleagues when the ceremony of giving up the seals of office and handing them to the new Ministers took place. It was therefore arranged that the Ministers

[24] The split had been evident then for nearly ten years, time enough, one would have thought, for passions to cool. In 1895, however, Lord Salisbury formed a Conservative Government, which for the first time included former members of the Liberal Party who disapproved of Home Rule for Ireland. Of these, the 8th Duke of Devonshire (formerly Lord Hartington) was one.

of the old Government should come at eleven and those of the new Government at twelve. The old Ministers would then attend a Council in the White Drawing-room at Windsor Castle and deliver up their seals of office. This always took some time and in the meantime the new Ministers would arrive and be shown into another drawing-room where they would be shut up until the Queen was ready to hand them the seals. This all worked perfectly, but unfortunately the Duke of Devonshire was very late, having driven over from some place near Windsor. As he came up the stairs he met all his old colleagues who had just given up their seals and who, of course, chaffed him on his joining the other party. No face was, however, more suited to a difficult situation like this and he was quite unperturbed and passed through them with his mouth wide open and his eyes half closed.

Being Junior Equerry, I was always sent for if any extra job had to be done. One day the Duc de Nemours [25] came to luncheon with the Queen; after luncheon she had had enough of him, but as his train didn't leave till 3.30, Princess Louise, Duchess of Argyll,[26] was asked to talk to him. Unfortunately she had an engagement and so he was shown into a sitting-room while I was sent for. I was told to talk to him in French for forty minutes, and as I had never seen him before, I began to wonder how I was going to fill up the time. It was far worse for the old man to have a young Englishman thrust on him and in all probability he would have been far happier sitting by himself. When I came in I found him seated in an armchair, and he told me to come close as he was deaf. He seemed relieved, however, to find I could talk French.

Having touched lightly on the state of the weather and been met with no response, I came rather to a standstill. I was fairly well up in French politics, and, as it was not very difficult to guess what his views were, I plunged boldly into the situation in France. Setting alight to a barrel of gunpowder would be a comparatively mild proceeding compared to the effect of my conversation on this old man. He got very excited, jumped up from his chair and paced up and down the room with one hand in his coat, while he shook

[25] Second son and heir of King Louis Philippe.
[26] Queen Victoria's 4th daughter.

52

the other in my face to give emphasis to his statements. He shouted at me that it was heartrending to see France in the hands of unscrupulous men who were only working for their own interests; what France really needed was a man who had the good of the country at heart and who would work disinterestedly for the State and not for purely selfish motives. He compared the politicians of years ago with those in power at the present day, needless to say to the detriment of the latter. I roused him to a state bordering on frenzy when I asked what he would do if he were Prime Minister. He roared that nothing would induce him to mix himself up with such *canaille,* but if he did then he would carry out the following reforms. It suddenly dawned on me that forty minutes was far too short for this interview and it was with the greatest difficulty that I got him downstairs and into the carriage. What I think happened was that he never got a chance of saying all this to the Queen and so determined to unload it on me, in the hopes that I would repeat it.

On another occasion I was sent for suddenly to prevent an unpleasant brawl taking place between two foreign diplomatists. Señor Cipriano del Mazo, the Spanish Ambassador, having been accused of attacking the Spanish Government in some speech he had made, had been recalled and was to be replaced by Señor di Casa Valentia, who was his chief accuser. Cipriano del Mazo, furious at this indignity, said that if he ever met di Casa Valentia he would spit in his face and insult him. So we were told that when they both came to Windsor, one with the letter of recall, and the other with letters of credence, they were on no account to meet. Cipriano del Mazo came down early, but unfortunately missed his train back to London so that he was still in the Castle when Señor di Casa Valentia arrived. I happened to be in the corridor at the time and Lord Edward Pelham-Clinton dashed at me and told me to take Cipriano del Mazo into one of the rooms and invent any excuse I could think of. I grasped at once what had happened. I seized him by the arm and told him I particularly wished him to see a picture in one of the adjoining rooms. Determined at any price to prevent any spitting, I almost pushed him through the door and shut it. He seemed rather surprised at my haste, but enquired which picture it was I wanted him to see. I pointed to one and said, 'We have never been able to find out for certain who it was of and who it was by.' But he said, 'I see clearly the name Winterhalter on the picture.' This was rather a facer for me, but I merely said, 'Ah! but is it by Winterhalter? That is the point!' The poor man was completely puzzled and proceeded to examine the picture carefully through his glasses. He probably thought I was drunk or mad, but mercifully a page came in and announced that the carriage was ready to take him to the station.

Once I was sent for a drive with the brother of the Khedive of Egypt, who had arrived an hour and a half before his time. The Queen didn't want to see him till half-past four, and by some mistake he had arrived at three.

Having given orders to the coachman that he was to drive round the park for an hour, I settled down to try and amuse this Egyptian Prince, but at first he was cross at being sent for a drive and only responded in monosyllables. Although he spoke English it was an obvious effort to him, as he never seemed to find the right word. So I changed into French and he at once responded. He opened the flood gates and hardly stopped for a moment. He told me all the difficulties of the Khedive's position and we plunged into the Egyptian situation.

Amongst the many complaints he made of Lord Cromer's [27] autocratic rule, he said that the old Egyptian aristocracy was being wiped out. 'We have an aristocracy', he said, 'as you have yours, and it is galling to see the heads of old families who have been there for hundreds of years ignored and trampled on simply because Lord Cromer does not like them, and will not look after them.' I repeated this to Lord Cromer some months later and he said, 'That is not true. I do look after them, for most of them are at this moment in jail.'

The Queen, I think, liked and admired Cromer, as she always did that type of man. There was, I suppose, a certain satisfaction in seeing a man of such autocratic character humble and diffident before her. Although she firmly believed that not only Kings and

[27] Evelyn Baring, 1st Earl of Cromer; Agent and Consul-General in Egypt, 1883–1907.

Queens, but even Princes, were on a higher plane than the rest of the human race, there was a certain simplicity and humility in her character that was attractive. The Duchess of Buccleuch once told me that she had met Cecil Rhodes at a party but that she had not asked to be introduced to him as she had heard that he disliked all women and that at times he could be very rude. She had told the Queen about this, but the Queen had replied, 'Oh, I don't think that can be so, because he was very civil to me when he came here'.

CHAPTER III

Assistant Private Secretary — The Diamond Jubilee — Shorthand — The diary and the birthday book — The Queen's ministers — Kitchener at Balmoral

In 1897, when the preparations for the Diamond Jubilee celebrations were being made, the work became very heavy. I had undertaken odd jobs, as even when there was much work the Junior Equerry still had nothing to do. When my father died in 1895, Sir Fleetwood Edwards was appointed Keeper of the Privy Purse and Sir Arthur Bigge Private Secretary, but they had no assistant. The work of the Private Secretary became so heavy that it was more than one man could do. There were no telephones at that time and shorthand writers and typists were unknown. Although I did as much of the donkey-work as I could and purchased a typewriter, I was only on duty for a month. The question therefore arose whether an Assistant Secretary should not be appointed, and whether there was anyone in the Household who would be suitable or whether it would be best to bring in someone from outside. Mercifully I was quite unconscious that I was in the running for the post, and I was preparing to leave after my month's waiting was over when Sir Fleetwood Edwards came to me and asked if I would like to take on the job. I really had not thought about it, and when I heard it entailed my being seconded and giving up soldiering I rather hesitated to accept. However, I finally consented and everyone thought I was very lucky. I was at once seconded and suddenly found that instead of doing occasional work I had a full-time job.

I was supposed to help both the Keeper of the Privy Purse and the Private Secretary, but I soon found that I was of little use to the former. His work, which consisted mostly of giving decisions,

57

could not be delegated to anyone else; so I merely took some of the routine work off his hands by dealing with the begging letters and the votes for charitable institutions.

My duties as Assistant Private Secretary were many and varied. I had to cypher messages from the Queen and decypher messages to her. I dealt with a mass of letters which the Queen or Sir A. Bigge had not opened and had to copy bits of despatches which the Queen wished to keep. In addition I had to do my four months a year as Junior Equerry-in-Waiting, but this merely meant dressing up in uniform on occasion or riding by the carriage.

At the Diamond Jubilee celebrations at St. Paul's I had to ride at the side of the Empress Frederick's carriage as the two Senior Equerries rode with the Queen. On the whole these celebrations went very well, and there is no doubt that they were far better organized than the original Jubilee in 1887. Of course, I was only told the mistakes that were formerly made and how the arrangements for the dinner of the foreign guests had practically broken down. One story amused me: as the downstairs rooms at Buckingham Palace were not sufficiently large for the large number of foreign suites, the Office of Works had constructed a large tent in the garden. This easily accommodated the guests, but apparently the question of ventilation had been overlooked. The result was that when the tent was full, the heat was so great that many nearly fainted. Reggie Brett (afterwards Lord Esher) was at that time Secretary at the Office of Works and therefore everyone appealed to him. He said that obviously a current of air was necessary, and that if windows were cut in the canvas at each end of the tent that would solve the difficulty. As there appeared to be no one capable of cutting holes in the canvas he determined to do this himself. He was in Court dress and had a rapier at his side. This he drew and at once thrust it through the canvas side of the tent. To his horror there was a piercing yell and it turned out that a housemaid was on the other side looking through a crack. Mercifully she was not hurt.

While all else went well in 1897, there was one lamentable exception: the reception of the House of Commons on June 23rd by the Queen was about the worst function it has ever been my lot to see. Who exactly was to blame I never knew, but I rather fancy it was one of those functions for which no one was really responsible. In those days the three main departments of the Household were in watertight compartments; if one department was responsible for a function, it was quite out of the question to ask for help from another department. There was a certain jealousy between the three departments and an official in one department was not allowed to help the officials in another.

On this occasion, however, I imagine that it was a case of dual control. The Lord Steward and the Lord Chamberlain were both supposed to manage this ceremony, and each thought the other was doing everything. There was practically no thought-out scheme. The House of Commons were to come and present an address of congratulation to the Queen in the ballroom. That was all there was in it, and yet the whole thing proved a fiasco.

I came in with the Queen's suite into an empty ballroom, and everything was most dignified. The Mistress of the Robes, the Lady-in-Waiting, the Women of the Bedchamber and the Maids of Honour accompanied the Queen, together with the Lord, Groom and two Equerries. Lord Pembroke,[1] Lord Steward, and Lord Clarendon,[2] Lord Chamberlain, received the Queen, and she sat down while all of us grouped ourselves round her.

The doors at the other end of the ballroom were then opened and in came the House of Commons like a crowd being let onto the ground after a football match. There seemed to be no order and the Speaker, Prime Minister, and Leader of the Opposition were lost in the struggling mass of M.P.s. This dishevelled mass of humanity came at the Queen, and instinctively the men of the Household felt that they were called upon to do or die. We moved out, formed a protecting screen, and stemmed the tide while the Lord Chamberlain and Lord Steward tried to find the Speaker, etc. Meanwhile the Queen was thoroughly put out at the mismanagement of the function and did not hesitate to let the two great officers of State know what she thought. The result was that they got thoroughly rattled; but they did wonders considering the

[1] Sidney Herbert, 14th Earl of Pembroke.
[2] Edward Hyde Villiers, 5th Earl of Clarendon.

chaos that existed, and succeeded with the aid of the Whips in getting the Cabinet Ministers together and in bringing them up one by one to the Queen. It was a thoroughly bad show, and after about a quarter of an hour the Queen had had enough and retired. So bad was it that eventually the Queen decided to give a garden party at Windsor ten days later to the members of both Houses of Parliament with their wives and daughters.

On thinking over what would be useful to me in my new post I came to the conclusion that a knowledge of shorthand and typewriting, ability to speak German (for although the Queen's German relations all spoke English fluently, their suites did not), and a certain superficial knowledge of the Almanach de Gotha in order to grasp the relationship of the members of the Royal Family would be most useful.

My efforts to master the latter were never crowned with any success, although I was fairly well up in the first and second cousins of the English Royal Family.

I took up shorthand enthusiastically, and having bought Pitman's Manual I devoted two hours every day to its contents. I had intended to have a teacher, but as I was always away from London, this was impossible. At the end of a year I had thoroughly mastered the whole system and all I wanted was practice. I therefore got the Telegraph Clerk, Mr. Hiley, to come to my room every morning at 8 A.M. and read me out the leading article in *The Times* slowly. I then read it back to him, and by degrees I gained a certain proficiency in the art of writing shorthand. When I had a month's leave and was in London I determined to go to Pitman's Metropolitan School for shorthand and decided to give the name of Powell. I was afraid that if they knew I was in the Grenadiers and in the Queen's Household they would not treat me seriously, and therefore called myself Frank Powell to account for initials in my hat. I was shown into the Headmaster's room and found quite a nice man with a cockney accent. After some commonplace remarks he asked me what post I had in view, and when I replied shorthand reporter to one of the leading newspapers, preferably *The Times,* he could hardly conceal a smile as he knew that I had little or no chance of this. But he grasped that I wanted to do serious work. He ended by saying that there were two points which he wished to impress upon me: the first was that I was to be careful to come sober to the classes. Considering that I had to be there at 10 A.M., this did not appear to be very difficult, and I said so, but he interrupted me, 'Not what *you* call sober, but what *I* call sober—not after you've had one or two whiskies and soda at the station'.

The other point he said was that when I met any of the female pupils he hoped I would not indulge in undue familiarity. This also I promised to observe, but as everyone was always in such a tearing hurry in that establishment, the warning seemed superfluous. Finally, I was taken before an expert to be tested. The expert, however, on learning that I was practically self-taught, made short work of me. He said, smiling, 'Let us see how much you know', and handed me a card where to my horror I saw Latin names of flowers and medicines, and hardly a word I had ever seen before. I had scarcely written more than a few lines when he said, 'Thank you, that will do. I see you don't even know the rudiments.'

I felt inclined to throw the inkpot at his head for giving me such an unfair test. Repressing an almost overwhelming desire to say something rude, I left the room humiliated and feeling that I had wasted a whole year. I was sent to the beginners' room, and I sat down mournfully and was given a foolscap sheet and told to write *P's* and *B's*. I looked round at the other pupils, middle-aged men most of them. None seemed the sort of person who would come drunk to the classes. The teacher came after I had finished my exercise, and I found him a charmingly human man. I told him of all my troubles and he said that he would give me an exercise on each chapter of the Manual every day, and if I did it correctly he would let me go on to the next chapter. The exercises he gave me were child's play to begin with, and as I never made a mistake I was only kept at this work for a fortnight and then allowed to go to the speed rooms. Sixty words a minute I found easy, and I was promoted to eighty and then to a hundred. There I stuck for a day or two, owing to careless mistakes, but later when I reached a hundred and twenty I obtained a certificate and left.

One amusing incident occurred in connection with shorthand

and that was that I went in for a competition in one of the short-hand newspapers. Feeling it more discreet I gave the name of my housekeeper, Bethia Williams, and the address of my house at Old Windsor. I was busy at the time and quite forgot all about the competition, but six months later I asked the housekeeper whether she had ever heard anything about this. She brought me a beautifully bound book on the first page of which was inscribed 'Presented to Bethia Williams, winner of the Prize Essay, etc.'. She confessed she had been very much puzzled at getting this book as it was printed in shorthand, but she had kept it carefully. The curious part was that she had got quite fond of the book and hated parting with it, but when I gave her a sovereign she let me have it.

The advent of the safety bicycle produced a bicycling craze in London, but while it took some time for it to reach the Royal Household, I was one of the first to buy a bicycle and go for long rides. Prince Henry of Battenberg asked me one day to go out with him, and we went all round Windsor Great Park, but as neither of us was sufficiently expert to take our hands off the handle-bars we got our eyes full of flies and gnats and had to stop and get down several times to wipe away the insects in our eyes.

Princess Patricia of Connaught [3] told me that when a Cyclist Corps was started at Aldershot the Duke of Connaught, who was in command of the troops, was made Colonel-in-Chief. He therefore took lessons as he thought he ought to be able to ride a bicycle when he attended any parade of the new Corps. When he was asked to inspect them, he was still very wobbly on his machine, but he gallantly rode forth from Government House. On the road he met an orderly who was also a beginner. The orderly in trying to salute him went end over end on the road, and the Duke, in attempting to return the salute, fell on the top of him.

One difficult duty that I had to do as Assistant Secretary was on certain occasions to write the facts for the Queen when she wrote her diary. She liked to get the facts and statistics absolutely correct before she wrote her impressions. When in 1897 she reviewed the Colonial troops it was stated in the accounts in the newspapers that the Queen had spoken in Hindustani to the Indian

[3] Daughter of the Duke of Connaught; later Lady Patricia Ramsay.

officers when they were brought up to her. When I was therefore told to write an account of this review for her I was uncertain whether I had better add this or not, although I knew it was not true. I had long learnt that history was not an account of what actually had happened, but what people generally thought had happened. So I put it in my account and Mrs. Grant told me that she read my account out to the Queen who said, 'That's not true. I did not speak in Hindustani but in English.' Mrs. Grant asked if she should scratch it out, and the Queen replied, 'No, you can leave it, for I could have done so had I wished'.

On another occasion I wrote something about the Duchess of Connaught. The Queen sent this account back to me for further information, and opposite the words 'Duchess of Connaught' she had written 'Always put H.R.H., otherwise it would look as if she was an ordinary Duchess'.

The Queen was very particular about people writing their names in her Birthday Book. She took the last volume of this about with her wherever she went and on occasions it had been mistaken for the Bible. Everyone who visited her had to write their name, and it became a mass of names of celebrities and nonentities all mixed up together. Mercifully the German Secretary, Herr Muther, was in charge of this book and had to keep the index, which he did indifferently well. When he was away or the Queen was abroad, one of the Equerries was responsible for this most tiresome book.

Sir Harry Legge was once the Equerry at Osborne in charge of the book, and a Siamese Princess came to see the Queen. He knew he would have to obtain her signature and so took the book to her while she was waiting to see the Queen. He asked her what day her birthday was, but this apparently conveyed nothing to her. To make it clearer he said, 'On what day were you born?' and she replied, 'On the ninth waxing of the moon of the season Pyatto in the year San Yow'. Now the whole point of the Birthday Book was that people should write their names on their birthdays, but as he didn't feel equal to spotting this date in the Christian calendar, he thought it safer to ask her to write on a separate sheet of paper.

When I went with the Queen to Aldershot for the big review in

1897 it never occurred to me that I was in charge of the Birthday Book; in fact I didn't even know that it had been brought to Aldershot. The Queen gave a dinner of about forty to all the Generals, Colonels of Battalions, and principal Staff Officers, and I never even saw the book, much less thought of asking anyone to write in it.

The next morning the Queen was leaving for Windsor and I thought I would go for a ride before breakfast. I got up at 6.30 and was just starting out at seven when I received a note from the Queen (written the night before) in which she said she presumed I had got the signatures of all those who dined. I was flabbergasted. The Queen was leaving at 10.30 and the troops were to line the road. To attempt to go round Aldershot in a carriage would take too much time, and so I determined to play the mountain to their Mahomets. I sent away my horse and summoned all the orderlies. There were luckily plenty: four on horses, four or bicycles, and four on foot. I sat down and scribbled notes to all the guests of the previous night and sent them off by degrees as soon as I had written them. I then found that the Brigade of Guards had already started off for Pirbright, and this meant I should be five signatures short. In about forty minutes Generals, Colonels, etc., arrived at full gallop imagining that the Queen was sitting waiting with the Birthday Book. By 9.30 all had written except the five at Pirbright. I therefore wrote with my humble duty reporting I had all the signatures except the Guards'. The Queen seemed satisfied with this, but sent a message to say I must get the other signatures as soon as possible.

My other adventure with the Birthday Book occurred at Nice. Sarah Bernhardt came to act at the theatre there, and the Queen was pressed by several people to hear her recite. At first she refused as she doubted Sarah Bernhardt's code of morality being quite what it should be, but eventually she agreed to receive Sarah Bernhardt in the drawing-room at the Hotel Regina. It was a great success and the Queen was delighted with the performance of a small play, *Jean Mari*.

I instinctively felt this was a case for the Birthday Book, and after the Queen had left the drawing-room I produced the book

and asked Sarah Bernhardt to write her name. She startled me by
insisting on kneeling down on the floor to write. Then she took up
nearly the whole of one page by writing *Le plus beau jour de ma
vie* and signed it with a flourish.

I felt I had done my duty nobly and when a message came from
the Queen asking me whether I had got Sarah Bernhardt's signature I sent the book in with pride for the Queen to see. To my
surprise I got no marks. First of all it was the wrong book, and
I ought to have used the artists' book, and secondly, I ought to
have prevented her taking up the whole page. I was told that the
Queen was much put out at this, but in any case I was to get Sarah
Bernhardt's signature in the artists' book. By the merest chance I
heard that she was leaving Nice for Marseilles that night after the
performance in the theatre, so there was only one thing to do, and
that was to catch her before she left; but this was not as easy as
I imagined, as I found out that she never saw anyone before going
to the theatre. I therefore had an early dinner and took a stall for
La Tosca. After the first act I went round to the box office and
said I wished to see Madame Sarah Bernhardt, but the man, who
no doubt had often to grapple with many others who had the same
wish, replied with a pitying smile that it was hopeless to try and
see her, and hinted that I had better fasten my affections on someone else. It was impossible to argue with a busy man who kept on
being interrupted and so I contented myself with asking to see her
secretary, and after some trouble he said he would arrange this.

As soon as the next *entr'acte* began I returned to the box-office
and after an interminable delay the secretary came, and although
polite was very short in his answers. So I had to play the Queen
and said, *'Je viens de la part de Sa Majesté La Reine d'Angleterre'.*
He at once was all over the place and took me to the back of the
theatre, where I found in a sort of antechamber a lot of people
waiting for a chance to see Sarah. But the Queen's name worked
like a talisman, and I was taken at once to her dressing-room,
where she received me most cordially. There were two dressers,
two sort of ladies-in-waiting, the secretary, and another whom I
took to be the lover. I explained my errand, and she said in her
voix d'or, 'Je l'ai déjà écrit'. I replied that this was so, but I had

been commanded to obtain her signature in another book, and I murmured something about its being *'plus intime'*. She said certainly she would write, but although the whole party looked everywhere, there was no ink. The lover did find a property inkstand and an old split quill, but no ink. There was nothing to do but to come back during the next *entr'acte,* and the secretary was told to get busy and procure some ink and a pen. Accordingly I sat through the next act and returned, not without difficulty, to her dressing-room. The ink and pen were produced and Sarah wrote her name, but of course there was no blotting-paper. I was so anxious that she should not see the other signatures that as soon as she had written I tried to take away the book, *'Un moment que ça sèche',* she said, and before I could stop her she glanced at the other signatures where several well-known artists' names appeared. The spell was broken. She handed back the book to me with a shrug of her shoulders. She understood.

The practice of having a Minister in attendance sometimes at Osborne and always at Balmoral enabled the Queen to make the acquaintance of many politicians, and she was never influenced by what was generally thought of the Cabinet Ministers or whether they were popular or unpopular; she had her own likes and dislikes.

Of course, in latter years Lord Salisbury stood out as her friend and adviser. He understood perfectly and was able to convince her that he was right in his policy while he treated her with great deference and asked her advice on foreign politics. He thought her great experience and her influence in Europe were factors that were not to be lightly despised, and he constantly made use of the exceptional position she occupied in Europe to gain some advantage or smooth over some difficulty. I was often engaged in cyphering messages to him and decyphering the replies.

I had an unfortunate experience with Lord Salisbury when he came to dine and sleep at Windsor. The Queen, for some unknown reason, decided to sit in the corridor, which she used only when there were no guests. It was quite the most uncomfortable place to spend the evening, but as all the men had to stand, it really made very little difference whether they stood there or in the White

Drawing-room. Poor Lord Salisbury, who was bad on his legs at any time, had to stand leaning against a glass door, and found himself alongside a young man, myself, whom he knew slightly. The Queen sent a message to say that she would talk to him in five minutes. So he had to resign himself to spending his postprandial moments standing up and talking to me. I decided to ask him a question that no one had ever succeeded in answering to my satisfaction. When the Sovereign, after a general election, sent for a Minister and asked him to form a Government, did she do it on anyone's advice, or was she to act entirely on her own initiative? Of course when it was a matter of appointing a Prime Minister after the retirement or demise of one, there was no difficulty, but what happened when a Conservative Government went out of office and the Liberal party came in with no well-defined leader?

Thinking there was lots of time I determined to work up slowly to the point, and I sketched out the Sovereign's responsibilities, dwelling at some length on the situation where a Minister had to defend the action of the Sovereign even when such action had been taken on the advice of his predecessor, who belonged to the opposite party. Lord Salisbury appeared interested and said that Ministers were often called upon to defend a policy with which they were not in agreement. I then dwelt, as a preliminary to the larger question, on the theory that the Sovereign can do no wrong, and I asked what happened when the Sovereign acted without asking the advice of anyone and the responsible Minister found he had to support a line of policy with which he was not in agreement. It was then that the Queen sent for him and asked him to sit down, a thing she never did with any other man. They talked incessantly till eleven, and then the party broke up and I never had an opportunity of continuing my conversation and getting to the whole point of the discussion. No doubt Lord Salisbury went away with the impression that I was trying to teach him the intricacies of our nebulous constitution.

On one occasion abroad I had an amusing experience with Lord Salisbury, who was asked to come to Cimiez, near Nice, have luncheon with the Household, and see the Queen afterwards. Luncheon was always at one o'clock, but apparently he thought it was at 12.30 and arrived half an hour too soon. The two French officers on guard always had luncheon with us, and as they usually had *café au lait* at some unearthly early hour and *déjeuner* at eleven, they found one o'clock very late and were famished by the time luncheon was ready.

When a footman announced that Lord Salisbury was waiting in the drawing-room and that there was no one else in to receive him, I went off at once, and in the passage met the two French officers who, hearing Lord Salisbury had arrived, hoped that luncheon might be earlier. I shook hands with Lord Salisbury and presented the two officers. Then there was an awkward pause, no one knowing what to talk about or in what language to speak. It so happened that Lord Salisbury was particularly anxious to know before he saw the Queen whether she had received certain despatches and what line she took. Thinking it was bad manners to talk English as the French officers would be unable to understand, he proceeded to address me in French without, however, mentioning any names. I told him all he wanted to know, and we talked away in French about the political situation. After some twenty minutes Lord Salisbury turned the conversation on to local topics, but the Frenchmen were quite tongue-tied: not that they knew who Lord Salisbury was, for after luncheon they asked me who he was, and when I told them I saw it conveyed nothing to them. I realized it was the pronunciation of the name that beat them, and I repeated it as the French pronounce it, Sullesbuerree, and then they were thrilled.

Once when I was at Cimiez the Foreign Office sent out a circular impressing on all concerned the importance of keeping the cypher book always under lock and key, especially in foreign countries. One day the Queen sent me to see Lord Salisbury, who was living at Beaulieu, and give him a message. When I arrived at the house I rang and rang, and apparently there was no one in. As the front door was open I walked in and determined to write him a letter. There on the table in the hall I saw the cypher book. Not only was it not under lock and key, but left out for anyone to see.

Lord Rosebery was also *persona grata* with the Queen, although a Liberal. He amused her and was always good company. He seemed to have a sort of historical veneration for her and took the greatest pains to explain his policy. When the Queen opened the Indian and Colonial Exhibition, he pressed her to wear a crown, but she flatly refused. He, however, maintained that a crown, and not a bonnet, was the symbol of Empire.

Lord Cross [4] was one of her favourites, probably because he invariably agreed with all she said. He was accustomed to do himself very well at dinner, and although in no sense drunk, he was very convivial afterwards. Unfortunately he was careless about his dress, and almost invariably his white evening tie used to work round and up. It was therefore not to be wondered at if perfectly untrue tales of his drunkenness were repeated.

Another favourite of the Queen was Mr. Fowler, afterwards Lord Wolverhampton.[5] He also agreed with all the Queen said, but it was because he understood her character that he was so successful. Lord George Hamilton the Queen liked as he was amusing and interesting to talk to, and although he often disagreed with her, he always did so in such a charming way.

Arthur Balfour was another who was a great success with the Queen, although to me he never seemed to treat her seriously. His philosophical outlook and his cynical view that nothing mattered made it difficult for anyone to disagree with him. All the same, the Queen admired him and thought his speeches brilliant. I was always surprised at the way he and Lord Rosebery disliked each other, when really they were so much alike and there seemed so little difference in the way they looked on the various questions of the day. They were both literary, both very cynical, and both lazy. One would have imagined that they would have had no difficulty in working together but there always seemed a certain rivalry between them. Rosebery said that for an amateur politician Balfour was wonderful; while Balfour told me that he always admired the glib way Rosebery spoke when he knew little or nothing of the subject on which he was speaking.

[4] Richard Assheton Cross, 1st Viscount Cross. Home Secretary, 1874–80, 1885–86; Secretary for India, 1886–92. Conservative.

[5] Sir Henry H. Fowler, 1st Viscount Wolverhampton; between 1892 and 1895 held the offices of President of the Local Government Board and Secretary for India. Liberal.

Once at dinner the Queen was talking about people's handwriting and how illegible it was. After enumerating the really bad handwritings she had known, she mentioned Lord Halsbury's [6] and compared it to a fly crawling out of the ink-bottle across the paper. 'Yes, Ma'am,' added Arthur Balfour, 'and a drunken fly, too.'

When Princess Beatrice became Governor of the Isle of Wight, a great deal was made of it, but of course it really meant nothing. Arthur Balfour came down to stay at Osborne and during dinner the Queen said to him, 'Did you see in the newspapers about the Governor of the Isle of Wight?' He replied that he had not, and added, 'I never knew there was such a post, and I have not the foggiest idea who is the Governor'. This threw cold water on the dignity of the office and the Queen let the matter drop without explaining why she had asked. Arthur Balfour was told afterwards about Princess Beatrice being appointed, but he said he rarely read the newspapers and when he did that would be the last thing he would read about.

Joe Chamberlain, when he became Colonial Minister in the Unionist Government, came to dine and sleep several times. It was curious to see him talking earnestly and deferentially to the Queen when I remembered what a firebrand he had been, and how he had attacked the Monarchy and even the Queen herself. I think the Queen liked talking to him as, although he was always respectful, he never hesitated to state his opinion. She felt it was like talking to a wild man who had been tamed.

He was very good company in the smoking-room, and always said he knew he could talk quite openly as if he was going to tell us highly confidential secrets, but as a matter of fact he never told us anything that we could not have read in the newspapers. I asked him once whether it was not very confusing changing from one Government office to another. He replied, 'No, they are all so different'. He added that he always made a point of asking as many ignorant questions as he could think of when he first started because, he explained, once you have settled down you don't dare

[6] Hardinge Giffard, 1st Earl of Halsbury; Lord Chancellor, 1895–1905.

ask them. He said he never delegated any work to a subordinate until he knew exactly what that work was about.

One night at Osborne everyone had gone to bed except Chamberlain, Count Mensdorff,[7] and myself. Chamberlain had only just lit a large cigar and so it looked like an all-night sitting. Mensdorff talked of art generally and painting in particular, and Chamberlain said what a pity it was that the Queen had never been painted by a good British artist. I asked him whom he would choose, and he said Sargent, but I pointed out that he was American. I tried to keep the conversation off Angeli, who I knew was a great friend of Mensdorff, for I was uncertain what Chamberlain would say. Unfortunately Mensdorff alluded to Angeli, and before I could cut in Chamberlain remarked that he was a caricaturist and that his pictures were no better than coloured photographs.[8] Mensdorff took it very well and said that he knew there were people who didn't admire Angeli.

We drifted on to palmistry and I didn't make out to begin with whether Chamberlain believed in it or not, but soon he made fun of the whole thing. He told us a story of the Duchess of Manchester, who hardly knew the elementary rules of palmistry, foretelling the disaster of H.M.S. *Victoria*[9] in Maurice Bourke's hand, and how Maurice Bourke had written to her after the disaster and reminded her of what she had foretold, but she had quite forgotten all about it. From palmistry we drifted to hypnotism and Chamberlain was most interesting, having witnessed some of Charcot's experiments. We again got back to foretelling the future and he told us that Miss Beatrice Potter, who later married

---

[7] Count von Mensdorff-Pouilly-Dietrichstein, later Austrian Ambassador in London, 1904–14. A strong Anglophile, he did all in his power to prevent the outbreak of war in 1914, and was later entrusted by the Austrian Government with the important but fruitless negotiations with General Smuts in Switzerland, December 1917.

[8] Posterity seems to have ratified Chamberlain's verdict.

[9] H.M.S. *Victoria*, the Flagship of Sir George Tryon, C.-in-C. Mediterranean Squadron, was lost in 1893 after a collision with H.M.S. *Camperdown* during manoeuvres off Tripoli. Sir George and more than half the crew were drowned. Captain Bourke, who was in command of the *Victoria* at the time, was later tried by court-martial and cleared.

Sidney Webb,[10] had once told the hand of a very clever man, Mr. Cross, who was permanent Under-Secretary of the Home Office. She was in the middle of a long dissertation on his numerous talents when she stopped, and a look of horror came over her face, but she positively refused to say what she had seen although Chamberlain afterwards pressed her to do so. She agreed, however, to write it down and place this paper in a sealed envelope which was not to be opened till Mr. Cross died. About a year later Mr. Cross committed suicide by hanging himself, and Chamberlain, remembering the envelope, found it in a drawer in his writing-table and opened it. He found she had written 'Suicidal mania'.

When in 1898 Kitchener came up to Balmoral after the battle of Omdurman to see the Queen, we had a most interesting dinner as Arthur Balfour was in a witty mood and was wonderful in drawing out Kitchener, who gave details of the battle. Kitchener related how he had been rather inconvenienced after the battle by having two thousand women on his hands. Princess Beatrice asked what the women were like and he replied, 'Very much like all women, they talked a great deal.' At the end of dinner the Queen monopolized the conversation and related how after Gordon's death she had sent a telegram to Gladstone upbraiding him for his callous neglect of Gordon. Gladstone had complained that the telegram was not in cypher, but she had deliberately sent it *en clair* so that everyone should know what she thought of him.

The following day after luncheon Kitchener said he could not go out as he had to write his speech for the Guildhall dinner in London. He said that as he was quite unaccustomed to make speeches he found it all very difficult: the facts he had at his fingers' ends, but the difficulty was to put them together in a speech. Arthur Balfour said there was no difficulty about this and generally it was the facts that were the stumbling-block. He said that he was going out but would be back about five, and if he could be of any assistance he would be very glad to help. About five the Queen sent for me and asked me to read to her some Foreign Office tele-

---

[10] Joint authors of *Soviet Communism: A New Civilisation?* and other works, not always showing the accurate foresight displayed on this dismal occasion.

grams. She then told me to ask Kitchener to come and speak to her. I went off to Arthur Balfour's room and there I found Kitchener seated at a writing-table with a large piece of paper on which he was laboriously writing with a quill pen. Arthur Balfour was seated or rather lying down in an armchair with Kitchener's notes and trying to dictate, but whenever he said anything Kitchener contradicted him. I told Kitchener the Queen wished to see him, and Arthur Balfour jumped up and said, 'We shall never get on like this'. He suggested Kitchener leaving his notes and asked if there was such a thing as a shorthand writer, as he found it impossible to concentrate his thoughts and dictate so slowly, more especially as everything he said appeared to be controversial. I explained that there was no shorthand clerk but that I could write shorthand if he did not speak too fast. He at once clutched at the idea and said he would dictate a speech and Kitchener could do what he liked with it. I sat down nervously at the writing-table with a shorthand notebook while Arthur Balfour subsided once more deep in his armchair and closed his eyes. Then off he went, never wanting for a word, and I raced away to keep up with him. Once or twice when he became very eloquent I had to check the pace, but on the whole I managed very well. I then took this away to transcribe into longhand, and to type it. This took me over an hour, although Arthur Balfour had left out all statistics, merely using the words so-and-so. I then took my typescript back to Arthur Balfour, feeling very much like a boy showing his exercises to a master. He read it through and said, 'Captain, that is just what I said, but I should like to express some of the phrases better'. He went to the writing-table and polished the speech up until it was very scholarly and literary production.

I took the result to Kitchener, who read it through slowly and then roared with laughter. He said, 'You don't really think I could make a speech like that. Why, the whole place would scream with laughter at such beautiful language coming from me.' I felt he was right. It would have been absurd for him to deliver such a literary gem as a speech. 'But', he said, 'this is just what I wanted, and now I can rewrite the whole thing in my own language.' He did so, and it was a great success at the Guildhall.

On one occasion when Arthur Balfour came to stay at Osborne for a week-end, golf was proposed on Sunday afternoon. It seemed doubtful whether the Queen would quite approve of this, although at that time golf was beginning to be played everywhere on Sunday. We therefore decided to say as little as possible about it and as we played without caddies on the private links in the grounds there was no reason why anyone should know. It was to be a foursome, the Duke of York (later King George V) and Balfour against Bigge and me. Immediately after luncheon the Queen sent for Balfour and after speaking to him about serious matters for half an hour, asked him what he was going to do. He replied he was going for a walk with us, but unfortunately the Queen sent for the Duke of York and asked him the same question. He scorned to tell even a white lie and replied truthfully we were going to play golf, and he felt sure she would not mind as we would carry our own clubs. This downright answer was clearly the right one, but of course it put Arthur Balfour in a difficult position, and the Queen was much amused at catching him out, as she expressed it, 'telling a fib'.

The Duke of York told me that when his brother the Duke of Clarence died, the Queen asked him to change his name to Albert. He consulted my father, Sir Henry Ponsonby, who replied that he would gladly lay down his life for the Queen, but if she asked him to call himself Thomas he would certainly refuse.

Arthur Balfour was once staying away from Saturday to Monday when he got a telegram saying that he was urgently required in London. It was of the utmost importance and therefore he took a special train back, but forgot to order any conveyance to meet him. He had his bicycle with him and, instead of leaving it with his servant, he determined to bicycle to 10 Downing Street. He went off as fast as he could through the traffic and a policeman tried to stop him, but he dashed on. The inevitable result was that the policeman promptly whistled to the next one, who barred his path and so stopped him. Before he could explain the second constable said, 'You ought to be ashamed of yourself, you are old enough to know better'. He felt so small that he did not dare say who he was, and as the policeman allowed him to go free he went humbly away.

When the Queen went for a drive in London she always drove in an open landau with one footman and a Highlander up behind, four horses with postilions, two outriders in front, and two grooms in rear. In addition two Equerries in tall hats and frock-coats rode on either side of the carriage.

Once when I was riding with her, an American in a hansom came along behind us, but it was an unwritten law that no carriage of any sort might pass her. I heard an altercation going on and finally the American shouted to the cabman, 'I don't care if there are forty Queens, I have to catch my train and I'll give you a sovereign if I do so'. Not unnaturally the cabman determined to earn this tip and whipped up his horse into a hand gallop to pass the procession in front. Green, one of the grooms in rear, however, thought this should not be allowed. He had been one of the whips of the Quorn and was a finished horseman. He cantered along the side of the hansom till he came to a side street; then he got the cab-horse by the head and turned him to the right smartly, giving him a flick with his whip as he left. The horse galloped down the street and disappeared, while the American was apoplectic with rage.

CHAPTER IV

State functions — Private entertainments — The Queen's taste — The Queen in France — The Queen's eyesight fails — Stalking near Balmoral — The Queen's daughters

DURING QUEEN VICTORIA'S REIGN functions out of London, especially visits to big towns, were hardly arranged at all. The main features were decided upon by letter, but the local or municipal officials were left to decide the details. There seemed little or no preparation and yet everything went well. Nowadays when every small detail is arranged beforehand and elaborate programmes are printed, it seems wonderful that in those days no hitch in the proceedings ever occurred.

The Queen herself lent so much dignity to even a trifling ceremony that nothing else really mattered. She, however, was very punctilious about ceremonies being well done and noticed any fault. It was the custom for all the officials to play for safety and ensure that everybody was in time by adding a margin of safety to the time the ceremony was due to take place. For instance, I remember that when the son of the Amir of Afghanistan came to Windsor, the Queen said he was to arrive at 12.30. The Lord Chamberlain ordred everyone to be in his place by 12.15. The Grand Staircase was to be lined by men of the Blues, and the Equerry, determined there should be no risk of their being late, ordered the men to be there at 12 noon. The Commanding Officer of the Blues determined also to be on time, so he ordered the men to be in their places at 11.45, and when the Adjutant received the order he made it 11.30. The result was that the men arrived one whole hour too soon.

All this was, however, unknown to the Queen, but once it happened to me to get involved in a miscalculation of this sort. There

77

was a small investiture, but it necessitated a guard of honour being mounted in the Quadrangle. I had nothing to do with the arrangements, but it so happened that Sir Henry Byng, the Senior Equerry, was not well on the day, and so I had to do his duty. I ascertained that all the orders had been given and everyone had been summoned. The ceremony was to be at 11 A.M. I happened to be walking across the Quadrangle about 10 A.M. when I heard the band coming up the Castle Hill, and that meant that the guard of honour would be in its place an hour too soon. I rushed off and with difficulty silenced the band. I explained the situation to the captain of the guard of honour and suggested they should go to the riding-school in the Royal Mews, pile arms, and fall out. He agreed that this would be best, and accordingly the band and guard of honour disappeared to the stables. Unfortunately the Queen had heard the band and sent down a message to me to ask where it was. I had therefore to explain that by some mistake (I didn't say whose) the band had come too early and they had gone to the Royal Mews. The next day she sent a note to Sir Henry Byng asking for an explanation, and as he had recovered sufficiently to do duty, he had to write a long nebulous explanation for which he got no marks.

Randall Davidson, the Archbishop of Canterbury, a man with a great sense of humour, told me of an amusing incident that occurred when he was Dean of Windsor and Clerk of the Closet. Mr. Matthews (later Viscount Llandaff), the Home Secretary,[1] being a Roman Catholic, did not wish to be in attendance on the Queen during a religious ceremony, and therefore when the Bishop of Winchester went down to Osborne to 'do homage', he asked Lord Knutsford, the Under-Secretary, to take his place. Having never done this before, Lord Knutsford did not know that he had to bring with him a copy of the oath which the Bishop had to read out, and so arrived at Osborne without it. When his mistake was pointed out to him he telegraphed to his private secretary in London and told him to open the official box containing the oath and telegraph the contents to Osborne.

Doing homage is a solemn ceremony and the Bishop has to

[1] 1886–92.

kneel down and place his hands together as if in prayer. The Queen then puts her hands over his and he has to read out an oath of allegiance ending with 'God bless Queen Victoria'. When the hour for the ceremony arrived there was no oath. It was anticipated that the telegram would arrive during luncheon and a clerk accustomed to engross documents was ready with a large sheet of paper, but nothing came. The Queen was actually coming into the drawing-room before an intimation arrived that the oath was coming through slowly. She sent word that there was no time to write it out properly and that the Bishop would have to read it off the official telegraph forms. These were quite dignified enough for the purpose, being foolscap-sized paper with the Royal Arms at the top. The ceremony went very well until the Bishop, reading the oath clearly word by word, ended up with 'God bless Queen Victoria, there is nothing more in the box'.

The Archbishop told me another amusing story that had happened in Queen Victoria's reign when he was Dean of Windsor. At that time there were naval as well as military Knights of Windsor,[2] but they were the source of constant difficulties as they were always getting into trouble with the police and the municipal authorities. Nominally they were under the Dean and Chapter, but when on one occasion there had been trouble, the Dean thought it would carry more weight if Count Gleichen,[3] who had been an Admiral in the British Navy, gave them a talking-to in his capacity as Governor of Windsor Castle. Accordingly it was arranged that he should see them and give them a lecture. Count Gleichen walked in accompanied by the Dean and the senior Canon of St. George's Chapel, but, when he saw all these old salts assembled, he felt quite at home and forgot the ecclesiastical atmosphere he was in. He proceeded to harangue them in language he had been accustomed to use on the quarter-deck. He ended up by saying, 'As

[2] A number of officers who have performed meritorious services but who are unable to maintain themselves suitably; they receive a pension of £50-130 *per annum*, with apartments in Windsor Castle.

[3] Admiral Prince Victor of Hohenlohe-Langenburg, for many years known as Count Gleichen. After a distinguished career in the Royal Navy, he became a professional sculptor. His most important work was a huge statue of King Alfred the Great at Wantage.

the Dean said to me just now, if these blasted fellows don't know how to behave, we'll damned well teach 'em'. The Archbishop added that it was distinctly trying to stand there and hear these forcible expressions put into his mouth.

The Queen was very fond of music and constantly had singers down to Windsor and Osborne: even at Balmoral there were private concerts. Usually such things were managed by Signor Tosti,[4] who was *persona gratissima* with the Queen as she admired his songs very much. He knew most of the artists and was generally able to gratify her wish to hear music. He once, however, made a mistake and treated the great operatic singers Jean and Edouard De Reszke as if they were itinerant musicians. The Queen had expressed a wish to hear them sing and everything had been left to Tosti to arrange it. It turned out that he did not consider them good enough to have any meal in the Castle and therefore took them to the White Hart Hotel in Windsor for an early dinner. They were then smuggled up with the accompanist through the back passages to the Red Drawing-room. The result was that they were very much annoyed. The programme was started by Jean, who didn't seem to care how he sang. Being too good an artist to sing badly he went through his song apathetically, and Edouard followed in very much the same tone. Now it happened that Lord de Grey, one of the syndicate who were financing the Covent Garden Opera, had been asked down to Windsor for the concert, and he found out the whole story, and taking advantage of the first pause between the songs he quickly explained to the Queen what had happened. The Queen almost immediately asked the Master of the Household, Lord Edward Pelham-Clinton, to present the two singers. She was in a charming mood and she treated them like Polish noblemen, asking questions about people she knew in Poland and telling them stories about Mario and Grisi, the great singers of her youth. Both Jean and Edouard were completely fascinated by her, and when they next sang it was quite a different thing. They were, so to speak,

[4] Later Sir Paolo Tosti (K.C.V.O., 1908). His songs which include *Come to my Heart, Good-bye,* and other sentimental favourites, were not admired by the Queen alone.

inebriated by her charm and let themselves go. It was such a success that the difficulty was to stop them, as they had practically discarded the programme and were singing their old favourites. While the concert was going on, orders for supper for them had been given, and so these two great singers went away in a completely changed mood.

At Osborne Kennerley Rumford [5] came down several times, as the Queen liked his singing, but he was often highly tried when he had to sing something from one of Wagner's operas. Once he and Leonard Borwick, the pianist, came to Balmoral, where unfortunately the Clerk-Comptroller, who was responsible for the food, had forgotten all about supper for them. There was a small gillies' ball that night, and this accounted for none of the other servants reminding him that the musicians would need something to eat. The result was that we had to send them back to Ballater without any supper. Kennerley Rumford was very nice about it, but I can imagine that driving back to Ballater without anything to eat and arriving at the hotel when everybody was in bed must have been very trying to the temper. Singers rarely eat anything before a concert, and therefore as the concert did not end till 11.30 they must have been very hungry.

Before the concert started the Queen wanted her chair moved to another part of the room, and although there were hundreds of servants in the Castle, she did not want to ring for anyone and asked me to do this. She sat with her feet straight out and I took a firm hold of her chair and lifted it to the place she indicated. It nearly made me laugh to find myself staggering about with the chair and the Queen in it, but mercifully I did not drop her.

Once before at Osborne I had been employed in furniture moving. After dinner Madame Albani,[6] Ben Davies, and Kennerley Rumford were to sing, and the Queen wanted the sofa in one place while Princess Beatrice maintained it had always been pushed into quite another place when there was music. I was appealed to as to which was right. I said that the last time there was singing I

[5] Clara Butt's husband, a fine singer in his own right.
[6] Later Dame Emma Albani. First appeared in Bellini's *Sonnambula*, 1870. Published memoirs in 1911, *Forty Years of Song*.

thought the sofa was out of the room. I don't think that Solomon ever gave a better decision because no one was then right and no one was wrong. 'The last time', said the Queen, 'there was singing in this room, Fritz was not here.' So I curled up at once. But Princess Beatrice argued that her suggestion should be carried out and the Queen said, 'Very well, let it be moved out.' As the only male besides myself was the Duke of Albany,[7] aged about twelve, we set to work. Carrying out the sofa presented no difficulties, but when it came to moving the grand piano on a carpet, it required all my efforts to start it. However, with the veins starting out of my head I managed with the help of the young duke to get it in its right position. He was delighted at being able to make a mess of the room. When the cloud of dust had subsided the singers were let loose.

On one occasion when Madame Albani sang at Balmoral the Queen ignored her impresario, Baron Caccamisi, who was quite furious. He insisted on coming with her and demanded an interview with the acting Master of the Household, Alec Yorke, who happened to be in his bath and who therefore asked me to tackle the irate Baron. He said he had been insulted and that unless he was asked to be present he would take Albani away. I pretended it was a mistake and asked him to sit down and wait. When, however, I presented the problem to the Queen's page, who asked her what should be done, the instructions I received were that he could have as much to eat and drink as he liked but he was not to come into the drawing-room until after the concert as he might make Albani nervous. I repeated this to Alec Yorke, who ordered a separate dinner for the poor man.

The Queen was especially fond of the playing of Maria Janotha, Court pianist to the German Emperor. Janotha was very eccentric and always knelt down at the Queen's feet and presented her with some white heather. She also placed a mascot on the piano while she played to keep away the evil eye.

Once or twice the Queen had an opera performed at Windsor and this was a terrific business. A special train was ordered to bring the artists, the chorus, the orchestra, down from London

[7] Later the last reigning Duke of Saxe-Coburg-Gotha.

and take them back after the performance. Then supper had to be provided for all, special scenery had to be made and the Waterloo Gallery had to be turned into a theatre. When all was ready and everybody was seated, two pages walked down from the Queen's room to make certain that there was no one standing about; then came the Queen, wheeled in her chair by an Indian attendant, preceded by the two Equerries. This procession came down the corridor and St. George's Hall to the entrance of the Waterloo Gallery where the Master of the Household received her. She then got out of the chair and walked in on the arm of the Indian.

The acoustics were not really good for opera, and singers usually came down early to try their voices. One of the difficulties was that the Queen herself sat in the front row within a few feet of the singers. When Francisco Tamagno came down to sing in one opera he arrived very late and had no time to try his voice. The result was that he nearly blew the Queen's cap off when he let himself go.

Once or twice whole plays came down, but this was expensive, and amateur actors in the Household were usually asked to produce something. There were two outstanding actors, Arthur Collins [8] and Alec Yorke, and these two alternately drilled the members of the Household and produced plays.

The first time I acted was in *She Stoops to Conquer,* stage-managed by Arthur Collins, who did the part of the Innkeeper. This was before I joined the Household. My brother Arthur [9] was Tony Lumpkin, while Arthur Bigge and I did the two lovers, and Princess Louise and Princess Beatrice the two principal ladies' parts. The Queen came to the rehearsals, which frightened us all very much, and when she saw me chucking Princess Louise under the chin (I was supposed to mistake her for the barmaid) she thought this was overdone. I received a message that I had better not indulge in any chucking under the chin. The next day I went through my part but never came within touching distance of Princess Louise, and again received a message to say I was overdoing

---

[8] Lieutenant-Colonel Arthur Collins, Gentleman Usher to Queen Victoria.
[9] Later 1st Lord Ponsonby of Shulbrede. For many years Socialist M.P. for Brightside Division of Sheffield.

it the other way. I consulted Princess Louise herself, who roared with laughter at my dilemma, and we finally hit off a happy medium.

Both Princess Louise and Princess Beatrice were quite good in their parts, but very sketchy with the words. I therefore learnt their parts as well as my own so that I could either say their words or prompt them. Everyone else did the same, but there was one small bit when they were both on together and of course they stuck, each one thinking it was the other's fault. After an awkward pause the servants gave a round of applause, which I thought was a very intelligent way of helping them, but although the prompter was able to start them again, they could not get going and the stage carpenter solved the problem by letting the curtain down.

Another time I acted in *A Scrap of Paper* at Balmoral, this time under Alec Yorke as stage manager. The Queen thought the performance so good that she invited Hare and his company, who were playing at Aberdeen, to come and witness the performance. They must have been amused as they all knew the play well, but of course they were loud in our praises.

There were also tableaux in which all the members of the Royal Family took part. They must have been very wearying for the audience, who had to sit for two and a half hours with very long intervals between the tableaux. The only person who thoroughly enjoyed them was Clarkson, the wigmaker from London. As he hob-nobbed with the Royal Family and as he supplied all the dresses, he probably made a very good thing out of it.

In literature the Queen's taste was said to be deplorable, and although she had little time for reading she never liked the works of the great authors. I remember a discussion taking place once at Balmoral between Queen Victoria and the Empress Frederick on the subject of Marie Corelli. The Queen said she would rank as one of the greatest writers of the time, while the Empress thought that her writings were trash. I was seated at the other end of the large dining-room table and therefore had not, unfortunately, heard the commencement of the discussion. The Empress suddenly called across the table to me and asked me what I thought of

Marie Corelli. Quite unconscious of the fact that the Queen was an admirer of this authoress, I replied that her books undoubtedly had a large sale, but I thought the secret of her popularity was that her writings appealed to the semi-educated. Whereupon the Empress clapped her hands, and the subject dropped with startling suddenness. It was not till afterwards that I learnt how I had put my foot in it.[10]

Queen Victoria had far too much character and individuality to have good taste. Apart from the creators of art, the majority of human beings acquire by degrees good taste by sinking their own individual likes and dislikes and adopting the suggestions thrust on them by experts. Now although the Queen had every desire to encourage art generally, she invariably refused to be influenced in any way by other people's opinions, and having very fixed ideas of her own she clung to what she liked.

In portraiture she considered the likeness to be of paramount importance and the artistic merit of the picture itself to be quite a secondary matter. Therefore she admired Angeli, while artists like Watts were unintelligible to her, and the Impressionist school she treated as a joke.

Every year the Queen went abroad, and before I joined the Household she had been to Aix-les-Bains, Grasse, Hyères, and Florence. After 1894, however, she invariably went to Nice, first to a small hotel, the Excelsior, with partitions which were made water-tight. This was very comfortably arranged, but it would never have done by itself, as of course the gardens round the hotel were always full of tourists. Mr. Cazalet lent the Queen the Villa Liserbe, which made all the difference as the Queen was able to go there in her bath-chair and sit out in the garden all the morning doing her routine work.

The curious thing was that she insisted on bringing with her all her English and Scotch servants. Altogether, counting the Princesses and the suite, there were about a hundred to be transported from England. Sir William Carington had a list made of all these servants and submitted it to her, but she said she had

[10] A common admiration for Marie Corelli was one of the few sentiments shared by the Queen and Mr. Gladstone.

85

gone carefully into it and found she could not do without one of them.

The Queen usually crossed the Channel in her yacht, the *Victoria & Albert,* escorted by torpedo-boats, and the crowds of people who came to see her pass were quite phenomenal. At Folkestone there were some thousands of people, but they could have seen little or nothing as no one was allowed near the Royal yacht, and on the pier there was a guard of honour and band with the General and his staff. Sometimes the Queen crossed in an ordinary steamer and every possible arrangement for her comfort was made. The only disadvantage of this was that the boat was crammed with both English and French railway directors and managers who thought it was their duty to accompany her. The Queen always insisted on a covered gangway being rigged up on the Royal yacht so that the crowd should not see her being carried in her chair, but with an ordinary steamer this was not possible, and an uncovered gangway was used. It was, however, usually so steep that no one would have expected an old lady to walk up it. At either Cherbourg or Boulogne there was a dense crowd of people who waved and cheered. The British were not popular at the time with the French, but I never saw anything but enthusiasm for the Queen. On the pier was a beautiful red velvet and gold lace tent for her to sit in, with a guard of honour of the French Army, while a host of Generals, Admirals, and officials hoping to be presented were drawn up near the tent. What with the band playing and the crowd continually cheering vociferously, it was difficult to hear anything. We travelled comfortably by train across France, but in those days the washing arrangements were very sketchy. I usually got the courier to telegraph to some station and order a jug of hot water to be ready to be placed in my carriage. This enabled me to wash and shave so that on arrival, when I donned my frock-coat and tall hat, I looked presentable.

We usually stopped at Cannes for five minutes to allow the Prince of Wales, the Duke of Cambridge,[11] or any other member of the Royal Family who happened to be there to board the train

[11] Queen Victoria's cousin; Commander-in-Chief of the British Army, 1856–95.

to meet the Queen. At Nice the whole town turned out and lined the streets from the station to the hotel. There were four regiments of infantry and a battery of artillery to keep back the ever enthusiastic crowd. At the station the Préfet, the Mayor, the General, and a host of men in evening clothes and tall hats were assembled.

The usual routine at the hotel was that the Household had their meals separately as in England, but one or two were invited to join the Queen's dinner. The English hours were kept: breakfast at half past nine, luncheon at one, and dinner at a quarter to nine. There was always a French guard mounted on the hotel with two officers, and this arrangement of meals was apt to upset them as they usually had their *café au lait* at six, *déjeuner* at eleven, and dinner at six.

After breakfast we retired to our rooms and worked till luncheon while the Queen did her official boxes in the garden of the Villa Liserbe and wrote out telegrams to be cyphered to London. In the afternoon we were not wanted and the men of the Household usually went to Monte Carlo. This somewhat ruinous way of spending the afternoon required careful management so that the little money I possessed could be made to last during the visit. I therefore only took with me five louis and when I had lost these I talked to anyone I knew till the next train went to Nice. One day, however, I was very unlucky; I lost my money and then lost the train: and when I eventually got to the station I found I had lost my ticket. I had to ask the stationmaster to give me one, and I paid him back the next day, but all this meant I was very late and I did not reach the hotel till 8.30. It was a great relief to me to hear that I was not dining with the Queen.

Divine Service was held at the hotel on Sundays in a room that was converted into a chapel. The servants formed the choir, and usually any distinguished clergymen who happened to be in the Riviera did the service. The Bishop of Ripon (Boyd Carpenter), a great favourite of the Queen, often came to officiate. Once Signor Tosti joined the congregation although he was a Roman Catholic, and tried to help the choir. He had a fruity tenor voice and sang the tenor part so lustily that the choir, completely upset, died away. I had my work cut out in showing him the place in the Prayer Book, as he was quite capable of singing the wrong part of the service. On one occasion he attempted to sing the Commandments.

In April 1898 Félix Faure, the President of the French Republic, paid a private visit to the Queen, who appreciated the civility. The only fault he made was that of trying to imitate royalty instead of remaining what he was—a President of a Republic. His successors never attempted this and were far more dignified in consequence. The Queen had an intense dislike for all Republics and while she had to admit that he was head of a soverign State, she flatly refused to treat him as a soverign. The Prince of Wales came over from Cannes to be present, and he was all in favour of a little difference being made. On account of the Queen's age and infirmity it was out of the question that she should go down to the door to receive the President, but there seemed no objection to the Prince of Wales doing so. After much discussion a compromise was reached and it was decided that the Prince of Wales should not go down to the door but should meet the President on the stairs. This was all the Queen would allow.

In the Hall Lady Southampton, Miss Phipps,[12] and Miss Evelyn Moore, Sir Arthur Bigge, Sir William Carington, and myself awaited the President. When he arrived, he looked round to see who was there to meet him, and seeing neither the Queen nor the Prince of Wales, kept his hat on to imply that the visit had not properly begun. He shook hands with the three ladies still with his hat on, and of course did the same with the men. Such a proceeding was hardly dictated by the Protocol, and it surprised us all. When Paris heard of this afterwards I was told that everyone said it was outrageous and very bad manners. The President was then conducted upstairs, and the Prince of Wales came hurrying down as if he were late. It was then and only then that the President took his hat off. He remained a quarter of an hour with the Queen while we talked to his staff. We all then came into the room and his staff was presented to the Queen. He then kissed the

[12] The Hon. Harriet Phipps, a Woman of the Bedchamber; the Hon. Evelyn Moore was a Maid of Honour.

Queen's hand and said goodbye. This he did very well and the Queen stood up with the help of her stick and said some polite remarks about the beauties of France. Later on the Prince of Wales returned the visit, but I did not accompany him.

The King of the Belgians [13] came to dinner one night, and after dinner it was interesting to see him talking to the Queen. He seemed very nervous and frightened of her and sat twisting his hands like a schoolboy. It was curious that she should like him, because his morals were notorious, but the Queen seemed to overlook this. Once he came all the way to Balmoral to see her and the Queen met him in the hall. When he kissed her hand she said, *'Mon cousin, quelle course!'* to which he replied, *'Ma cousine, quelle butte!'* I gave him marks for being so ready with an answer.

The Queen of the Netherlands,[14] then aged eighteen, came to see the Queen in 1898 and it was interesting to see the two Queens together as they were so different in age. It appeared to be the custom for the suite of the visited to write their names and leave cards on the suite of the visitor. I had therefore to go to Cannes and write the names of all the Queen's suite in the Queen of Holland's book. The farce of leaving cards struck me as being so absurd; as there were six of Queen Victoria's suite and twelve of the Dutch suite I had to leave seventy-two cards.

On one occasion I went to Cannes to bid farewell from the Queen to the Prince of Wales and I found that a train back to Nice started five minutes after the Prince of Wales' train left. I determined to catch this, but unfortunately so many people came to the station to see him off that I had only one minute in which to get to another platform and catch my train. I remained bowing on the platform till the Prince's train started and then ran like a hare. But a tall hat and frock-coat were never intended as suitable attire for running, and there was something ridiculous in my bounding over the line to catch my train. I reached the train just as it was starting, rushed to the first carriage I saw and swung myself in. Now the train on leaving Cannes goes immediately into

[13] Leopold II.
[14] Queen Wilhelmina, now Princess of the Netherlands.

a tunnel and it so happened that in the carriage which I had selected were two maiden ladies who had been nervous about travelling for fear of thieves and who had therefore tipped the guard
to give them a compartment to themselves. When they saw me
jump in as the train rushed into the tunnel they never waited a
moment but pulled the emergency cord, with the result that the
train stopped and glided back into Cannes station. There the stationmaster appeared supported by gendarmes, and the two French
ladies monopolized the conversation, but they were so excited and
incoherent that the stationmaster found it difficult to understand
what exactly had happened. I sat quiet to start with, but as I
wanted to get back I quietly pushed them aside and emerged from
the carriage. The gendarmes eyed me suspiciously, but I explained
in a few words what had happened, and I offered to go to another carriage. The stationmaster took me to another carriage,
and on the train went.

There was always much ado about Orders and presents when
the Queen left, as nearly everyone wanted an English Order,
which was like a rare stamp or an unknown egg to collectors. The
officials themselves were very jealous about others having Orders
besides themselves. The proprietor of the hotel was very anxious
to have the M.V.O.,[15] but the Queen said she would on no account
give her personal Order to an hotel proprietor, and in this she was
strongly supported by the Préfet, the Mayor, and others. The
difficulty was what to give him and finally the Queen decided on a
bronze bust of herself about two feet high on a black plinth. She
told me she would pretend to hand it to him, but as it was so heavy
I should have to lift it and give it to the hotel man. I brought him
in and presented him to the Queen, who made a pretty speech
thanking him for all he had done. I then came forward with the
bust, but I didn't know it was not attached to the plinth, and in
handing it to her and on to the man, the bust rolled off and fell
within a few inches of the Queen's feet, which rather spoilt the
ceremony. I was afraid she would be cross, but she roared with
laughter and so it passed off very well. I heard afterwards that the
hotel proprietor had prepared a beautiful speech saying how flat-

[15] Member of the Royal Victorian Order.

tered he was at receiving such a present, but adding that he would have preferred an Order. Fortunately this slight accident prevented his delivering this oration.

During the Queen's last visit to Cimiez I suddenly got a telegram from Sidney Greville [16] asking me to come to Cannes and play golf. I received permission from the Queen to do so and arrived about luncheon-time at the golf club. I found the Grand Duke Michael,[17] who was a very touchy and tiresome man, his wife, Countess de Torby, a delightful person, the Prince of Wales, Mrs. George Keppel, Miss Marie Hay,[18] Sir Harry Keppel and Captain Colin Keppel,[19] and a host of other people. We had an enormous *déjeuner* which quite ruined my golf. After playing in a foursome I drove back with the Prince of Wales and Sidney Greville to their hotel, and then back by train. The Prince of Wales plied me with questions on every conceivable subject on the way home and, as this was the first time I had talked to him since I was a boy, I was very careful about what I said. It occurred to me afterwards that the Prince of Wales wanted to see what I was like.

During the last years of her life the Queen's eyesight became very bad and the difficulty of writing so that she could read became greater. My handwriting was obviously unsuitable for this purpose, and I soon realized that if I wanted to succeed in making it legible for her I should have to alter it completely. It was all very difficult as I had constantly to write to her every day. Also I had to copy her letters, which was by no means easy, as her handwriting, especially as her sight got worse, became extremely difficult to read. These copies always looked so odd in my handwriting, especially sentences like 'William is quite wrong: he should remember that as German Emperor, etc. etc.' or 'Bertie and Alix must not do this'.

[16] The Hon. Sir Sidney Greville. Private Secretary to Lord Salisbury; Equerry to Prince of Wales 1898–1901; Groom-in-Waiting to King Edward VII; Paymaster to the Royal Household, 1911–20. Died 1927.
[17] The Grand Duke Michael Michailovitch of Russia.
[18] Afterwards Mme Herbert von Hindenburg. Wrote under her maiden name.
[19] The Hon. Sir Henry Keppel, Admiral of the Fleet. Capt. Colin Keppel, later Admiral Sir Colin Keppel, was his son.

I bought some copy-books issued for girls' schools and developed a completely new handwriting, very large, with perfectly formed letters. I also bought some special ink like boot varnish and Sir A. Bigge invented a copper tray the size of an ordinary letter with a spirit lamp underneath so that I could dry my letters quickly, since blotting-paper was out of the question. This was quite a success to begin with, but I soon received pathetic messages asking me to write larger and blacker still, and I got some more potent ink specially made. The disadvantage of this ink was that it came through the paper, and I got over this difficulty by writing on one side of the paper only. This worked very well at first, but when long cypher telegrams came, the amount of paper I used by writing very large and on one side only made the length of the telegram look so formidable that the Queen sent me a message to say that my writing on one side of the paper was very inconvenient and would I therefore write on both sides as I did formerly. Obviously the only solution was now to get thicker paper, and I took immense trouble over this and got the Stationery Office to make writing-paper stamped in the same way and looking exactly like the usual writing-paper, but very much thicker. This again was a success to begin with, but it appeared that the Queen kept all these decyphered telegrams in a case to refer to until they were sent to the archives at Windsor, and she soon found that the thick paper was far too bulky. I received a message that the Queen hoped I would revert to the ordinary paper in future. I grasped then that it was hopeless and I consulted Sir James Reid as to whether it would not be possible to explain all the difficulties to her, but he said he feared her sight was going and that any explanation would therefore be useless. So I went back to the ordinary paper and ordinary ink, and of course received a message to say would I write blacker, but as it was hopeless I didn't attempt to alter anything.

In May 1899 I married, having waited three years. The Queen had strenuously opposed the marriage, giving as her reason that a man always told his wife everything and therefore all her private affairs would get known all over London. Colonel and Mrs. Kennard not unnaturally thought me a poor match for their beautiful daughter, and so, faced with all this opposition, we felt unable to publish our banns. But after three years we determined to insist on fixing the date. Colonel and Mrs. Kennard at last gave their consent, but the Queen's opposition was more difficult to overcome. It was Miss Phipps who undertook to persuade the Queen that after three years' waiting she should withdraw her opposition. Eventually I was told I might marry, but I was to understand that I should never have a house given to me.

The Empress Eugénie [20] told me that she was certainly on my side but feared she could be of little help. She added that she had heard that my fiancée was beautiful, and that this was much more important than being good. The world was chock full of good women but there were very few beautiful women.

The marriage took place at the Guards' Chapel and the Prince of Wales and all the members of the Royal Family came to it, with the result that I and Charles Corkran, my best man, had to appear in full uniform. As so many members of the Royal Family came, all London flocked to it, and the Guards' Chapel was filled to overflowing.

Later in the year the Empress Frederick said she would persuade the Queen to give me the Saxon Tower at Windsor Castle, which was at that time vacant. Princess Christian, Princess Louise, and Princess Beatrice all agreed to help, but apparently it was overdone. They all swamped the Queen with arguments why I should have this Tower, with the result that she firmly refused to give it to me and had it turned into a store.

When it came to her giving me a wedding present, Miss Adams, one of the Queen's dressers, a most excellent woman and a friend of mine, told me that the Queen had ordered her to get me a silver tea service for this purpose. She herself thought it should be a tea and coffee service, and as she was a privileged person and allowed to say what she thought, she had told the Queen so, but Her Majesty had replied rather tartly, 'Am I giving this present or are you?' This, of course, put the lid on further discussion.

The Queen's eyesight became worse about 1898, when she first began to mistake people. The first time I noticed the difference

[20] Napoleon III's widow lived on at Farnborough till 1920.

was at Balmoral when before leaving the room she said, 'Where is Fritz?' Before I could interpose, Lord Balfour of Burleigh,[21] who was six-foot-five and weighed sixteen stone, came forward with a smile and a bow, not having heard what she said. The Queen, supposing him to be me, asked him how his mother was, which startled him considerably as his mother had been dead for years. Another time she thought Lord William Cecil,[22] who was standing by the door, was me, and congratulated him on his good shooting. It was particularly unfortunate as he had missed a stag while I had got two, and of course he thought she was ironical; but she suddenly realized her mistake and sent for me.

No one was really kinder to bad shots as a rule than she was, although the head stalker came in every night to tell her exactly what each person out stalking or fishing had done. She always pretended not to know the result of the day's sport and asked for information. Prince Francis Joseph of Battenberg, who was a very bad shot, unlike his brother Prince Henry, unfortunately didn't know this. Having been out stalking, he proceeded to give a rambling account of his day's sport, quite unconscious that the Queen knew every detail. All would have been well if he had left it at that, but he went on to say that it was a pity everything was so badly done and that the stalkers did not know much about stalking. Then the Queen turned on him and rent him. She asked him how many shots he had had, and when he replied he could not remember, she asked whether he had had seven, and had missed them all. She asked how far the stags were when he fired and he replied that he was no judge of distance, whereupon she said, 'I suppose about a hundred yards'. It then dawned on him that she knew exactly what had happened and he shut up like an umbrella. I was a very indifferent but keen fisherman, and as the Queen was always told about every day's fishing she was under no delusion about my piscatorial powers. One night she asked me what sport I had had, and when I replied that I had caught nothing, she said, 'Not a very good fisherman, I fear'.

[21] Alexander Hugh Bruce, 6th Lord Balfour of Burleigh.
[22] Son of 3rd Marquess of Exeter.

In 1898 the Neumanns [23] took Invercauld, the Farquharsons' place, which is a few miles from Balmoral, and when the Prince of Wales came up to stay with the Queen they invited him to a deer drive. I was also included amongst the rifles.

Everything went wrong. In the first place the deer refused to be driven in the proper direction; whether this was sheer bad luck or owing to the lack of skill on the part of the keepers it is difficult to say. Deer when they are conscious of being driven invariably go straight back through the beaters and therefore it has to be done in a subtle manner. Whatever the cause was, the drive that lasted two hours proved a failure and no one got a shot. The Prince of Wales, who knew the difficulties, took it with great equanimity and made light of it, but when the luncheon proved a fiasco, it was quite a different matter. Neumann, full of apologies for the failure of the drive, led us off to luncheon. He had made all the arrangements himself so that there should be no mistake. We walked down a path in single file and he assured us that it was not far. After half an hour's walk we came to a wood and Neumann explained he had chosen this sheltered spot in case it was a windy day. It seemed an ideal place but there were no signs of anything to eat. He told us to wait a moment while he looked about and, like a hound who is trying to pick up the scent, he circled round and round but with no success. The Prince of Wales, who by that time was getting very hungry, began to make very scathing remarks about rich men undertaking things they knew nothing about and ended by shouting suggestions to the wretched Neumann, who was still scouring the countryside at a trot. I then went after Neumann and asked if I could help. He produced a copy of his orders and said he had looked out the place on a map, which didn't seem to help much. While we were talking he caught sight of a shepherd and raced off after him. The shepherd explained that the place he had written down was over five miles off and that the one we had come to was differently pronounced, although spelt very similarly. The problem was how to get the luncheon and the guests together. Neumann begged me to explain the situation to

[23] Later Sir Sigmund Neumann, 1st Bart.; prominent in Edwardian banking circles.

the Prince of Wales and tell him that he would go as fast as he could to get a conveyance if the guests would walk as far as the road and wait there. H.R.H. on hearing the explanation called Neumann every synonym for an idiot, but urged by hunger he agreed to walk to the road, which took us about half an hour. It was then past two and there, on a heap of stones, we sat silently waiting for a conveyance. Conversation was at first tried, but eventually we all relapsed into gloomy silence. It was past three when a wagonette arrived and we all bundled in. When we did find the right place we thought the luncheon was the best we had ever eaten. But it was too late to have another drive in the afternoon and we returned home.

Queen Victoria's daughters were all very talented and would have been remarkable in any class of society. The Empress Frederick was the cleverest as she was a great reader. Princess Alice I never knew, as she died in 1878. Princess Christian was a very good musician and played the piano remarkably well. She had been well grounded in classical music when young and delighted in playing duets with professionals on two pianos. An amusing incident occurred once at Osborne when Sir Walter Parratt, the celebrated organist at St. George's Chapel, was staying there. A new footman was told by Princess Christian to ask Parratt to play after tea, but he didn't know anyone by sight. On going into the Equerries' room he found Sir Henry Byng (later Lord Strafford) seated at a writing table and thought he must be Parratt. 'Princess Christian', he said, 'asks if you will come and play four hands after tea.' This was quite unintelligible to Byng, who merely said, 'Will you repeat all that slowly?' and then the mistake was explained.

Princess Louise had a remarkable talent for drawing and painting and having worked at her art for many years was almost professional in the way she painted. Princess Beatrice played very well on the piano and also sketched in water-colour but was rather eclipsed by her more brilliant sisters.

They all had a great facility for writing letters or telegrams. I was often surprised, when I was called upon to help them, at the easy manner in which they could dictate telegrams. I always thought that had they belonged to the Jones or Robinson families, they would have been considered very remarkable women, but people seemed to take it for granted that they were remarkable because they were Princesses. Later in life, when their talents were of no use to them, they often failed owing to their total inability to assess men at their proper value. They were usually taken in by a fraud and were unable to distinguish a second-rate from a first-rate man.

CHAPTER V

The Irish visit — Sorting the archives — Acting Private Secretary

THE QUEEN'S VISIT to Dublin in April 1900 was a great success. She cleverly led up to it and decided upon it entirely on her own initiative and without any persuasion from any of the Ministers. It was, I think, the Duke of York (later King George V), who first put the idea in her head, as his visit to the Horse Show in 1897 had gone so well, and even in the South of Ireland he had been well received.

The Irish people always resented the coldness of the Royal Family towards Ireland and complained that their Sovereign had not set foot in Ireland since 1861. They quite overlooked the fact that there had been occurrences which were calculated to implant in Her Majesty's mind a distrust and even a dislike of Ireland. The first was that when the Prince Consort died the Queen presented a statue of him to the city of Dublin, but the Mayor and Corporation refused to accept it and sent it back to her. This occurred when she was in such deep grief that it completely overshadowed her whole life, and she is reported to have said that she would never forgive Ireland.

Then in 1885 the visit of the Prince of Wales was hardly encouraging, although at first a certain semblance of loyalty was kept up. The Dublin City Council flatly refused to take any official part in his reception, and his visit to the South was nothing more or less than a dismal failure. At Mallow ugly incidents were only just avoided, while at Cork the town was hung with black, and coffins were placed in the streets through which he passed.

In the Queen's Jubilee of 1887 addresses and telegrams of congratulation came not only from the Dominions and Colonies but from most of the countries in the world, but nothing from Dublin or the South of Ireland. On the Diamond Jubilee of 1897 the same thing happened. It is hardly to be wondered at that the Queen resented all these slights and regarded Ireland with antipathy and even dislike. The remarkable valour and loyalty displayed by the Irish regiments in most of the battles in South Africa, however, seemed to have changed the Queen's opinion and she began a series of little attentions that were much appreciated by the Irish. After one of the victories she sent a telegram of congratulation specially for the Irish troops. The warm-hearted Irish people responded to these attentions and soon a more favourable atmosphere for a better feeling between the Queen and Ireland was created. The formation of the Irish Guards had been suggested some months previously, but at that time she did not like the idea and so nothing was done. When she finally decided to pay a visit to Ireland she sent for all the papers and not only approved of the creation of a battalion of Irish Guards but even pressed it forward. She stipulated, however, that this was not to be publicly announced until she was in Ireland. First of all the announcement was made that she intended to pay a visit to Dublin, and after she had arrived the Creation of the Irish Guards was made public. The Irish people welcomed all this enthusiastically although, of course, the extremists remained hostile.

The Queen was accompanied by Princess Christian and Princess Beatrice, and the following members of the Household were in attendance: the Countess of Antrim, the Hon. Harriet Phipps, the Earl of Denbigh,[1] Sir Fleetwood Edwards, Sir Arthur Bigge, Sir William Carington, Sir James Reid, and myself. Sir Matthew White Ridley [2] was Minister in Attendance.

We crossed over from Holyhead in the Royal Yacht *Victoria & Albert,* in April 1900, and arrived at Kingstown in the morning amidst much booming of guns and hoisting of flags. The Queen landed about eleven, and the procession, consisting of three carriages escorted by the Life Guards, drove off to Dublin. Carington and I rode behind the Queen's carriage and we went at a slow trot, but it was a long way and it must have been very trying and

[1] Rudolph, 9th Earl of Denbigh; a Catholic Lord-in-Waiting.
[2] Later Viscount Ridley.

hot for the Escort. There were crowds of people practically all the way, but when we got into Dublin the mass of people wedged together in the street and in every window, even on the roofs, was quite remarkable. Although I had seen many visits of this kind, nothing had ever approached the enthusiasm and even frenzy displayed by the people of Dublin. There were, however, two places where I heard ugly sounds like booing, but they only seemed like a sort of bagpipe drone to the highly-pitched note of the cheering. One of these was the office of some Nationalist newspaper, and the other a house on the Quay. The latter was noticeable as the crowd was not so numerous there and the cheering therefore less noisy.

We settled down at Viceregal Lodge for three weeks while Lord Cadogan [3] with his family and staff went to Dublin Castle. It had been arranged that the Queen should not have functions every day, but lead her ordinary life, merely giving dinner-parties.

The Church was divided in its attitude towards the Queen. Archbishop Walsh [4] refused to come to Ireland during the visit, but Cardinal Logue [5] not only came, but also dined with Her Majesty. It was most curious to see the Queen and the Cardinal talking together and they both seemed surprised to find how well they got on together. The Queen went out of her way to make herself agreeable, while the Cardinal was quite captivated by her charm. He said afterwards how much struck he had been by her conversation and how he felt he was talking to a great personality.

The Queen went for long drives every afternoon and there was always a scene of loyal demonstration whenever she went through any village. At first the *cortège* consisted of :

> Two mounted Constabulary men
> One outrider
> The Queen's carriage
> Two Equerries
> Two N.C.O.s of the Constabulary
> Two grooms
> Two Constabulary men

[3] George Henry Cadogan, 5th Earl; Lord-Lieutenant of Ireland, 1895–1902.
[4] The Most Rev. William J. Walsh, Catholic Archbishop of Dublin.
[5] Archbishop of Armagh and Catholic Primate of all Ireland.

There were also cyclists about a mile in front and behind, but these were only in case of trouble and were not recognized, as they were in plain clothes. The numbers were reduced later and only one Equerry, one N.C.O., and one groom accompanied Her Majesty.

The Queen went for drives of about twenty miles taking about three hours every afternoon, and, as we never stopped jogging along at a trot, it was rather trying. I was always afraid I might have a stitch and have to stop, but mercifully I was never afflicted in this way. When there were two to ride Sir Arthur Bigge took his turn, but with a great deal of work to be got through it was very hard work having to ride for three hours two days out of three. When only one had to ride, it became easier, but the heat and perpetual jogging began to make us very sore. I was, I am ashamed to say, the first to retire from the contest, as after a particularly hot and long ride I was quite raw. However, I quickly recovered, and when Bigge and Carington eventually became raw I was able to ride every day.

The Queen often went to sleep during these hot drives, and in order that she should not be seen like this by a crowd in a village, I used to dig my spurs into the horse whenever I saw a large crowd ahead and make the astonished animal jump about and make a noise. Princess Beatrice always knew that this meant a crowd, and if the Queen didn't wake with the noise I made, she woke her herself.

One day when passing through a small village there were a certain number of people and one woman yelled, 'God bless the Queen' while another on the other side of the road piped up, 'And down with the Minister in Attendance,' pointing at me. I told Sir Matthew White Ridley this afterwards and he was much amused and said that this was indicative of the attitude of the Irish people.

When the Queen arrived at Viceregal Lodge two little girls sent her a bunch of shamrock and primroses and she sent me word that £5 was to be sent to each of the children as she was much touched by their kind attention. Sir Fleetwood Edwards, an old hand at this sort of thing, advised me not to do anything until quite the end of the visit. I waited therefore till two or three days before we left and sent off £5 to each little girl. Two days later this incident was published in every newspaper. The result was that just before we left shamrock began arriving from all parts of Ireland, and the Post Office announced that there were hundreds of bunches yet to come. I left this as a legacy to Lord Cadogan's staff and asked that all these flowers should be acknowledged, but no more £5 notes.

The Archbishop Alexander, the Protestant Primate of all Ireland,[6] came to dinner one night, and as he was extremely infirm on his legs he was totally unable to do more than shuffle along slowly. There were two long rooms between the room where the guests assembled and the dining-room, and whenever a clergyman dined the Queen always waited until everyone was in the dining-room before sitting down, so that grace might be said. The dear old Archbishop shuffled along so slowly that I saw that the Queen in her chair had nearly reached the dining-room before he had gone very far. I therefore explained to him that the Queen was waiting standing up for him to say grace. Most gallantly he responded, but in his frantic efforts to go faster he nearly fell on his nose. I caught him, and, after struggling together for a few moments, we started off like two men in a three-legged race and somehow reached the dining-room, where he said grace although much blown with his efforts. The Mayor of Dublin dined and seemed much pleased at the attention paid him.

The Duke of Connaught was commanding the troops in Ireland and in addition to his official residence occupied a house in Phoenix Park which Lord Iveagh [7] lent him. It was a lovely house with oak and tapestry and the Duchess of Connaught and Princess Patsy preferred it to the official house. One day I walked with Princess Beatrice to pay a visit to the Duke and Duchess of Connaught and rather an amusing incident happened. The Duchess of Connaught, pointing to an old black chair with a high back, said to me, 'That is a most comfortable chair. Do try it.' I ought to have suspected that there was some sell as it was most unlikely that she would wish to have my opinion on a subject like this. I at

[6] Archbishop of Armagh (Church of Ireland).
[7] Edward Cecil Guinness, later 1st Earl of Iveagh.

once sat down, when to my horror some spring worked and two iron clamps came out and closed with a snap, holding me fast. There were roars of laughter in which I joined, although I could not move. Then the Duchess explained that all she had to do to release me was to touch a spring at the back of the chair, and she proceeded to show how easily this was done. 'Come here, Patsy', she said. 'You know how to do it better than I do.' Princess Patsy went to help and there was much fumbling behind the back of the chair, but still I remained pinned to the seat. 'I am afraid it is broken', said Princess Patsy, and I had visions of remaining there for days. 'Nonsense', said the Duchess, scarlet in the face from pushing at every likely place at the back of the chair, while I sat with an idiotic smile on my face pretending I was amused. By now the laughter had quite died away and I had become an extremely tiresome incubus. 'Ring the bell for the butler', suggested someone; but no one came, the butler having gone out with the Duke. Where were the footmen? One had gone with the carriage, and the other had just been sent off with a telegram. So we had tea, and as the Duchess and Princess Patsy felt responsible for my detention, they brought me every sort of biscuit and cake to pass the time. Meanwhile Princess Beatrice was itching to go, feeling that she was outstaying her welcome, but she hardly liked to leave me still imprisoned. Someone then suggested that the gardener knew the secret and we all cheered up. Princess Patsy offered to go and find him, but minutes passed, the conversation languishing when no gardener appeared. Again I felt like the skeleton at the feast, but after another twenty minutes the gardener appeared and at once touched the right spring. I sprang out of the chair with alacrity in case anything should go wrong again, and when taking leave of the Duchess I said that never again would I sit down on any chair in her house.

One day the Queen paid a State visit to the Cadogans at Dublin Castle. Carington and I in uniform had to ride immediately behind the carriage. She was met at the door by the Cadogans with their whole staff and then went round the rooms, which she remarked had not been changed much since she was last there forty years ago. While the Queen was at tea, I slipped away with Lord Langford [8] and joined the party that was staying in the Castle where I found many friends. Suddenly a message arrived to tell the party to come as quickly as possible to the hall as the Queen was leaving. We all ran down the passages, the women gathering up their voluminous skirts to enable them to quicken their pace. Lady Erne, a *grande dame* of stately appearance whom I had never seen before out of a sedate walk, bunched up her gown and ran like a hare. However, they were all in time to be presented, and I went to my horse.

The Queen held a review of the troops in Phoenix Park and the Duke of Connaught as Commander-in-Chief of Ireland was in command. It was a scene of unparalleled enthusiasm. Hamilton, afterwards Duke of Abercorn, who was in command of the escort, had the greatest difficulty in preventing people from trying to get into the carriage, and in one place the police were swept off their feet. The review itself was not much to look at, but the troops were reinforced by the Navy, which the Irish always liked, and when they doubled past with their guns there was loud cheering. The 21st Lancers looked very well and so did the King's Dragoon Guards. It was very stirring at the end when three cheers were given and the men took off their headdresses and yelled while the crowd joined in. The bugler sounded his bugle several times to try and stop them, but they went on and on.

We returned to England on April 26th, and for six months we continued that serene unhurried existence which was such a feature of Victorian England. In November 1900 Herr Muther, Queen Victoria's German Secretary, retired. Primarily his work consisted of drafting telegrams in French and German to European Sovereigns and Princes whom the Queen did not know personally, since telegrams to her relations she invariably wrote herself. His work in this direction was practically nil, but he had charge also of the archives and was responsible for keeping the official papers in such a way that they could be readily produced and could eventually be bound for the archives at Windsor. Originally the Prince

[8] Hercules Rowley, 4th Lord Langford; a representative Irish Peer.

Consort with the help of Stockmar [9] had devised a system of keeping papers with a cross-reference (in those days unheard of) which could hardly be improved upon today, but it entailed constant work. Under this system all the Prime Ministers', Foreign Ministers', and other Ministers' letters were kept in chronological order, and in addition each political question of the day had a particular file. It therefore entailed extracts relating to the particular question being copied from the Prime Ministers' and other Ministers' letters. I don't know exactly how a successor to Muther was chosen, but I believe Baron Schroeder [10] was responsible for recommending Herr von Pfyffer, who was given the appointment. In view of his freshness to the Court I was astonished to hear that all the secret papers and family letters were to be entrusted to him, but fortunately he turned out to be a gentleman with a high sense of honour and he never abused the trust that was placed in him. When he went through the cupboards and archives he found to his surprise that little or no work had been done for forty years. The papers were simply piled up one on the top of the other; no notice having been taken of the instructions written by the Queen, 'Please place this among the so-and-so papers' or 'This should be copied'. The elaborate system devised by the Prince Consort had proved too much for Herman Sahl, who was Baron Stockmar's successor, or for Herr Muther, and the whole thing was a whited sepulchre. It was curious to see by the way the papers were kept the history of the manner in which each German Secretary had tackled this task. Herman Sahl began by trying to carry out the methods of Baron Stockmar, but as the correspondence increased he soon gave it up and contented himself with placing the papers he was given in cupboards without attempting to sort them in any way. Muther, who succeeded him, was horrified to find that nothing had been done for a great number of years, but was not man enough to tackle the arrears. He therefore decided to begin afresh, and one saw how conscientiously he set to work, but after a year

[9] Baron von Stockmar was sent by King Leopold I of Belgium to act as Queen Victoria's confidential adviser in 1837.
[10] Head of H. J. Schroeder and Co., bankers.

or two he found this very hard work and ended by tamely copying the methods of his predecessors.

Von Pfyffer quickly grasped that he would be held responsible for all this confusion when the Queen died, but to tackle some forty years of unsorted correspondence was a Herculean task which he did not feel he could take on. He therefore came to me and asked my advice. I told him to write out a clear statement of the condition in which he had found the archives, and, since the Queen ought not to be worried, to give his report to Sir Fleetwood Edwards.

Von Pfyffer's report naturally startled Edwards, who after consulting Bigge came to the conclusion that the Queen would be very much upset at finding that the archives, which she had always imagined were perfect, had been entirely neglected. Bigge, however, said there was really no alternative to letting the Queen know the truth. It was decided that in order to soften the blow Edwards should not actually send her the report to read, but should tell her about it, quoting passages from it. The result was surprising. The Queen was in no way put out and refused to believe it was as bad as von Pfyffer had reported. She said that obviously he was no sort of use, although she didn't blame him, for it was difficult for a newly appointed man to understand the intricate system on which the archives had been kept. She added she would appoint me to take charge of the whole thing and von Pfyffer would assist me and learn how to do it.

After dinner the Queen sent for me and explained the problem. She made very little of it and said she was sure that I would soon put the archives in order and get them as perfect as they were in old days: it would only take me a week or two and I should then be able to report to her that everything was in order. Any comment from me was superfluous, and indeed I had been told by Edwards and Bigge to say as little as possible. I grasped that I was to undertake to cleanse this Augean stable in addition to my usual work, and I did not imagine that a German who knew little or nothing of the political history of England would be of much assistance. I told Edwards and Bigge, who were very much amused by my account of my talk with the Queen, but much relieved to hear that she was not worried. I repeated to von Pfyffer the instructions I had received, but he said that he didn't think that a dozen men would be able to do the job in ten years and added that he thought I ought to see the archives before I committed myself.

The next morning I started my labours by making a thorough inspection of all the archives. I went down to a dungeon in which the Prince Consort's papers were kept and found it perfectly dry and well ventilated. There were long letters from every conceivable person of the time, beautifully bound with an index, and extracts had been copied in a copperplate handwriting into books relating to various questions. It was astonishing that the Prince Consort should have devised such an excellent system of keeping papers at a time when little or nothing was known of the businesslike methods that prevail to-day. I noted that 1861 was the last bound volume of letters. I was then taken to two rooms with cupboards from the floor to the ceiling all round the walls with papers tightly fitted into them. Finally I saw the room in which the German Secretary worked and in which were apparently kept the latest letters. In addition to these rooms which formed the various archives I was shown the confidential family letters in a large cabinet in one of the drawing-rooms. These had all been bound and each son and daughter of the Queen had a certain number of volumes.

I must own that I was appalled at the work and I could not help feeling that von Pfyffer had been right in thinking that little or no impression could be made on them by two men however hard they worked.

I quite grasped that anything so intricate as the Prince Consort's system was out of the question, but I thought that if I worked hard I might possibly get the papers under certain headings and then by degrees get them indexed and eventually have cross-references to the letters dealing with certain events. In order that I should not get behind with my ordinary work I decided I would devote to this one hour before breakfast, one hour in the morning, two to three hours in the afternoon, and one hour after dinner. Von Pfyffer worked very well but complained that I was driving him too hard as he had no time now to go for a walk. He knew absolutely nothing of English history and asked questions like 'Who is Gladstone?' but he was very keen and did exactly what I told him.

I had never seen such a conglomeration of valuable and valueless papers all piled one on the top of the other. The German Secretaries had apparently exercised no discrimination as to what letters should be kept and therefore everything was kept. Letters from Ladies-in-Waiting and Maids of Honour merely announcing the time of their arrival, letters of thanks for Christmas presents, and even advertisements had all been kept, together with the more important political letters.

Naturally the first thing to do was to burn all unimportant letters, but in order to make sure that nothing of importance was being destroyed, I kept a rubbish-heap during the day, and every day after dinner I went through this heap, paper by paper. It was very hard work, but as I did not do this too long at a stretch I think I made no mistakes. The temptation was to read some of the letters which were deeply interesting, but this would have been fatal as one would never have got through the work.

This superficial sorting of papers, that is, putting the Cabinet reports, the Prime Minister's and other Cabinet Ministers' letters together, worked well enough while I was at Windsor, but as the Queen was seldom there I came to the conclusion that I should have to make other arrangements for Osborne and Balmoral. I therefore had black boxes made with a lock and I took with me as many papers as I thought I could index when I went to Osborne. I had just succeeded in getting the letters into different categories in the month von Pfyffer and I had been at work, but there were innumerable letters which did not come under these categories and which I had called 'miscellaneous'—a dangerous heading, since one was tempted to put all letters the signature of which one could not read into this category.

The night before we left Windsor the Queen said to me, 'I hope you are teaching Herr von Pfyffer the system on which the archives have been kept', and I replied that he was doing very well, having quite decided never to let her know how bad everything was. The only thing I asked was whether the family letters could be placed under the care of Princess Beatrice. They seemed all sorted and it did not seem right that I, much less von Pfyffer, should be allowed access to this cupboard. This the Queen thought would only be right.

So I took a great deal of work to Osborne and settled down to carry out a scheme of indexing the letters, but I had not got very far before the Queen was seriously ill. I had of course to give up this work, and when she died I had all the letters brought back to Windsor.

When King Edward came to the throne he asked me about the archives and said that he heard I had done wonders (I don't know who could have told him this). He asked many questions, and when I told him the whole story he said he had never thought much of Sahl and Muther. He ended up by telling me he intended to entrust the archives to my charge and that he would give me a clerk to do the spade work. I thanked him for the confidence that he placed in me, but told him frankly that with my other duties, which necessitated my accompanying him wherever he went, it would be practically impossible for me to undertake the job. Secondly, the papers were so interesting that it was worth while to have them properly indexed, and I urged that they should be placed in the charge of a literary man aided by a clerk. The King said he would talk the matter over with Sir Francis Knollys,[11] his Private Secretary. Eventually Reggie Brett, who had been Secretary of the Office of Works and therefore in close touch with the Household of Queen Victoria, undertook the task and was given a clever lady clerk to help him—Miss Williams. The only thing he asked for in return was to be made Deputy Governor of Windsor Castle, which would give him some status in the Household.

Brett, later Viscount Esher, managed to get all the papers sorted during King Edward's reign, but when King George ascended the throne their importance had become so great that the Hon. John

[11] Later 1st Viscount Knollys of Caversham. Private Secretary to King Edward VII and King George V till 1913.

Fortescue,[12] the Librarian at Windsor Castle, took charge of them and had under him the Rev. Albert Lee and three expert archivists. After some twenty years the indexing was still unfinished, which only shows how optimistic I was in tackling such a colossal job.

Although I had for over two years been Assistant Private Secretary, I had never done the work of Private Secretary, nor had I ever seen the Queen about business. Occasionally after dinner she would talk to me about letters that had interested her, but all the work was done by boxes.

In September 1899, Sir Arthur Bigge had to go away for some reason and left everything in my hands, with instructions that if I was in any difficulty I was to refer to Edwards. During the first ten days I never saw the Queen to speak to except at dinner, and carried on the work with boxes. Every morning in addition to the ordinary routine work, a great deal of which had to be done without troubling her, there were several questions that required her decision. Letters from her Ministers, although addressed to the Private Secretary, were really intended for her, and an average of five or six official leather boxes were sent in to her every morning and did not return to me till the evening—unless it was something very pressing. Sometimes the Queen would keep a box two or three days or even a week, and therefore one had to keep a careful note of what boxes were sent in to her.

The outstanding subject in these ministerial communications was that of South Africa, where the situation had been growing in tenseness for several years, and during the next few weeks I came into closer contact with the Queen than ever before.

[12] Later the Hon. Sir John Fortescue; historian of the British Army.

CHAPTER VI

The South African war — Some amateur strategists — White and Buller — The Queen's war album — Lord Marcus Beresford

I HAD BARELY TAKEN OVER the reins of Acting Private Secretary when the situation between England and the Dutch Republics suddenly took a very threatening turn, and the constant cypher telegrams added to my work enormously. The Queen insisted on knowing everything and insisted on her prerogative of reading and approving every dispatch before it was sent off. Sometimes her approval had to be telegraphed to avoid delay. This caused a peculiar position to arise when, early in October 1899, an emergency Cabinet drafted a very moderate and even conciliatory dispatch to President Kruger, which merely recapitulated our demand for the franchise and made no mention of the delicate question of suzerainty. The Queen wished to study this and therefore her approval was not telegraphed immediately. Meanwhile an arrogant telegram from Kruger had been received, peremptorily calling on the British Government to send all troops away from South Africa and practically amounting to a declaration of war.

The question arose what should be done with the conciliatory dispatch that had been drafted by the Cabinet. It seemed out of the question that it should even be considered. Sir Fleetwood Edwards said that according to the Constitution the Queen must approve of a dispatch or alter it, but I argued that this was making an absolute farce of her approval, as she could neither approve nor alter it after Kruger's telegram had been received. We had a long argument and finally it was agreed to submit the matter to Harry Chaplin,[1] the Minister in Attendance. He knew little or nothing

[1] Later 1st Viscount Chaplin.

113

about constitutional methods as far as the Sovereign was concerned and decided that the best thing he could do was to back up
Edwards, because he was the older and more experienced man.
Between them they drafted a telegram to be sent to Chamberlain,
saying the Queen had approved of the dispatch before Kruger's
telegram had arrived. I pointed out that this was useless, but as it
would have to be submitted to the Queen before it was sent I was
quite ready to wait until her consent had been received. She knew
far more about the Constitution than any of us and would therefore be the best judge, but I asked that both sides of the controversy should be fairly put to her. Edwards therefore saw her and
dispassionately stated the question, whereupon she unhesitatingly
took the same view as I did and sent back the dispatch to Mr.
Chamberlain not approved.

When war was declared a few days later I found the Queen in
a bellicose mood after dinner; she seemed all in favour of teaching
Kruger a sharp lesson, but later she became lachrymose about the
senseless waste of human lives all this might entail.

Troops were dispatched to South Africa with feverish haste,
and while some people said we were overdoing the whole thing
and sending out too many men, others were of opinion that we
were not sending enough.

The Guard at Ballater was ordered to join the headquarters
of the regiment to which it belonged and to go off to South Africa.
The Queen determined to wish them godspeed and make them a
little speech, and told me to arrange for this. I went to Ballater,
saw Captain Ker, who commanded the Guard of a hundred men,
and mapped out a miniature review. I then wrote to the Queen and
reported what I had done, asking for her approval. I had often
noticed that she liked some definite command being given as a
signal for her to begin speaking. Usually her carriage was drawn
up in front of the men and then she had to begin. I made quite
different arrangements. The Queen was to drive up to the place
where she would be when the miniature march-past took place.
The Guard would then march up close to the carriage and the
Captain would give the command 'Order Arms', which would be
the signal for her to begin. This apparently pleased her very much.

The next day to my surprise the Queen sent for me to go through the details of the little ceremony and was glad to hear I had kept it to quite a simple small parade. It really was quite a pretty little scene and everything went like clockwork. Her speech was admirable, and as her voice carried very well (I think she must have been taught to pitch it just right) all the men were able to hear.

This was the beginning of a new epoch for me, and I could hardly believe my ears when the Queen's page told me to come out in the garden and bring any letters and papers I wanted her to read. Donning my frock-coat, which it was necessary to wear in her presence even at Balmoral, I went out and found her seated in the verandah of a bungalow she had had built about a hundred yards from the Castle. She asked me to open a box from Lord Halsbury, the Lord Chancellor, and read out its contents. Now his handwriting was practically illegible and, as I was naturally nervous working with the Queen for the first time, I soon came to a part I could not decypher and stopped. She told me to puzzle it out and make a copy. She added that several attempts had been made to induce him to have his letters written by a secretary, but that he had always insisted on writing them himself. The next box was from Mr. Goschen,[2] the First Lord of the Admiralty, who sent in his resignation. The Queen feared I was again in difficulties about the handwriting and was guessing wrong, so made me read it again. It came as a great surprise to her.

After this experience I was sent for regularly and although at first I was pleased and flattered, it turned out not altogether to be a blessing as she would send for me at all hours. Once when I was going out fishing the Queen sent for me. I was in rat-catcher costume and a reddish tie, but I managed to pull on a pair of trousers and put on a black overcoat. I happened to meet Lord James of Hereford [3] in the passage and he was much amused at my costume, especially the tie. I remember being sent for at Wind-

[2] The Rt. Hon. George Joachim, created 1st Viscount Goschen, 1900. A former Chancellor of the Exchequer.
[3] Henry, 1st Lord. A former Liberal Attorney-General, who seceded over Home Rule for Ireland.

sor while she was having breakfast. Everything on the table was gold, which seemed all in the picture, and she was eating a boiled egg in a gold egg-cup with a gold spoon. Two Indian Khitmagars in scarlet and gold remained motionless behind her chair, while outside a page and a Scotchman in a kilt waited till she rang.

Meanwhile, I had decided that my proper place at this period was with the Army again, and I made every attempt to get out to South Africa, but I should have known from my previous experiences how difficult this would be. In 1896 I had tried to go to Ashanti, but as there was only a small force required it is hardly to be wondered at that I did not succeed. Again in 1896 I made every effort to go to Egypt and possibly I might have succeeded, but unfortunately the Household got wind of this and both Bigge and Edwards sat very heavily on the idea.

When the South African War broke out I again made every effort to go, but at first only one battalion of the Grenadiers went out and it was quite hopeless my trying to go when all the officers of the other battalions were applying. I therefore tried to go out on the Staff and wrote confidentially to one or two Generals. Most unfortunately one of them happened to see the Princess of Wales and told her of my efforts, and she told the Queen, who was furious. She sent for me and told me she had never heard of such a thing: she had just trained me to learn her ways and she was getting old, yet there I was calmly proposing to go off to South Africa. There was a great deal of truth in what she said, and I could only reply that if I was wanted by my regiment I feared I should be forced to go. She thought a moment and said that was quite right—certainly I should have to go, but there was no necessity for me to go on the Staff. I said I thought the Princess of Wales was wrong in thinking I should not go because I was married, and she said, 'You were quite right there, it should make no difference'. Nevertheless, I did not get out to South Africa until nearly a year later.

Arthur Balfour always imagined that had fate decreed that he should be a soldier he would have been a great tactician. All that was necessary was to apply the principles of logic and you pulverized the enemy. When he came up to Balmoral in October 1899, he had made a study of the whole position in South Africa and was anxious to unfold his plan of campaign to someone who was sufficiently educated in military campaigns. There was, however, no one who could lay claim even to the most rudimentary knowledge of war and he had therefore to fall back on me.

One night before we went to bed he brought out his map of South Africa and laid it on the billiard table. Then with unanswerable logic he proceeded to point out what Kruger should do with his forces. Having pinned flags to denote the Boer Army, he then showed what tactics the British Army should adopt to inflict a crushing defeat on them. I was quite unable to find any flaw in his reasoning and contented myself with saying that it was no certainty that the Boers would take up the positions he had assigned to them. He said that, always assuming that they had Generals who had studied campaigns, it was evident to the meanest intellects that these positions were the right ones. He said afterwards that he was disappointed to find how ignorant I was, but when the Boers did eventually begin fighting they never went anywhere near the places Arthur Balfour had selected.

One night at Osborne I was taken from my lowly place at the bottom of the dinner table and put one off the Queen next to Princess Francis Joseph of Battenberg, as my French was supposed to be better than that of Lord James, Sir Fleetwood Edwards, and the other men. I was conscious at first that the Queen was listening to my French, although she appeared to be looking the other way, but I got on very well with Princess Francis Joseph. The Queen was in a charming and fascinating mood and soon she chipped in to our French conversation and was very witty and amusing. She suddenly broke into English and laughed so much I was afraid she would have a fit. I had written out a memorandum in which her approval was asked for the Royal Irish Fusiliers to wear a green hackle in their busbies. Instead of 'busbies' she had read 'breeches', and wondered on what portion of these garments a hackle could be worn.

After dinner I had to read out to her a long telegram about the war while the Royal Marines string band was playing Wagner, and although her hearing was good, I had to speak very loudly to make myself heard. Every now and then, however, the music stopped abruptly whilst I was left shouting at her, much to the amusement of the rest of the dinner party who were crowded at the end of the room.

When Bigge returned I told him my work as Assistant Private Secretary was now quite different as I constantly saw the Queen. I was, however, most careful not to interfere in any way with the Private Secretary's work, which Bigge did so admirably, but there was plenty of work for two men and there never was the slightest difficulty.

The Queen would often break down and cry at the long lists of casualties—at least we thought them long in those days; she seemed impatient for victory and unable to understand why the British Army did not have one great victory and put an end to the war.

When the news of the disaster of Nicolson's Nek [4] came and it was reported that Sir George White had lost a whole battalion and a battery of artillery, she was in a great state of mind. She said, 'I suppose we could not expect to have no reverses, but we must win, if the whole Army has to go out.' She sent a telegram to Lord Lansdowne [5] in which she said Sir George White was in no way to blame, but I ventured to point out to her that this implied that it was the fault of the officer in command of the party, and this apparently Sir George White had wished to disguise. So

[4] By October 1899, the Boers had succeeded in forcing the British troops in Natal to fall back on Ladysmith. Before the investment of the town was complete, the British Commander, Lieutenant-General (later Field-Marshal) Sir George White, V.C., ordered a general attack at Lombard's Kop; this was a complete failure. A large part of the left column was forced to surrender at Nicolson's Nek. Two days later Ladysmith was isolated. General Sir Redvers Buller, V.C., after three unsuccessful attempts, finally relieved it in February 1900, by which time the inhabitants were at their last gasp. Some of the ill-feeling between White and Buller may be explained by the fact that Buller had advised White to surrender, which White refused to do. Ian (later General Sir Ian) Hamilton distinguished himself at Elandslaagte and in the defence of Ladysmith, and finished the war as Chief-of-Staff to Kitchener. He later commanded the Dardanelles expedition.

[5] Henry Petty-Fitzmaurice, 5th Marquess of Lansdowne. Secretary for War, 1895–1900; Foreign Secretary, 1900–5. In 1916, as Minister without Portfolio, suggested possibility of negotiated peace with Germany; later wrote famous letter to the *Daily Telegraph* on this subject.

she altered the telegram and expressed every confidence in him although he chivalrously took the blame on himself.

When Sir George White came to Windsor in 1900 after the relief of Ladysmith, I had a long and interesting conversation with him. At first he was reserved, but after a time he became more communicative. He said that in public he would always appear to be grateful to Buller for having relieved Ladysmith, but as a matter of fact the way in which Buller had behaved to him was disgraceful. Buller had pretended to be his friend and yet he never lost an opportunity of saying unkind things about him even in public. On one occasion, when Sir Ian Hamilton was appointed to command a brigade, Buller had remarked before everybody that it was a pity he (White) spent his time in pushing the officers of his old regiment into every conceivable billet. Buller had let it be understood in Natal that he had several times been asked to supersede White, but had refused to do so; there was no word of truth in this, as no one had ever suggested that White should be superseded. When they met after Ladysmith was relieved, it would only have seemed natural for Buller to have greeted White, but he barely spoke to him and made a point of avoiding him, which of course was much remarked upon by all the officers of the two forces. All of this I repeated to the Queen. When the Prince of Wales (King Edward) came to stay at Windsor a fortnight later, he talked to me about the war and said it was remarkable how White and Buller had worked so well together. I told him that nothing was further from the truth and I confidentially repeated what White had told me.

Before the tide turned in South Africa someone proposed a 'Day of Humiliation' and the two Archbishops warmly supported the idea, but the Queen told me she was very much opposed to it. She said that in the first instance she objected to people being ordered to pray: 'Let them pray,' she added; 'I hope and trust they will do so, but it should be without any order from me'. She added that she thought that if we were justified in going to war and if we thought we were doing right by South Africa, there was no reason why we should 'humiliate' ourselves, but if on the other hand we thought we were wrong, the sooner we stopped the war the better.

Lord Lawrence,[6] one of the Lords-in-Waiting, at dinner found great fault with the Generals in South Africa and expressed his views freely as to what they ought to have done. The Queen the next day told Bigge of this and added, 'I said to myself, I wonder how much he knows about it?'

When the news came through that Kruger had bolted, I read the telegram to the Queen and she expressed herself freely about his conduct. She said it was disgraceful his going away with all the money he had squeezed out of the people. I remarked, 'Yes, Madam, and leaving Mrs. Kruger behind too', to which she replied, 'I don't know about that; he probably was right'.

Lord Wolseley,[7] then Commander-in-Chief, came to stay at Osborne in January 1900, and had a long talk with the Queen both before and after dinner. It was quite late when she sent for me and asked me to tell Wolseley something she had forgotten. Apparently they had both forgotten something, for when I knocked at Wolseley's door and gave him the message, he wanted to add all sorts of things he had omitted to say. For three-quarters of an hour I listened to him talking about his schemes for the Army, which all seemed admirable. I always thought he was by far the cleverest man we had in the Army, and the most far-seeing. He was very violent about the civilian element at the War Office, but I ventured to argue that the work at the War Office required special training and that if officers were employed for four years they would be practically useless until they learnt the work. The civil servants in other Government Departments would be too clever for them and so the War Office would always get the worst of any argument between Government Offices. He, however, would not listen to this and said that when he retired he would spend his life in condemning the ridiculous system of civilians running the Army.

[6] John Hamilton Lawrence, 2nd Lord. Son of Viceroy of India.
[7] Field-Marshal 1st Viscount Wolseley. Commanded Gordon Relief Expedition.

George Wyndham [8] came down to Osborne soon after and I was afraid that his literary studies might have made him priggish, and that now that he was Under-Secretary of State for War he would be too great a man to speak to; but I was most agreeably surprised to find that he was a delightful human being and full of humour. The Queen talked to him also for a long time before dinner and a short time after dinner, and again she forgot to ask something. I went to her about eleven and she was much pleased with him and thought him charming. She was glad to hear the steps that had been taken to send out more men and more guns to South Africa, but she had forgotten to ask him what provision was being made for the wounded men when they were discharged, and whether men totally incapacitated through fever were to be given pensions.

I went off in search of Wyndham and found him in the billiard-room talking to Lord Lorne [9] and Charlie Harbord.[10] Lorne, who liked to play billiards to aid his digestion, proposed a four game, but as no one was any good it was not till 12.30 that we managed to finish. So I had to follow George Wyndham up to bed. The Queen had told me to apologize to Wyndham for his not being put into the Minister's bedroom, which was undergoing redecoration, and as we mounted the stairs I explained the matter to him and apologized, adding that when Chamberlain had been there he also had to be put into this ordinary bedroom. Wyndham replied sarcastically that it was surely a great honour to have the same bedroom as Chamberlain had.

However, when we arrived at this bedroom any annoyance he may have felt at my allusion to Chamberlain had vanished and he listened attentively to the questions I asked. He then addressed me as if a question had been asked in the House of Commons, and having all his facts and figures at his fingers' ends, he more than answered the questions. He was so interesting about the war that it was not till 1.30 that I went off to bed.

In 1899 the Queen had started an album for photographs of

[8] Secretary for Ireland, 1900–5.
[9] Later 9th Duke of Argyll. Married Princess Louise.
[10] Later 6th Lord Suffield.

all the officers killed in the war. It was a sad business writing to widows and mothers and asking for these photographs, but it seemed to give them some consolation. This gave endless work as it was necessary to write a special letter in each case, and some-times to get involved in a long correspondence. The Queen liked to see all the answers I received, and in addition to this I had to see that the date and circumstances under which every officer was killed were written under each photograph. Mercifully the gum-ming-in of the photographs was done by an expert, also the writ-ing of the names and particulars, but in order to ensure that no one was forgotten, the lists had constantly to be checked. After a year, the Queen came to the conclusion that the book was too sad to look at, and therefore the living should be added in order to make it less mournful, but as it was obviously impossible to in-clude all the officers fighting, it was decided to confine it to all Generals holding commands in South Africa. This did not give so much trouble, as the same letter did for all.

Not content with this, the Queen wished a special letter to be written to all parents who had four sons or more fighting in South Africa. This was another long business, but really the War Office supplied the names, verified each case, and dealt with masses of letters that arrived claiming a number of sons fighting. At Christmas the Queen had special boxes of chocolate made with her effigy on the lid and these were sent to every officer and man in South Africa. It was a pretty idea, and the personal touch was much appreciated, but I imagine it must have given the Army organizations in South Africa a great deal of work.

Up to the end of her life the Queen continued to take the great-est interest in everything connected with the war, and the sick and wounded were constantly in her thoughts.

Lord Marcus Beresford [11] was the most spontaneously witty man I ever knew; when he was in good form he would keep peo-ple in roars of laughter. There are many stories of his witty re-partees, but usually witty remarks said on the spur of the moment are no longer amusing when written down. I remember his trying to play bridge once at Brighton when King Edward was staying

[11] Son of 4th Marquess of Waterford.

with Mrs. Arthur Sassoon.[12] King Edward came in and said, 'Hallo, Marcus, playing cards. I didn't know you knew one card from another'. He replied, 'I know a king when I see one'. Another story that always amused me was when he went to a theatre and on arrival was met by the cloak-room woman who said to him, 'Shall I take your hat and coat, sir?' 'No, thanks', he said. 'Shall I take your cap and apron?'

When, therefore, Bill Carington organized a night out in London for Sir James Reid, the Queen's Physician, he asked Beresford to be one of the party to enliven the proceedings. First there was dinner, then a play, and afterwards supper. After the play was over they decided to walk the short way down the Strand to the Savoy for supper. Reid and Beresford came last of the party, and as they passed another theatre which the audience was leaving there was a smart brougham drawn up at the door with a beautiful woman in it waiting for her husband. Beresford seized Reid before he understood what was happening, pushed him into the brougham, slammed the door and said 'Right' to the coachman, who drove away. Of course, Reid was furious, and after he was finally released told everyone that the beautiful lady had said to him, 'You ought to be ashamed of yourself. You're drunk'. What with hammering at the window to stop the coachman and the lady shouting at him, he had no opportunity of explaining his case. However, the husband to whom he apologized, had seen the incident and roared with laughter. So it all ended happily.

[12] At 8 King's Gardens.

CHAPTER VII

The Queen's illness — The Prince of Wales arrives — The German Emperor — The Queen's death — The funeral — The Queen's character — John Brown

In 1900 the Queen made a new arrangement which necessitated my sleeping at Osborne House instead of Barton Manor. Fleetwood Edwards, the Keeper of the Privy Purse, and Bigge, the Private Secretary, were given houses close by and, when they had finished their work in the evening, they returned to their homes. The Equerries slept at Barton Manor. This worked very well during her reign, but the increasing number of telegrams in addition to occasional telephone messages that were often received at night made it necessary for someone who could deal with them to sleep at Osborne House. The Queen therefore decided that I was to sleep at Osborne House instead of Barton Manor in future and deal with any emergency that might arise.

Once in February 1900, the Queen's health not being good, Sir James Reid asked me to take steps to ensure that no bad news should reach her by telegram. I had not found this quite so easy to arrange as I anticipated, for when I told Mr. Hiley, the telegraph clerk, to bring me any telegram that might come for the Queen before sending it to her, he replied he had strict orders from her that all telegrams addressed to her were to be sent in at once to her and to no one else. I had spoken in a careless manner so that there should be no suspicion that anything was wrong, but I grasped that I should have to take him into my confidence. I therefore told him the Queen was unwell and that Sir James Reid had impressed on me the necessity of her not being worried by bad news, and I finally wrote down and signed instructions to him

125

enjoining secrecy. However, the next day the Queen recovered, and as no telegrams arrived, all was well.

When, therefore, Reid came to me on January 16, 1901, and told me the Queen was not well, I did not think it serious, but repeated the former instructions to the telegraph clerk. The next day, however, things began to look bad, and Sir Douglas Powell [1] was sent for. Still, no one outside knew anything, and we all hoped it would pass off. On the 18th both Reid and Powell thought it very serious and said that the Prince of Wales, the Duke of York, and the members of the Royal Family should be informed. So with telephoning, telegraphing and cyphering, we all had a very busy time. On the 19th the Queen rallied and there was a slight improvement in her condition. Meanwhile the Prince of Wales arrived and the Princess of Wales was to come later that evening. The arrival of other members of the Royal Family soon followed and the house was full to overflowing. Then the German Emperor announced his intention of coming, and this upset everyone. Bedrooms were taken for the various suites in adjoining houses, but the arrangements that had to be made by Lord Edward Pelham-Clinton to feed all these people, and by Sir John M'Neill to convey them all to and from Osborne House in carriages, became most intricate.

When Reid announced a change for the better in the Queen's condition the Prince of Wales decided to go back to London but to be ready to return at a moment's notice, and a telegram was sent to the German Emperor asking him to remain in London. A bulletin was issued warning the public of the state of the Queen's health and this brought in masses of telegrams from all parts of the world.

On January 21st everything went on much the same as before, but after dinner a long telegram about the war in South Africa arrived and I went off to ask Reid what should be done with it. He said with a grave face that there had been a change for the worse and that he feared that the end might come at any time during the night. I therefore dispatched a mounted groom to summon

[1] The heart and lung specialist. Physician-in-Ordinary to Queen Victoria, King Edward and King George V.

Edwards and Bigge and I also sent a carriage for the Bishop of Winchester (Randall Davidson). They all came and we had a long consultation and it was decided that the Prince of Wales should be told at once. The telephone in those days for long-distance calls was very uncertain, but after some delay I managed to get on to the Prince of Wales himself, and he decided to come at once by special train.

M'Neill had retired to bed and so I had to make the arrangements about the yacht *Alberta* going off at once to Portsmouth to meet the Prince of Wales, but just as I was telephoning to Captain Broad I received a message that the Queen had again rallied and that therefore Princess Christian, Princess Louise, and Princess Beatrice thought there was no necessity for the Prince of Wales to come down that night. To cancel the instructions to the yacht only took a minute, but stopping the Prince of Wales was more difficult. However, eventually I got a message through to Marlborough House. The Bishop of Winchester retired to Whippingham Rectory and the others to their various houses. Bigge insisted on remaining and helping me to sit up all night to be instantly ready if any change should take place. I was to sit up until 6 A.M., when he would relieve me. I suggested his going up to my bedroom and lying down with rugs on the sofa. This he did, but it was already past one when he retired. I sat in the armchair in his writing-room and read, but at 4 A.M. I got so cold that I had to get a rug. Everything seemed ghostly and still, but curiously enough I did not seem at all sleepy. As I sat there I thought of all the people crowded into Osborne House and what the Queen's death would mean to them, what would happen when the Prince of Wales came to the throne, and what changes he would make. Gloomy thoughts in the small hours of the morning with only myself and a few policemen awake. At six Bigge turned up without my having to wake him and we had a cup of tea. I then retired to bed and slept till 9.30.

When I came down to breakfast at ten I found somewhat better news about the Queen; the Prince of Wales had returned and the German Emperor had arrived. Although the rest of the Royal Family seemed to resent his coming and no one had asked him to come, he behaved in a most dignified and admirable manner. He said to the Princesses, 'My first wish is not to be in the light, and I will return to London if you wish. I should like to see Grandmamma before she dies, but if that is impossible I shall quite understand'. Nothing could have been better.

The whole house was crammed and even all the houses in the vicinity were full. I expected every minute to be turned out of my bedroom, which was large and comfortable, but no one even suggested this.

When the Prince of Wales went in to see the Queen she became conscious for a moment and recognized him. She put out her arms and said 'Bertie', whereupon he embraced her and broke down completely. Another time during a moment of consciousness she sent for her dog, a little white one, and called it by its name.

About luncheon-time we heard the Queen was sinking and I sent for Bigge and Edwards. A carriage was sent for the Bishop of Winchester and Clement-Smith, the Rector of Whippingham. No change, however, occurred for several hours.

Arthur Balfour arrived and discussed the action of Parliament. He was astounded at the accumulation of official boxes that had taken place during the last week and said it showed what a mass of routine work the Queen had to do. Still there was the point to be considered how the machine could go on without her. Judges, for instance, could not function without a warrrant signed by her: all sorts of appointments could not be made without her sanction. He impressed on Bigge the necessity for summoning a Privy Council, no matter what happened. But we all knew it was only a matter of hours.

At about half past six we were told that the end had come. The Duke of Argyll told me that the last moments were like a great three-decker ship sinking. She kept on rallying and then sinking. The behaviour of the German Emperor was beyond all praise. He kept in the background until they were all summoned. The Prince and Princess of Wales, Princess Christian, Princess Louise, and Princess Beatrice stood around the bed, while the German Emperor knelt down and supported the Queen with his arms, while Reid held her up on the other side. The Emperor never moved for two and a half hours and remained quite still. His devotion to the Queen quite disarmed all the Royal Family.

When the news came, Bigge sent and stopped the telegraph wires until the official telegrams to the Lord Chancellor, Prime Minister, Archbishop of Canterbury, Lord Mayor of London, etc., had been dispatched. I was told the scene on the hill down to Cowes was disgraceful. Reporters in carriages and on bicycles were seen racing for the post office in East Cowes, and men were shouting as they ran, 'The Queen is dead'.

As the last death of a sovereign had occurred in 1837, no one seemed to know what the procedure was. We spent the evening looking up what had been done when George IV and William IV had died. A Privy Council seemed urgent, but at first the Prince of Wales refused to go and argued there was no immediate hurry. When Lord Salisbury cyphered to Arthur Balfour that there must be no delay, the Prince consented to go to London the next day.

When he returned he brought with him Francis Knollys, George Holford,[2] and Sidney Greville, and a difficult situation arose. The relations between the two households had always been very cordial so that there was no chance of any unpleasant rows taking place such as were reported to have happened in Germany when first the old Emperor William and later the Emperor Frederick died.[3] The difficulty we had at Osborne was quite the reverse because everyone behaved so tactfully that whenever a telegram or letter arrived no one would open it. The Prince of Wales's people hated the idea of taking everything over abruptly, and yet, of course, we had ceased to hold any appointment. At last Sidney Greville came to me and said that the Prince of Wales had decided that we were all to continue our duties until further orders and go on just as usual with our work, only referring questions

[2] Later Sir George Holford. Equerry to Edward VII as Prince of Wales and later as King; then to King George V. Married daughter of Mr. Arthur Wilson, of Tranby Croft.

[3] Frederick III, King of Prussia and German Emperor, succeeded his father, William I, in 1888 and reigned for only 99 days. As a strong Liberal, neither he nor his entourage were in sympathy with the old Emperor's circle of conservative advisers, or with the clique which had formed itself round the Crown Prince (who succeeded his father as William II).

to him that required decision. I was therefore temporarily employed in answering his telegrams, but this did not give me much work. When I heard that Princess Louise was in difficulties I at once offered my help. This she gladly accepted and I found her trying to deal with two hundred and eighty-one telegrams; after answering hundreds daily this number did not frighten me. I asked her to go through them and dictate answers to those she wished to reply to personally while I took down what she said in shorthand. She, just like the rest of her family, found no difficulty in expressing herself and dictated some really first-rate answers. The remainder I told her I would answer myself. This took about a quarter of an hour, and I went off to write out the telegrams. Afterwards I heard that she complained of having nothing to do while her sisters remained hard at work.

The 6oth Rifles had been sent for from Parkhurst Barracks to provide the guard over the coffin, but when they arrived and asked for orders no one quite knew what the procedure was. The men had never been taught to reverse arms and the drill book was dumb on the subject. I was appealed to under the misapprehension that I had done this sort of thing before, but I was really very hazy about the subject. A most intelligent and smart captain, however, after consultation with Sir John M'Neill and myself, evolved a ceremonial for relieving the men every hour, as the strong perfume of the flowers seemed to upset them at first, and it was arranged that four men should stand with reversed arms at the four corners while one of the Household should keep watch at the foot of the coffin.

The Duke of Connaught, however, found out that it was the privilege of the Queen's Company, Grenadier Guards, to mount guard over the defunct Sovereign, and a telegram was sent off summoning them at once. They arrived with two officers, St. John Coventry and Myles Ponsonby. Coventry was extremely sketchy about the whole thing and simply copied the 6oth Rifles. When however, Arthur Lloyd, the Captain of the Queen's Company, Grenadier Guards, came along it was a very different thing and the changing of the sentries became a most impressive sight, all done in slow time. In addition to the Grenadiers one member of the late Queen's Household kept watch. I found this very trying, not only on account of the very strong scent of the tuberoses and gardenias, but because I could ill afford the time. The dining-room was turned into a mortuary chapel and was hung round with curtains and draperies. The coffin was covered with crimson velvet and ermine with the crown in diamonds on a cushion, and the Order of the Garter which the Queen had worn was on a raised platform covered by the Royal Standard. The room was lighted by eight huge candles and there were palms round the room in addition to masses of wreaths. It was all gorgeous with colour and most impressive.

The Princess of Wales refused to be acknowledged as Queen and would not let anyone kiss her hand. She said that there could only be one Queen until the funeral and that she wished for the present to remain as Princess of Wales.

King Edward then took charge of the funeral arrangements and had all the difficult points submitted to him for decision. He sent for me and told me he wished me to take charge of all the funeral arrangements at Windsor. He impressed on me that the service at St. George's Chapel would be arranged with the Dean by the Lord Chamberlain, and that I would have nothing to do with that. All I had to do was to arrange the procession and give orders to the troops, police, etc., at Windsor.

I therefore decided to go to Windsor the next morning by the earliest train, and telegraphed to the Mayor, the head of the police, and the Officer Commanding the troops, to meet me. I was not sure that it was a wise thing to put someone in charge of the Windsor part of the funeral who would have to take part in the funeral *cortège* starting from Osborne.

When I arrived at Windsor I went to the Town Hall and discussed all the arrangements with the Mayor. He called in the police officials and everything went well. The officer commanding the troops was luckily David Kinloch,[4] a most capable and first-rate organizer, and I went over all the ground with him. We decided that in view of the fact that there would be colossal crowds the procession, instead of going straight from the station to St.

---

[4] Later Brigadier-General Sir David Kinloch, 11th Bart.

George's Chapel, should go down High Street, Park Street, and then up to the Castle through the gates at the bottom of the Long Walk. I told him that the funeral procession itself was being managed by the Earl Marshal and that, beyond having a few officers available to marshal the procession, he need not trouble about that. As everything seemed satisfactorily arranged I returned to Osborne in the evening. Knollys and Greville had practically taken over the whole of the secretarial work and therefore there was no reason why I should remain at Osborne, but when on my return I asked whether anything had been decided about the funeral at Windsor, I was told that nothing of any sort had come from the Earl Marshal's office about Windsor as they were still concentrating on the London part.

I naturally became anxious. The next morning, Thursday, January 31st, in case it was supposed that I was doing the funeral procession as well as the arrangements of troops, police, etc., I determined to go to London and make sure what was expected of me. A second time I rushed off to London and went at once to the Earl Marshal's office where I found absolute chaos. The Heralds, who claimed the right to manage the funeral under the direction of the Earl Marshal, had little precedent to work on since there had been no Sovereign's funeral for sixty-four years, and being accustomed to work out coats of arms and genealogical tables at their leisure, were swept off their feet with the urgent arrangements for the funeral. There appeared to be no system and everyone was engaged in working out the little bits of detail most suited to their capacity. I asked for the programme of the Windsor part of the funeral and was told that they had not yet begun it. 'We haven't finished Osborne and London yet', cried one of them. 'But', I argued, 'has it occurred to you that the funeral starts from Osborne tomorrow?' I suddenly realized that the Windsor part would be a fiasco, and I should be blamed. Finding everything so confused I asked to see the Duke of Norfolk,[5] the Earl Marshal,

---

[5] Henry FitzAlan-Howard, 15th Duke of Norfolk. His efficiency and despatch are further attested by the fact that he was Lord Mayor of Sheffield and Postmaster-General simultaneously.

and here I found a thoroughly businesslike and capable man dealing with telegrams, letters, ceremonials, enquiries from the Lord
Chamberlain, Lord Steward, Master of the Horse, telephone messages from the Foreign, India, and Colonial Offices, but quite
unconscious that the work he was delegating to his subordinates
was not being done. Although he was working like a cart-horse he
at once saw me. He was under the impression that a skeleton programme was being made out and that all that was necessary was
to fill in the names, but I explained that nothing had even been
started. He seemed rather put out about this and explained that
the Lord Chamberlain was constantly supplying him with fresh
Kings and Princes who were to attend the funeral, and this made
any definite printing of a ceremonial impossible. He said that the
best plan would be for me to consult Lord Roberts and then make
out a skeleton ceremonial for his approval. So off to the War
Office I went, but when I got to the Commander-in-Chief's room
I was told that Lord Roberts could see no one. I, however, wrote
on my card, 'Funeral arrangements—urgent'. I was at once
ushered in and I briefly explained that the funeral began at Osborne the next day and that nothing had been decided about the
Windsor part. Lord Roberts said that he had nothing to do with
the funeral itself, but if it came to giving orders to any troops, I
had his permission to give whatever orders were necessary, and
say that they were given with his approval.

This was excellent, and I returned to the Earl Marshal's office
and sent for a shorthand writer, who told me that it was the first
time he had been employed. It was astonishingly difficult to dictate
a programme with practically nothing to go on, but I kept everything in categories: English Royal Family, Foreign Sovereigns,
Foreign Princes, Representatives of Foreign Countries, Foreign
Suites, etc. Apparently it was impossible to get any accurate lists
on account of the constant changes. I think I covered the ground
pretty well and let everyone know what they had to do. When this
was typed I took it to the Duke of Norfolk, who made some corrections. He said that some of the Heralds had complained of my
rudeness and had resented some remarks on their inefficiency
which I had made. I at once apologized to him, but I pointed out

that had I not come to London no arrangements of any sort, no orders for the battery of the Horse Artillery, for the Life Guards, Foot Guards, Naval Guard of Honour, would have been issued. He asked me who was now going to give the orders, and I told him that Lord Roberts had given me *carte blanche*. I told my shorthand friend to have this skeleton ceremonial printed and sent to the various authorities concerned and then went to the Admiralty and War Office to see that the orders were understood. I returned to Osborne that night and arrived at 2 a.m.

I had to get up very early and put on full-dress uniform. Arthur Davidson had been put in charge of all the funeral arrangements at Osborne, and I must say it was beautifully arranged. Everyone knew what to do and where to go, and it all went without a hitch. We Equerries were to march on either side of the gun-carriage and to assemble at the front entrance of Osborne House. Punctually the bluejackets from the Royal yacht, under Lieutenant Pelly, carried the coffin down the stairs and placed it on the gun-carriage. The Queen's Company, under Arthur Lloyd, marched in single file on either side of the procession and the whole *cortège* moved in slow time all the way to Trinity Pier, where the coffin was placed on board the Royal yacht *Alberta*. It was a lovely still afternoon and the immense crowd was most impressive. At three the yacht started. Battleships and cruisers were anchored in two lines all the way to Portsmouth. The sun was setting in a red sky as we arrived and it was a very pretty sight to see the little yacht *Alberta* going through this avenue of immense ships. She was followed by the *Victoria & Albert,* the *Osborne,* and the Admiralty yacht, but these anchored in the harbour while she went alongside the jetty. I was told to go on board the *Osborne,* where I found a cabin prepared for me.

About seven o'clock King Edward sent for me and I went in a steam pinnace to the *Victoria & Albert*. He said he wished me to undertake the arrangements for the final service in the Mausoleum at Frogmore on the Monday, and he hoped I should be able to have a printed ceremonial ready for him to see on Sunday morning.

There I was at Portsmouth on board the *Osborne* with nothing to refer to, no precedent to go by, and no idea of who would attend this last ceremony. I was to walk with the other Equerries alongside the gun-carriage through London, and yet I had not only to stage-manage the final ceremony, but also to have a ceremonial printed. I was dead tired, having been all day on the go with very little sleep the night before. I realized that the next day all the shops would close early to enable people to see the funeral and that the day after was Sunday. Up to that moment Arthur Davidson had managed everything so well that he had set a very high standard and I felt that there was every possibility of the Windsor part being a fiasco. If in addition to this I mismanaged the final ceremony, what little chance I had of being taken on by King Edward would evaporate.

When I grasped all the difficulties I felt I had undertaken a hopeless task, but of course there was no alternative but to tackle it. It occurred to me that if I was to have anything printed by Monday, the printers must be warned, and I therefore sent a telegram to Oxley, the printer at Windsor, saying I should want a ceremonial printed by Saturday evening and that he was to meet a messenger whom I was sending by an early train and receive from him the written ceremonial. I sent for one of the King's Home Service Messengers and told him to come to my cabin early the next morning, by which time I should have written out a draft. As the King told me that only those who were staying at Windsor would attend the last ceremony, I grasped that it would be quite a different list from that of the larger ceremony through London. The only possible way I could think of to obtain a correct list was to telegraph to the Master of the Household's clerk at Windsor Castle and ask him to telegraph the names of all those who would be staying in the Castle. After dinner I retired to my cabin, where I proceeded to write out a ceremonial in suitable language. Under ordinary circumstances I should never have attempted such a thing, but there seemed to be no alternative, and although in some places it seemed rather bald, I succeeded in producing a dignified programme for the printer. Late that night I received a sheaf of pink telegraph forms giving me, as I had asked, the names and precedence of the guests staying at Windsor for the final ceremony. I filled in all the names and sealed up my draft ready for the Messenger.

The next morning, February 2nd, we all landed at Portsmouth in full uniform and went by special train to Victoria Station. The train with the coffin and one or two of the oldest members of the Queen's Household came later. We all stood waiting with the King and the male members of the Royal Family for this train to come in. The coffin was then carried by men of the Coldstream, under Leslie Hamilton, on to the gun-carriage and the procession started through London with the Equerries on either side. The streets were lined all the way with troops and the densely massed crowd was a wonderful sight, most reverent and silent. As we marched in slow time it took quite a long time to get to Paddington, but on arrival the coffin was again taken from the gun-carriage and placed in the train. We were all told off to various carriages, and so to Windsor.

When we arrived at Windsor I at once got hold of David Kinloch, who had done wonders on the very meagre instructions which I had given him. He had arranged everything perfectly and had managed to form up the outline of the procession, leaving plenty of room as he had no idea of the numbers.

As soon as the King and the other foreign Sovereigns had taken up their places (they were to walk this time), I went and asked His Majesty's permission to start the funeral procession. It had been previously arranged that I should hold up my hand and the band would begin the *Dead March,* while the officer in charge of the gun-carriage would start at the same time. When I received the King's commands to start the procession, I stepped out well to the side so that everyone could see me and held up my hand. The drums at once began to roll and the procession started.

The horses on the gun-carriage had, however, been standing still in the cold for some time, and as the lieutenant in charge never gave the command 'Walk march', the two wheelers suddenly started off before the leaders, and finding an unusually heavy load, began to kick and plunge. Away flew the traces and the gun-carriage remained still. I had contemplated all sorts of things going wrong, but such a mishap had never occurred to me.

Meanwhile the front of the procession, unconscious that anything was wrong, had slowly marched on and the band had already turned the corner when I sent a non-commissioned officer to
stop them. I found then that the traces were broken and everyone
was trying to get the horses clear while several officers were engaged in trying to devise some makeshift, but naturally the first
thing was to inform the King of what exactly had happened. I did
so, and on coming away Prince Louis of Battenberg said, 'If it is
impossible to mend the traces you can always get the naval guard
of honour to drag the gun-carriage'. I went back to the horses
where I found that it was contemplated getting two horses only to
drag the gun-carriage with the leaders' traces. The general impression, however, seemed to be that this was a most hazardous
solution of the difficulty as it seemed very doubtful whether the
two horses would be able to drag the gun-carriage up the steep
hill into the Castle with traces that were only makeshifts, and
which might easily snap. Another solution was suggested, and that
was that the gun-carriage should go up by the shortest way to St.
George's, but this I dismissed as it would have meant disappointing a crowd of several thousands.

So I determined to adopt Prince Louis's suggestion and accordingly went a second time to the King and said, 'Have I your Majesty's permission to take out the horses and let the men of the
naval guard of honour drag the gun-carriage?' The King said,
'Certainly'. I told the captain of the naval guard of honour to pile
arms and bring his men up to the gun-carriage. While he was doing this I went to the officer in charge of the Artillery team and
told him to get the horses clear as the men of the naval guard of
honour were to take their places. This raised a storm of discussion, all carried on in a whisper. There were several Artillery
officers among the A.D.C.'s to the Queen who resented very much
the orders I had given, and they assured me that all would be well
if I would leave things alone. Bigge was particularly angry and
told me I was ruining the whole ceremony as I knew nothing
about Artillery horses. I replied that I was merely carrying out
the King's orders and that I could not allow anyone to interfere.
He was furious, however, and went off to expostulate with the

King, who merely said, 'Right or wrong, let him manage everything; we shall never get on if there are two people giving contradictory orders'.

So all the men of the Artillery stood sulkily looking on while I went in search of a rope, feeling this was a necessity for the sailors. The stationmaster to whom I applied rushed off and returned with a steel hawser which was all he had. This was, of course, out of the question as it would have cut the men's hands to the bone. The Artillery A.D.C.s were triumphant and said, 'You'll have to come back to the horses after all'. I went to the Officer commanding the naval guard of honour and explained to him the situation. He said that if he could have the remaining traces off the horses he could manage and I told him to order his men to get them. The men of the Artillery remained looking on while the sailors swarmed round the horses and took off the traces. In an incredibly short time they had got into a compact group and were ready to start.

The whole of this lasted about ten to fifteen minutes, but it seemed to me about two hours. I went off to the King and reported that everything was ready, and having received orders to start the procession, I stepped out for the second time and held up my hand. This time all went well and I returned to my place alongside of the gun-carriage. The procession moved slowly along High Street and Park Street and then turned up towards the Castle through the gates at the bottom of the Long Walk. It was very heavy going and the gun-carriage seemed to sink in, but the sailors experienced no difficulty. One of the A.D.S.s called my attention to the brake and said that if no one understood how to work it there might be serious trouble when we descended the steep hill to St. George's Chapel. So I moved out of my place and consulted the naval lieutenant, who said he had a petty officer who understood all about the brake, but that if I liked he would place three men on each wheel so that, in the event of the brake not working, there would be no danger of the gun-carriage going too fast downhill. I asked him to do this. But everything went well and I was able to dismiss from my mind all dangers of another mishap and admire the beauty and dignity of the whole procession.

On arrival at the west door of St. George's Chapel, the bearer party of the Coldstream took charge of the coffin and carried it into the choir. We all followed in procession and found the Chapel crowded with people. It subsequently turned out that the Earl Marshal's people had forgotten to give seats in the choir to any-one, but Sir Spencer Ponsonby-Fane, to whom the Earl Marshal had entrusted the arrangements in the Chapel, had grasped that a mistake had been made and had taken suitable people from the nave and placed them in the choir. The service was most impressive and most beautifully sung.

At the conclusion all the Foreign Sovereigns, Princes and Representatives went up to the Castle where there was a stand-up buffet, where I was able to get something to eat and drink; but a message that the King wished to see me interrupted my post-prandial moments, and I hurried off to Edward III's Tower, where the King was temporarily lodged. He told me he wished me to do all the arrangements for the final funeral on Monday, and that as the sailors had done so well that day he would like them again to drag the gun-carriage. I ventured to point out to him that the Artillery had been deeply mortified at their failure that day, coming as it did so soon after the experience at Ladysmith when so much had been made of the handy-man taking the place of the artilleryman, and that therefore they would be much hurt if the sailors took their place again. He talked it over for some time and said that he had no wish to hurt the feelings of the Artillery. He quite realized that they were not to blame and that it was only an unlucky accident, but he really thought that the sailors had been most effective and had really added to the dignity of the procession. I, however, pressed my point and finally he said, 'Very well, the gun-carriage will be drawn by the Artillery, but if anything goes wrong I will never speak to you again'.

I was determined therefore that nothing should go wrong and I wrote to Sir Arthur Bigge, Sir Henry Ewart, the Crown Equerry, the Officer Commanding the battery of Artillery, the lieutenant in charge of the Artillery team, the captain of the Queen's Company Grenadiers, and asked them to come to the door of St. George's Chapel at 6 a.m. the next morning, Sunday.

I told the Artillery to have their team of horses there, and Arthur Lloyd commanding the Queen's Company to have all his men there. I received charming letters from all of them, but an especially nice and forgiving letter from Bigge saying he was so glad to hear the Artillery were to have another chance and promising to help me in any way he could.

When the printer's proof of the ceremonial for Monday arrived, I took it to the King, who made several small alterations and sent it back to the printer.

Lord Esher, the Secretary of the Office of Works, suggested that we should have a rehearsal of the final ceremony at the Mausoleum. He asked me to order the bearer party and the gun-carriage and horses to be down at the Mausoleum at eleven that night and he would have a box approximately the same size and same weight as the coffin made by the men of the Office of Works ready at the lodge leading to the Mausoleum. We drove down in a carriage and found all the men waiting. It was a pitch-dark night and there was something very ghostly about the lanterns that were carried to light up various points. It was a weird scene and the two bearer parties, one from the Life Guards and one from the Foot Guards, remained motionless on the steps of the Mausoleum. The gun-carriage with the Artillery team was standing at the lodge with the box on it and had been told not to move until ordered to do so. Lord Esher had thought of everything and had told the men that all was to be done exactly as it would be on the Monday. We then began the rehearsal, and the gun-carriage with the sham coffin advanced slowly to the steps of the Mausoleum. It had been arranged that as the coffin was very heavy one bearer party should carry it up two flights of steps and then be relieved by the other bearer party, who would carry it into the Mausoleum. The first part went very well and the relieving bearer party took over the sham coffin, but when they advanced up the remaining steps, we realized that they would have to place the coffin on the tomb the reverse way to the marble figure of the Prince Consort. We came to the conclusion that this would never do and we halted the men. While we were discussing what should be done, I noticed that although the bearer party consisted of enormously powerful men they were staggering under the weight of the sham coffin, and I suggested that they should put it back on the gun-carriage while we decided what should be done. The sham box coffin was therefore carried back again and placed on the gun-carriage. We discussed whether at St. George's Chapel it would be possible to make the change, but Esher pointed out that the space in the choir was small when the Chapel was full and it would be difficult and perhaps irreverent to attempt to turn the coffin round the other way. At last we came to the conclusion this would have to be done on the steps of the Mausoleum. We made the bearer parties try various methods, not carrying anything but merely walking slowly. When the relief took place the relieving party had to face the other way and slowly turn round before going into the Mausoleum. After one or two rehearsals this somewhat intricate manoeuvre worked perfectly. Eventually everything went smoothly and we dismissed the men. If it had not been for Esher's forethought in having this rehearsal we should undoubtedly have had another fiasco.

The next morning I was on the Castle Hill just before six and all the different people whom I had asked to help me arrived. Remembering King Edward's remark that if anything went wrong he would never speak to me again, I had ordered ropes cut in suitable lengths and with hooks like traces to be kept hidden in a place in the Cloisters. The only person I told about this was Arthur Lloyd. In the unlikely event of the horses again kicking over the traces I gave him instructions that the Queen's Company was to pile arms and pull the gun-carriage as the sailors had done. I impressed on him the necessity of keeping this strictly confidential as the Artillery would undoubtedly be hurt if I had shown want of trust in them.

Bigge, who was most kind and forgiving, was invaluable, and discussed with the officers of the Artillery what should be done to ensure the horses being quiet. Ewart, with his great experience of processions and his knowledge of horses, joined these discussions, and I felt that as far as it was humanly possible to ensure that no mishap would occur again, every precaution was being taken. We walked behind the gun-carriage along the whole route to the Mausoleum and I halted the procession at awkward places to see how the horses would behave, but everything went perfectly. The rest of the day I spent in seeing the various officials and in arranging for tickets of admission into the private grounds of the Castle.

At 6 a.m. on Monday I again attended a short rehearsal with the horses. It was very cold and we kept them standing ten minutes before moving off, but they behaved perfectly.

After breakfast the King sent for me and I found him in the corridor. The list of Sovereigns and Princes staying in the Castle had been telegraphed to me by the clerk to the Master of the Household, but the name of the Duke of Fife [6] had been omitted. The curious part of this was that, although the King and several Court officials had seen the draft of the ceremonial, no one had noticed this omission. Unfortunately the ceremonial had been published in the newspapers and everyone was reading it.

I found the German Emperor, the King of the Belgians, and the King of Portugal [7] standing by the fire all smoking cigars, which rather shocked me as, of course, no one had ever smoked there before. The King was standing a little further down the corridor with the Duke of Fife, and on seeing me proceeded to reprimand me severely. He said that the Duke of Fife's name had been omitted from the list and he could not understand how I could have made such a bad mistake. How could he have any confidence in me when I made omissions of this sort? It was inconceivable to him how anyone like me, accustomed to arrange ceremonies, should have omitted so important a person as his own son-in-law.

Naturally, I didn't say a word and the Duke of Fife, who seemed pleased to hear me abused, walked off satisfied. As soon as he had gone I said I could not apologize sufficiently for the mistake, which of course I ought to have seen and corrected when the proof came, but I reminded him that the proof had been on his table all Sunday and that no one else had noticed the omission. He at once became quite different and, taking me by the arm, said

[6] 1st Duke of Fife. Married Princess Royal, King Edward's eldest daughter.
[7] Don Carlos, King of Portugal since 1889; assassinated with the Crown Prince, 1908.

confidentially to me, 'I know how difficult it has been for you and I think you did wonders. I had to say something strong, as Fife was so hurt that he came to me and said he presumed that he could go to London as he was apparently not wanted.'

A curious incident happened at the last funeral ceremony. An officer in khaki came to see me and applied for tickets for the Mausoleum. I told him that no one but the Royal Family would go to the Mausoleum, but I would give him a ticket for the private grounds. He was a dignified gentlemanly-looking man with several medals. I never gave him another thought, but it appeared that in some unaccountable way he stepped out of the crowd and joined the German suite in the procession. They very naturally thought he was connected with the arrangements and took no notice of him. However, I knew nothing of this.

The whole ceremony went beautifully and it was most impressive to see the foreign Sovereigns, headed by the King, walking behind the gun-carriage. When the gun-carriage reached the steps of the Mausoleum the two bearer parties did admirably. There was dead silence, no whispering or hesitation, simply the slow tread of the men. The doors were closed and the service began. Suddenly a voice whispered in my ear, 'Who is the old bird with a beard?' I looked round and saw the khaki officer, who was pointing to the King of the Belgians. I said 'Hush', took him by the arm, led him to the door, and forcibly ejected him. The service was really beautiful and the singing of the St. George's Chapel choir was perfect. At the conclusion of the service we all retired, leaving the Royal Family by the tomb. When I got outside I espied my khaki friend and told him what I thought of his conduct. I said his behaviour was disgraceful and that I had not thought it possible that an officer of the Army should push himself forward and intrude in a purely family service like that. I added that I wanted his name and regiment as I should report him to the Commander-in-Chief. He gave me his name and regiment, saluted, and walked away. We walked back to the Castle and on the way we were passed by carriages containing the Royal Family and their suites. When I entered the Quadrangle I saw the Royal Family and foreign Sovereigns and Princes talking together at the Sovereign's Entrance, and in the midst of them was my khaki friend. He had apparently come up in a carriage with the German suite. I went off at once, took him by the arm, and much to the relief of the Royal Family, led him away to the gate, where I luckily found a policeman. I sent for one of the detectives and gave him instructions to take the officer to the station and send him off to London. I then wrote to the Military Secretary and reported the incident. It later turned out that the poor man had been invalided home from South Africa suffering from sunstroke and that he was mentally deficient.

If absolutely true records of the reigns of the Kings and Queens were now to be found they would in all probability prove that all the histories that had been written were entirely wrong in many respects. Unfortunately untrue history, that is to say, tales repeated by people of the time, are so much more amusing and interesting than the dry hard facts, that they eventually become history and are accepted by historians; even true stories become overemphasized or distorted in the course of years. In the Middle Ages this was undoubtedly the case, but as late as Queen Victoria's reign stories often without foundation were bound to be repeated about her because, from the death of the Prince Consort to the Jubilee in 1887, she lived such a retired life.

After her death Edmund Gosse [8] wrote a character sketch of her in the *Quarterly Review* and this was generally supposed to have been inspired by a conversation with my mother. How far she was responsible for what he wrote I do not know, but of course discussing a person's character in conversation is a very different thing from writing an article and he probably over-emphasized traits in her character that had only just been touched upon in conversation. I think that he really meant to make her out a great personality, but it was too soon to treat her like Queen Elizabeth or Queen Anne and discuss her character as a human being shorn of all glamour that surrounds a Sovereign. He appeared to give the impression that she was a person of very commonplace ability,

[8] Later Sir Edmund Gosse. Librarian to the House of Lords, poet and essayist.

which she certainly was not, and his article gave great offence to her friends and admirers.

Queen Victoria's life was so hidden from the public that all sorts of myths were bound to gain credence. The stories about John Brown, her Highland attendant who died in 1883, were at one time so numerous and so obviously made-up that it hardly seemed worth while to correct them. I thought at first that while they were untrue there might have been some grain of truth in the popular idea that John Brown had been something more than a faithful servant. The story that they were secretly married rested on no foundation whatever, and I asked several people in the Household who must have known the truth, and they all laughed at the idea. Even the old Duchess of Roxburghe, who was generally supposed to have been present at the marriage, told me that the whole thing was a fabrication inspired by people who wished to ridicule the monarchy, and that certainly she had never heard such a thing mentioned. It appears to have originated when a scurrilous pamphlet entitled *Mrs. John Brown* was privately published. Many people who didn't believe a word of it shook their heads and said that there was no smoke without some sort of fire. Although the tale was not generally believed, no one took the trouble to contradict it. Whether there was any quite unconscious sexual feeling in the Queen's regard for her faithful servant I am unable to say, but judging by what I heard years afterwards, of course, I am quite convinced that if such a feeling did exist, it was quite unconscious on both sides, and that their relations up to the last were simply those of employer and devoted retainer.

John Brown was certainly a privileged servant and could do practically what he liked with the other servants. His word was law with them and his relations with the gentlemen of the Household were difficult to define. Like all Scotchmen of that class he never became familiar and as a rule was always respectful, but that did not prevent his being an autocrat with the servants. My father, Sir Henry Ponsonby, seems to have got on very well with him, but Brown always treated him with deference and respect. It was, however, not always so with the Equerries. When General Sir John M'Neill was appointed Equerry he was accustomed to command troops, and although the most charming of men with a great sense of humour, was apt to be rather abrupt in his manner with the servants. On one occasion he was in the Equerries' room at Osborne when John Brown came in with a message about some carriages that were to be ordered. After delivering his message Brown remained standing by the writing-table, whereupon M'Neill told him to wait outside and he would send for him when he had written the order. Brown complained that he was over-- bearing in his manner and that he had shouted at him as if he was a private soldier. In the evening M'Neill received a letter from the Queen asking him whether he would like a command in India. The one she referred to was quite a small command which would mean his going down and not up in the military world. Unable to understand why he was summarily to be got rid of, he took the letter to my father, who guessed the cause of the trouble and advised him to reply that he would of course be glad to accept any command that Her Majesty was pleased to offer him, but as people would naturally ask why he was giving up his post in the Household, he begged that he might be told the reason he should give. He followed this advice and heard nothing more, as of course the Queen could not give the real reason; but she never spoke to him for some years and so arranged his month's waitings that he never came to Balmoral or Osborne where she might have to speak to him.

Doctor Profeit, the factor at Balmoral, disliked Brown intensely and resented his constantly interfering with local matters, but was in such awe of him that he never dared stand up to him. Still, it was a well-known fact that these two were enemies. When Brown died in March 1883, the Queen, who was quite unconscious of the bad feeling between the two, presented Profeit with a tiny miniature of Brown set in diamonds and made up like a tie-pin. Profeit realized that if he wore this everyone at Balmoral would laugh at him. He therefore hit upon the idea of keeping it in his coat pocket so that when he had to see the Queen he could take it out and put it in his tie, returning it to his pocket when he came away.

General Sir Lyndoch Gardiner, one of the Queen's Equerries, was one of Brown's pet aversions, although he was quite unconscious of the fact. While he treated Brown well, he was a great stickler for adhering to the rigid methods by which things were done in those days, and if a carriage was wanted he insisted on knowing all the facts before he would write the order. On one occasion he came into waiting and on meeting Brown he enquired how the Queen was and what she had been doing lately. Brown replied, 'The Queen's very well. It was only the other day that she said to me "There's that dommed old fool General Gardiner coming into waiting and I know he'll be putting his bloody nose into everything that doesn't concern him".' History does not relate what General Gardiner replied.

The Queen often quoted John Brown and seemed amused by his quaint expressions. At one time the Duchess of Roxburghe and Miss Stopford [9] were not on speaking terms and when Miss Stopford was ill, Sir James Reid, the Queen's doctor, suggested that perhaps the Duchess might go and see her. 'Oh dear no,' exclaimed the Queen. 'There would only be what Brown calls Hell and hot water.'

Often the Queen used expressions that had long since passed out of the slang vocabulary of her contemporaries. Once when a picnic was arranged by the members of the Household, the Queen was asked whether the Maids of Honour might go. She replied that they might, although she did not altogether approve of the ladies 'junketing' with the gentlemen.

[9] The Hon. Horatia Stopford, a Woman of the Bedchamber.

BOOK II

BOOK II

CHAPTER VIII

The new King — Changes in the household — Milner —
Lord Lansdowne's faux-pas

WITH THE FUNERAL of Queen Victoria there passed an age. Naturally the Victorian tradition took some time to die and the new era was not ushered in within a few weeks of King Edward's accession to the throne, but gradually new methods were being introduced into the Royal Household and every department was being overhauled.

For myself there was little change, for soon after the funeral King Edward sent for me and told me he intended to appoint me Assistant Private Secretary and Equerry. This was good news to me as I knew he meant to make drastic changes in the Household, and I felt he must have thought of all sorts of people whom he knew and whom he intended to give some post in the Household.

There was Sidney Greville, who had been with him as Prince of Wales and who seemed a likely appointment because he had been Assistant Private Secretary to Lord Salisbury at one time. There was Lord Algy Gordon-Lennox whom the King, when Prince of Wales, had constantly pressed on Queen Victoria on account of his having been with the Duke of Cambridge, but curiously enough Gordon-Lennox was never given any post at all, while Sidney Greville had been appointed Private Secretary to the Queen, an appointment which I don't think he liked. There were any number of men whom King Edward knew and who would have done very well, and I was therefore surprised at his at once offering me the appointment. Of course there was no room for Sir Arthur Bigge, as Sir Francis Knollys would obviously continue to be Private Secretary, having served the King in that position for thirty years. Among the Equerries Sir John M'Neill wished to retire as he was getting old, and Bill Carington King Edward didn't like, but I don't know for what reason, and therefore he was not reappointed. Arthur Davidson and Harry Legge, however, continued as Equerries and Brocklehurst was appointed Equerry to the Queen.

The King made a clean sweep of the Grooms-in-Waiting and decided to appoint in future soldiers and sailors of distinction to be Gentlemen Ushers, a position similar to that of Chamberlains abroad. In Queen Victoria's reign these appointments were held by any type of man and there was a certain amount of nepotism. The King's plans were not at first understood and he was hurt at the refusal of several old friends to serve as Ushers. Later many soldiers and sailors accepted, but it is doubtful whether they were really suited for managing large crowds of society people at Buckingham Palace.

When the King and Queen went to London, Buckingham Palace was undergoing great changes and they therefore had to remain at Marlborough House, which had been the King's London home since his marriage.

Having been appointed Assistant Private Secretary I imagined that I should have a great deal of work to do, but when I came the next morning at 10 a.m. I was told by Francis Knollys that it was quite unnecessary for me to stay as he wanted no help. This surprised me considerably as I knew there must be a lot of work to be done, but as there is nothing more tiresome than a person hanging about idle when everyone else is busy, I made myself scarce. Even the Equerry had so much to do that he had no time to speak to me.

I learnt later that while there was no friction of any sort between the new and the old Household, Marlborough House was firmly convinced that Buckingham Palace was hopelessly out of date and that none of Queen Victoria's Household were any good. There was a great deal of truth in this, but while the other Departments were certainly out of date, the Private Secretary's office under Sir Arthur Bigge was not only up to date, but far better managed than the equivalent office in the Prince of Wales' Household. Bigge had organized the office on business lines, and since I had joined the Household typewriting and shorthand had been introduced, and the filing of papers brought up to date.

The new appointment of myself as an Assistant Private Secretary was not altogether popular. In the first place Francis Knollys considered it quite unnecessary, and in the second place a member of Queen Victoria's old-fashioned Household had been nominated, which probably meant incompetence. There were clerks at Buckingham Palace, but they were probably hopeless, therefore quite obviously the Marlborough House staff had better carry on as before, and the Assistant Private Secretary, who was a fifth wheel to a coach, could join the ceremonial Household.

Such were the thoughts that prevailed at Marlborough House, but after a few days the whole machinery began to creak. Francis Knollys, who was accustomed to write every letter himself, could not keep pace although he worked all day. Mr. Bryant,[1] the chief clerk, and his brother worked till midnight but were totally unable to get through the work. They all thought that after a few days the torrent of letters would cease and that they would then have time to make good the arrears.

Although unable to open all his letters himself, King Edward always looked through them and opened those he thought were of a semi-private nature. One day he received several letters asking for answers on more or less urgent matters and pointing out that no reply had been sent to former letters dispatched nearly a week ago. He therefore suspected that something was wrong and sent for me. He asked me what work I was doing, and when I replied I was doing nothing he became thoughtful. Finally he said I was to go down and see Francis Knollys. I was to tell him that I had been appointed to take as much work off his hands as possible and I was to induce him to confine himself to the really important stuff. The King added that several letters had not been answered and that he didn't like this. I asked if I might employ the clerks at Buckingham Palace, and he said that of course I was to bring them in.

I did not realize at the time that I should have to tread on people's corns, and I thought that all I was asked to do was to bring

[1] Later Sir Francis Bryant.

relief to a much overworked staff. I saw Knollys and repeated what the King had said. He had just begun to open his letters and I begged him to go through them with me, select the important ones and give me the rest to deal with. I am sure that had I proposed this the first day I should have met with a rebuff, but he was tired and the accumulation of arrears made him uneasy, and I managed to collect two big baskets full of letters. I then went to see Mr. Bryant and told him what the King had said. He was a very businesslike man and he had realized that he was undertaking more than he could do. So I arranged with him that all he had to do was to separate the important from the unimportant letters, and send all the latter to Buckingham Palace. It was impossible to say which were important without reading them through carefully, and as Francis Knollys would have to be consulted and in most cases the King himself asked what answer should be sent, it was essential that someone who knew the ropes should do this. I told him for the present to do nothing more and I impressed on him the importance of merely making a note of what answer should be sent and letting the clerks at Buckingham Palace write the letter.

I then saw Sir Dighton Probyn,[2] who had been appointed Keeper of the Privy Purse, who also wrote all letters himself, and induced him to send for Mr. Gibson, the Secretary of the Privy Purse, from Buckingham Palace, who would take a great deal of the work off his hands.

Then to Buckingham Palace where I found Mr. Gibson and all the clerks bored at twiddling their thumbs. We soon organized the work and, of course, they were all accustomed to writing letters, so there was no difficulty. After two days I was able to report to the King that all letters up to date had been dealt with. From having nothing to do I suddenly found I was busy all day, but the rather delicate machinery I had devised worked quite well. I did not realize at the time that both Francis Knollys and Bryant looked upon my efforts as an affront to Marlborough House, and that they very much resented my butting in.

[2] General Sir Dighton Probyn, V.C.; Colonel of the 11th King Edward's Own Lancers (Probyn's Horse).

At the end of February 1901 Sir Alfred Milner [3] arrived in London from South Africa and received a great ovation from the people of London. Lord Salisbury and Joe Chamberlain went to the station to meet him, and unkind people said that the reason there was such a crowd in the streets was not because everyone wanted to see Milner, but because they wished to see Joe Chamberlain sitting with his back to the horses opposite Milner and Salisbury.

They arrived at Marlborough House and while Milner went straight up to the King, Salisbury went home, leaving Chamberlain to bring Milner to an official reception. Chamberlain came to my room and after talking of incidents at the station, where the enthusiasm of the crowd was extraordinary, asked me whether the King was likely to keep Milner long. I replied that I didn't think so, and added, 'Being given a peerage apparently takes no time'. 'What!' said Chamberlain, 'is the King going to make Milner a Peer?' I replied that I had been told so. 'Well,' said Chamberlain, 'isn't that like Lord Salisbury! I wrote to him twice about this and he never answered my letters. So this is the first I have heard of it.'

As it seemed inconceivable that this peerage should have been decided upon without Chamberlain's knowledge, I murmured that I must be mistaken. Pom MacDonnell, [4] Salisbury's Private Secretary, came in at that moment and I asked him whether there was any truth about the statement. He replied that I was perfectly right and that the King and Salisbury had arranged this, but he could not understand why Chamberlain had not been informed.

Suddenly Milner came in and at once Chamberlain went up to him, dropping his eyeglass from his eye, held out his hand and said, 'I congratulate you'. There came a look of blank astonishment in Milner's face and he said, 'What on?' 'On your peerage', replied Chamberlain in a tone that implied he had known it all along. 'But', said Milner, 'I haven't been given a peerage, and I've heard nothing about it'. An ugly look came over Chamberlain's

---

[3] Later 1st Viscount Milner. First Governor of the defeated Boer Republics, and High Commissioner for South Africa, 1897–1905.
[4] Sir Schomberg MacDonnell.

face and he turned menacingly to me, suspecting I had made a fool of him. I interposed at once, asked Milner to wait a minute, and dashed from the room. I rushed upstairs and caught King Edward as he was just coming down. I hastily explained the matter to him and he said, 'How stupid of me! Milner was so interesting that I clean forgot all about it.' I got hold of Milner again and it all ended happily.

The number of addresses to be presented to the King and Queen and the deputations to be received was so large that the King decided to devote whole mornings to these ceremonies. Some of them necessitated the King wearing uniform, and these were all fixed on certain days, while those which the King would receive in plain clothes were fixed on other days. The King also decided that he would take first those that he alone had to receive and that the Queen should only come at midday, when together they would receive the more important addresses and deputations.

One day the King came down in full uniform and received addresses beginning at 10.30, but when it came to twelve o'clock there was no sign of the Queen. Meanwhile the second deputation arrived and then the third, fourth, and fifth, which upset all the arrangements. In order that they should not get mixed up, a different room had been allotted to each, and soon every room was filled with eminent men in uniform, but in spite of repeated messages there was no sign of the Queen. The King in full uniform sat in the Equerries' room drumming on the table and looking out of the window with the face of a Christian martyr. Finally at ten minutes to one the Queen came down looking lovely and quite unconcerned. All she said was, 'Am I late?' The King swallowed and walked gravely out of the room.

The Queen's unpunctuality must have been very trying, but by then he had accepted it as inevitable and never attempted to remonstrate with her. Generally she was twenty to thirty minutes late for dinner, but I remember once at Windsor her being five minutes too soon. Pages and footmen were sent running to warn the guests and the members of the Household.

It was in March 1901 that we Equerries suddenly had a windfall. Something so wonderful happened that it seemed as if a fairy godmother must have come to our aid, because only under the following curious circumstances could we ever have been so well treated.

For many years during Queen Victoria's reign the War Office officials had meant to tackle the Equerry question, but they were doubtful how she would regard any interference. The advent of a new reign seemed an opportune moment to raise the question. The War Office thought it was preposterous that an Equerry should be drawing full pay from the Army while he was doing Equerry's work, for which he was paid £500 a year. It was also questionable whether an Equerry who held the post for ten years and then retired should be allowed to count those years for pension, and it was thought that five years in any case was quite long enough for an officer to be an Equerry. We all knew this storm was brewing, but there seemed to be no way of fighting it and all we hoped was that, like so many similar questions, it would eventually end in smoke.

One day King Edward opened a box and found in it one of the usual submissions sent by Lansdowne, who was [5] Secretary of State for War. As he read it he became more and more angry, and finally exploded with rage as he chucked the paper at me. I read it with consternation as I saw it was proposed that Equerries should only hold the appointment for five years, that they should receive no Army pay, and that the five years should not count for pension. I was so taken up with the details that I failed entirely to grasp the King's point, but he soon made this abundantly clear in a voice that shook the roof of Buckingham Palace. He said that no one was more willing than he was to discuss these points, but to have a submission about his own staff thrust at him in this way without a word of explanation was more than he could stand. How simple it would have been for Lansdowne to come and see him to ascertain his views and discuss the question with him, but instead of doing so Lansdowne coolly sends him a submission without any explanation. The box was put aside and I was told to ask Lansdowne to come and see the King the next day.

Lansdowne came the next day quite unprepared for the storm,

[5] Or, rather, had been. Lord Lansdowne was by this time Foreign Secretary.

and the King told him frankly that he considered it lacking in courtesy, to say the least of it, to make changes in the regulations governing his Military Household without even mentioning the subject to him, and then to send a submission for his approval without a word of explanation. Lansdowne, however, completely took the wind out of the King's sails by at once apologizing and saying he entirely agreed with all he said; he explained that as Secretary of State he often had been called upon to sign submissions that were the result of long-protracted negotiations between His Majesty and the War Office officials, and he had naturally assumed that this was the outcome of discussions that had been carried on for some time. He was much put out to hear that this was the first the King had heard of these proposals. He was so apologetic that the King, who had expected a fight, calmed down, but His Majesty asked who was responsible for drafting the submission, and was told it was Sir Evelyn Wood [6], the Adjutant General.

I was then told to ask Sir Evelyn Wood to come and see the King. He arrived fully prepared for a storm, but what exactly passed during this interview I do not know.

The result was that an Army Order was issued to the effect that Equerries held their appointments at the King's pleasure without any limit; that they would in future continue to draw Army pay in addition to their Equerry's pay, and that their period of service as Equerry would count for pension. This exceeded our wildest dreams.

[6] Field-Marshal Sir Evelyn Wood, V.C.

CHAPTER IX

The Emperor William — The Empress Frederick's letters — The Empress Frederick's death and funeral — King Edward at Homburg — Lunch with the Emperor

SOON AFTER his accession the King began to receive alarming accounts of the health of his sister, the Empress Frederick of Germany, and at once decided to go to Cronberg and see her. Her son the Emperor William was to meet him there. To my surprise he decided to take only his physician, Sir Francis Laking, and myself. He had not realized yet that being a King was a totally different thing from being Prince of Wales, and he argued that as he had formerly taken only one Equerry, one would be quite sufficient on this occasion.

I had seen the German Emperor at various times when I was a boy, but the first time I had an opportunity of speaking to him was when he came to Cowes in his yacht. Of course he was at once invited to luncheon by the Queen at Osborne. It so happened that the same day the Duke of Connaught had asked the Officer Commanding a battalion of the Rifle Brigade at Parkhurst Barracks to send over a man wearing the new equipment that was proposed for the Army. He was anxious that the Queen should see this equipment as there had been much discussion about it.

After luncheon we were all asked to come into the drawing-room and bring the man with us. A particularly smart-looking sergeant of the Rifle Brigade arrived and waited outside. We found the Royal Family talking together and at once the Duke of Connaught sent for the sergeant, who came in looking rather uncomfortable in his dark-green full-dress uniform over which various khaki belts and straps had been put. It all looked very odd. The Duke of Connaught walked round explaining the object of the different straps to the Queen, while the German Emperor merely nodded and grunted to signify that he understood the explanations. I thought that this was all there was to be done, but the Emperor had not had his say. He called me up and asked whether I did not think the greatcoat that was rolled up was too high, and whether it would not interfere with a man firing his rifle lying down. Without waiting for an answer he told the sergeant to lie down and get into a firing position. He then proceeded to lie down alongside and point out that even with a Rifleman's head-dress, which was flat at the back, the greatcoat prevented his putting his head back far enough. He maintained that with a helmet or *Pickelhaube* it would be impossible. It was a very hot afternoon and beads of perspiration broke out on the sergeant's face as he found himself lying down in front of the Queen, with the German Emperor lying down beside him glaring at him and plying him with questions without ever giving him time to answer them. However, all this was intended for the Queen's edification and she seemed much amused. The Duke of Connaught merely replied that this equipment was intended for khaki uniform and that obviously it was unfair to judge it when worn with a full-dress uniform.

For the now proposed visit to Germany I entrusted the travelling arrangements both in England and on the Continent to the courier, while all I wanted to know was the time of departure and arrival of the trains. I myself had to give orders to the police. I had to send instructions to the Royal yacht and arrange with the Admiralty to have two escorting cruisers. I had to inform the War Office that no guard of honour was wanted anywhere, and made it clear that no General, Admiral, etc., was expected to be at the port of embarkation. There were a hundred and one little things to think of, but I knew the game pretty well. The journey was to be kept a profound secret, but, needless to say, the presence of extra police and the arrival of the Royal special train gave the public sufficient indication of His Majesty's movements.

We started on Sunday afternoon and I was horrified to find a crowd lining the streets all the way to the station. King Edward was much put out and made caustic remarks about the ease with which he travelled formerly.

We crossed in the old *Victoria & Albert,* and when we were alongside the jetty at Flushing we heard a large number of people apparently singing hymns. I thought this a very proper way of spending Sunday evening, but what I could not understand was why they sang the same hymn over and over again *ad nauseam.* I asked Sir Henry Howard, His Majesty's Minister at The Hague, who came on board as soon as we arrived, and he explained that it was the Boer National Anthem, and that the mass of people who were singing had originally intended to sing it on the jetty, but that owing to his representations, the authorities had kept them outside.

I got to know this hymn very well, as it was sung at several stations at which the trains stopped, but perhaps the most trying was the singing of 'God Save the King' at Duesseldorf. At two o'clock in the morning a girls' school, led by the headmistress, who had a piercing voice, sang the National Anthem. Of course it was too late to take any notice of it as everyone was asleep, but it woke up the whole train. Afterwards the *Daily Mail* referred to this and said that the young ladies were much disappointed at the King not appearing. I wonder if they expected him to come out on the platform in his pyjamas!

We arrived at Homburg, and found the Emperor at the station in very good spirits and most cordial. We drove at once to Fried-richshof and were shown to our rooms. The house is very much like an English country house, a great deal of it having been copied from Flete, the house of the Mildmays in Devonshire. Herr Ihne, the architect, who built it, was half English, and fell in at once with the Empress Frederick's idea of making it like an English country house. The bedrooms seemed quite English except for the stove. Otherwise the house was like a museum filled with a collection of works of art and curiosities.

The arrival of Laking was not very welcome, for I found that the German doctors resented him coming, and he was therefore in a very difficult position. King Edward had brought him, as he thought that he would be able to induce the German doctors to give morphia in larger doses than they were accustomed to give.

King Edward, Princess Victoria of Schaumburg-Lippe, the

Duchess of Sparta, Princess Frederick Charles of Hesse [1], and I, walked round the garden in the morning. Princess Victoria I had known as a girl, and I found her full of go, but unhappily married. The other two were charming and most anxious to help and make the meeting between King Edward and their brother, the Emperor William II, a success.

In the afternoon we drove in sledges to see an old *Schloss* which belonged to the Emperor. The King and the Emperor went in the first sledge, while Sir Frank Lascelles, the British Ambassador, Count Seckendorff, the head of the Empress's Household, and I drove in the second sledge. We seemed to go at a great pace, and I had a very agreeable drive.

When we arrived the Emperor was most affable and full of chaff, but went off at once with King Edward. We were shown into a room with a huge stove and massive furniture covered with dark-green cloth. There we found Count Eulenburg, the head of the Emperor's Household, a most able organizer, Count Metternich, the German Ambassador in London, cynical and taciturn, General von Kessel, the Empress Frederick's pet aversion, and said to be very anti-English, and General von Scholl, a very tall A.D.C. to the Emperor.

King Edward was very superstitious about thirteen being at dinner and told me to impress on Eulenburg the importance of avoiding thirteen at any meal. Unfortunately I forgot about this, but I never took it seriously because in the first place I didn't believe there was anything in this, and in the second place I had constantly had meals with the Household in Queen Victoria's reign when we had been thirteen. I had often come in last or got up first, according to the variation of the superstition which existed in the minds of the superstitious.

The third day at Friedrichshof the King sent for a list of those who had dined the previous nights, and to his horror found we had been thirteen each night. He seemed much upset by this, but later told me it was all right. Feeling I was getting out of my

[1] 2nd, 3rd, and 4th daughters of the Empress Frederick. The Duchess of Sparta was later Queen to King Constantine of Greece.

depth I said, 'Why?' and he explained that Princess Frederick Charles of Hesse was *enceinte*.

Most unfortunately I sat next to von Scholl whose conversation was limited to the weather. After ten minutes the conversation languished and von Scholl, feeling he ought to do something, produced a photograph-book of places in Germany. Now there is nothing more tiresome in this world than photographs of places, but there was no getting away from it. After half an hour's talk we returned to our sledges to Friedrichshof.

The dinners were not altogether lively, although the Emperor kept the conversation going. The Duchess of Sparta and Princess Frederick Charles of Hesse were always ready to dash in if the conversation seemed to get into dangerous channels, and one always felt there was electricity in the air when the Emperor and King Edward talked. The German doctors, Renvers and Spielhagen, remained silent, and Laking, having grasped that not only they but the whole of the suite resented his presence, kept very quiet. The suite themselves were not very talkative and seemed more inclined to listen to the Emperor than to talk.

I was glad to retire early as I had such a lot to do. I had no clerk and had to write everything myself and to keep a note of my replies. Sometimes it was necessary to make a copy of a letter. The King's Messenger brought daily a number of official boxes, and while some of them only contained submissions requiring the King's signature, others required carefully worded answers on instructions given to me by the King, all of which I had taken down in shorthand.

After I had been at Friedrichshof for three days I received a message that the Empress wished to see me. At the hour named I went upstairs and into her sitting-room where I found her propped up with cushions; she looked as if she had just been taken off the rack after undergoing torture.

She asked me all sorts of questions about England, the South African War, the King's position, but after half an hour this intense conversation and hurricane of questions seemed to tire her. The nurse came and told me I really must go, but the Empress said, 'Only a few minutes'. When the nurse left the room she said, 'There is something I want you to do for me. I want you to take charge of my letters and take them with you back to England.' When I expressed my readiness to undertake their custody she seemed pleased and went on in a dreamy sort of way: 'I will send them to you at one o'clock tonight and I know I can rely on your discretion. I don't want a soul to know that they have been taken away, and certainly Willie must not have them, nor must he know you have got them.' Our conversation was again interrupted by the nurse and this time I felt I had to go. I retired to my room wondering whether the Empress had said all there was to be said on the subject.

After dinner I went as usual to my room and had plenty to do.

The Castle clock boomed one and I waited expectantly, but there was dead silence, and I was coming to the conclusion either that I had misunderstood or that some unforeseen obstacle had prevented the letters reaching me. Then I heard a quick knock at my door. I said 'Herein', and four men came in carrying two boxes, the size of portmanteaux, and covered with black oilcloth. The cords round them were quite new and on each box was a plain white label with neither name nor address. I noticed that the men wore blue serge breeches and long riding-boots and I came to the conclusion that they were not trusted retainers but stable-men quite ignorant of what the boxes contained. They put down the boxes and retired without saying a word.

It now dawned on me that I had undertaken no easy task and I began to wonder how I was to get such large boxes back to England without anyone suspecting their contents. I had assumed, perhaps not unnaturally, that the expression 'letters' meant a packet of letters that I should have no difficulty in concealing in one of my portmanteaux. But these large corded boxes were quite another matter.

I came to the conclusion that the Empress intended these letters to be published. To attempt to smuggle them away was to court disaster as the whole place was full of secret police. I therefore wrote on the label on one box 'China with care' and on the other 'Books with care' and the next morning had them placed in the passage with my empty luggage.

On March 1st we left Friedrichshof for London and I was talking to the Emperor in the hall when a procession of soldiers passed carrying our luggage. When these two boxes came past they looked so different from the rest that I feared someone would ask what they were, but no one noticed them and the Emperor went on talking. Most unluckily they were placed last on the top of a heap of luggage on one of the wagons and there appeared to be something wrong with the tarpaulin cover. The other wagons were all covered up, but this particular wagon remained uncovered and the boxes with their new cords and labels staring at me. The Emperor was, however, still holding forth and so no one noticed them.

In 1927 I consulted King George V about their publication, but he seemed opposed to the idea and told me to consult Princess Louise, Princess Beatrice, and the Duke of Connaught. Princess Beatrice was the one of the three who was doubtful; the other two approved of my idea of publishing the letters in book form. So the King withdrew his opposition but said he neither approved nor disapproved and that I had better do what I thought best.

I sent for the letters and found there were sixty volumes, each volume containing approximately four hundred pages. Of course the letters varied in length, and while some of them were thirty pages long, others filled only just the four sides of note-paper. It took me nearly a year to read through them carefully and to point out to my confidential typist, Mr. Marten, which ones I wanted typed. I finally had a large mass of typewritten material, far too much for my purpose, but while I was careful to keep any letters of historical interest, I cut out a great deal of private family matters which could be of no interest to the public. Having written only sufficient running commentary to enable the reader to understand the letters, I was advised by the publisher, Sir Frederick Macmillan, to invoke the aid of Mr. S. F. Markham, who had assisted Sir Sidney Lee in his *Life of King Edward*. He proved invaluable, and not only did he find corroborative material in other books that had been published years ago, but he brought the whole thing together.

In 1928 the book came out and received a very good Press. On account of the allusions to the German Emperor, there were not only long and excellent reviews of the book, but big headlines in most of the newspapers.

It was curious to find how divided the Royal Family were on the subject, but, while those who thought the publication of the letters was wrong were loud in their abuse of the book, those who thought I was right were singularly inarticulate.

The King at first seemed interested in the book, but when his sister the Princess Victoria [2] denounced it as one of the most dreadful books ever published, he joined in the general abuse of it. The Queen remained impartial and thought that while I was justified in publishing the letters, I should have cut out many of them. Princess Beatrice, who had not read the book but only the extracts in the newspapers, said it was a dreadful book; Princess Helena Victoria [3] most naturally sided with her brother, Prince Abby, who, of course, was all for the German Emperor. On the other hand, the Duke of Connaught was entirely on my side, and wrote me two long letters saying that I was undoubtedly right in publishing the letters, more especially as the Emperor had written his side of the controversy; there was also Emil Ludwig's book which would form history unless contradicted, and he had no doubt that the Empress Frederick had intended to have the letters published. Princess Louise wrote a charming letter of approval, but the letters that pleased me most were from the Empress Frederick's daughters, Queen Sophie [4] and the Landgraefin of Hesse. Unfortunately they did not wish to be quoted, but they both were convinced their mother had given me the letters with a view to their publication. They thanked me for carrying out her wishes, and the Landgraefin ended her letter, 'Yours gratefully and sincerely, Margaret'.

When the announcement that I intended to publish the letters was made in Berlin, it caused much uneasiness. The German Emperor was determined to stop the publication and began by writing to tell me that the letters belonged to him as his mother's heir and that I had therefore no right to publish them; that it was my duty

---

[2] Second daughter of King Edward VII.

[3] Daughter of Prince and Princess Christian. Prince Abby (Albert) was Duke of Schleswig-Holstein.

[4] Of Greece.

to return them to him as it was too soon to publish them. He added, 'The clandestine removal of these letters is next to theft', and that he intended to place the matter in the hands of a lawyer versed in international publication law and to try and stop the publication.

I had no intention of arguing with the Emperor and I merely acknowedged the receipt of this message. Herr von Kleist, the Minister in charge of all matters relating to the Royal Family in Berlin, then wrote me a long letter first of all on the legal position, arguing that in giving me the letters the Empress had not handed over the copyright, which still remained the property of the Emperor. He then appealed to me to withdraw the book on the grounds that its publication would be detrimental to the interests of the German Royal Family.

I consulted Sir Frederick Macmillan on the legal question, and he, after consultation with an eminent lawyer, told me that, according to the law, the ink and paper belonged to the person to whom the letters were addressed, but the copyright belonged to the person who wrote the letters. Therefore the Emperor might be right in thinking that, as heir to the Empress, he owned the copyright. There was, however, the question of the deed of gift when the Empress gave me the letters. As the copyright at that time belonged to her, she had a perfect right to give it to me. The Emperor would therefore have to prove that the copyright was not given before he could lay claim to it.

I therefore replied to Herr Kleist that my right to publish the letters was undeniable, and on sentimental grounds I maintained that, as I was selected by the Empress as a person in whom she could trust implicitly to carry out her dying wishes, I could not betray that trust.

The next I heard of this was that Sir Frederick Macmillan told me the Emperor had employed an eminent K.C., with instructions to bring an injunction against me prohibiting the publication of the letters. As it depended, however, on whether the Emperor could prove that there was no deed of gift, and that the letters were stolen, all this ended in smoke.

After the book appeared Herr Emil Ludwig, the German

historian, wrote an article in the *Observer* in which he chivalrously recanted his former views on the Empress's character, and owned that, had my book been published earlier, it would have 'caused substantial changes to be made' in his book on the Kaiser. He asked why the book had not been published sooner, and why only a selection from the letters had been given.

The *Observer* rang me up and asked me to write a reply but unfortunately I was in bed with influenza. I therefore replied that I could not write one by the following Sunday, but I would have it ready by the Sunday after that. The editor said that the only Sunday available was the next one, and after that the following four consecutive Sundays had been promised. I therefore wrote my answer and sent it to *The Times,* as I felt that to wait five weeks would give a wrong impression. *The Times* kindly gave me the centre page. I explained in my letter that there were sixty volumes of letters and that it was clearly impossible to publish them all; that I had hesitated to publish them at first, but that after the Emperor's own book and Emil Ludwig's *Kaiser Wilhelm II* appeared, it seemed obvious that if the Empress's letters were ever to be published, and if historians of the future were to have an opportunity of correcting the entirely misleading portrait of her given in these two books, it was imperative that the letters should be published with as little delay as possible. I then gave an account of the Emperor's efforts to stop the publication, and I asked why he had never made any attempt to defend his mother and why no one in Germany stood up for her when slanderous attacks were made on her memory. It was a long letter which took up two columns, but it appears to have carried conviction, as many people who were interested in this controversy told me that I had entirely disposed of all the criticisms.

The curious part of this was that the Emperor complained that the publication was too soon, while Ludwig said it was too late.

In my letter to *The Times* I said at the end: 'While purporting to be a dispassionate description of the Emperor, Dr. Emil Ludwig's book is really a most one-sided picture based on the evidence of those inimical to him. Had the Emperor died in 1913 at the zenith of his career and had Herr Ludwig been asked to write his biography, the sources from which the biographer would have derived his estimate of the Emperor's character would have been very different from those he made use of in his famous book.'

This roused Herr Ludwig, who made a spirited reply in the *Observer,* in which he admitted that in 1913 very little was known about the Emperor. When he wrote his book, however, he had the Emperor's own speeches and letters in addition to the papers and dispatches in the Government archives for material. It could not therefore be said that his opinion of the Emperor was based on the evidence of those inimical to him. He ended up by saying that I had succeeded in putting the Emperor in an even less favourable light than he had.

Although the Emperor was unable to prevent the publication of the letters, he decided to mitigate the effect they would have in Germany. He therefore bought the German rights on condition that he would be allowed to write the preface, and he then wrote a very clever preface in which he said that the Empress 'was very sensitive and everything wounded her; she saw everything in shadows, everything hostile, saw want of sympathy and coolness where there was only a helpless silence, and her temperament made her use bitter words about everybody. Therefore the reader should not believe implicitly everything she wrote.' This was far cleverer than an attempt to vindicate his own conduct towards her.

On August 5, 1901, the poor Empress Frederick died at Friedrichshof and of course King Edward attended the funeral. He left London for Cronberg on August 10 attended by Lord Clarendon, the Lord Chamberlain, Admiral Sir John Fullerton,[5] and Sidney Greville, Grooms-in-Waiting, Stanley Clarke,[6] Equerry-in-Waiting, and myself as Acting Private Secretary. It was curious that none of these could speak German: in fact amongst the Household there was a dearth of German scholars.

As regards myself, I must go back a year or two to explain how I stood as regards German.

At the end of Queen Victoria's reign I had seriously considered

[5] Extra Groom-in-Waiting.
[6] Major-General Sir Stanley Clarke, later Paymaster and Acting Master of the King's Household.

what I ought to do to qualify myself for the post of Private Secretary and how I could best employ any leisure moments I had. I came to the conclusion that obviously I ought to learn German. All the German Royal Family talked English fluently but their suites did not, and I had often experienced the difficulty of making myself understood to a German whose knowledge of English was very elementary. Of course Count Seckendorff and Baron Reischach, who were with the Empress Frederick, talked English perfectly: in fact you would hardly have known that the former was not English. Most of the Emperor's suite talked English, but when one of the minor Princes came to see Queen Victoria, it often happened that he brought with him a man whose knowledge of English was practically nil.

Obviously German should be learnt, but the question was how to set about it without having to go to Germany. I had learnt a little German at Eton, but not only had I forgotten the little I learnt, but when I learnt Hindustani in India, it drove out of my head the few German words I knew. I had always remarked that people who began to learn foreign languages were unable to speak because of their limited vocabulary, and I therefore determined as a start to learn ten German words a day. These I pinned on my looking-glass so that when I got up in the morning, washed my hands for luncheon, dressed for dinner, and went to bed I repeated them over and over again. Then at the end of the week I recited the whole seventy. The difficulty of course was to look out the words, and after a time this became more and more difficult. However, I kept this up for a year, by which time I had learnt 3,650 German words. To learn a language, all that is needed is a parrot-like ability to reproduce strange sounds and a good memory.

When I had a month's leave, I went to the Berlitz School in London and paid for a course of lessons. I was then ushered into a room where a learned-looking man explained in English the methods they adopted. After that he told me he would always speak German. He then pointed to various things in the room and I replied in German. He then produced picture-books and I told him what the German was for everything he showed me. Of course, this was mere child's-play. He then got other books illustrated, but I never made a mistake. He seemed puzzled but took to abstract things, pointing to words in an ordinary English dictionary, but he never put me down. At last he said he had taught a great many people German, but never had he come across anyone who had such a varied vocabulary. I had to explain in English that, while I knew the German for a boa-constrictor, I couldn't say 'Where is my hat?' in German. This he said he would soon rectify, and I must go through a course of written exercises. So away I worked at grammar and translations till I became completely fogged. I became tongue-tied and hopelessly mixed with the genders, verbs and prepositions. The harder I worked the worse I became, and then I began to forget my vocabulary. This depressed me a good deal, but I stuck to it for three weeks, by which time I became convinced that, at the age of thirty-four, I was too old to learn, and certainly past the age when one could cram. I gave up the whole thing and determined to try something else.

When, therefore in the course of our journey to Cronberg, Stanley Clarke showed me a telegram saying that the Emperor was sending an A.D.C. General to explain what the arrangements were on our arrival I merely remarked, 'If he can't talk English you must do your best in German, because I can't speak a word. There are things I can do and things I can't, and this is one of the things I can't.' He laughed and said no doubt he could get on. The General arrived and Stanley Clarke greeted him warmly, but when they were seated in the railway carriage they found they could not make themselves understood. Stanley Clarke had no German and the General had no English, but while Stanley Clarke could talk French, the German General, curiously enough, could not. As it was sufficiently important for the Emperor to have sent a General to explain, Stanley Clarke felt that something must be done, and therefore came and told me of the *impasse* he was in. There seemed no other solution but for me to have a try. So I went into the compartment when I was duly presented to the General. I began cautiously in German and said that while I could not speak German I could, I thought, understand if he did not talk too fast. He then began to explain a somewhat intricate programme the Emperor had sketched out at Frankfort, and I found to my surprise that I had no difficulty in understanding every word he said. But what fairly astounded me was that when I began asking questions, I never hesitated for a moment and German flowed easily from my mouth. The General then rattled on naturally and I talked away with the greatest ease. When I had taken notes of all that was going to happen at Frankfort, the General paused and said with a puzzled expression that he had understood me to say I couldn't speak German. He seemed to think there was a sell somewhere, but I told him of my efforts and how I had learnt German words, etc. He laughed hugely and said he would at once learn English in this way.

This was so encouraging that I determined to pursue my German studies. I read German novels and when I was at Marienbad I had an Austrian schoolmaster to talk to every day, and I finally got fairly fluent in German; but of course it is never the same thing as learning a language when one is a child.

The point of all this was that the German Emperor had stage-managed an official reception at Frankfort, and intended to meet the King there and travel on to Homburg with him. I was so busy talking to my German General that I quite forgot to warn my servant that I would change into uniform before reaching Frankfort. He was unfortunately travelling in another part of the train and there was no connecting corridor. When I tried to open the tin case containing my uniform I found it locked, and of course he had the key. There was therefore nothing to be done but to break open the tin case, but I had no implement suitable for the purpose. The attendant had no hammer and I foresaw not being properly dressed in time. All the other suite came to help with suggestions, but we all failed. Finally the only weapon that could be found was the iron key used for winding up the beds, and with this I proceeded to batter the lock, but it was difficult to use a handle as a hammer, and I knocked all the paint off the tin case. The others stood by cheering me on and eventually I managed to smash the lock. I had rather a scramble to get ready, but succeeded in appearing impeccably dressed at Frankfort, and there the Emperor and all his suite met us. We all travelled together on to Homburg and found a guard of honour drawn up with a mass of officials to receive us. King Edward inspected the guard of honour, shook hands with the leading officials, and then drove to the Hotel Adler accompanied by the Emperor.

The first part of the funeral ceremony was to take place at Homburg on Monday and we spent Sunday quietly in the Ritters Park Hotel, but all of a sudden the King sent word that all our gold lace, aiguillettes, etc., were to be covered with crape. Personally I thought this was quite wrong. In the British Army we simply wear a mourning band, and although it was the custom in the German Army to cover themselves with crape, I saw no reason why we should copy their methods. There was no time to argue the point and the courier was sent out to collect women who would be willing to sew on crape; not by any means an easy thing to do on a Sunday night, but eventually three women were induced to do this work for a high wage. We all brought our sword-belts, shoulder cords, and aiguillettes, and placed them on chairs with our names written on a card so that they should not get mixed up. The next morning the funeral service was to begin at Cronberg Church and the Emperor was to drive there with the King. Imagine my horror when I went to find my things after breakfast, to be told they had not yet been begun. Naturally as I was the junior they decided to do my things last, but they had miscalculated their agility with the needle and found that it took longer than they estimated to cover things with crape. I exhorted the women to further efforts and then changed as far as I could into uniform. Finally I walked into the room where the women worked, and pinned crape over the remaining accoutrements. I rushed downstairs only to find that all the carriages had gone, as it had been assumed I could not be ready in time. To come all the way to Germany to attend a funeral and then miss it seemed to me idiotic, although of course I had a perfectly good excuse. I shouted to the courier to get me a carriage, but after a few minutes he returned to say there were none left in the town. I was, however, determined to have a try and sent out both *concierges* to find a cab of any description, while the courier explained that the Emperor might come at any moment and that even if I started I could not possibly arrive in time as the roads would be stopped by police, but I swept him aside and drove off in a one-horse cab which one of the *concierges* produced. I explained to the driver that he was not to take the road on which the Emperor would drive and he said there was a shorter way, but it was a very bad road. I promised him twenty marks if he arrived at Cronberg before the Emperor. The distance was about six miles and away he went at a hand gallop, but some cavalry threatened to stop us, whereupon I stood up and shouted at them and they allowed me through. I kept on looking back nervously to see whether there was any sign of the Emperor's carriage on the other road, which was plainly visible about a mile away. I heard that he intended to have four fast-trotting horses and I knew that if I saw the carriage too soon I was bound to be beaten. After a mile or so the cabman showed signs of tiring and appeared to be taking it easy, so I stormed at him, determined to keep further inducements of money till later. The horse turned out to be quite a good one, but the cab, which was a very old victoria, threatened several times to fall to pieces. Once when the wheels caught in a deep rut, the victoria was pulled out like a concertina, but righted itself when we got on more level ground.

I was feeling fairly confident of winning this race when I saw a cloud of dust on the other road and I realized that this must be the Emperor and King Edward. I at once got up and doubled the original sum I had promised the driver. This roused him to further efforts and he proceeded to flog the horse. I explained to him that all that was necessary was to keep the horse cantering along and that it was useless to use the whip, which apparently had not the smallest effect on the horse. So we ambled along, the victoria swaying from side to side, but still holding together.

It occurred to me that I should present a somewhat undignified appearance if I had to drive through the streets of the village which were lined with troops, and as I should be able to walk up the hill to the church quite as quickly as the horse could go, I determined to dismiss the cab at the entrance to the village. I explained this to the driver, who seemed to have looked forward to a neck-and-neck finish with the Emperor. It was well that I did so, as the poor horse had had quite enough by the time we reached the village and to urge him up the hill would have been cruel. I dismissed the cab at the bottom of the hill and told the man to come to the hotel in the afternoon when I would pay him. I walked quickly through the lines of troops and had just reached the church door when I heard behind me the orders being given to salute the Emperor. I had won only by a short head. I walked leisurely into the church and joined the others, who were much surprised to see me. The service was simple but well conducted and we returned to our hotel in time for luncheon. This time I went in one of the specially ordered two-horsed carriages.

In the evening we all dined quietly with the Emperor at the old castle near Homburg. The next day we went by train to Potsdam, where the second and principal part of the funeral ceremonies were to take place. The majority of the British suite was at the Neues Palais, but I was sent to the old castle at Potsdam, which was not unlike an hotel; long corridors with masses of bedrooms. Frederick the Great built the Neues Palais and conceived the somewhat barbarous idea of having three nude life-sized figures made into likenesses of his three greatest enemies, Catherine of Russia, Maria Theresa of Austria, and Madame de Pompadour, supporting a huge crown on the roof of the Palace.

I had brought with me an old soldier who had been in the Grenadiers and later valet to Eddy Gleichen.[7] This man, named Herbert, was an excellent servant, but having just returned from the South African War and being a man of limited intelligence, he appeared to confuse the Germans with the Boers. When I arrived I went to luncheon at the Neues Palais and returned afterwards to change my clothes at the Alteschloss. We all were attended by *lakais* dressed in livery with aiguillettes, top-hats, and boxcloth gaiters, and the one I had was admirable and never left me. I could find no trace of my English servant or luggage and so, accompanied by my *lakai,* I drove back to the Neues Palais thinking that probably he had gone to the wrong palace. There I found him seated in a cab with all the luggage round him. He explained that he had been unable to understand a word anyone had

[7] Later Major-General Lord Edward Gleichen; only son of Admiral Prince Victor of Hohenlohe-Langenburg, known for some years as Count Gleichen.

said to him, but as he did not trust any of them he refused to budge and determined to remain in a conspicuous position outside the Neues Palais on the chance of my seeing him. I spoke to him rather strongly on his stupidity but explained that now my *lakai* would look after him, see he had luncheon, etc. I turned to the *lakai* and asked him his name, whereupon he at once produced a card from his pocket, and this I handed to Herbert, who looked horrified when he read it. On it was printed 'Paul Kruger' which was the name of the President of the Transvaal Republic. It was simply a curious coincidence, but unfortunately it confirmed Herbert's suspicions that the Germans were the same as the Boers. However, my excellent *lakai*, ignorant of all this, looked after him so well that I never had any difficulty.

The funeral was most impressive, the road being lined all the way with troops four deep, while the magnificent hearse drawn by eight horses was followed by the Emperor and all the Royal Family on foot. We, the English suite, kept all together, and as we found all the deputations from other countries jockeying to take precedence of each other, we decided to go last of all. When the procession wound round a corner, however, the Emperor looked back and caught sight of us in rear of the whole procession. He at once sent an A.D.C. to bring us forward and place us immediately behind the Royal Family. While we were far back I was rather shocked at the levity displayed by many of the German officers. The hearse was quite a quarter of a mile ahead and we could not hear the massed bands playing the Dead March. This may have accounted for the way in which many German officers greeted their old friends with facetious remarks.

The funeral service took place in the Royal Mausoleum of the Friedenskirche on August 13, but there was only room for the Royal Family and the procession, and all the troops had to wait outside until carriages came to drive everyone back to the Neues Palais. The next day the King returned by motor to Homburg accompanied by Stanley Clarke, Sidney Greville, and myself, while the rest of the suite returned to London.

We arrived at the Ritters Park Hotel and the next morning went down to the place where people drink the waters. On the

King's previous visits, as Prince of Wales, no one had paid much attention to him, but it was now different. Wherever he went he was followed by a host of people who stood round in a circle and stared at him, for as his photographs were in every shop-window the crowd never had any difficulty in spotting him. He was furious and swore he would never come there again.

After the first few days the crowd behaved better and the King was able to move about more freely. We walked about drinking the waters from 7.30 to 9 a.m., and then had breakfast consisting of a cup of coffee and a boiled egg. All the morning I worked away at the letters and official boxes: luncheon at one and then a motor drive in the afternoon, usually with Stanley Clarke, which enabled me to play golf on a small links where the English community generally assembled.

There was a curious mixture of people at Homburg, and although the King knew many, only a few were ever asked to luncheon. There were Count Benckendorff,[8] at that time Russian Minister in Copenhagen, who interested the King; Sir Condie Stephen, who was Minister at Dresden, and therefore knew the German Royal Family very well, a charming man with a great sense of humour; Lord and Lady Cork [9]—he was tiresome, but she amused the King; and Sir George Lewis, the famous solicitor, who was a fund of amusing legal stories. The latter told me a curious thing, which was that among all his clients he had never known of anyone making money by gambling on the Stock Exchange. Several had consistently made money for fifteen or even twenty years, and had lost it all and a great deal more in two years. Among others at Homburg were Captain and Lady Lilian Boyd, she like the White Queen in *Alice Through the Looking-Glass,* he uncouth, giving the impression of a rough diamond, when really he was the most cultivated of men; Mr. A. Wagg, a racing man of good value from the racing point of view; and Arthur and Venetia James, he charming but not having much in common with the King except racing; she full of humour and high spirits, walking

[8] Later Ambassador in London.
[9] Richard Boyle, 9th Earl of Cork and Orrery, married a daughter of 1st Marquis of Clanricarde.

with the King and keeping him amused. The old Duke of Cambridge went about with his son Colonel FitzGeorge and Mrs. Vyner, but only met the King at the Golf Club, where everyone went for tea.

On August 23, 1901, the King went to pay a visit to the Emperor at Wilhelmshoehe, four hours by train, which seemed a long journey for only a luncheon. We, of course, had to go in uniform, the King attired as Colonel of his German regiment. We started at 9 a.m. and did not get back till past 10 p.m. When we arrived there seemed to be an enormous number of troops in the streets and they told me afterwards that the Emperor had sent for 15,000 men, which seemed to me to be overdoing the whole thing in view of the fact that the visit was supposed to be private on account of the mourning. When we arrived at the castle all the troops marched past the Emperor and the King. This seemed to be interminable, and having had an egg at 8 a.m. we were all getting very hungry by two o'clock. At last we went to luncheon, the King and the Emperor sitting one side of the table whilst Stanley Clarke and I sat next to Eulenburg on the other side, there being about twenty at luncheon.

The Emperor presented the King with a large gold cup surrounded by a sort of gold railings to keep the flowers on the table tidy. He had invented the railings himself and was much pleased with his present. He was in great spirits and full of stories and chaff. At the end of luncheon he suddenly drank my health. Now I knew it was the custom to stand up and drink to him, but I was caught napping and had nothing in my glass. So when he said 'Fritz', I tried to get up, but tripped up over my sword. Finding I had nothing in my glass, I seized the nearest decanter and poured out some wine, but it was simply sediment at the bottom of an old claret. There was, of course, nothing else to do but to drink it. Whereupon the Emperor chaffed me about drinking the dregs of bottles, and everyone seemed much amused.

This visit being purely private had no political significance. It was only natural that King Edward, taking the waters at Homburg, should pay a visit to his nephew. At that time there was no jealousy on the Emperor's part, nor had anyone then started the cry of the encirclement of Germany. There is no doubt that the Emperor did all he could to make himself agreeable, but King Edward never liked him and therefore while the conversations in public were ostensibly very amicable, one always felt that it was an effort on both sides to keep them so. They had a private talk at which Sir Frank Lascelles [10] was present, but it was so full of chaff that nothing was taken very seriously.

While out driving in the afternoon the Emperor said to the King, 'I hear you have trouble at Malta and that you are contemplating giving them self-government.' Now the King had heard nothing of this and was very much put out in consequence. Afterwards he told me to write to Joe Chamberlain and enquire why he had not been kept informed of what was going on at Malta. I did so and received a very stiff reply pointing out that constitutionally the Secretary of State for the Colonies was responsible to Parliament only and that he did not have to consult the King before taking any action like the Secretary of State for Foreign Affairs. I replied that His Majesty had no wish to interfere in any way with the work of the Colonial Office, but thought he should be kept informed as to what had been decided instead of undergoing the humiliation of learning the facts from the German Emperor.

Chamberlain melted at this and wrote saying he quite understood how distasteful it must have been to the King to be instructed by the Emperor and that he would therefore take steps to ensure that in future His Majesty was kept well informed on all Colonial matters. When I returned to London I saw Ampthill, Chamberlain's Private Secretary, and fixed up the details with him.

One day the King motored to Wolfsgarten, the country residence of the Grand Duke of Hesse.[11] In those days motors were very rare and we had constantly to stop when frightened horses in carriages and carts threatened to bolt. The Grand Duke and Duchess of Hesse, Prince and Princess Louise of Battenberg,

[10] Ambassador to Germany, 1895–1908.
[11] King Edward VII's nephew. His marriage was dissolved later in the same year.

Princess Sandra of Coburg, and Princess Helena Victoria, met us there.

The house was like a Swiss cottage with a garden like the scene in *Faust,* stunted trees and rather sham-looking flowers and grass, but on the whole a fascinating place. Inside it was composed of every style of mural decoration, but predominantly what was called 'art nouveau' or 'secession'. In some of the rooms the walls were a deep blue with green woodwork and red furniture; in others gold carved doors and marble walls. The furniture was of the weirdest shapes and description, but every now and then one came across lovely things. We had an amusing and talkative luncheon and sat about in the garden afterwards.

CHAPTER X

Household reforms — A court martial and its consequences — The King and Lord Lansdowne — Sir John Fisher — Lord Charles Beresford — Curzon — Visits to Eton — King Edward's golf — Two Assistant Private Secretaries

I FOUND THE KING very businesslike but exacting, and far more considerate and human than Queen Victoria was. The Queen rarely considered the feelings of her Household and it never occurred to her to ascertain whether any wish of hers might cause inconvenience, whereas King Edward was always thinking of small acts of kindness and often, without being asked, suggested to some married man that he should go away and spend the week with his family.

King Edward was a born organizer, and, had he been an ordinary man, he would certainly have made his mark as a business man. Hedworth Lambton [1] always said that had King Edward been a very poor man he would have become a Hyde Park orator. He also had the great gift of selecting good men for posts and never made a mistake with an important appointment. Once he trusted a man he would leave him entirely in charge and never interfere with details.

When he first came to the throne the whole system was antiquated. Queen Victoria had reigned so long and had disliked any change so intensely that abuses had sprung up everywhere. King Edward at once set to work to remedy this and completely revolutionized every department. To all who had been in Queen Victoria's Household it was almost miraculous to see how things were

[1] Later Admiral of the Fleet the Hon. Hedworth Meux (he assumed the name Meux in 1911); commanded the Royal Yacht 1901–3; Commander-in-Chief, Portsmouth, 1912–16.

gradually altered and improved. Naturally these changes were not carried out without some grumbling, especially amongst those who had been found to be incompetent and who were therefore pensioned. In the Lord Steward's department, which was concerned with service and catering, the whole machinery was reorganized. A Committee composed of Sir Arthur Ellis,[2] Lord Farquhar,[3] and Sir William Carington advised the most drastic reforms, which were immediately carried out. Many found great fault with this reorganization on the grounds that it took all the power from the Lord Steward (a political office of State) and transferred it to the Master of the Household.

The Lord Chamberlain's office under Sir Arthur Ellis, which was concerned with ceremonial issues, was also reorganized and all sorts of innovations and improvements were introduced: the most effective of these was the 'Drawing-rooms', as they were then called, being held in the evening instead of the afternoon. They were in future called 'Courts' and were held in the ballroom instead of the throne-room. Ellis, who had visited every Court in Europe with King Edward when he was Prince of Wales, had an unrivalled knowledge of the way things were done abroad and was able to adapt the best features of the Continental receptions. The King went into every detail and between them they stage-managed perfectly a new piece of pageantry.

When I attended a 'Court' I was always struck by the incongruous music the band played, and determined to do what I could to have this remedied. The majority of the Household, being quite unmusical, clamoured for popular airs, and Sir Walter Parratt, the Master of the Music, who cared only for classical music and looked down on any other sort of music, complied with the demand. I argued that these popular airs robbed the ceremony of all dignity. A presentation at Court was often a great event in a lady's life, but if she went past the King and Queen to the tune of 'His nose was redder than it was', the whole impression was spoilt. I maintained that minuets and old-fashioned airs, operatic music

[2] Major-General Sir Arthur Ellis; Comptroller in Lord Chamberlain's Department.

[3] Later 1st Earl Farquhar. Master of the Household to King Edward.

with a 'mysterious' touch, were what was wanted. I wrote to Sir Walter Parratt, who welcomed my opposition, to counter the pressure for popular airs; not that he carried out my proposals, but he played music that he liked.

I also took up the question of the music played by the band of the guard of honour at investitures and wrote to the Senior Bandmaster, Captain Rogan, on the subject. What I disliked was seeing eminent men being knighted while comic songs were being played by the band outside: also when the Home Secretary was reading out impressively some particularly heroic deed which had been performed by a man who was to receive the Albert Medal, the band outside played a two-step, which robbed the whole ceremony of any dignity. I suggested operatic music of a dramatic nature being played, and he entirely agreed, and circulated my letter amongst the other bandmasters.

But the difficulties that bandmasters had to contend with were not always so easily settled, and I remember that once at Windsor contradictory orders were sent to the band. King Edward liked French and Viennese light operas, whereas Queen Alexandra preferred grand opera, particularly Wagner. One morning the bandmaster received a message from the King to play Offenbach, and one from the Queen to play Wagner. Finding himself unable to comply with both, he thought he would hit upon the happy medium and selected Gilbert and Sullivan operas, and as always with people who compromise, he got into trouble with both the King and the Queen.

It was in June 1901 that one of those unfortunate cases which suddenly get out of all proportion and involve far-reaching effects happened. A certain captain who was in command of a company at Sanna's Post during the action there in 1900 had suffered, owing to the exposed position of his company, the loss of over half of his officers and men, and decided to hold up the white flag and capitulate. Upon which the whole of Adye's small force surrendered under the impression that the white flag referred to them, and six guns were captured by the enemy.

At the conclusion of the war, when the prisoners were released, Captain X was tried by court martial according to the regulations, and although he was acquitted of cowardice he was found guilty of an error in judgment. Lord Roberts was Commander-in-Chief in South Africa at the time and quite approved of the findings of the court martial, but when the papers came home Lord Wolseley, who was Commander-in-Chief at home, took the view that it was necessary to make an example as the white flag had been used too freely in South Africa. He therefore reversed the decision and ordered Captain X to be cashiered for cowardice. He persuaded St. John Brodrick,[4] the Secretary of State for War, to support him and give his approval.

Captain X, however, on returning home was determined to appeal and found he had a perfect right to appeal to the King as long as he did so through the proper channels. Guided by a first-rate lawyer he sent his appeal through his General and on to the War Office for submission to the King, who came to the conclusion that the sentence had been unduly harsh and that the military authorities should be content with forcing Captain X's resignation. Meanwhile Lord Roberts had succeeded Lord Wolseley as Commander-in-Chief at home and naturally agreed with the King's view, as he had approved of the findings of the court martial in South Africa; but in order to save everyone's face he decided that a special Court of Inquiry should be held composed of Generals who had been in South Africa, and presided over by Kelly-Kenny,[5] the Adjutant-General. These Generals heard all the evidence and eventually supported the verdict of the original court martial, which was that Captain X was not guilty of cowardice but of an error in judgment.

When, however, the case came again to Brodrick for confirmation he refused and said it was impossible to reverse a decision arrived at on the advice of the former Commander-in-Chief. Lord Roberts urged him to give way but he was adamant. He wrote to the King at some length and added that if His Majesty insisted on reversing the decision there would be no alternative for him but to resign. The King was furious and apparently contemplated

[4] Afterwards Earl of Midleton.
[5] General Sir Thomas Kelly-Kenny.

accepting Brodrick's resignation. Then suddenly the whole principle of constitutional monarchy was at stake and Brodrick appealed to Balfour, the Prime Minister. Balfour took the view that he was bound to support one of his Cabinet and wrote to the King that if Brodrick resigned, he feared the whole Cabinet would tender their resignations. Here was a very awkward situation for the King, because if the Government resigned and had an election with the cry that His Majesty was acting autocratically and was overriding the decisions of his responsible Ministers, the whole country would support them. The King quickly grasped this and told Balfour he would leave the matter in the hands of the Cabinet and would abide by their advice. This was considered by the Cabinet a very adroit way on the King's part of extricating himself from a delicate and dangerous situation. The King always prided himself on being entirely a constitutional monarch, but at heart he was a born autocrat. The matter came before the Cabinet, but of course it was a very one-sided affair, for Brodrick presented his case and there was no one to represent the other point of view. The Cabinet supported Brodrick: Captain X was cashiered and disgraced, and the British Constitution saved at his expense.

The King never seemed to get on with Brodrick, although he always seemed anxious to please His Majesty. They had different types of minds. The King adored uniforms and decorations, both of which were Greek to Brodrick. On the other hand, Brodrick was so busy trying to reform the whole system of the Army that he was supposed to let everything else slide and to deal with Army problems in the light of what the House of Commons would say. He seemed to give a totally erroneous impression of his personality to people he met for the first time and appeared at first sight to be a pig-headed pedant, whereas he was a man with big ideas, a good speaker, and a hard worker. When the King invented a new forage cap copied from the Russian Army and it turned out to be very unpopular, Brodrick most gallantly allowed it to be thought his creation and got soundly abused by the Press.

I was just settling down to my work as Assistant Private Secretary and was working very well with Knollys when I nearly got into severe trouble. The King took up some question about Sandhurst [6] and got very cross about it. Apparently he saw Lord Roberts, who promised to enquire into the matter, but when he did so he wrote more or less supporting the Sandhurst authorities. The King on receipt of this letter was furious and dictated a stinging reply. I took this down in shorthand and wrote using the *ipsissima verba* of His Majesty. It was a subject of which I knew nothing and I therefore thought it safer to reproduce the King's words, but I showed my letter to Knollys, who merely handed it back to me without comment. I think he should have told me it was worded too strongly. It turned out that Lord Roberts was much offended at the tone of my letter and told Arthur Ellis, not without reason, that he did not consider any Private Secretary ought to write in such a tone to the Commander-in-Chief. As soon as I heard this I at once wrote to him and humbly apologized, explaining the circumstances under which my letter had been written, and I received a charming reply to the effect that he quite understood.

The King never appeared to hit it off with Lansdowne, and I was unable to guess the reason, for no one treated His Majesty with more consideration and as far as I knew there had never been any real difference of opinion. Possibly Lansdowne may have been jealous at the King being supposed to run the foreign policy of the country and felt he had been ignored, being only told when matters had so far advanced that it was difficult for him to do more than give his approval. I always had the impression that, if the King ever made a false move, Lansdowne, so far from defending him, would stand and look on. He was said to take so much trouble with small questions that he quite lost sight of the big issues and often to be so busy correcting the English phraseology of dispatches that he forgot what the dispatch was about. Whether this was true or not I don't know, but he certainly will rank amongst the best Foreign Ministers.

Another Minister with whom the King had little in common was the First Lord of the Admiralty, Lord Selborne, and in most naval matters the King preferred the vigorous opinions of Ad-

[6] Royal Military College.

miral Sir John Fisher.[7] When King Edward came to the throne Fisher was Commander-in-Chief in the Mediterranean, but in 1902 he became Second Sea Lord, and in 1903 was transferred at his own request to the Portsmouth Command; while holding this office, he began to draft plans for the entire reorganization of the Navy.

It was at Balmoral in October 1904 that I first made the acquaintance of this tempestuous personality. I was going for a walk one afternoon just as he decided on the same form of recreation. I rather fancy he was bored to tears at the sight of me and would have done anything he could to avoid me, but without being rude he could not avoid my company. As we walked on he began by asking me whether I liked dancing. At the time I thought he had chosen the only topic which he imagined would suit my intelligence, but I found later he was passionately fond of dancing. I determined, however, to get the conversation on more interesting topics and I asked him about the row between Archibald Hunter and Hedworth Lambton and he told me his views, but still he didn't appear to wish to talk. So I got on the problems of national defence which I had been studying and stated my opinions with a view to drawing him out. This had the desired effect and away he went. He said that unless we kept up the Navy to a two-power standard we were done. London would starve in a week unless the seas were kept clear to bring in supplies. He sketched out what was later called 'the blue-water school'. I told him that I quite agreed with him but unless he had an Army at home large enough to prevent raids and make it necessary for a foreign enemy to land large numbers of men, the Navy would be useless. If 20,000 men could dodge the Fleet and land somewhere in England, they could march on London and create such a scare that we should be forced to capitulate without striking a blow. He was delighted with my arguments and got so excited talking that he had to stop and hold my arm to prevent my going on. He sketched out rather a wild scheme which was to reduce the Army and Navy to experts alone, and then keep a huge reserve of men who could become either

[7] Later 1st Lord Fisher of Kilverstone, Admiral of the Fleet. First Sea Lord, 1904–10 and 1914–15.

soldiers or sailors. A beginning had been made in this direction by the nucleus crew system, but he wanted to carry the idea much further and make it apply to the Army. I told him that I very much doubted whether an Army composed of 90 percent raw recruits would be any good, and I imagined that the highly trained German Army would soon make mincemeat of them, but he maintained that any idea of our fighting the Germans on land was absurd. By this scheme he would be able to reduce the income-tax by half, and that alone would be a blessing. We were out over two hours and when we returned he was still talking and holding me back from opening the door.

Personally I always had a great admiration for his genius and there seems no doubt that had it not been for the reforms which he pushed through in King Edward's reign, and which were resisted by the majority of naval officers, we should have come off second-best on the sea in our struggle with the Germans.

It was curious how he and Esher seemed to hit it off together, and I think the reason they got on so well was that they had the same type of mind. Both were very clever; both preferred to come in at the back door instead of the front; both had the early Italian type of mind. There was something tortuous about both of them, but while Fisher loved a fight and was prepared to stand or fall by his measures, Esher was very susceptible to public opinion and shrank from any responsibility. I always think that Esher's strong point was that he never minded who got credit for any measure he devised so long as it was adopted by the authorities.

Fisher was always very good company and loved telling naval yarns, which he did remarkably well. He had not, however, sufficient popularity or individuality to carry out his reforms single-handed, although he practically dominated every First Lord, no matter on which side of the House. It was King Edward's support that enabled him to carry out his reforms.

He very soon realized that if he was to retain King Edward's confidence he must make friends with the King's *entourage,* and he therefore with subtle flattery proceeded to make me one of his adherents. He would write me long letters apparently intended only for me as they were so outspoken, but really for King Edward to read. Unless he marked them private, which he rarely did, I always gave them to the King to read, and King Edward delighted in reading what he imagined was not intended for his eyes.

In April 1904 the King went down to stay with Jackie Fisher at Portsmouth. At that time the majority of the officers in the Navy were strongly opposed to Fisher's schemes while only a few of the cleverest officers supported him. The King, however, believed in Fisher and without quite understanding all the intricacies of the various questions involved, saw clearly that some reforms were needed. His Majesty consequently backed him while Charlie Beresford,[8] who hated Fisher and all his works, became the leader of the reactionary officers. These asserted that the reforms were quite unnecessary, that Fisher's methods were Machiavellian and un-English, and that Fisher had Malay blood in him; but as Fisher had the powerful backing of the King, these attacks proved harmless. Fisher always said that had it not been for King Edward's support he would never have succeeded in carrying out his various schemes. He always seemed to get the various First Lords of the Admiralty in his pocket, and Selborne, Cawdor, Tweedmouth, and McKenna [9] went about repeating his cogent arguments, but they carried little or no weight with the officers of the Navy. His energy was marvellous, and although he had insisted on having no routine work when he became First Sea Lord, he used to get up at 5 a.m. every morning and do four hours' hard work before breakfast. He always said that these four hours of uninterrupted work were worth more than eight hours during the day. He interested and amused the King and often kept him up late at night propounding his theories of reform, and dilating upon the virtues of his newest toy, the submarine. The King's wonderful gift of listening as if keenly interested, and his knowledge of human nature, were exemplified in a remarkable degree during this visit to Portsmouth. Fisher had explained the general principles on which the submarine worked and had outlined the

[8] Rear-Admiral Lord Charles Beresford, later 1st Lord Beresford and Admiral. After distinguished Naval career became Conservative M.P. Brother of Lord Marcus Beresford.

[9] Successive First Lords of the Admiralty.

various problems which had not yet been satisfactorily solved, so that the King knew a good deal before Captain Bacon, who later made a great name for himself [10] and became Admiral Sir Reginald Bacon, came to dinner, but he listened attentively to all Captain Bacon said when he practically repeated all that Fisher had told him. The following day we went on board a submarine and a very keen young officer showed us round. When he began at the beginning explaining things I felt inclined to say 'We know all about that', but the King listened attentively a third time to these explanations and asked several questions as if he were hearing about the submarine for the first time.

In 1907 Fisher sent me confidentially the draft of a memorandum which he had written on invasion for the Cabinet. I told him in my answer that a memorandum on such a subject without any mention of the Army, small as it was, would carry no conviction and I sketched out a short paragraph on the part the Army would have to play.

He replied: 'The codicil you propose is an excellent and valuable idea. *Bless you for telling me.*'

Later he wrote, 'Your words on the Army the most lucid and to the point ever yet written. Like Saul I don't believe you quite knew you were a prophet when you were prophesying. I am going to give them to the Prime Minister as they so exactly hit off the situation. I mean the following words: "In order to create a large reserve for great emergencies and in order to prevent a panic, it may be necessary to have a Territorial Army, but do it as cheaply as possible. My point is that if we are not safe from invasion then make us so. Spend money on submarines, etc., but don't waste money on an armed mob." ' Naturally Fisher was delighted with this, but Haldane [11] on the other hand wrote a scathing minute on it because the Territorial Army was his creation.

Some time later Fisher wrote again: 'I sent your bit to the Prince of Wales and he is delighted with it. You will go down to posterity for that short paragraph—the best you ever wrote or

[10] As Commander of the Dover Patrol, 1915–18.
[11] Later 1st Viscount Haldane of Cloan. Secretary for War, 1905–12; Lord Chancellor, 1912–15 and 1924; Army reformer and philosopher.

can write. It's all in a nutshell. I call it the "Ponsonby Pill". It regularly clears them out and is damned hard and nasty to swallow.'

When McKenna became First Lord of the Admiralty Fisher was very much pressed by the Liberal Government to reduce the naval estimates, and to everyone's surprise he cut them down considerably. King Edward told me to write privately as from myself and enquire how it was that with former First Lords he had stoutly maintained that the millions he had asked for were the minimum he could accept, and yet here he was cheerfully acquiescing in a substantial reduction of the naval vote now that McKenna had become First Lord. I asked what new factor had made this reduction possible. This was a very awkward question, but he wrote at once, beginning 'My beloved Ponsonby. I call you beloved as you ask me a question which I just love answering.' He then wrote a long letter which, however, didn't answer my question at all.

Once an officer in India wrote to me and ended his letter 'Yours till Hell freezes'. I used this forcible expression in a letter to Fisher, and he adopted it instead of 'Yours sincerely' and used it a great deal.

In 1914, when he again began writing memoranda for the Cabinet, he sent me his drafts, but this was before he was brought back to the Admiralty during the War and he found that as a retired officer he didn't cut much ice. He wrote a sad PS. to one letter: 'No chance of being anything now: let alone Viceroy of India. Another Pharaoh has arisen who knows not Joseph.'

The last time I saw him, towards the end of the War, he told me that the Labour party had asked him to be First Lord of the Admiralty if they came into office. I advised him not to go into politics at his age, but he never lived to have to make the decision.

In September 1907 I heard the other side of the controversy from Charlie Beresford when I stayed with the Londonderrys at Wynyard. One evening he gave me forty minutes breezy conversation on the Navy, presumably hoping I should pass on to the King what he said. He always began by saying 'I wish to keep all argument impersonal', but after a short time he forgot and went on 'If it were not for that damned fellow Fisher'. The whole of his conversations was impregnated with a hatred of Fisher, whom he accused of having poisoned him with the King. The chief points he made against the present administration were:

(1) That the firing which had attracted so much attention was really a farce. Fisher and Prince Louis of Battenberg had been duped by the Flag Captain, Mark Kerr,[12] who had produced wonderful results under unfair conditions.

(2) The firing on the *Dreadnought* had been a farce and was laughed at by the Navy.

(3 The Home Fleet was a fraud and a deception. The ships were really a lot of lame ducks produced for effect.

(4) The nucleus crew system, although sound in theory, was really unworkable in practice and had really broken down owing to the details not being properly worked out.

(5) The whole Navy was dissatisfied, and until we had a real Board of the Admiralty we should never advance on sound principles. At present it was packed by Fisher.

Whenever I tried to bring him to the point by asking what he would do if he were to be appointed First Lord, he never seemed to have any satisfactory answer.

His last complaint was that there had been no cut-and-dried scheme of attack for the Channel Fleet; but this, as I told him, was really an attack on Wilson,[13] who commanded the Fleet before him.

I repeated all this to the King, who listened attentively but made no remark. He was so much in favour of Fisher that he didn't pay much attention to Beresford.

St. John Brodrick was there, and I had some talk with him. He touched lightly on the difficulties he had had at the India Office, but we got on to Germany, and as he apparently had a great wish to talk on this subject, I did not attempt to turn the conversation

[12] Later Admiral Mark Kerr, Commander-in-Chief of the Adriatic Squadron, 1916–17; attempted the Atlantic flight, 1919.

[13] Admiral Sir Arthur Wilson preceded Beresford as Commander of the Channel Squadron.

back to India. He said that the King was always so busy and had so much to think about that he had never had a chance to tell His Majesty how much he deplored the strained relations with Germany. He laid great stress on the point that it was very necessary to find a successor to Sir Frank Lascelles from outside the Diplomatic Service. He said that all diplomatists were the same and followed the same groove. Unless someone was appointed who would help Englishmen to visit Berlin and *vice versa* we should never get on better terms with the Germans.

I had also some talk with George Curzon,[14] who struck me as not being well at all. I asked him whether he did not consider that the liberty of the Press was a paradox in India. I remarked that however well it might work with a self-governing community, it was apt to be abused by a people under the autocratic rule of another race. He said he quite agreed, but it was hardly to be expected that John Morley [15] would relinquish one of the most cherished ideals of the Liberal party, however unsuitable it might be. He praised Morley and said that he had imagination. It fascinated him (Morley) to think he was indirectly governing this vast and mysterious empire, and he thought he was one of the great Moguls.

He indirectly attacked Kitchener, and said that a great deal of the unrest in India was due to the military authorities, who were striving for military efficiency at the cost of the religious customs and beliefs of the natives. I asked him incidentally how he found good men and how he judged them. He replied 'by seeing them and drawing them out'. I said I thought this method unsatisfactory and that it was a mistake to judge a man socially. The only way was to see a man at his work. He said this might be so at home, but in India everyone was full of their work, and that you could much more easily draw a man out in India than here.

In April 1901 the King and Queen with Princess Victoria went

[14] Later 1st Marquess Curzon of Kedleston. Viceroy of India, 1899–1905; Foreign Secretary, 1919–24.

[15] Later 1st Viscount Morley of Blackburn. Secretary of State for India, 1905–10; Lord President of Council, 1910, till resignation with John Burns on outbreak of war, 1914; wrote *On Compromise* and lives of Gladstone, Cromwell and Cobden.

to Sandringham by train with Seymour Fortescue [16] and myself in attendance. It was supposed to be a private visit but there was a huge crowd all the way from Marlborough House to the station. On arrival at Wolferton the King inspected the volunteer guard of honour and then drove off with the Queen and Princess Victoria, escorted by the Norfolk Yeomanry under the command of Prince Frederick Duleep Singh.[17] Fortescue and I rode on each side of the carriage with the two officers of the escort on the outside, but it was most uncomfortable as on several parts of the road there did not seem room for a carriage and four horses abreast. When we arrived at Sandringham House the King first inspected the Sandringham Company of the Norfolk Volunteers. It is sad to think that all these men, who were tenants and keepers on the estate and who eventually became Territorials, were killed in Gallipoli in 1915. The King and Queen walked down the lines of tenants and shook hands with all old friends.

Sandringham was of mid-Victorian type with polished light oak panelling, masses of photographs on tables, but hardly one really good thing in the house. It was extremely comfortable and for those days there were quite a number of bathrooms. The library looked imposing, but, while there were many valuable and interesting books, it was mainly filled with trash, masses of presentation books in beautiful bindings but quite unreadable. King Edward soon revolutionized this and cleared out all the rubbish. Mr. Humphreys from Hatchard's shop in London came down and was told to supply books suitable for a country-house library.

Twice I went with the King to pay a visit to Eton. The first time it was as ill-managed a show as it is possible to conceive. The arrangements were, to say the least of it, very sketchy, and beyond a few letters that had passed between Francis Knollys and Dr. Warre, the Headmaster, no definite programme had been drawn up. The King motored down from London to Windsor and stopped on his way at Eton. Having inspected the guard of honour of

[16] Captain the Hon. Sir Seymour Fortescue; Equerry-in-Waiting to Edward VII as Prince of Wales and later as King.

[17] Son of Maharajah Duleep Singh of Lahore; served in 1st World War with Norfolk Yeomanry.

Eton Volunteers, the King walked into School Yard and stood on the steps of the chapel. The Head of the School came forward and read an address, but when it came to a reply being made, the King turned to me and asked where it was. Harry Legge, the other Equerry, was appealed to, but neither of us knew anything about a reply. His Majesty thereupon came to the conclusion that for some reason or another no reply was to be made, and walked down the steps. It turned out afterwards that Esher had arranged the whole thing with the Provost, Dr. Hornby, and had assumed that Francis Knollys would be responsible for the reply to the address. Francis Knollys, however, said he didn't even know there was going to be an address as the Provost had never mentioned it in his letters.

Another time the King and Queen went down and paid a private visit to Eton. Having gone round Upper School, Hornby and Warre took them to see the block on which boys were flogged. To Their Majesties this was very much like going to the Chamber of Horrors at Madame Tussaud's, or to the torture-chamber at the Tower of London. The Queen whispered to me, 'Were you ever flogged?' and when I replied that twice I had undergone this punishment, she asked who had flogged me. 'Dr. Hornby', I replied, whereupon she went up to him and said, 'You cruel man! You flogged poor Captain Ponsonby', which disconcerted him very much.

We then went through the School Yard and I asked Mr. Cornish, the Vice-Provost, whether the King was going the right way as he appeared to be leading the party without anyone to guide him. Mr. Cornish with a smile replied that His Majesty seemed to be taking the line of least resistance and as all the doors of School Yard except the one leading to the cloisters were locked, he would eventually of his own volition end up at the Provost's House.

The King had told me that as he possibly might want to retire when he got to the Provost's House, I had better arrange that the Provost should ask him to come and see some particular picture which would give him the excuse of leaving the room. I therefore explained all this to Dr. Hornby. When we got to the Provost's drawing-room the Provost said in a rather sheepish way, 'There is a picture I should like to show Your Majesty in the next room', and then blushed all over, having probably never told a lie in his life. But the King didn't want to retire and replied that he would come and see it after tea, whereupon the Provost must have felt like a naughty boy who has been caught telling lies.

At Sandringham the King ordered a golf-links to be made in the Park: the putting-greens were good though small and the fairways were properly mown, but there were no bunkers. To remedy this the agent, Mr. Frank Beck, had placed wicker hurdles to indicate the places where the bunkers would eventually be dug. He argued that they could easily be moved to any position that the King eventually decided upon. This was perfectly sound in theory, but in practice it worked out very badly.

The first match we had on these links was the King and I playing the same ball against Seymour Fortescue. Nature had not made the King's figure suitable for driving a long ball, but he fancied himself at approaching and putting. Having blinked at the hurdles on the right and left of the fairway, the King proceeded to drive off and of course hit those on the right. The agent, who had come out to see whether the sites for the bunkers were right, looked horrified, but the King merely said 'What a silly place to put a bunker! See that this is altered to-morrow; have them put much more to the right and further off the tee.'

Every other hole the same thing happened, and the King got louder and louder in his denunciation of the stupidity of the person who had placed the hurdles, while the agent took copious notes, but not being a golfer himself he had left the whole thing to the head gardener. However, as Seymour Fortescue kept on driving into the long grass we had quite a good game, and as the King did a very good approach shot at the eighth hole and sank a long putt at the ninth (we played only nine holes), we won on the last green and he quite recovered his temper.

The second day we played he took the even holes and of course drove into the hurdles again, when precisely the same thing happened and he ordered the hurdles to be moved. The third day was the most unnerving for the agent, because the hurdles at all the holes had been moved to different spots indicated by the King.

The agent had taken the precaution of bringing out two men to move the hurdles anywhere. Again after viewing the hurdles distastefully the King never failed to drive into them and, in a voice of thunder, asked who had been stupid enough to place them there. When the agent replied by reading out his notes, which proved that it was the King himself who had selected the spot, the King exploded with rage and ordered all the hurdles to be taken away. This was done and orders were given to the head gardener to make proper bunkers. But unfortunately he knew little about this, and the following year erected only two bunkers on the nine holes and made them like fortifications.

On one occasion I proposed to the King to get the professional over from Hunstanton to make a fourth, and I thought that he would be able to get the King over the ground. It was, however, not altogether a success to begin with, as the professional was so nervous that he made all sorts of bad strokes. He wanted to play the game of his life and developed a terrible hook on his drives. The King, who had to play the second shot out of a bush, or out of long grass, cursed him freely, which made him worse. Then he made a mess of his short game and couldn't putt at all, with the result that Seymour Fortescue and I won very easily.

On the way back to the house the King said that quite obviously the man was a very bad player and that no doubt I had selected him because I knew that I could beat him easily. As a matter of fact, the man could give me a stroke a hole any day.

I was so sorry for the professional that I sent him word that I would play him before breakfast the following morning. I explained to him that it was not necessary to play a super game. I had a handicap of nine and Fortescue of fifteen, so that all he had to do was to go straight and give the King a chance of doing well at the short game. The poor man was, however, still so nervous that he couldn't play at all the first three holes, but I got him to tell me some of his triumphs at golf, and he forgot his bad play with the King and settled down to his ordinary game. When the King came out to play at 11.30 he played beautifully and had quite got over his nervousness.

In the afternoon Queen Alexandra and I played against Princess

Victoria and Francis Knollys. The Queen seemed to confuse it with hockey and was under the impression that one had to prevent the opponent putting the ball in the hole. This usually ended by a scrimmage on the green. She also thought that the person who got into the hole first won it, and asked me to hurry up and run between the strokes. It was very good fun, and we all laughed. Francis Knollys always played in a square-shaped billycock hat and a London tail coat, and hit so hard that his hat almost invariably fell off.

As golf proved so popular, the King gave orders that a golf course should be made at Windsor and wished it to be eighteen holes, but as we always took one and a half hours to do nine holes, I persuaded him to limit it to nine holes. I asked Mr. Muir Fergusson, a distinguished amateur player who had laid out a course called New Zealand at Woking, to come down and sketch out the Windsor Castle links. He came down and took infinite trouble. We had men with stakes to mark the right and left of each bunker, and a man with a tape measure. Muir Fergusson succeeded in laying out nine good holes ending up just below the East Terrace, and I gave instructions to the farm bailiff to have the bunkers made.

I did not go to Windsor for two months as I presumed that a competent firm had been employed, but I suddenly received an irate telegram from the King to the effect that the private Park at Windsor had been ruined and that I was to order the bunkers to be rased to the ground. When I went to Windsor I was aghast at what I saw. The man who had undertaken to make the bunkers had obviously no knowledge of golf grounds and didn't know the ABC of the business. At each post which had been driven into the ground to make the right and left of the bunkers he had erected a mound four feet high and a ditch four feet deep but only ten yards long. The result was that the ground looked like a graveyard with tombstones dotted about. I was furious and went in search of the man. I found him talking to the farm bailiff. He said that he proposed to make the last bunker in the shape of a Victoria Cross with flowers! I told him what I thought of him and said it was criminal of him to undertake a job like this when he had not the most elementary knowledge of bunkers. I gave orders that he and his men were to leave the ground at once, and I told the farm bailiff to see that they never returned. We had a breezy five minutes, and I closed the discussion by saying that unless he and his men cleared out in an hour I would instruct the police to push them out. I gave orders that the bunkers were to be rased to the ground, and sent for the professional from the Datchet links close by and explained to him how the bunkers should go, asking him to superintend the work. Eventually this came out all right and Muir Fergusson came down and made a few alterations. He was a big red-faced man and probably accustomed to have his way, but when the King happened to come along he became tongue-tied. It was unfortunate that I did not have an opportunity of explaining what a swell he was in the golfing world because the King thought he was a professional. However, when I explained everything afterwards to the King he sent him a cigarette-case with the Royal cypher on it.

Other leading golfers were invited to play with the King. First of all Kirkaldy came down from Scotland, but he got rather drunk and was sent back. Then Ben Sayers came and was a great success. He was always anxious to praise the King's shots and once when the King topped his drive, he exclaimed 'Very good direction, Your Majesty'. Once when the King said he would play at three o'clock Sayers teed up two new balls ready but received a message that the King would not play till four, so he went away. Meanwhile Queen Alexandra came out to play and, finding two new balls, played a sort of hockey with them till they were battered into a three-cornered shape. She then replaced the balls on the tee and went in. At four the King came out and asked Sayers if he had got any golf balls. He replied that they were ready on the tee, but when the King saw them he thought Sayers was trying to be funny. Luckily Sayers had plenty more, but it was not till tea-time that the King learnt that the Queen and Princess Victoria had played golf at three, and grasped why the balls were so battered.

About this time an amusing incident occurred with Benjamin-

Constant,[18] the eminent French artist who painted a splendid portrait of Queen Victoria. I had always taken an interest in this picture as when I was with Queen Victoria I had to deal with the request from the *Illustrated London News* that Benjamin-Constant should be given a sitting. When the letter came I had heard of Benjamin-Constant but never realized what a really great artist he was. When, however, I made enquiries and found he was the greatest living painter in France, I urged Queen Victoria to grant the request, but she was not at all anxious to be painted. Then it appeared that no less a person than the Prince of Wales (King Edward) was responsible for the request being put forward, and later he wrote to her pressing her to give a sitting. So a sitting was arranged, but I was to make it clear that it was not to last more than twenty minutes.

I saw Queen Victoria after the sitting and she said that Benjamin-Constant was a most extraordinary artist as he never painted at all, but sat with his face between his hands gazing at her during the whole sitting in a most embarrassing way. Of course Benjamin-Constant realized that twenty minutes was ridiculously inadequate for the purpose: he had therefore tried to stamp an impression of her on his brain. The result was a magnificent picture.

Years later many inaccurate stories were told about this incident. One of them was the sitting took place in the Waterloo Gallery, which is the size of a ballroom, and that Queen Victoria, after looking at the picture, said, *'Nous ne sommes pas si rouge'*; this story was originally told of Queen Anne.

The King purchased the picture from the *Illustrated London News,* but with his love of accuracy and his great knowledge of orders of chivalry, was much put out at the colour of the Garter ribbon in the picture being light blue instead of a deep blue. He told Sir Arthur Ellis to send a piece of the riband in the picture to the artist. As it was simpler, Ellis sent him a whole Garter riband and for some reason this arrived before the letter. Benjamin-Constant, who was ignorant of the fact that the Garter could

[18] Jean Joseph Benjamin-Constant, famous painter of Oriental scenes. His portrait of Queen Victoria took the Grand Prix at the Universal Exhibition in Paris.

only be given abroad to crowned heads or Crown Princes, jumped to the conclusion that the Order of the Garter had been conferred upon him. It was quite a natural mistake to make as he had the Grand Cross of the Legion of Honour. When, however, he approached the British Ambassador in Paris, Sir Edmund Monson, he was surprised to find that nothing was known about this: in fact Monson appeared to think there must have been some mistake. When the letter eventually arrived, Benjamin-Constant at once saw his mistake and was so much put out that he absolutely refused to alter the picture. He said that was the colour he wanted for his effects and he had no intention of substituting any other colour.

I had really given up all ideas of going to the South African War, although I had made frantic efforts to go at the start. It was only on my return from Homburg that I received a letter from the Colonel of the Grenadiers telling me that Curry's wife had been taken dangerously ill and that Curry would only be allowed to come home if he could get someone to take his place. Would I volunteer to do this? It was in September 1901, but I determined to to go. I saw King Edward and he was all in favour of my going.

My experiences in South Africa were similar to those of all junior officers at that time, monotony relieved by moments of great excitement, and I therefore do not mean to attempt to describe what I saw.

A short time before peace was declared I unluckily had enteric fever, and spent some time in hospital, after which I was invalided home.

When I returned to London at the beginning of June, I found myself in a very difficult position. Francis Knollys was a very clever and charming man, but he had never wanted an Assistant Private Secretary and had from the beginning been opposed to my appointment. For some forty years he had kept everything in his own hands, and even when the King, as Prince of Wales, went abroad, all the letters were sent to him in London. He had been the pivot on which everything moved and had made it a one-man job. It is hardly to be wondered at that he resented my coming in and practically doing his work.

King Edward on the other hand, while he still relied on Knollys for advice, wished to show that he could get on quite well without him, and found that when he went to Friedrichshof he managed very well with me as Secretary. When he subsequently went to Homburg he decided to take me and cut adrift from Knollys altogether.

When I went to the South African War, Arthur Davidson took my place as Assistant Private Secretary, but during the time I was away King Edward never went abroad. Francis Knollys, having resigned himself to the inevitable and accepted the fact that there must be an Assistant Private Secretary, came to the conclusion that two would be preferable to one, and that if they did alternate months they would not have the same power as one who took his place when the King was away from London. He also had the false impression that I was trying to cut him out and take his place, which was the last thing I wanted to do.

The first I heard of this was when Sir Dighton Probyn told me it had been decided to have two Assistant Private Secretaries and therefore in future I should only be expected to do six months' duty. Two hundred a year would in consequence be deducted from my salary.

At the time I did not say anything, but the next day I again went to see him and expostulated with him. I pointed out that I had been seven years with Queen Victoria and that now, through no fault of mine, I was to lose £200 a year. The prospect of having six months' leisure every year certainly did not attract me. Dear old Probyn, who was the kindest man in the world, was not prepared to argue with me as he really didn't know enough about the matter. When he grasped that I wished to argue the point he rang every bell he could lay hands on to get hold of Francis Knollys. However, Francis Knollys was not long coming, and when he came he merely said there would be no objection to my resigning if I wished to, but that the appointment of two Assistant Private Secretaries had been decided by the King and the deduction of £200 from my salary was irrevocable.

It seemed waste of time arguing any further, and I had, of course, to accept the new conditions. It was arranged that I should do month on and month off with Davidson, and a more charming and loyal man to work with could not have been found. We never had the slightest difficulty during all the years of King Edward's reign.

CHAPTER XI

The Coronation and the King's illness — Life on the royal yacht — The naval review — The Shah and the Garter — The Isle of Man — Martino, Soveral and Austen Chamberlain — Drinking at Balmoral — Christmas at Sandringham

I HAD RETURNED from South Africa just in time for the Coronation, which was fixed for June 26th.[1] As this date came during my period of 'off duty', I was not wanted at Buckingham Palace and I was attached to Prince and Princess Henry of Prussia[2] who were at Wimborne House. Lord Clanwilliam[3] and Admiral Sir John Fullerton were the other two attached and were naturally quite at sea about all the ceremonies. I liked both Prince and Princess Henry very much and they were both charming, but as they went about with their own suite there was practically nothing for Clanwilliam, Fullerton, or me to do but to hang about.

At the first function that took place there was a row which promised to be interesting. Field-Marshal Count von Waldersee[4] came to represent the German Army, but as far as I could gather had nothing to do with Prince Henry's suite. There was to be a reception at Buckingham Palace and it had been arranged by Prince Henry that he would take the first three carriages from Wimborne House and that the fourth carriage should be left to Waldersee. Then the fun began. Waldersee flatly refused to go after the suite, while they maintained they must keep up close to

[1] 1902, eighteen months after the King's accession. The delay was largely caused by the protraction of the Boer War.
[2] Prince Henry of Prussia was younger brother of the German Emperor, William II.
[3] Richard James Meade, 4th Earl of Clanwilliam; Admiral of the Fleet.
[4] German Chargé d'Affaires in Paris, 1871; later Chief of the Prussian General Staff; commanded International Forces in China, 1901. Died 1904.

Prince Henry. A fierce discussion followed and soon the hall was filled with irate officers all talking at the same time. Clanwilliam and Fullerton asked me what the row was about, and when I told them, they were quite unable to understand why anyone should want to go before anyone else. It seemed, however, that the two staffs were working up for a fight and I therefore intervened and told them that I would submit the problem to Prince Henry. I found Prince Henry in a sitting-room and explained all the trouble to him. He seemed to grasp the importance of the quarrel and the difficulty of giving an answer that would not hurt someone's feelings. I suggested to him that as Waldersee was not attached to him in any way he should go separately, and that as I was sure that Prince Henry himself did not mind where he went, he should let Waldersee in the fourth carriage go first and then wait five minutes before he went himself. Not only did he like this solution, but when I explained it in the hall, it seemed to meet with general approbation. So at last we all got to Buckingham Palace.

The next day the news arrived that the Coronation had been postponed and that the King was to undergo an operation. All the foreign guests left at once, including Prince and Princess Henry of Prussia, and again I had nothing to do.

It was not till the middle of July that I received a message from the King that I was to go with him on board the *Victoria & Albert* where he would convalesce after his operation. I travelled down with Harry Legge and Harry Stonor [5] in the same train as the King and Queen. The King was carried to the train on a stretcher, and we went down to Portsmouth at a slow pace. When we arrived the King was carried on board the yacht by bluejackets. The deck cabin where we usually sat or played bridge had been fitted up as a sick-room with a bed in the middle and tables with bottles of medicine and dressings.

We went in to luncheon, but of course the King did not come. To me it was like a fairy-tale, coming after South Africa, where I had become accustomed to bully beef and other tinned foods. Moreover, after having come to the conclusion that my position

[5] Later Sir Harry Stonor. Gentleman-Usher and Groom-in-Waiting to King Edward and King George V.

was very precarious and that I should soon have to find some other job, it was astonishing to find myself not only 'in waiting' but again as Acting Private Secretary.

At the luncheon table there were gold cups and masses of roses. The Queen sat at the end of the table and rang a tinkly bell when the servants were wanted. The Marine band under Lieutenant Miller played soft music outside on the deck. I sat between Princess Maud, later Queen of Norway, and Sir Frederick Treves, the great surgeon, a man with a keen sense of humour but a certain contempt for the human race. After luncheon the King sent for me and I found him in a blue flannel suit lying on the bed puffing a cigar. He greeted me with 'Hallo, Fritz. I little thought the last time I saw you that I should be like this now.' He added, 'You can't think what a pleasure it is to get out of my sick-room at Buckingham Palace.' I asked him if he had suffered much pain and he said that at first it had been very painful but he hoped that was all over now. The Queen then came in and talked away for a few minutes to me, but I felt I ought to make myself scarce, and when Caesar, the King's terrier, was brought in, I discreetly left.

The King began doing a little business and sent for me twice a day to give me letters to answer, but I soon saw that no one was sending him any difficult stuff. He was still in bed or else lying on the bed, but able to write. It seemed a great pleasure to him to be able to make a start.

After dinner the Queen took me down and showed me her cabin, which was lovely and not in the least like a cabin but more like a drawing-room. It was painted white and panelled with bookcases, with a boudoir grand piano and very comfortable armchairs around what looked like a fireplace. She was in great form and full of jokes. She showed me with pride her bookplate which she had designed herself. On it there were her favourite books, her favourite music, her favourite dogs, a picture of Windsor, a picture of the Palace at Copenhagen, and a little strip of music, the first bars of her favourite song; a most elaborate bookplate, and she said she had been told it would be quite impossible to have so many different things portrayed, yet there it was.

Divine Service on board was an interesting sight as all the

yacht's crew attended and sang lustily while the Marine band played. Hedworth Lambton, the Commodore, officiated, but naturally refused to intone, and read the service and responses like short snappy words of command while the band and two hundred men responded with full choral effect. The Queen, Princess Victoria, and Princess Maud with the members of the Household sat facing the yacht's crew, and the King had his bed wheeled up to the window of his deck cabin and looked on benignly.

The Queen, accompanied by Treves and myself, paid a surprise visit to Netley Hospital. We went in a steam pinnace and, although the doctors and nurses were in the secret, the patients had no idea who she was. She was delighted when she asked one of the men whether he was better and he replied, 'Yes, Miss'. It was, however, unlikely that none of the men should recognize her and soon all those who were able to walk came crowding round, and we had some difficulty in restraining them. One man lying down with his head all bandaged up attracted the Queen's attention and she asked him about South Africa. He replied he had been out at the war for two and a half years and had taken part in almost every big battle. The Queen asked him at what battle he had been wounded and he replied that he had never been wounded at all but that, on arrival at Southampton, he had slipped and fallen down the hatchway!

The King fixed the Coronation for August 9 and said that all the arrangements for the original Coronation were to stand good, but of course there would be no foreign Princes or Representatives from the Dominions and Colonies.

As I was not to have taken any part in the original Coronation beyond being attached to Prince and Princess Henry of Prussia, I rode in the procession with the other Equerries some way ahead of the King and Queen. Usually London is empty in August, but as so many people had to take part in this ceremony and as the crowd was anxious to see it, there seemed little or no difference between July and August. There were thousands of people in the streets, which were all lined with troops. I saw the procession in the Abbey very well but was too far away to see much of the actual coronation. The King stood the strain very well although it must have been very trying for a man who had just been operated on to undergo such a tiring ceremony. Everything went perfectly and there was no hitch.

On August 17 the King and Queen with Princess Victoria went down to Cowes, taking with them only Miss Charlotte Knollys, Seymour Fortescue as Equerry, and myself, Acting Private Secretary. Francis Knollys, who was still deeply hurt at being left behind, made things as difficult as possible for me by never telling me anything about the arrangements and never letting me see any papers or former correspondence relating to current subjects. It was not malice but a wish to wash his hands of all business.

I had read in the newspapers that the Mayor of Portsmouth would present an address and that the King would hand a reply. Neither the address nor the reply would be read because it was considered inadvisable that the King should be kept standing long on the jetty.

I as Acting Private Secretary had to deal with addresses and the replies, but I was told that Francis Knollys had given the reply to Seymour Fortescue. I was getting so accustomed to this sort of thing that I made no protest, but in the train on the way down to Portsmouth I remarked to Seymour Fortescue that unless one person was made responsible there was every chance of a misunderstanding. Fortescue listened thoughtfully and suddenly jumped up saying he had left the reply by mistake in London. This was certainly awkward because the reply was not to be read. Had it been arranged that the King should reply, he could certainly be trusted to do so extempore, but it was impossible to hand nothing after the Mayor had gone down on one knee and presented the address.

I went to my stationery box and selected a piece of folio-sized paper, and from a War Office box in which there were some documents for the King to sign I abstracted some broad blue ribbon and tied this round the paper. We arranged that Fortesque should tell the King about this and that I should warn the Mayor not to open it and tell him that the reply itself would be forwarded to him later. It all went very well and the King gravely handed the blank paper to the Mayor, who took it with a low bow while the crowd cheered.

The Naval Review which followed was a splendid sight and the Royal yacht steamed through streets of ships which were all manned. The King sat on the bridge in full uniform and took the salute of each ship. In the evening there were illuminations but these were a good deal spoilt by the rain. The yacht was anchored in the centre of the huge fleet, and when the King pressed a button all the ships were illuminated. At eleven he again pressed a button and all the lights went out together like magic. I never grasped how this was done, as it seemed unlikely that all the ships extending over several miles were connected by cable.

The next day there was an interesting ceremony. The Boer Generals came to see the King. The Queen said they looked like undertakers, but I thought they looked like Scotch elders of the kirk in their Sunday attire, for they were all dressed in black frock-coats, black trousers, black gloves, and top-hats. It was interesting to see the steam launch come alongside with Roberts, Kitchener, Botha, De Wet, and Delarey when one remembered that it was only a short time ago that they were fighting.

Lord Roberts presented each of the Boer Generals in turn while Kitchener looked on sardonically, and the King tactfully alluded to various incidents without touching on anything of an unpleasant nature.

If there was one thing the King liked doing it was presenting medals. He loved doing a kindness to anyone and he always thought a medal gave human beings the greatest pleasure in life. To a certain extent he was right because a man who had war medals was always glad to have another medal, but when a man had none it was very doubtful whether he liked wearing a Coronation medal by itself.

It sounded a simple matter when the King announced that he intended to give medals to the officers commanding all the ships as well as to the representatives of foreign navies, but it required a little arrangement. I could find no list of officers nor could anyone tell me what number of medals would be required. As it was essential to get the names of each recipient, I flatly refused to allow the ceremony to begin until I had got everything prepared. A signal was made that all admirals and officers in command of ships were to come on board the yacht; also all foreign officers in command of ships. I asked the officers of the yacht to help and arrange that, first, the foreigners should go by and then the British, after a list of names had been properly drawn up. Unfortunately the Japanese and Italian captains whose ships were nearest to the yacht came some time before the others, and Hedworth Lambton brought them up to the King, who was much put out at having no medals to give them. I was at the time getting the medals ready in my cabin, while the yacht officers didn't like to interfere although they had not got the names of the foreigners. An irate message reached me telling me to come at once on deck, and there I found the King very angry. I explained that this method of doing things was quite impossible and would inevitably end in confusion, and that unless all the officers were there and the names were available it was out of the question to begin. I suggested that the King should go and have tea while I got everything ready. The Prince of Wales backed me up, and finally the King, who saw the logic of my remarks, told Lambton to leave things alone. About a hundred and twenty officers came on board and with the help of the yacht's officers I got their names and lined them up to come up to the King, while two pages brought a table with the medals all ready. When the King came up I explained what I proposed and he had quite recovered his temper. I read out each name and they all came past and received their medal. At the conclusion the King made them an impressive speech, which he could always do so well.

The Shah of Persia [6] had intended to pay an official visit to the King, but this was postponed owing to the Coronation being delayed. All that could therefore be arranged was a visit to the King on board the yacht on August 20, and with this the Shah was satisfied. He wanted the Order of the Garter, and he did not mind much whether it was given to him in London or on the yacht.

Francis Knollys had given me no papers on the subject: in fact I didn't know that there had been any correspondence about this between Lord Lansdowne, who was Secretary of State for Foreign

---

[6] Muzaffar-ad-Din; succeeded Nasir-ad-Din, who had been assassinated in 1896; succeeded in 1906 by Mohammed Ali, who was deposed in 1909.

Affairs, and the King. He left me to deal with this most explosive material as best I could.

When the visit was first arranged the Shah had made it clear that he expected to be given the Garter and that he would accept no other Order. Originally the Garter was only given to Christian Sovereigns and infidels were not considered eligible; but Queen Victoria had made exceptions in the cases of the two Sultans of Turkey when they came to England, and had also given it to the Shah's father, and this had created an awkward precedent. When Lansdowne found that the Shah would not be content with anything but the Garter, he asked the King to make another exception and give that Order in this case. Here there was a misunderstanding: Lansdowne understood from the King that he approved of the Garter being given while the King maintained that he had never agreed. It was a pity that there was nothing on paper because in a discussion a wrong impression may so easily have been given.

Lansdowne, under the impression that the King approved, let it be understood by the Persian Minister that the Garter would be given, but as one of the non-Christian Sovereigns had raised an objection to the star of the Garter having a Christian emblem— the Cross—he hit upon the idea of having a special star made without the Cross of St. George and sent the design down for the King to see.

Such was the position when I was brought into the dispute. A Foreign Office box came down looking harmless enough, but when the King opened it, read Lansdowne's letter and saw the design, there was an explosion. He was so angry that he flung the design across his cabin and it went through the porthole and, as I thought, into the sea. Later, however, I found that it had fallen into a steam pinnace and had been brought back by the stoker, who presumed it was a picture of some value. Of course this was all Greek to me and I was at first totally unable to understand why the King was so angry. He dictated some very violent remarks for me to incorporate in my letter to Lansdowne. From these and from further conversation on the subject I grasped that it was a serious matter. I therefore suggested to the King that I should write to Knollys and ask him to convey His Majesty's wishes to Lansdowne, but this proved impossible as Knollys had already gone up to Balmoral. I therefore wrote a bowdlerized version of the King's withering remarks and pointed out that His Majesty had never approved of the Shah being given the Garter. If this Order was to be given to non-Christian Sovereigns, surely the Emperor of Japan should be the first to receive it, but once this was begun we should have to consider all sorts of Eastern potentates. I added that the King had been shocked at the proposal to omit the Cross of St. George and wouldn't hear of such a proposal.

Lansdowne replied that the mistake was entirely his and that he must have misunderstood what the King said, but as he had, in his capacity as Minister for Foreign Affairs, said that the Shah would be given the Garter, there was no alternative for him but to place his resignation in the King's hands. He then appears to have laid the whole matter before Arthur Balfour, the Prime Minister, who took the view that as he had, rightly or wrongly, as Minister of Foreign Affairs, practically promised the Garter, he must of course be supported, but the proposal to eliminate the Cross of St. George was fantastic.

Lansdowne then came down to see the King on board the Royal yacht and His Majesty promised to reconsider the matter carefully. Eventually the King agreed with Arthur Balfour and so the trouble subsided; but relations between the King and Lansdowne, which had never been good, deteriorated still further.

The Shah brought down a large suite and there was not sufficient room for them in the dining saloon. The King therefore arranged that I should take half of them to luncheon on board the *Osborne,* the second of the Royal yachts. When, however, I tried to do so, they flatly refused to come and sat down and sulked. They thought they had been insulted and all sat together whispering. I didn't know enough of the Eastern mind to be able to handle them. I addressed them slowly so that they would understand and told them that unless they came with me on board the *Osborne* they would get no luncheon. I added that in any case they could not sit where they were as the King and Queen and the Shah would want those chairs after luncheon, but I would come back in five minutes to conduct them to their luncheon. When I did so they rose reluctantly, and with some more coaxing I induced them to come with me. The officers of the *Osborne* were drawn up to receive them and played up well, making much of them.

The King determined to go for a cruise round the coast and to end up in Scotland. Austen Chamberlain [7] was to come as Minister in Attendance and I was to do the Private Secretary's work. The Marquis de Soveral, the Portuguese Minister,[8] came as a guest and Chevalier Martino the artist.[9] To begin with, I had a delight-ful time with nothing to do and I was able to play bridge in the evening after dinner. The King had been getting stronger every day and soon he became restless about the routine work being behind-hand. Treves raised no difficulty about his doing any work and he therefore told me to telegraph to the different Government Offices and tell them to send by messenger all boxes as usual and also all the arrears. I had no idea what this entailed, but when the first messenger arrived I grasped I should have to take my coat off and work. Not only were there masses of letters and official boxes but cypher telegrams arrived. Knollys had not allowed me to take a clerk with me and so I had not only to write all the letters myself but also to keep a copy. I began usually at 8 a.m. and put in an hour's work before breakfast. Then between eleven and one I was with the King and during the afternoon I worked on. I found it necessary to drink water at dinner so that I could start work again immediately afterwards. Yet in spite of this I often had to sit up till one or two.

We went slowly round the coast escorted by a cruiser and two torpedo-boats, which were useful in bringing off the messenger from different ports. All this took a bit of arranging. I had to consult Hedworth Lambton each day and, when the yacht's course

[7] Later the Rt. Hon. Sir Austen Chamberlain (K.G. 1925). Chancellor of the Exchequer, 1903–6 and 1919–21; War Cabinet, 1918; Foreign Secretary, 1924–9.

[8] 1891 and 1897–1910. During the interval he became Portuguese Foreign Secretary.

[9] Commendatore Eduardo de Martino had been Marine Painter-in-Ordinary to Queen Victoria. A Neapolitan, served in the Italian Navy till 1867; sketched his way to the Paraguayan War and painted several pictures for the Emperor Pedro II of Brazil; settled in England 1875.

was decided upon, select a suitable port and telegraph instructions to London.

On August 24 the King and Queen landed at Pembroke Dock and had luncheon with General W. Lambton. This meant a seven-mile drive in a carriage, and although it was all very private, masses of people turned out and lined the road.

We arrived at the Isle of Man on the 30th, and it was said that the last British Sovereign to visit that island was Canute. We dropped anchor without telling anyone, but the unusual presence of a cruiser and two torpedo-boats alone attracted attention. Soon the news was telegraphed that Their Majesties were paying a visit to Douglas, the capital, and thousands of people came over from England. As there seemed to be only about half a dozen police-men on the island, the crowd did very much what it liked. When we landed, however, it was still too early for the crowd to assemble and so we had no difficulty. We drove in motors round the island and got smothered in dust. The President of the House of Keys met Their Majesties and one or two distinguished Manxmen were presented, but they were all swept into the background by Sir Hall Caine,[10] the novelist, who thought he was the only man worth speaking to on the island. After luncheon a photograph was taken of the party with Hall Caine as the central figure and the President of the House of Keys and distinguished Manxmen in the back-ground. We drove back to Douglas, where we got into an electric tram, and here the fun began. Steamers full of people had been arriving all the afternoon and there must have been four or five thousand people round the tram waving and cheering with no one to keep them back. A tram, however, is a dangerous thing and the crowd kept at a respectful distance, but when it arrived at the end of its line and we had to get into carriages, the pressure of the crowd was almost frightening. The crowd was so big and so anxious to see the King and Queen that it swept them about in whirlpools. Queen Alexandra had a charming way of treating the crowd as if they were intimate friends, and she was so nervous that people would get hurt that she appealed to those nearest to

---

[10] An early protégé (or protector) of D. G. Rossetti, and author of a stream of popular novels, including *The Deemster* and *The Manxman*.

her to look after the children. The King roared at the coachman to go slowly, but got very cross with him when the carriage stopped, and no one seemed capable of clearing a way, but eventually the carriage got through and arrived at the pier.

When we left the tram to get into the carriages, we found that Martino was lost and in that sea of faces it was quite impossible to find him. I told the King that the only possible place to look for him would be the police station, as an excited Italian gesticulating and asking to be taken to the King would inevitably be mistaken for an anarchist. However, luckily Spencer, the police officer who always went about with the King, caught sight of him in the crowd and rescued him.

Chevalier Martino was marine painter to the King and it was in that capacity that he accompanied His Majesty, but the real reason was that he was a sort of Court Jester, a butt for the King's jokes. As a painter of ships he was unrivalled, for not only did he paint really first-rate sea pictures, but his knowledge of detail was marvellous and he never made any mistake. Like all jesters he was really a very shrewd man, but he liked being singled out for the King's wit and he never failed to amuse people with his quaint remarks in very bad English.

Soveral, the Portuguese Minister, was a very clever diplomat who did all he could to disguise the fact, having found by experience that both men and women fight shy of a clever man. He therefore played the fool and was the most delightful companion anyone could have. As a talker he was quite wonderful at keeping the ball rolling, and without being exactly witty his conversation was always sparkling and amusing. It was only when he had to talk seriously that one realized how clever he was. On European politics generally no one was better informed and had he wished he could have become one of the leading statesmen of European politics, but partly from indolence, partly because he had a supreme contempt for the Portuguese Government, he preferred to remain Portuguese Minister in London. He was universally popular in England, where he made love to all the most beautiful women and where all the nicest men were his friends. He was an excellent friend to King Edward and was able to discuss international politics with him and keep him interested. I once asked him what he had talked about to King Edward at breakfast (both of them usually had nothing but a bit of toast and a cup of coffee), and he replied, 'I know him well enough not to talk at all and so we don't really begin till we have finished our coffee'.

Austen Chamberlain was a great acquisition on board. At first we feared he would be too serious a politician to talk nonsense to and that he would hold himself aloof from all the silly games and nonsensical chaff which a yachting party of this sort indulge in, but we were quite wrong. He turned out to be very good company and joined in everything. He had a delightful sense of humour and amused and interested the King and Queen.

He had been told that King Edward was very particular about dress, and had provided himself with impeccable yachting attire, but he was always on the lookout when we went on shore in case he should not hit the right note in dress. He was very much amused at the King's niceties about dress when we reached the Scotch coast and he heard His Majesty say to his Swiss valet, '*Un costume un peu plus ecossais demain*'. He appreciated the subtlety of not overdoing the thing and making the transition from English to Scotch dress too abrupt.

At Skye the Duchess of Hamilton asked everyone to shoot, but I had to remain on board and work. At Dunrobin the same thing happened, but there we dined and I sat next to the Duchess of Sutherland [11] and talked of old days. Before we left she gave me her book and said she was anxious that the King should write something in it. This book consisted of the signatures of great men, authors, composers, and artists, who had all written quotations, done sketches, or written a few bars of their favourite music. When I returned on board I told Austen Chamberlain in chaff it was the duty of the Minister in Attendance to put forward suggestions for the King to choose from. He took what I said quite seriously, screwed his glass in his eye and said that it would be difficult enough to think of something he himself could write, but to suggest something for the King was beyond him. Of course this writing of *bons mots* is nothing more than a trick and most

[11] Wife of 4th Duke of Sutherland.

people who stayed at country houses had something always ready, but Austen Chamberlain had never come across these books and spent a sleepless night thinking out something. The next morning I took the book to the King, who was an old hand at the game, and he wrote a quotation from La Rochefoucauld which was most pointful and which delighted the Duchess.

We went straight from Dunrobin by train to Balmoral and there was great rejoicing at the arrival of the King and Queen after the Coronation. A great many changes had been carried out and the drawing-room, which formerly was all tartan, was entirely changed and was made like a room in one of the Gordon hotels.

The King at once took strong measures to stop the drinking that went on, but, I think wisely, did not try to stop it altogether. In Queen Victoria's reign whenever anyone went out stalking, a whole bottle of whisky was given out, and whatever the guest did not drink became the perquisite of the stalker. It was quite a common thing for a stalker to come to the Castle and drink off a glass of neat whisky before he started. Of course if he went out stalking no harm was done, but when the weather was impossible and the mist came down he retired to his house and started the day slightly intoxicated. The amount of whisky consumed by the servants was truly stupendous. Whenever the Queen went out driving, a bottle of whisky was put under the coachman's seat and was supposed to provide stimulant to anyone who had had an accident. It was said that early in the Queen's reign a poor man had been found at the side of the road in a state of exhaustion and that Her Majesty had remarked what a pity it was that no one had any stimulant to revive him. This was at once rectified and innumerable bottles of whisky must have gone astray in this way. But the whole atmosphere was wrong. A drunken man was so common that no one ever remarked on it. Before my day there were what was called 'larders'. The stags that had been shot during the day were taken from the larders and placed in a row and all the gillies carried torches. The Queen came out after dinner and dancing took place, all of which was very pretty, but after she left it became an orgy of drink.

Another occasion when whisky was freely given was the anniversary of the Prince Consort's birthday. All the stalkers, gillies, and people on the estate were expected to attend dressed in top-hats (what the people called a funeral hat) and black coats. A prayer was said in front of the Prince Consort's statue, and the Queen drove there in her carriage with two grey horses and an outrider. Then whisky was sent out as light refreshment at the back of the wood. The result was that the whole community was three parts intoxicated and when we went for a walk in the after-noon it was no uncommon sight to find a man in a top-hat and frock-coat fast asleep in the woods. Sir James Reid, the doctor, helped the King, as he knew the men so well that he could do al-most anything with them.

All this was now altered, and although a flask of whisky was provided with the luncheon for anyone going out stalking, bottles were no longer the perquisite of the stalker.

The King therefore, without overdoing it, took steps to stop the unfortunate amount of drinking that used to take place for-merly, but the regulations he made were enforced with the utmost severity. I was really very sorry for one of the stalkers, a splendid-looking man with a white beard, of the name of Cameron. A deer drive was ordered and all the stalkers and gillies turned out, but the weather made everything impossible, for not only were there sheets of rain, but the mist was so low on the hills that no one could see anything, so the deer drive was cancelled. No sooner had all the men been sent back to their houses than the sun came out and it cleared up completely. The King therefore said he would have luncheon out on the hill and the deer drive would take place afterwards. Cameron, who lived some way off, feeling sure that he would not be wanted, had commenced drinking, when a mes-senger arrived summoning him. Had it been later in the day he would have been too drunk to obey the summons, but as it was he was only rather drunk. He turned up for luncheon and instead of keeping out of the light he insisted on going up to the King and talking. Of course His Majesty saw he was drunk although he could just walk. The King called up the head stalker and told him that Cameron was drunk and that he was to be dismissed at once, and dismissed he was, without a pension. This was making an example with a vengeance, and it was said that the stalkers and gillies were partly resentful at a man with thirty years' service being sacked, and partly frightened lest the same thing should happen to them. Cameron, who hailed from Inverness-shire, returned to his birthplace a broken man, but the King told me confidentially that when the affair had blown over he would see that Cameron was given a pension on the understanding that he did not return to Balmoral.

In December the King and Queen went to stay at Gopsall with Lord [12] and Lady Howe and took with them Lady Emily Kingscote, Harry Legge and myself. By this time the arrangement whereby I should do alternate months with Arthur Davidson was in full swing and it worked very well. We worked in together keeping each other informed of all that went on during our month's waiting, with copies of all the correspondence that took place.

At Gopsall there was a large party, but George Howe most kindly asked either Harry Legge or me to shoot every day. It was all very well done and the house had just been done up with bathrooms galore and everything most comfortable. About the fourth night I sat next to Lady de Grey, who sat by the King, and she whispered to me 'For Heaven's sake suggest a topic for me to discuss with the King as I have sat next to him for three nights.' I replied, 'Give away your relations and friends and repeat any secrets about them'. She laughed and said, 'But I did that the first night!'

The King undoubtedly liked masses of pheasants driven over his head about the height of an ordinary tree, but while most people would get rattled at the number he slowly selected one and shot it, generally behind him. He was quite good at shooting with a crowd looking on, as he never seemed to miss; but then he never fired at a difficult bird.

At Christmas-time I went to Sandringham, where I found that the festivities began on Christmas Eve. The King and Queen did the presents themselves and spent hours in the ballroom arranging everything. In the centre of the ballroom was a large Christmas-

[12] Richard Penn Curzon, 4th Earl Howe; Lord-in-Waiting, 1900–1903.

tree and round this were arranged trestle tables the whole length of the room, covered with a white tablecloth. Every member of the party had a bit of these tables portioned off to them, and the clergy, doctors, etc., also came and had their share. It was all beautifully done, and the pleasure of giving seemed never to leave their Majesties, as it so often does with rich people. Before dinner on Christmas Eve we all assembled in the corridor outside the ballroom and one by one we were called in. It was always a rather trying experience as one found the King on one side and the Queen on the other explaining who gave what present and giving particulars about the various articles. One stood gasping one's thanks to each alternately, and it was always a relief when the next person was called in. It was impossible to make a set speech, and most people, including myself, continued gasping 'Thank you so much'.

I was quite overcome at first by the number of presents I received. There were prints, water-colours, silver cigarette-cases, a silver inkstand, pins, studs, and several books. Gottlieb's band played in the gallery, and every evening after dinner we went to the ballroom and looked at everyone else's presents. The King and Queen, of course, received wonderful things from their relations in Europe, the Emperor of Russia sending particularly lovely things by special messenger.[13]

On New Year's Eve all the presents were taken away and the tables were arranged differently and closer to the Christmas-tree. All the servants and workers on the estate came in and remained outside the row of tables while the presents were massed round the Christmas-tree. Each servant and employee drew two numbers on entering the room, and the Princesses and members of the Household took the numbers and found the present. Of course often a present didn't fit the recipient and a housemaid might get a razor and a footman a powder-puff, but these could be ex-

[13] Some of the fantastic novelties concocted by M. Carl Fabergé for the Russian Imperial family have recently been shown in London. They included Easter eggs in gold and enamels; precious stones with tiny coaches, etc., inset; cigarette cases carved of jade; minute sprays of cornflowers and ears of corn set in a rock crystal vase. All were a little gaudy, but unsurpassable in ingenuity and finish.

changed later. Some eight hundred presents were given in this way and it seemed to give much pleasure. At the conclusion the Christmas-tree was stripped and all the toys and sweets were given to the children.

CHAPTER XII

The King's first official trip abroad — Portugal — Gibraltar — Malta — Naples — The visit to the Pope — Rome — Paris — L'Entente Cordiale

KING EDWARD had always been a lover of European travel, but as Prince of Wales his various visits to European capitals or spas were strictly unofficial. Shortly after his accession to the throne, however, he determined to make a Mediterranean tour which should include several official visits. Whether he anticipated opposition on the part of the Government to these official foreign visits I never knew, but the arrangements which he made for his tour early in 1903 were kept a dead secret and most of the suite had no idea where they were going. The King kept the whole arrangements in his own hands and knew that he could rely on the discretion of the various members of his Household to keep everything as quiet as possible. Everything was in water-tight compartments, so that the person who was responsible for the orders to be given to the yacht knew nothing about the telegrams and letters that were being sent to foreign capitals. Beyond the fact that I was to form one of the suite, I knew nothing at all about the arrangements.

The suite consisted of the Hon. Charles Hardinge,[1] Minister Plenipotentiary and Assistant Under-Secretary of Foreign Affairs; Major-General Sir Stanley Clarke, Acting Master of the Household; Rear-Admiral the Hon. Hedworth Lambton, Equerry and in command of the Royal yacht; Captain the Hon. Seymour Fortescue, Equerry; Sir Francis Laking, the King's physician;

[1] Later 1st Baron Hardinge of Penshurst. Assistant Under-Secretary of State for Foreign Affairs, 1903–4; Permanent Under-Secretary of State for Foreign Affairs, 1906–10 and 1916–20; Ambassador to Russia, 1904–6; Viceroy of India, 1910–16; Ambassador to France, 1920–22.

Chevalier de Martino, the marine painter; and myself as Equerry and Acting Private Secretary. The Marquis de Soveral, the Portuguese Ambassador, came as far as Lisbon, which was to be our first port of call.

In Queen Victoria's reign it was the custom for a Cabinet Minister to accompany the Sovereign, but King Edward made a new departure in taking with him a comparatively unknown Secretary from the Diplomatic Service. At first it was said that Hardinge had been selected because he had married one of Queen Alexandra's Ladies-in-Waiting, but this was quite wrong. King Edward had with unerring judgment discovered Hardinge as the rising man in diplomacy, and thought he would be far more useful than a Cabinet Minister, who would probably be unable to talk French or German. It was certainly a very happy selection, for Hardinge proved to be a man of exceptional ability.

The decision to take three Equerries, and make one do the work of the Master of the Household, never seemed quite a success as the duties of the latter practically ceased when we landed, but everything went smoothly and there was rarely any difficulty. I am sure it was the King's original intention to leave Martino on the yacht, but with that kindness of heart which characterized all his actions, he ended by allowing Martino to accompany him. Anybody more inappropriate in the suite of an English King than an Italian painter it is impossible to imagine. First of all Martino objected to ranking last in the suite, and King Edward told me to bring him the list so that he might decide what should be done about this. I told him that I had no objection to ranking last and possibly Martino would be satisfied if he was placed above me, but complications followed because Seymour Fortescue, hearing of this ridiculous protest on Martino's part, also offered to rank last. Then Hedworth Lambton, the Commodore of the Royal yachts, had to be placed among the suite, and on hearing about Martino also asked to be placed last. This amused the King very much, but he definitely decided that Martino should rank just above me to satisfy him, and that the others should be placed in their proper order.

We arrived at Lisbon on April 3rd, and as soon as we dropped anchor the Embassy staff came on board. The King of Portugal came later in a green and gold barge rowed by eighty men in red. It was just like the Middle Ages, for these barges had been used for centuries.

King Edward was dressed as Colonel of a Portuguese cavalry regiment, a uniform that certainly was not becoming to a stout man as the coat was very short and showed an immense expanse of breeches. The King of Portugal welcomed His Majesty effusively and then both Kings presented their suites by name. We were all new at the game at that time, and did not know we had to be presented, so that the King found us scattered all over the yacht when he wanted to present us.

In the evening we went ashore in three picturesque barges while bands played, guns boomed, and spasmodic cheering was heard on shore. The municipal magnates were drawn up on the quay and an address of welcome was read in Portuguese, to which the King replied in English. We were then all conducted to gilded coaches amidst more cheering. These coaches were not unlike the one that Cinderella had, to take her to the ball, with exquisitely painted panels in the style of Boucher, but they were so old and cracked that I feared lest the floor-boards of the one in which Martino and I drove should give way and we should have to run inside the coach. The first four coaches were each drawn by six white Arab ponies and the last two by black English horses, while a large body of cavalry formed the escort. The drive through the streets of Lisbon lasted an hour and a half, and everywhere there were dense crowds.

On arrival at the Palace the King was received by the Queen Mother, Maria Pia, in the absence of the Queen of Portugal, and we were shown to our rooms. I had a suite of rooms given to me which were magnificently ugly, but not comfortable as we understand comfort. There was a musty smell about the rooms which gave me the impression that they had not been used for years, although bathrooms had been specially installed for our ablutions. My sitting-room was quite medieval, having heavy red velvet curtains, not only on the windows but also over the doors, old-fashioned massive furniture and huge pictures, while the bedroom contained a four-poster bed with heavy curtains. Soveral had obviously written to ask that every effort should be made to provide us with English luxuries, for whisky and soda was placed in our rooms at night and a cup of tea was brought us in the morning.

The following day the two Kings went to Cintra for luncheon and returned in the afternoon, when the King received the Corps Diplomatique. This was one of the most trying ceremonies a Sovereign had to undertake, for the Ambassadors and Ministers, supported by their staffs, were drawn up round the room and the King had to speak to each one while the others remained listening. The King was a past master at this and never seemed to find any difficulty in doing it quite naturally. His method was to talk to A and then draw B into the conversation, move on imperceptibly and while apparently listening to B, draw C into conversation, and so on, but it required a very alert mind not to make a mistake and to recognize each country by the uniform and decorations so that the Peruvian was not mistaken for the Bulgarian Minister.

The next day, April 4th, was one of the most tiring I have ever spent in my life, for I had to stand practically the whole day. In the morning the King received addresses at the museum of the Geographical Society and we all stood behind him on a platform. After luncheon we went to see pigeon-shooting in the gardens of the Ajuda which lasted from two to five. According to the etiquette, no one was allowed to sit except the two Kings, and we had to stand in an enclosure in the hot sun, bored to death with the competition. The King of Portugal was most anxious to win but only got third prize although he was a wonderful shot. At five we went to tea with the Queen Mother, but there again it was contrary to etiquette to sit and we had therefore to stand for an hour. We got back to our rooms soon after six, but as the banquet in full uniform took place at 6.30, we only just had time to dress.

There were a hundred people at the banquet, and it seemed very well done, but we had hardly time to drink our coffee before we were hurried off to a gala performance at the Opera. The Royal Box was in the centre of the house, and contained only three huge gilt chairs for the two Kings and the Queen Mother, and I could hardly believe my ears when I was told that according to the etiquette we all had to stand throughout the performance. I had already stood about for four hours in the afternoon and an hour in the morning, and I was expected to enjoy the performance dolled up in uniform and standing to attention. I stood it for an hour and twenty minutes and then I told Hedworth Lambton that I really could not stand any more and he agreed to retire quietly from the box and go and sit down outside somewhere, but when we tried to slip out quickly, the Portuguese thought we were being polite and were putting them in front of us. They said 'Please, please', and insisted on our remaining in the front row. We were so much taller than the Portuguese that it was impossible to escape detection. At the end of a scene there was frantic applause and bouquets were passed up to the prima donna, which gave us the opportunity of gliding back and then leaving the box. When we got out into the corridor there were no chairs or seats of any description, but on peering about I found two in the ladies' cloakroom and there we sat and smoked cigarettes, though not for long, for an aristocratic-looking female appeared at the door and not unnaturally resented our presence. She went off to find someone to turn us out and soon the corridor was full of irate women. So we thought it wise to beat a retreat, but nothing would induce me to return to the box, and after sauntering about we found a bench in the foyer and there we sat till we thought the performance was nearly over, when we mixed with the crowd of officials in the Royal Box, and this time when they said 'Please, please', we allowed ourselves to be pushed again into the front row.

An awkward thing happened to me on Sunday the 5th. Sotheby, one of the Privy Purse clerks, who was with me as typist and secretary, asked for leave to go out with one of the attachés at the British Legation. I at once gave him leave as I could not imagine that anything would be wanted on a Sunday, but all of a sudden after he had left the King told me that he was going to Cascaes, and as a purely formal business the Mayor of that place intended to hand an address which would not be read and a typed reply would be all that was necessary. I went to Sotheby's room and found everything carefully locked up. I wanted some paper with the Royal Arms on it and his typewriter, but all his boxes were locked. I had therefore to break the padlock on his typewriter and prise open his stationery box, all of which took some time, but I managed to produce some non-committal reply with commonplace remarks for the King to hand to the Mayor.

One afternoon we went for a motor drive round the outskirts of Lisbon, and Hedworth Lambton and I went in a car driven by the Duc d'Oporto, the King of Portugal's brother, who was a most frightening driver and who insisted on playing practical jokes. These so unnerved Lambton, who said he didn't think it funny to have his neck broken for a joke, that he insisted on getting into another car the first time he stopped. I was unfortunately seated by the Duke and I came to the conclusion that while he might possibly kill someone on the road, there was little danger of anything happening to him or to me. As we drove home he asked whether I would like to see him put the cars behind us in the ditch, and I nervously replied that I did not understand what he meant. 'You will see', he replied, and looking back he waved them to come on, at the same time quickening his pace till he must have been going about fifty miles an hour. We arrived suddenly at a T-shaped cross-roads and he put the brakes on so suddenly that I was nearly shot out of the car, but by this means he was just able to turn sharp to the left. The cars behind being quite unprepared had no chance and two of them got into a ditch, which was luckily not very deep, whilst a third skidded into a wall, all of which seemed to amuse him immensely. Another time he pretended to run straight into the crowd and then jammed on the brakes so that the car stopped suddenly within a few feet of them. The crowd rushed away in confusion, men, women, and children tripping and falling over one another in every direction. This made him laugh heartily, while I sat with my hair standing erect on my head. He ended up by careering over a draw-bridge, through an archway and into a courtyard, only missing the wall by an inch, and I made a mental resolution never to drive with him again.

Then came the giving and receiving of decorations, a very tiresome business, but I was young enough to be pleased at being given my first star, that of the Order of Our Lady of the Conception. The King had assumed that as Charlie Hardinge was in the Diplomatic Service he would know all about the interchange of decorations, but of course he knew little or nothing about such trivial things. He was, however, given charge of all this to begin with. Stanley Clarke was told to look after the presents. On this occasion this arrangement worked well to begin with, as Soveral made out the list, but when difficulties arose I was called in as I had had some experience of both decorations and presents with Queen Victoria. Eventually the King decided that I had better take over all this and be responsible for both. What annoyed the King was that Stanley Clarke quite forgot to look up the names of those who were to receive presents on this occasion in the lists of presents His Majesty had already given in former years. When the King presented one of the Secretaries at the British Legation with a silver cigarette-case, it turned out the Secretary had already received a precisely similar one a few years ago. So I was put in charge of this in future and both Charlie Hardinge and Stanley Clarke were glad to be rid of what was really an unimportant and tiresome job.

At the State banquet the King of Portugal read a speech of welcome in French, and the King replied in French without a note.

The next day we went to a bull-fight, which was certainly a beautiful sight. Bull-fights in Portugal were different from those in Spain because the bull was never killed nor were the horses ever hurt. The horses were beautiful animals for which large sums were paid—very different from the old worn-out horses ridden in Spanish bull-fights. The bull has rubber balls on his horns, but in any case the horses must never be hurt, and it was wonderful to see the riders turn on a sixpence to avoid a charging bull. The performance began very much like a Spanish bull-fight, and a procession of old-fashioned coaches drove into the arena in which the picadors, matadors, etc., were seated, and the crowd cheered the celebrities. Having deposited their illustrious occupants, the coaches drove off and the bull was let loose. I thought it very fine, but I was told that those accustomed to the gory Spanish bull-fights looked upon it as a very tame affair.

On the 7th we returned on board the yacht and left Lisbon amidst the booming of guns and cheering. What struck me most during this first State visit abroad was the fact that the King himself made all the arrangements and supervised every detail. After having been on the Viceroy's staff where the Military Secretary practically arranged everything and told the Viceroy what to do, I was surprised to find that it was the King who told us what to do. Of course, except for Stanley Clarke, we were all lamentably ignorant of the conventionalities of European Courts and we had no idea of what the usual routine was during State visits, but later we got properly trained.

It was while we were at sea that I grasped that the King intended to go to Paris and Rome. When we started we were told we were going to Lisbon and the Mediterranean, but I soon was convinced that from the first Paris was the King's real objective. When telegrams poured in and I had to decypher them I began to understand the whole programme, but of course I never said a word to the others. Hardinge was sending messages from the King to various European countries, but I doubt whether he knew when we started what was in the King's mind. One evening the King said, 'You know we are going to Paris' (he didn't mention Rome), and I replied that I had gathered so much from the telegrams. All he said was that I was not to tell anyone about this.

The yacht steamed on to Gibraltar where Sir George White and his staff received the King. There was an official dinner, and at the end of dinner His Majesty announced that he had made Sir George a Field-Marshal. This was a clever touch on the part of the War Office, as they thought an announcement from the King was better than an official communication. The following day we went to the top of the Rock on hill ponies: there was no difficulty about going up there, but when it came to going down the King flatly refused to ride, for he considered (wisely, I thought) a small Arab hill pony, twelve hands high, was hardly a safe conveyance for a man of his weight when it came to going down a slope as steep as a roof: so he walked down and was very stiff the next day in consequence.

A curious incident occurred while we were at Gibraltar. A 'dangerous' anarchist, that is to say, a man described by the police as an active anarchist who was prepared to do things and not merely write and talk about communistic ideals, suddenly arrived. It appeared that the man was under police surveillance in Italy and that when he suddenly disappeared telegrams of warning were sent to the police in the neighboring countries. He was easily traced in France and then to Spain and Gibraltar. In order to ensure that he would have no opportunity of shooting or stabbing the King, the authorities had him arrested on a charge of stealing as this enabled the police to keep him locked up for three days. It was proposed to release him as soon as the King left, but it occurred to all of us that if he had really come with a view to assassinating the King it would be perfectly easy for him to go on by boat and overtake His Majesty. I therefore spoke to Sir George White and asked him whether he could do anything, but at the same time I pointed out that this man might be a perfectly harmless individual who had merely come to Gibraltar for his health. Sir George White replied that it was a curious place for an anarchist to come for his health, but in order to be on the safe side, he would have him again arrested as soon as he was released by the civil authorities on the charge of entering a fortress armed. Apparently he had not only a revolver but also a long knife, so there would be no difficulty about this. It all sounded very thin and I feared there might be trouble when the man was released, as the Press would make fun of anyone being detained on such a ridiculous charge, but I heard afterwards that when he was eventually released he made no protest or complaint but went off to Barcelona.

On we went to Malta, delightful hot days with a smooth sea, no letters, no telegrams, no work to do. We arrived at Malta on April 16th and as King Edward was the first British Sovereign to visit Malta, the inhabitants gave him a great reception. General Sir C. Mansfield-Clarke had just been appointed Governor and had not had time to get properly in his saddle when the King's visit was announced. The result was that there appeared to be no system at all in the way things were managed. He had brought with him a chef from Paris who turned out to be a fraud, and so the food

231

was bad; moreover the staff had not time to get together and everything seemed left to chance.

There was the usual review of the troops, presentation of addresses, and a gala performance at the Opera. The performance itself was very indifferent, but the audience, which contained all the notabilities of Malta, was interesting to look at. The last night after dinner there were fireworks and what was known as a water carnival. Each man-of-war had a steam launch made up to represent in miniature some period in shipbuilding, beginning with the Ark and ending up with the most modern type of battleship. The men had entered eagerly into this and really the galleys and old three-deckers were most beautifully represented. The Ark went so far as to have a dove on board which they let loose as they passed the Royal yacht.

On the 21st the King left Malta, escorted by what was quite a small fleet, and proceeded to Naples. Owing to bad weather we stayed one night at Syracuse and on passing Stromboli there was an eruption of the volcano which had apparently been inactive for some months. Martino said this was Italy's first salute to the King. I had telegraphed on to Naples to say that the King would arrive incognito, which seemed rather absurd as no other human being in the world could come with eight battleships, four cruisers, four destroyers, and a dispatch vessel.

On arrival Sir Francis Bertie,[2] the Ambassador, and Mr. Rolfe, British Consul at Naples, came on board. The latter was a most erudite scholar and it was said that he knew more about Italian works of art than the Italians themselves. Then came a stream of visitors: the Duke of Abruzzi,[3] the Crown Prince of Portugal, the German Crown Prince and Prince Eitel Friedrich, General Pedotti and many others. Last but not least came Mrs. Vanderbilt accompanied by Lady Lowther.

The next day the King landed and went to see the museums but refused to listen to the police, who wished to take precautions.

[2] Later 1st Viscount Bertie of Thame. Ambassador in Rome, 1903; in Paris, 1905–18.

[3] Son of Duke of Aosta. Polar explorer and mountaineer; Commander-in-Chief of the Italian Navy, 1915–17.

They proposed to close the museums which he intended to visit and have innumerable police in each gallery. They seemed nervous about his going about like an ordinary individual, but the King laughed at the idea of police protection and refused to allow any precautions to be taken. We were then asked whether it could not be arranged that two of us should always be behind him, no doubt with a view to guarding him from bullets and knives, and we agreed to this as there seemed no objection; but when we tried to put this into practice the King got irritated with finding two of us at his heels and sent us off in different directions.

On the 26th we went to have luncheon with Lord Rosebery at Posillipo [4] where he had a famous villa. The King, Queen Amélie of Portugal, Hedworth Lambton, and I went there in a steam launch across the Bay of Naples. The King was in a meditative mood and rather sleepy; Hedworth Lambton could not manage any French at all, but Queen Amélie was in a talkative mood and selected me as the only possible person to talk to. We talked without stopping for forty minutes while the King and Lambton merely listened. I found this rather trying as of course the presence of the King rather cramped my style, but she was witty and amusing and there was no difficulty in keeping the ball rolling.

We had an interminable luncheon of about twenty courses, which I thought would never end, but Lord Rosebery, who said it was like a nightmare, explained he had been obliged to put the whole thing in the hands of a Neapolitan caterer.

The King went to a gala performance at the Opera House, which is reputed to be one of the most beautiful in Europe. The interior was decked with roses and there seemed to be a great many pretty women in the audience. All the men were in uniform which always adds colour to a scene, and the jewels worn by the women gave it a sparkle. The King had a great ovation when he came into the Royal Box.

We had some difficulty over the King's wish to visit the Pope.[5] He said that among his subjects were millions of Roman Catholics and that they would be inclined to take offence if he took no

---

[4] A beautiful promontory near Naples.
[5] Leo XIII.

notice of the Pope when he was in Rome. There was no doubt he firmly intended to pay this visit and the Cabinet in London had been told that such was His Majesty's intention. Had it been left at that there would have been no difficulty, but unfortunately the King sent another telegram asking their advice, and Arthur Balfour, the Prime Minister, found himself in an awkward position. If he advised and approved of the King visiting the Pope, he stood to be shot at by members of Parliament and religious bodies, but if on the other hand he officially told the King not to go, it looked petty and small-minded. When Hardinge's second telegram was read before the Cabinet they came to the conclusion that as their advice had been asked they could not be expected to sanction such a visit, and they therefore said that they adhered to their original decision and thought it most inadvisable that His Majesty, who was a Protestant, should see the Pope. When the King received a long cypher telegram to this effect, he was perfectly furious and dictated to Hardinge a strongly worded message, such a message as would have put the backs up not only of the Cabinet but the two Houses of Parliament. Hardinge, who at that time did not know the King's ways and did not understand that messages of this sort had to be toned down, wrote it out practically verbatim and asked me to cypher it to the Prime Minister. As I read it I felt instinctively that if this message was sent there would be no alternative for Arthur Balfour but to send in his resignation, and after reading it several times I came to the conclusion that it was impossible to send such a plain-spoken provocative message as it was. I perfectly understood that the King wished to see the Pope, but this message could have but one result, and so far from furthering the King's wishes, the Prime Minister would probably send a reply which would make the visit impossible.

My difficulty was that everyone had gone on shore to an official dinner and I was left alone on board as I had so much to do. It would have been a comparatively simple matter had I been able to go to the King and show him the draft of an amended message or even to consult Hardinge, but every moment was precious and they might not return till midnight. I determined to rewrite the message on my own responsibility and sent it off. It was a telegram from the King and not from Hardinge, and I felt that I should not risk getting Hardinge into trouble. I therefore altered the whole telegram and in conciliatory language said that the King quite realized the difficulties of the Cabinet and that he did not wish to put them in a false position. He would take the initiative himself and if he found that circumstances rendered it advisable that he should pay a visit to the Pope, he would do so without consulting them and entirely on his own responsibility. They must, however, leave it to him to decide. The gist of the message was that he withdrew his former request for advice and would act on his own responsibility. This telegram I sent off at once in cypher. When everyone returned on board about midnight, I thought I ought to tell Hardinge what I had done and showed him a copy of what I had sent. He was extremely angry. He said I had no right to alter the King's words. He accused me of putting him in a false position and said it was an unheard-of thing to tamper with a message from the King to the Prime Minister. We had a heated discussion on the subject and I replied that all I had done was to further the King's wishes. Had the message been sent as he had written it, the visit would have been out of the question. The Cabinet had but to publish the telegrams and the whole of the British nation would be on their side. I maintained that it was my duty as Private Secretary to do all I could to help the King to carry out his intention to visit the Pope and that therefore I was right in altering the telegram. The King often dictated telegrams couched in too forcible language, and, as he never found any difficulty in expressing himself, he rattled them off and it was my duty to see there was nothing in them that would give offence.

Hardinge, however, was not appeased and pointed out with some truth that in this case it had not been a matter of softening the language used. I had, he said, altered the message and given it quite a different interpretation. If things went wrong, as he feared they would, he would have no alternative but to send in his resignation. I replied that he was blameless and that he was at perfect liberty to throw the blame on me.

He was so much put out at this that instead of going to bed he continued to pace the deck for some time meditating what he ought to do. Finally about one o'clock he came down to my cabin where I was still writing and said he would await Arthur Balfour's reply before coming to any decision.

The next morning came a long cypher telegram from Arthur Balfour and I nervously decyphered it. It was a great relief to me to find that what I had predicted had come true. Balfour at once accepted the situation and said he had explained the whole matter to the Cabinet, who were quite willing to withdraw their advice and who quite agreed that it was best to leave the matter in the King's hands. This was a great triumph for me, and I took it at once to Hardinge, who most generously agreed that I had done the right thing.

Later I explained to the King that I had altered his message as I feared that it might put up the backs of the Cabinet and that they would feel it their duty to protest, which might make a visit to the Pope difficult if not impossible. As Balfour's answer had been just what the King wanted, he said he thought I was quite right.

This was the only difference of opinion I had with that brilliantly clever man Hardinge, who was years later to become Viceroy of India. Probably had I possessed a crystal ball and known to what eminence he would rise I should never have dared to alter his interpretation of the King's message.

When it became known in England that the King was to visit Rome the Roman Catholics, headed by the Duke of Norfolk, took the view that it would be an act of discourtesy if the King did not call on the Pope, while Protestant societies stirred up anti-Catholic feeling vigorously. All this was reflected in a mass of letters and telegrams and resolutions passed by these societies that were sent to the King in Rome. I took all the telgrams to the King, who read them carefully and said he did not intend to be guided by such narrow-minded people. I had of course to be most guarded in my replies and the King told me not to be drawn into any discussion. I merely acknowledged the receipt of the telegrams and assured the senders that their messages and resolutions would receive every consideration.

As the duties of Minister in Attendance were ill-defined, Hardinge was uncertain what exactly he was supposed to do. Quite early in the cruise he came down to my cabin and found official boxes from the Foreign, War, Home, Colonial, and Indian Offices, from the Admiralty and many smaller Government Offices, and he asked whether it was right for me and not him to deal with these. I told him that usually the Minister in Attendance was a Cabinet Minister whose duty it was to discuss with the King lines of policy and advise him in political matters, but it was out of the question for him to write to permanent officials at the different Government Offices or to deal with the routine work. He agreed but said that he was astonished at the mass of letters I had to write in addition to the boxes. He had no idea there was so much work to be done.

We arrived in Rome on April 28th and the King was met at the station by the King of Italy [6] and two of the Italian Princes in addition to a host of civil, naval, and military authorities. There was the usual inspection of the guard of honour and then we drove in open carriages to the Quirinal. The crowd was most enthusiastic, as the Italians have always had a great love of England, and they were delighted at the visit of an English King. On the way the Syndic of Rome, Prince di Sonnino, and civic authorities presented an address of welcome.

On arrival at the Quirinal we were shown our rooms and I was glad to find mine were the most comfortable, comprising a sitting-room, bedroom, and bathroom, all luxuriously furnished and fitted up with all modern requirements. The only disadvantage was that my rooms were a long way from the King's, and as I had to be constantly running backwards and forwards to see him, I had to take a great deal of exercise during the day.

The Italian letters and telegrams that awaited me on arrival were terrific. In Italy it was still the custom for uneducated men to employ letter-writers and one man alone would turn out a hundred a day. There were basketfuls of them, about 1,500 in all, and in addition about twenty-five very long telegrams. I at once wrote to Frank Bertie, the Ambassador, and explained that with the best

[6] Victor Emmanuel III; succeeded his father, Humbert I (who was assassinated), in 1900.

will in the world I could not grapple with these letters. To start with I knew no Italian, and in the second place I had not sufficient time. I asked whether it would not be possible for some member of the Embassy staff to take these off my hands, and he replied that if I would pack them up and send them to the Embassy he would see that they were all dealt with. The letters continued to come in during the visit at the rate of a thousand a day, but the telegrams were more difficult and these I had to deal with myself, including those that still poured in from irate Protestant societies in England.

The evening of the State banquet the King was not at all well. He seemed overcome by the heat and was distinctly peppery in his temper. Those who had to ask him unimportant questions did not dare to come a second time; he was in a difficult mood and sent the servants flying about in all directions. I kept out of the way as much as possible, but there were many things I was obliged to consult him about, though while he seemed to resent trivial matters being referred to him, he became quite calm when anything important required his decision.

I therefore only troubled him with big stuff and got on very well, but there came a tiresome little question which he alone could deal with and this made him distinctly cross. The Italian Prime Minister sent his Private Secretary to me to ask for a copy of the King's speech which he wanted to give to the Press after the banquet. I was obliged to ask the King for it. He was dangerously calm about this and explained that he always spoke extempore, that he never attempted to commit a speech to memory nor did he ever read it. I repeated this to the Secretary, but after ten minutes he returned and explained that, although there were hundreds of Italian shorthand writers, they naturally had no one who could write English shorthand. I had therefore to go a second time to the King and explain this. He exploded with rage and said that he couldn't be bothered about the Press. When I argued that if nothing was given to the Press they would invent something, he said I must take it down in shorthand myself and not bother him any more. I told the Secretary of this arrangement and added that as I understood there would be about two hundred at dinner, I hoped that I might be placed where I could hear, for if I was at the bottom of the table it might be difficult for me to record His Majesty's speech. When we went in to dinner an official came up to me and said that for some reason which he did not know I had been taken from the lower part of the table and placed immediately opposite the two Kings. I understood the reason and went to my place firmly grasping a shorthand note-book and a pencil. Speeches abroad are made in the middle of dinner, and Italy was no exception. The King of Italy made a long speech in Italian which was quite wasted on me, and we then sat down and had something more to eat. When King Edward stood up, everyone again got up. There I was in full uniform, the scarlet coat of an Equerry, with aiguillettes and decorations, standing up in front of the two Kings, note-book in hand, with a lovely Italian lady on each side wondering what on earth I was doing. I managed, however, to take down easily what the King said, as he spoke slowly, but towards the end of his speech an officious seneschal behind me asked whether I required a pen and some ink. He spoke in broken English, but I didn't understand him and thought I was infringing some rule. After he had repeated his question I shook my head, but I lost two or three sentences. Immediately after dinner we got into State coaches and drove to the Opera, cheered by masses of people in the streets. As soon as I arrived a messenger from the Prime Minister came up to me and asked for a copy of the speech, as it would have to be translated into Italian. I replied that I had not had time to transcribe it into longhand but would do so at once. Instead of looking at the opera I retired into a lobby adjoining the box and asked Charlie Hardinge to come and help. To take down a speech is one thing: to edit it for the Press is quite another. The King had been rather led away by the enthusiasm of his audience and had made use of some expressions which required modifying. In one passage he said, 'We have often fought side by side', but, as I explained to Hardinge, I could think of no instance where English and Italian troops had fought side by side except when the Sardinians had joined with the English and French in the Crimean War. He suggested omitting the word 'often', and made one or two alterations. He luckily remembered something of the sentences I had lost, but he said that clearly this report of the speech must be submitted to the King before it went to the Press. When I got back to the Quirinal I found my friend the Secretary to the Prime Minister in despair at not getting a copy, but I explained I must see the King first. When I attempted to do so I was told by Laking, the doctor, that His Majesty had gone to bed and must on no account be disturbed. I had no alternative but to give the speech to the Press as I had written it out. It all turned out right, for the King the next day said it was substantially correct.

The next day, April 30th, there was a review of twenty thousand Italian troops. It was arranged that as the King had not quite recovered from his indisposition he should drive with the Queen of Italy in a carriage, and that Stanley Clarke should go with an Italian General in the second carriage while the rest of the suite followed. I, however, was to ride with the staff of the King of Italy. We motored down to some cavalry barracks near the review ground and mounted our horses. I was given a beautiful black charger whose acquaintance it was difficult to make while walking to the parade ground, but it seemed a very quiet animal and perfectly trained. The King of Italy rode first, followed by the Italian Princes, and I came immediately after them and in front of a number of Generals. We walked slowly through some streets till we came to the review ground, when the King of Italy broke into a canter and then into a gallop. The horses were perfectly trained and we all started off at full speed. I was just admiring this spectacular arrival of the King of Italy and was thinking, as we swept over the ground, how well it must look from the crowd's point of view, when the King of Italy suddenly stopped dead and all the horses of the staff stopped as if they had been shot. Although one naturally sits fairly tight when galloping (and had it not been for this I should undoubtedly have shot over my horse's head), I was totally unprepared for this and found myself sitting on my horse's ears. Possibly the animal may have been accustomed to riders sitting there, for he never moved and I slowly slid back into the saddle. I was terribly conspicuous, being the only one in a red coat, and had I shot over the horse's head I felt I should have brought disgrace to the whole British Army, but as it happened no one noticed my acrobatic efforts. At first I was rather angry at no one having warned me this was going to happen. It would have been so easy to tell me that all the horses would stop as soon as the King of Italy did so, but later I came to the conclusion that as this was an everyday occurrence in Italy, it never occurred to the staff that I didn't know this spectacular manoeuvre. In England, even at Aldershot, it is not the custom for a King or a General Officer in Command to come on the ground at breakneck speed and then stop dead.

We returned to the Quirinal for luncheon and afterwards the King paid the much-discussed visit to the Pope, but not before a few more awkward little problems had been solved. Even when the visit had been practically settled a difficult question of precedence arose. Cardinal Rampolla [7] insisted on the King taking the initiative in asking for an interview, whereas the King wished the invitation to come from His Holiness. Eventually Cardinal Merry del Val [8] tactfully arranged that the Pope should express a wish to see the King so as to make it easy for His Majesty to pay his visit. Hardinge, Stanley Clarke, and Lambton accompanied His Majesty, and I was not included. As it was impossible for the King to go to the Vatican in one of the King of Italy's [9] carriages, it was necessary for King Edward to start from the Embassy and drive there in the Ambassadorial carriage. This intricate manoeuvre meant driving in one of the King of Italy's carriages to the British Embassy, then changing into the Ambassador's car-

[7] Cardinal Secretary of State and later Arch-Priest of the Vatican Basilica.

[8] Master of the Robes and acting private chamberlain to Pope Leo XIII, of whom he was a great favourite. He was, in fact, made a Cardinal later in the year when the new Pope, Pius X, appointed him Secretary of State. Educated in England, he had previously been Papal Envoy at King Edward's coronation.

[9] Since 1870, relations between the Vatican and the Italian State had been bad or, in fact, non-existent. Successive Popes claimed that the occupation of Rome by Italy was illegal, and that their independence was jeopardized by the abrogation of their temporal powers. They accordingly forbade Catholics to take any part in Italian political life and refused at all times to go outside the Vatican. With the accession of Pius X in 1903, relations improved, but complete agreement was not achieved until 1929, when the Lateran Treaty, signed by Mussolini and Cardinal Gasparri, created the new State of the Vatican City under the sovereignty of the Pope.

riage to go to the Vatican, and repeating this procedure on the return journey. But in spite of these little difficulties the visit went off very well indeed.

The next evening Laking, Martino, and I accompanied the King to dine with the King and Queen of Italy. After dinner the King of Italy came and spoke to me for some time. He struck me as being a very clever man and he certainly had all Italian politics at his fingers' ends. He said that the first thing he did on ascending the throne was to make every effort to restore Italian prosperity: unless that was achieved nothing would be of any use. He spoke for some time on the difficulties Italy had to contend with and then asked me questions about the political situation in England. He asked for information about the British Army and had apparently followed closely the South African War.

He then brought Laking into the conversation. Now Laking was a keen student of psychology, and his success as a doctor was mostly due to that; but while he was shrewd and clever in many ways, he was lamentably ignorant of all European countries and his knowledge of the strained relations between the Quirinal and the Vatican was nil. After the King of Italy had made one or two remarks to him the conversation seemed to flag. Laking thereupon determined to initiate a new topic and to my horror said, 'How do you get on with the Pope, now?' The King of Italy looked rather astonished at such a delicate topic being bluntly started, but finding that Laking had no intention of being impertinent replied quietly that he had 'no wish to make the Pope a prisoner'. He said that he respected the Pope as head of the Church, but that he would not have Cardinals like Rampolla meddling in Italian politics. They must keep to Church affairs and not interfere with the interior policy of the country.

I was relieved to find that he had taken this question so well and had been quick enough to see that Laking was ignorant of all that was passing between him and the Pope. Laking then began to speak again and I trembled lest he should commit another indiscretion; his next question was as tactless as his first. 'There are a lot of anarchists here in Rome, are there not?' he said. 'Are you frightened of them?' Considering that the King of Italy's father had been blown up by an anarchist, it seemed an unfortunate question. The King of Italy again looked rather surprised but answered calmly that anarchy came entirely from unrest, hunger, and discontent: if people were contented and happy there was no such thing as anarchism. His aim and ambition had always been to make the people in Italy happy and contented, but it was by no means easy. I was relieved when he turned away to talk to other people as I felt Laking had put his foot into it quite enough for one evening.

There is no doubt that King Edward's visit to Rome was a great success. The Italians were pleased at his going there before visiting other countries and the King of Italy became a firm friend.

On May 1st we left Rome amidst great enthusiasm and travelled to Paris. I tried to find out who was in favour of this visit. Sir Edmund Monson, the British Ambassador in Paris, as he told me later, was certainly not. Lord Lansdowne and the Foreign Office very much doubted the wisdom of a visit in view of the hostile attitude of the Parisian crowd towards England. Arthur Balfour and the Cabinet didn't quite know enough about it to be able to express any opinion on the subject, but as apparently they were not consulted they were quite content to let the King do as he liked. Hardinge told me it was entirely the King's idea and while no one was in favour of the visit, the Government hardly had sufficient grounds for actually opposing it.

At Dijon the Ambassador, Sir Edmund Monson, joined the train together with the French officers attached to the King during the visit. This necessitated our making conversation with them all the way to Paris, but they were all charming and easy to talk to. We arrived at the station in the Bois de Boulogne, where we found President Loubet and a large number of officials. We drove in six carriages each drawn by four horses with postilions, and were escorted by a large number of French cavalry. There was an immense crowd in the streets and all along the Champs-Elysées. Whether the King had a good reception or not I didn't know, but I was told afterwards that the cheers were mostly for the President. As regards myself in the last carriage I received anything but a pleasant ovation, for the cheers had become jeers by the time

I came, and being in a red coat I was selected by the crowd for witticisms. There were cries of *'Vive Marchand!'* and *'Vive Fashoda!' 'Vivent les Boers!'* and occasionally *'Vive Jeanne d'Arc!'* which seemed to be going back a long way in history. On one or two occasions a voice shouted quite a long sentence which I was unable to catch, and the crowd was convulsed with laughter, all of which showed that we were anything but popular in Paris.

At the British Embassy we were not very comfortable, as the Monsons only lived in certain rooms and usually left the main apartments, except the drawing-rooms, empty of furniture. The *'Garde-meuble'*, where all the best furniture from the old palaces was stored, sent some lovely bits of furniture and these empty rooms were luxuriously furnished. Half an hour after we arrived we had to get into carriages again and pay a formal visit to Monsieur and Madame Loubet. The first speech the King made was to the British Chamber of Commerce and this made a great impression on the French mind when it was translated and published the next day. In the evening we went to the Théâtre Français where we saw *L'Autre Danger*. During the *entr' acte* the King insisted on walking about in the crowd in the foyer, much to the terror of the police.

The following day we had a long drive down to Vincennes, where eighteen thousand men marched past. We drove through the poorer parts of Paris and although the crowd were not very enthusiastic there were no rude remarks.

It was at the Hôtel de Ville that the King made a short speech which entirely changed the whole atmosphere and brought all the French round at once. The actual speech in all its brevity was as follows:

'Je désire vous exprimer combien je suis vivement touché de vos bonnes paroles. Il aurait été fâcheux, en passant par votre belle ville, de ne pouvoir m'arrêter à l'Hôtel de Ville. Bien sincèrement, je vous remercie de l'accueil que vous m'avez fait aujourd'hui.

'Je n'oublierai jamas ma visite à votre charmante ville, et je puis vous assurer que c'est avec le plus grand plaisir que je reviens à Paris, où je me trouve toujours comme si j'étais chez moi.'

That last phrase went home, and as he sat down he received a tremendous ovation. He seemed to have captured Paris by storm. From that moment everything was changed wherever we went. Not only the King but all of the suite were received with loud and repeated cheering. It was the most marvellous transformation, and all in three days. The first day distinctly antagonistic, the second cold, and finally frenzied enthusiasm.

In the afternoon we went to the races at Longchamps where a race meeting was specially held in honour of the King. He was seated in a box with Madame Loubet on one side and the wife of a French General, the Governor of Paris, on the other, and was intensely bored, but having very good manners he didn't like to get up and leave the box. He remained there for two races and then sent for me. He whispered in my ear, 'You must get me out of this. Go to the Jockey Club and ask someone to send me an invitation to come and see the new wing they have built or anything that will get me out of this.' I went off at once to the Jockey Club, but I was not sure whom I should confide in. I found Prince d'Arenberg whom I knew slightly and gave him the King's message and he at once understood. In a few minutes three members went to the President's box and asked the King as a special favour whether he would come and see the alterations that had been made. The King turned to Madame Loubet and said he was sure she would excuse him, and away he went leaving the two French ladies sole occupants of this beautiful box. He remained in the Jockey Club until just before the last race and then returned to the box. He told me to thank Prince d'Arenberg for having arranged this so well and to ask him to come to the Embassy the following day. I raced off and gave this message, but when I tried to get back to my carriage the crowd was so great that I found it quite impossible. I pushed and pushed a way through the crowd until I was stopped by a sturdy gendarme. I explained in French that I was one of the King's suite, but he replied, '*Vous êtes la cinquième personne qui m'a dit cela*', and the crowd roared with laughter at his having spotted an impostor. I was prepared to be left behind, but Hedworth Lambton happened to see me and shouted to the gendarme that it was all right, and I came through and got into the carriage just as the procession was starting.

During this visit I found the work as much as I could do. Having to attend all functions, banquets, etc., mostly in uniform, it left little time for the letters, telegrams, etc., but these I did at night, sometimes sitting up till 2 a.m. All the arrangements for the functions had to be done at odd moments during the day, and in addition there were the orders and presents to be given.

When we arrived I received a long letter from M. Armand Mollard, Chef du Protocole, enclosing a programme which went into great detail. It was apparently the custom in France for the Protocole to arrange functions and have everything printed and distributed to the persons concerned. The programme sent to me not only described what the President should wear and do, but went so far as to describe in detail the dress to be worn by the King on each occasion. Being totally ignorant of such things, I took it as a matter of course and showed it to the King. He read it through and appeared to think it was impertinent. He said it was going rather far when they laid down what he should wear and what he should do, and taking a blue pencil he erased all particulars about himself. Having once started he pulled his chair up, lit a cigar, and got really to work on the whole programme. He found several mistakes and proceeded to amend the programme, explaining that it was written by a man who obviously had had no experience of State visits.

I sent it back to M. Mollard with a polite letter in French asking that these corrections should be made before the programme was circulated. In the evening he came to see me and seemed very much put out. He was a tallish man with whiskers and a low persuasive voice and was very polite. He said that no doubt I had not understood that the programme emanated from the Protocole, and he implied that once the Protocole had decided the procedure at a function it could not be altered. I replied that I was perfectly aware that the Protocole had drawn up the programme, but that the King was not accustomed to be guided by foreign authorities when he paid a State visit. I reminded him that no one had a larger experience of State visits than the King and that it was therefore only natural that His Majesty should know what was most fitting. He again expostulated, but I ended up by saying more or less 'Le *roi le veult'*, and that ended the discussion. I was amused to see later that the Protocole, so far from resenting the King's attitude, always sent to ask what he wished before attempting to issue more programmes.

I was much struck with the importance everyone seemed to attach to what the King said or did. He had such a dominating personality that I had only to quote him and all opposition vanished. I was perfectly aware that, strictly speaking, little importance could be attached to these State visits. The King was not accompanied by a Cabinet Minister, who alone could commit the country to a definite policy. Hardinge was not a political Minister, but he was the rising man in diplomacy, and although in theory the King could do nothing with his aid, in practice he was really able to do all he wished, as the Secretary of State for Foreign Affairs was bound to ratify any agreement made.

In the evening there was a State banquet at the Palace of the Elysée to which 130 people were invited. I was amused to see that although France was a republic, everything was done in exactly the same way as in monarchical countries. There were hundreds of footmen with powdered hair, and the whole banquet was precisely the same as we had had in Rome and Lisbon, the only difference being Monsieur and Madame Loubet instead of a King and Queen. At the conclusion of dinner the President proposed the King's health in a speech prepared by the Protocole. He was obviously nervous and had pinned the speech to one of the candlesticks in front of him, which necessitated his leaning forward to read it. The result was that only a certain number of people near him could hear what he said. When he had finished, the King got up and replied in French. He never seemed at a loss for a word and without any notes or paper in his hand he made an admirable speech, speaking like a Frenchman, which captivated all the guests. They had been accustomed to hear a President mumbling a speech and they were carried away with enthusiasm. The King spoke clearly and distinctly so that all the people at the further ends of a long table were able to hear, and this no doubt accounted for the enthusiastic ovation he received when he sat down. There are very few people who can make a telling speech in a foreign language, but His Majesty was able to do this both in French and German. On the 4th we left and returned to London.

The visit eventually had far-reaching effects, and it was all very well for Lord Lansdowne to claim afterwards the credit for the *Entente Cordiale,* but neither he nor the Government could ever have got the French people round from hostility to enthusiastic friendship in the way King Edward did. As M. Paul Cambon, the French Ambassador in London, remarked, any clerk at the Foreign Office could draw up a treaty, but there was no one else who could have succeeded in producing the right atmosphere for a *rapprochement* with France. After the banquet the King cleverly singled out Prince Radolin, the German Ambassador, to talk to, obviously with a view to smoothing the ruffled feelings of Germany.

The visit to Paris always seemed to me to strain the limitations of a constitutional monarch to breaking point. The King went to Paris with no Cabinet Minister to advise him or to act as a liaison between him and the Government, and yet he reversed the whole policy of this country.

The idea of an *entente* with France was by no means new. In 1891 Chamberlain met Clemenceau in London and discussed the possibilities of France and England coming to some arrangement, but partly because they could not agree and partly because Salisbury refused to budge from his policy of splendid isolation the whole thing ended in smoke. After this England appeared to drift towards Germany and in 1899 Chamberlain attempted a *rapprochement* with Germany but met with a humiliating rebuff from Bülow.[10]

When King Edward went to Paris only two years later public opinion was still turning towards Germany. It must, therefore, have been difficult for the officials at the Foreign Office to readjust their ideas and turn the ship of State in the opposite direction. At the time it was only thought that the King had succeeded in settling our differences with France—nothing more. Not that the

[10] Bernhard von Bülow (Prince, 1905) became German Foreign Secretary in 1897 and Chancellor in 1900. His relations with the Emperor William gradually deteriorated, and he resigned in 1909.

King ever contemplated doing more than that when he decided to go to Paris. He never imagined that in ten years' time it would become practically a defensive alliance. His decision to go to Paris and not Berlin during his first tour abroad was arrived at without any discussion with his responsible Ministers, but whether the Government attached no importance to his movements or not, there is no record of their having suggested Berlin or of any discussion on the question.

The visit to Italy may have astonished them if they paid any attention to these visits, as Italy was at that time one of the Triple Alliance. There was, therefore, no reason why first Portugal and then Italy should have been selected as the first objects of the King's tour in Europe. Without doubt he selected these as a screen to conceal his real object. Had he gone only to Paris it would have roused the anger of the Germans, but to take Paris on his way back from Rome seemed only natural.

The King's first official tour of 1903 was to be followed by many travels abroad, sometimes official, sometimes incognito, but whilst future official visits were viewed with perhaps an exaggerated importance by Europe, none surpassed his visit to Paris in 1903 in terms of results. Not least of these results was a feeling of irritation in Berlin, and it was perhaps with the hopes of minimizing this that his official visit of 1904 was to Kiel.

CHAPTER XIII

The King's visits to Germany — Kiel, 1904 — Orders and decorations — Hamburg — Homburg, 1906 — Kassel, 1907

NOT LEAST OF THOSE who were irritated at King Edward's apparent preference for France was the German Emperor. To him Berlin was the centre of the earth, but here was King Edward visiting France, Portugal, Italy, and Austria, and absolutely ignoring Germany. The difficulty was that the bad feeling between the two countries hardly admitted of a visit to Berlin. However, King Edward decided that a friendly visit to the Emperor at Kiel might do some good, and accordingly went there in June 1904.

The party on the Royal yacht was an odd mixture. There was Baron D'Estournelles de Constant, a French pacifist known in France as 'L'ange de la Paix', who had written articles on disarmament in every European magazine, but who had a certain reverence for monarchs generally. The Emperor treated him as an amiable lunatic, but King Edward liked to hear him expound his theories, without apparently taking them very seriously.

Then there was the Prince of Monaco, a scientifically-minded man who cared only for deep-sea fishing, but who seemed to get on very well with the Emperor. Why these two were included in the party it is difficult to say. Possibly D'Estournelles was asked to please the French and provide antidote to the German poison, while the Prince of Monaco might be useful as a smoke-screen. Prince Louis of Battenberg, a popular Admiral in the English Navy, who was a great friend of King Edward, Lord Selborne, First Lord of the Admiralty as Minister in Attendance, Sir Frank Lascelles, the British Ambassador in Berlin, Major-General Grierson,[1] who had been Military Attaché, Captain O'Callaghan,[2] a leading light in the Navy, Captain Tyrwhitt [3] and Captain Troubridge,[4] reputed to be coming men, Captain Allenby,[5] Naval Attaché in Berlin, Count Gleichen, Military Attaché in Berlin, Lord Ormonde,[6] the Commodore of the Yacht Squadron, Chevalier de Martino, the marine painter, Lord Churchill,[7] Lord-in-Waiting, Johnny Ward,[8] Equerry, and myself as Private Secretary were also on board; in fact, every available cabin on the yacht was filled.

Selborne as Minister in Attendance did very well but I missed Charlie Hardinge very much as there were difficult letters to answer, difficult messages to send in addition to a thousand small matters connected with the visit to Kiel where his great experience would have been invaluable.

The meeting of the King and Emperor took place at night after the Royal yacht had been made fast to the jetty. It was pouring with rain and pitch-dark when King Edward went on shore to inspect the guard of honour, and as I got accustomed to the darkness I found the whole pier was bristling with troops while the band thundered 'God Save the King'. It was no easy matter to inspect a guard of honour under such circumstances, but King Edward, after greeting the Emperor, went round slowly and did it very well in spite of the rain. They both returned on board the Royal yacht and then the presentation of suites began. First of all the Emperor presented his retinue, and the King had a particularly charming way of showing he remembered old faces. When it came to the King presenting all the guests on board, the Emperor also greeted old friends warmly, but when I came forward the King said 'And of course you know Fritz Ponsonby', whereupon the Emperor looked at me as if he had never seen me before in his life.

[1] Later Sir James Grierson.
[2] Later Admiral. Naval A.D.C. to the King.
[3] Later Admiral of the Fleet Sir Reginald Tyrwhitt; commanded Destroyer Flotillas at Heligoland Bight and Dogger Bank.
[4] Later Admiral Sir Ernest Troubridge.
[5] Later Admiral Reginald Allenby.
[6] James Butler, 3rd Marquess of Ormonde.
[7] Victor Spencer, 1st Viscount Churchill of Wychwood.
[8] Later Major the Hon. Sir John Ward; Equerry to King Edward VII, King George V, King Edward VIII and King George VI.

He didn't even shake hands but made a little formal bow and passed on to the next person. I thought that he had forgotten me, although this seemed unlikely, but in any case this did not account for my being the only person with whom he didn't shake hands. However, as there was nothing to be done about it I dismissed the whole thing from my mind.

Apparently the Emperor had taken it into his head that I was the person who always dissuaded the King from visiting Germany and that I was very anti-German, and he therefore wished to show how much he resented my hostile attitude. His refusal to shake hands with me seemed so trivial that I wondered whether all I was told was true, but an incident occurred the next night after dinner which left no doubt whatever as to the Emperor's feelings towards me.

We dined on board the *Hohenzollern* which was really a man-of-war fitted out as a yacht. This was always a sore point with the Emperor who envied the comfort of the *Victoria & Albert*. I was talking to Captain O'Callaghan when Prince Henry of Prussia came up and we began a friendly discussion on some trivial matter. The Emperor, hearing laughter, came up and asked his brother what we were discussing. When he was told he joined in at once and gave his opinion. There was a pause when he concluded his remarks and I chipped in with some light jest which made the others laugh, but the Emperor turned towards me, looked straight at me, and then turned on his heel and walked away.

I told the King about this and he chuckled and said that the Emperor wished to be offensive to some one and had selected me. He had, of course, noticed the incident when the Emperor refused to shake hands with me.

Selborne as Minister in Attendance was in mortal fear of being offered the Red Eagle and wished me to make it clear that as a Cabinet Minister he was precluded from accepting a decoration. He said St. John Brodrick had been so unmercifully chaffed at being given it, and *Punch* had had such a very funny skit on him, that he hoped there would be no mistake about it. But the first morning when he went to his cabin after breakfast there it was on his table, sent by command of the Emperor. He arrived in my cabin pale with rage and gasping maledictions. He explained that he particularly wished to avoid having to refuse it, and now he was placed in the impossible position of having either to accept it or write a letter of refusal. He certainly blamed me for putting him in this position, but I explained that I too had found the Red Eagle on my table and that although the Emperor was always in a hurry with decorations, it was impossible for me to foresee that he would send them while we were at breakfast. I rang for the steward and enquired how the Red Eagles had apparently dropped from the sky through our portholes, as I had seen no emissary from the Emperor. He replied that a naval officer had come from the *Hohenzollern* while we were at breakfast and had asked to be allowed to leave decorations from the Emperor in each cabin. I told him to go at once to the officer of the watch and tell him that the Emperor's naval A.D.C. was to be prevented from leaving the yacht until I had seen him, and meanwhile all the Red Eagles were to be collected from the cabins and brought to me.

Selborne seemed pacified by my efforts, but still questioned my ability to stop his particular Red Eagle. Meanwhile many of the guests seemed to resent my taking their Red Eagles from them and crowded round my cabin asking for an explanation. I, however, went off at once to catch the Emperor's A.D.C., and ran him down in the wardroom where he was being entertained by the officers of the yacht. I explained to him that according to the regulations we were not allowed to accept foreign decorations without special permission of the King, and that although I was sure this would be forthcoming I had been obliged to collect all the decorations the Emperor had so kindly sent us. If he would kindly leave me the list I would at once see the King and ask for his permission. On receiving the list I pointed out to him that Selborne, as a Cabinet Minister, was not allowed ever to accept foreign decorations, and asked him to explain this to Count Eulenburg, head of the Emperor's Household, who I knew would understand. After an hour the naval A.D.C. returned with a huge framed picture of the Emperor for Selborne and took back the First Class of the Red Eagle. Selborne was overcome with joy and one might have thought that this huge framed print of the

Emperor was the one thing he had wanted all his life. So everything ended happily.

Orders and decorations played a great part in German life and the Germans were quite unable to understand English customs. The different value set on orders and decorations by us puzzled them. Whereas in Germany they gave yearly thirty thousand, in England the most that were ever given at that time was about eight hundred, and therefore a British decoration was far more difficult to get. Then on State visits foreign Sovereigns scattered three hundred to five hundred decorations, whereas the King only gave about thirty. So British decorations became like a rare stamp or rare egg, and were much sought after. Even France, a Republican country, scattered decorations during State visits, and President Loubet gave six hundred Legion of Honours when he went to St. Petersburg.

The first night after dinner on board the *Hohenzollern* Count Eulenburg came up to me and became as affectionate as an old friend. He said that of course he knew all about our customs about decorations, but might he send me a list of officials who he thought might be decorated? I replied certainly, as long as he realized that the King didn't give decorations on European principles.

Soon after Richthofen, the Secretary of State, went through practically the same conversation. Finally Prince Bülow, the Chancellor, came up and said he understood the others were 'helping me' with the question of decorations, might he do the same and send me a list, although he knew how ridiculous all these trifles were?

The next day I received the lists and found there were about two hundred names on each list. I showed the lists to the King and repeated to him the purport of the various conversations I had had. He said he wondered how men who pretended to know British customs could seriously produce long lists of persons the majority of whom were not even at Kiel but in Berlin. He added that in order to avoid unpleasantness he would give one decoration to each Minister and they were to choose the person on their list to whom it was to be given, but he stipulated that the person should be at Kiel and not in Berlin.

The next evening I had a distinctly unpleasant time. To begin with, Eulenburg came up and said, 'Is it all right about my list?' and I replied, 'No, it is all wrong'. I explained that only one decoration would be given, and he bowed and retired hurt; the same thing happened with Richthofen and Bülow, who were icy in their attitude towards me. The friendly spirit had evaporated and we were back on bowing terms.

The Germans were natural decoration-hunters, as, continually wearing uniform, decorations meant so much to them, and when the alluring prospect of receiving a rare decoration was torn from them, they determined to put up a fight. All the disappointed went to their respective chiefs and said there must be some mistake: obviously the whole thing was in the hands of an ignoramus who understood nothing about the European conventionalities on State visits. Bülow, Richthofen, and Eulenburg, having burnt their fingers once, had no intention of doing anything more, but they suggested that the senior officers should approach Sir Frank Lascelles. The following day poor Lascelles had a hectic time; high Court officials, Admirals, Generals, etc., tackled him and told him the whole decoration question was being mismanaged. He was a very experienced diplomatist and knew all about decorations. He merely pointed out that we did not give decorations on the German principles, but that he would make enquiries. He came to me and was much amused at what I told him about these three big men having sent me long lists. He said they had laid themselves open to a snub and they had got one. He quite approved of all I had done, but made one or two suggestions about the Kiel authorities.

The decoration-hunters, finding they could get no change out of Lascelles, went off to Metternich, their own Ambassador in London, who was the guest of the Emperor on board the *Hohenzollern,* but he was far too wily an old bird to burn his fingers with a question of this sort. I was in my cabin on board the *Victoria & Albert* when a bluejacket announced that Metternich had come on board to see me. I at once went on deck and greeted him, but when I asked him to come down to my cabin he said how much nicer it would be to sit on deck. Two armchairs were sent for and he then suggested our sitting on the upper deck of all, as it was nice being in the sun, etc. There we sat and talked of every conceivable subject: Cowes, yachting, hunting, shooting, London society, and finally foreign politics. I wondered when he was coming to the point as it seemed inconceivable that he should merely talk about trivialities, and was on my guard for fear of a trap. When we got to the European situation I was all attention, but he seemed to avoid the relations between England and Germany, which might have been interesting. I let him do the talking and merely kept the ball rolling. After half an hour he rose and said he must be going. As he went down the gangway he said, 'Is it all right about the decorations?' and when I replied 'Yes', off he went.

Afterwards I learnt that he had been so bullied by all the disappointed that he had finally consented to go and plead their case with me. The reason he had insisted on going to the upper deck was that he was conscious that telescopes and glasses from the *Hohenzollern* and other ships were fixed on him to see that he was really carrying out his promise. He wanted to give the impression that he was pleading their case and begging for decorations, while he was really talking to me about yachting, and as he was engaged with me for half an hour they were all under the impression that they had a most persistent advocate.

The King spoke in German at the dinner on board the *Hohenzollern*, and was most impressive, but he insisted on seeing a draft of the Emperor's speech as he didn't trust him and didn't want any indiscretion that would upset other European countries.

Count Eulenburg was a wonderful organizer. When any function was going on he looked as if he had nothing to do with it and was merely a spectator, when really he was running everything through his trusty staff. Another was General von Kessel, who was the Governor of Berlin, and had been the Empress Frederick's *bête noire*. He had been originally with the Emperor Frederick, but finding which way the wind blew, had quickly joined the Emperor William. The King treated him coldly, but apparently he didn't expect more. Another who avoided the King was Admiral von Senden und Bibran, who was generally supposed to have been the instigator of the Emperor's telegram to Kruger after the Jameson Raid.[9]

The King seemed to like Bülow and had a long conversation with him, but whether an account of this was ever written by the King I do not know. The conversation with the Emperor seemed to pass off well, but I cannot imagine they ever touched on anything difficult.

The King having agreed to pay a visit to Hamburg, the arrangements were at once made, the Emperor tactfully deciding that he would not accompany His Majesty in order to emphasize the fact that this was to be a visit to the German people. Hamburg was practically a republic within the German Empire, as the councillors, who had unlimited powers, were elected on democratic principles. In the old days the people groaned under the extravagance of monarchs, but at Hamburg they had been crushed by municipal extravagance. On arrival at the station we drove to the Rathaus, a most magnificent building of various coloured marbles with golden gates, and I was told that many millions of marks had been spent in making it a fit place for the town councillors. The King was received by a host of officials, and a procession was formed. In order to dazzle the King with the splendour of the building, it was arranged that we should wind our way through the various pillared halls, making a complete tour of the building and ending up by mounting the grand staircase to the principal chamber. Knowing how scant of breath the King became when mounting long staircases, I was nervous lest His Majesty should arrive in an unfit state to make a speech. I therefore left my place in the procession and pushed my way until I came up to him on the landing halfway up. I found him, as I expected, blowing like a grampus. There was most unfortunately nothing remarkable on the landing to call his attention to, and I was forced therefore to become enthusiastic about the ceiling. I stopped him and pointed out to him the beautiful work right up in the roof. At first he seemed to resent my quite uncalled-for enthusiasm about the ceiling, but he soon

---

[9] This supposition was incorrect; the instigator was Baron von Marschall, who hoped that this empty gesture would divert the Kaiser from dangerous thoughts of armed intervention.

grasped the reason, and, looking up, he listened attentively while I talked more or less nonsense about Michael Angelo, St. Paul's Cathedral, and anything else that came into my head. The officials at first seemed rather to resent the procession being stopped without apparently any orders from anyone, but when those in front turned round and saw the King overcome by the architectural beauties of their building while I, no doubt an expert in ceilings, was calling his attention to them, they smiled with satisfaction. As soon as the King had recovered his breath he made it abundantly clear he had had enough of my talk, and I retired hastily to my place. There was, however, no cause for my fears, for when we reached the Central Hall, the President made a speech that lasted quite a quarter of an hour, and the King thus had ample time to compose himself. His speech, in German, received a great ovation, although there seemed nothing much to evoke such enthusiasm.

When we returned to London, the Press in both countries was very guarded in estimating the value of this visit. Still the King and the German Emperor had met and made amicable speeches, but whether this was any indication that the attitude of the two countries would change and become less hostile to each other, it was impossible to say.

My next visit to Germany was in the August of 1906 when King Edward preceded his 'cure' at Marienbad by a formal visit to the German Emperor at Homburg.

The King left London on August 15, 1906, and crossed over in the *Victoria & Albert* to Flushing. Here we got in the train and at Frankfort we were joined by Hardinge and the British Ambassador, Sir Frank Lascelles. I do not think that Lascelles quite liked Hardinge being out there; after all he was the Ambassador, and anybody from the Foreign Office was rather poaching on his preserves. Hardinge, however, was full of tact and allowed Lascelles to do everything.

When we arrived at Homburg we found the Emperor, very much like his pictures, in his steel helmet and light-green uniform with a red collar. He was accompanied by Prince and Princess

Frederick Charles, Eulenburg, Scholl, Reischach, Hohenau, and a large number of officers. The King and the Emperor embraced and then we were all presented. The Emperor was most cordial with me. He said, 'How are you, my dear Fritz? Haven't seen you for some time. See you are getting grey like me. How old are you? Thirty-eight; well, I'm forty-six, nearly ten years older than you. Uncle says you have been playing tricks with your health. Very silly at your age, with grey hair too.'

Princess Frederick Charles was also most cordial, and the Duchess of Sparta, both of whom I had met some years ago.

We drove to Friedrichshof and found that it had not been altered at all. At luncheon the Emperor was in great spirits and spent most of the time in chaffing Lascelles. I sat next to the Kaiser's doctor, who could talk only German. After luncheon we all smoked on the terrace and I talked to the two Princesses. Suddenly the King shouted to me and asked me the name of the architect who had done Queen Victoria's memorial in London. I said that Brock was the name of the sculptor, but that I could not remember the name of the architect. The Emperor rapped his knuckles on my forehead and said, 'Come on, out with it, I am sure it is there', but this made it all the more impossible for me to remember.

There was always a feeling of thunder in the air whenever the King and the Emperor were together. Both were such big personalities that they each tended to dominate the conversation. I was glad when the talk kept on family topics and things that did not matter. After luncheon we all got into motors and drove to the Roman camp at Salzburg, which the Emperor had had rebuilt entirely as it was in the Romans' time. It was rather a curious idea. There were originally only ruins and the Emperor got the leading professors of Germany to say how they thought it must have been in the Roman days. He then spent a lot of money on rebuilding the whole place, and in creating a museum for the exhibition of the many antiquities excavated. Added to this he had some rams and machines for shooting arrows constructed exactly on the Roman designs.

We had coffee in one of these museums at a long table and the

Emperor told us at length how he started this idea. Afterwards we motored back to Homburg. The Emperor had a standard attached to his motor and a trumpeter on the box who blew long bugle-calls at every corner. The inhabitants thus had no difficulty in making out where the Emperor was, and all the traffic cleared out of the way when they heard the trumpets blow. The King, however, detested what he called 'theatrical methods' and drove about like anybody else.

In the evening we dined with the Emperor and we all wore German decorations, while the Germans wore English ones. After dinner I talked to the Emperor's Minister in Attendance, the clever von Jennisch. Afterwards I talked to Tschirschky, the Under-Secretary for Foreign Affairs.[10] He was very interesting, but of course very guarded in his language.

I had a short talk with the Emperor who laughed at the idea of The Hague Conference, and said all questions of limitation of armaments were Utopian. He added that he had not the slightest intention of diminishing the armaments of Germany in any way or sort, and that he was quite convinced that if he did it would mean war with some European power.

We only stayed one day and went the next to Marienbad.

The following year, 1907, the King's annual stay at Marienbad was again preceded by a meeting with the German Emperor, this time at Kassel.

We crossed in the *Victoria & Albert,* and when we got three-quarters of the way across to Flushing the fog was so bad that we could not see any of the lighthouses, so we anchored. Admiral Colin Keppel, normally a man of iron nerve and daring, did not like to take any risks, so we had to remain where we were until the fog had lifted. It was trying, remaining there with the siren whistling the whole time. We had had dinner and were quite prepared to go on shore and get into the train. They came and told us, however, that there was no chance of landing for another two hours.

We stood about on deck for another two hours and at 3 a.m.

---

[10] As German Ambassador to Russia, he had been closely connected with the signing of the Two Emperors' Treaty at Björkö.

we managed to land. We were all very tired and slept very well in the train.

The second evening in the train an amusing incident happened. While we were playing bridge we arrived at a big station. The King did not think it looked well to be seen playing cards, and so we put the cards dealt to us in our pockets so that we could resume the game when the train moved on. Colin Keppel had been dealt a smashing hand, with four aces, three kings, and two queens, and he had to put it in his pocket. It was a long wait of half an hour, and Colin had to walk about the station with his precious hand of cards in his pocket, half afraid that something would occur that would prevent our continuing the game. However, we did continue when the train started and he got Grand Slam.

At half past one we arrived at Kassel; we were three hours late. The Emperor and all his staff were at the station, and as there were not sufficient troops to line the streets the Emperor had ordered an army corps to come from manoeuvres. There were therefore some fifty thousand men lining the streets four-deep. I was sorry for the crowd; they could have seen very little. The Emperor was most cordial at the station and said, 'I tried to read in the newspapers some account of the yacht-racing at Cowes, but all I could see was that your wife looked remarkably well and wore a new hat'. I replied that no doubt His Majesty was a supporter of the *Daily Mail,* and the Emperor owned that it was from this source that he tried to get the news about yachting. This eventually turned out to be a regular joke, and some time afterwards when the King told the Emperor about some interesting article in *The Times,* the Emperor turned to me and said, 'I know I shall only read what colour your wife's gown is'.

We drove up through masses of people and troops and arrived at the castle, which stands in very pretty grounds. There we stood on the steps of the palace whilst the troops marched past. Having only had a cup of coffee in the train, we were all getting rather hungry, but the review seemed interminable. I said to a General next to me that I hoped it would not last long, and he replied, 'I hope so too, as we have to get into motors and go for a drive at once'.

I mildly remarked that we should like something to eat at some time. I said that we had only had a cup of coffee and if the Emperor contemplated taking us for a long motor drive, it might be well if we had a little luncheon. The General, who was apparently temporarily on the Emperor's suite, said, 'Of course the Emperor thinks you have had luncheon'. I begged him to disabuse the Emperor of this, and he went off to the Emperor and told him that we were all very hungry. The Emperor turned to the King and said, 'I thought you had had luncheon before you got out of the train. We have all had luncheon here long ago.' It was then nearly two o'clock. The King explained he also would like a little luncheon before we started on the drive, and orders were given accordingly.

The review lasted till nearly three, when we sat down to luncheon. The Emperor and Empress and all the German suite sat down too but did not eat anything; the Emperor was charming and talked and chaffed with me across the table. He was in his delightful mood, but of course I had known him in quite another frame of mind.

Later we went to see Jerôme Napoleon's gaudy palace. We had coffee on the balcony, and the Emperor discoursed about Jerôme Napoleon. He was as usual wonderfully accurate in all his facts and went glibly through the whole history of that time. He must have a remarkable memory, because he never seemed to make a mistake and was never at a loss for a date. On the way back the motor I was in broke down but was repaired after a short time, and we managed to get back at ten minutes past eight. I had to dress in full uniform for dinner at nine. I had half a dozen telegrams to answer, and I had to decorate half a dozen of the Emperor's suite. In addition to this the King sent for me, and I wasted much time in finding His Majesty's room through a labyrinth of corridors. I dictated the answers to the telegrams and with the help of my servant got out the decorations. I dressed in full uniform and turned up at ten minutes to nine. I went to the various members of the suite and handed them their decorations. It was most unfortunate that I had asked Stanley Clarke to do one. This was the General Commanding the Army Corps. It appears that Stanley Clarke had a bad servant, and being an old man he found some difficulty in dressing so quickly. He was therefore not only late for dinner, but he had not given the decoration.

The King sat down and was much put out at seeing the General opposite without the Victorian Order. Stanley Clarke turned up after soup had been served carrying the Victorian Order intended for the General under his arm, and the King at once understood.

Immediately after dinner I rushed off and told Stanley Clarke that it must be given at once. He took the General off to a side room and decorated him accordingly, so all was well.

The dinner was most beautifully done. I was told afterwards that they had a regiment of infantry in to help the servants, and everything was done with military punctuality. After dinner I had to talk German the whole time. My ordinary German was pretty good, but when I got on to politics and tried to argue about anarchists with some official, I got rather stuck.

At eleven o'clock we went to the train and the Emperor came to see us off. The whole garrison had turned out with torches and at every hundred yards there was a band. It was really a very fine sight as we drove down the masses of troops. As the train moved off the Emperor had a parting shot at me, and he said he looked forward to reading about my wife's gown again in the newspapers.

When we left Kassel something went wrong with the third carriage in which I was to drive to the station. Reischach came to me and asked if I would mind coming down to the station in a bus with him and some others. I replied certainly. When the King and the Emperor had driven off through the line of troops with torches, with the band thundering 'God Save the King', Reischach told me to follow him and took me round the corner to a big bus. We got in and quickly the bus filled with German officers, but it was dark and I could not see who they were. Last of all a big Prussian General climbed in and as he sat down he said, '*Gott sei Dank! Diese verfluchten Engländer sind weg*' ('Thank God these cursed Englishmen are off'). Reischach at once saw he must do something to prevent the conversation continuing in this dangerous strain, and promptly presented me to all the officers in the bus. It only took a few minutes to reach the station, during which time I was unable to think of a stinging reply and translate it into German. The only replies that occurred to me were distinctly rude. I told the King about this when we got into the train and he appeared to be disappointed at my lack of repartee, but added that if the Germans came to Windsor he was sure that when they left I should say, 'Thank God these d——d Germans are off'.

CHAPTER XIV

The King's visits to Scandinavia — Copenhagen, 1904 — King Christian IX — Copenhagen, 1908 — Stockholm — Christiania — Visit to the Russian Emperor at Reval

THE KING paid several visits to Copenhagen during his reign, usually in the spring in order to be present at the birthday celebrations of Queen Alexandra's father, King Christian IX of Denmark. The children and grandchildren of King Christian were a very devoted family and made a point of being present at the family reunion on his birthday.

In addition to Queen Alexandra, who was his eldest daughter, there were the Empress Marie of Russia and the Duchess of Cumberland and her three brothers, the Crown Prince Frederick of Denmark, King George of Greece, and Prince Waldemar.[1] It was, of course, difficult for King George of Greece to be present on these occasions, and the Empress Marie of Russia only attended them occasionally.

The first time I went to Copenhagen was in April 1904. The King and Queen, accompanied by Charlotte Knollys, Charlie Hardinge, Seymour Fortescue, and myself, stayed there for three weeks. The King was wonderful. I knew he was quite as much bored as we all were at the stiff formality of the Danish Court and yet he never showed it, but on the contrary seemed to be quite happy, and did his utmost to please Queen Alexandra, who was in the seventh heaven and delighted to be in her old home surrounded by friends of her youth. Having visited every museum, picture gallery, or house of historical interest, the King was even-

---

[1] All children of King Christian IX of Denmark. The Crown Prince Frederick succeeded his father as King Frederick VIII, 1906–12; the author's unflattering portrait of him below is hardly fair to such a liberal and well-liked man. The Empress Marie of Russia was the widow of Czar Alexander III.

tually reduced to visiting a farm which supplied quantities of butter to England.

Of course, living in any foreign capital with nothing to do would have been a trying experience, but life in the Amalienborg Palace was particularly tedious. The food was heavy, not to say indifferent, and the rooms were uncomfortable according to English standards. At first walking through the streets seemed my only diversion and exercise, but later I discovered a golf-course on a racecourse a few miles from Copenhagen, and played generally with the Goschen family [2] and the members of the British Legation, who were really the creators of the links. One particular stroke I made still lives in my memory. The professional and Prince Demidoff [3] of the Russian Legation played against Ralph Peto of the British Legation and me, and although the professional and I had only a ball on the match, the others were playing for £5 a hole and £25 on the match. We were all square at the 17th hole and in playing his approach shot Peto overshot the green. When we came to find the ball it was lying in a rut on a road and was almost unplayable, but as there was £25 on the match I had to do my best. With a niblick I quite by chance played a perfect shot, just missing the edge of the rut, and up went the ball straight up in the air. It landed on the green and ran into the hole, much to Peto's astonishment and delight. So we won the match, and Peto instead of losing £25 + £5, won £30, a difference to him of £60. Many times I tried that shot later, but never repeated it.

At the Amalienborg we had breakfast in our rooms, after which I went and did routine work with the King until luncheon. The Royal Family had luncheon separately and all the suite went to the Household luncheon. The evening was the worst part, dinner being at 6.30 p.m. This was a joint meal, and the Households were all drawn up round a large room when the Royal Family came in. The old King of Denmark was still a sprightly-looking man,

[2] Sir (William) Edward Goschen was Minister in Copenhagen, 1900–5; Ambassador in Vienna, 1905–8; in Berlin, 1908–14.

[3] Later Russian Minister in Athens; author of several books on travel and hunting.

although nearly ninety years of age, and went solemnly round the
room saying something to everyone. Dinner consisted of several
courses and many wines, and usually lasted one and a half hours.
We then all filed out arm in arm to the drawing-room, where
again the King of Denmark and all the Danish Royal Family circled round the room. At eight we retired to our rooms to smoke,
but as the Danish suite accompanied us the conversation was limited to polite enquiries into the customs of the two countries. At
nine we returned to the drawing-room where we played round
games, generally Loo, without stakes.

At ten we were mercifully released and allowed to go to our
rooms. These evenings were a high trial to everyone, but the
King behaved like an angel, playing whist, which was then quite
out of date, for very low points. After a week of this, however,
he determined to play bridge, but only after the King of Denmark had retired to bed. We went through the usual routine till
ten o'clock, and then Prince Demidoff of the Russian Legation
came to the King's rooms and played bridge with the King, Seymour Fortescue, and myself, for fairly high points. We continued
thus till the end of the visit, and it was a pleasure to relax ourselves from the stiffness of the Danish Court.

It occurred to me that the conventional conversation which the
octogenarian King of Denmark had to indulge in every night
after dinner might be greatly improved, or at least rendered less
dreary for him, if I could get him to talk of the things that interested him. People when they reach the age of eighty-five are quite
incapable of remembering what happened the previous day, but can
still recollect wonderfully well all the details of their early life. I
determined therefore to find out particulars of his youth, and after
much difficulty I succeeded in borrowing a book in German which
was extremely dull, almost unreadable, but which purported to be
his biography up to the age of fifty. I cannot pretend that I made
an exhaustive study of the subject, but I read enough to provide
me with sufficient material for my purpose. When the King of
Denmark came up to me after dinner I plunged boldly into the
early part of the nineteenth century, and started the ball rolling
by asking the somewhat crude question whether there had been any

truth in the report that at one time he was going to marry Queen Victoria; I also asked whether he had attended her Coronation. He at once started off and said that people had imagined he was going to marry her but that there had never been any truth in the report. He had not attended her Coronation, but had paid her a visit ten years later. He was thoroughly interested and found it most amusing to talk of those days. After this he rushed through his perfunctory questions to the others and came straight back to me, continuing his reminiscences, always talking as if I had lived in those days whereas in reality I had just read enough to draw him on. One evening he said to me, 'You will remember General Stewart', and I afterwards ascertained that this distinguished officer had died at a ripe age some thirty years before I was born. It was all a great success, so much so that one night while we were playing bridge, King Edward asked me what on earth I talked about to the old King, as he always seemed so interested. When I replied that we were talking about his early life, the King looked puzzled, but thought he had better leave it at that.

Prince John of Glücksburg, King Christian's youngest brother, was far easier to talk to, and was full of stories. He had a great admiration for King Leopold of the Belgians (the 'Uncle Leopold' of Queen Victoria), who had been such a factor in European politics. He said that King Leopold had given up corresponding with Queen Victoria after her marriage as the Prince Consort had resented his influence over her, but on the Prince Consort's death had begun again to be her adviser, only to find she didn't want his advice. Prince John had no words bad enough for the second King Leopold, who, he said, had done all he could to drag down the position of monarchs in the mud and who was famous for his low friends and his second-rate *demi mondaines*.

The Crown Prince seemed to me to be a nonentity, having none of the ability of his brother, King George of Greece. He seemed anxious for popularity and to gain this he was quite willing to don the cap of liberty and promise anything to the people. His son,[4] however, was much cleverer and a stronger character. The Crown Princess was one of the ugliest women I have ever seen, but re-

[4] Later King Christian X.

puted to be charming. As the French Minister said, *'Ce n'est pas permis d'être si laide'*.

Prince Waldemar had married a Bourbon, a daughter of the Duc de Chartres, and it was curious to see a vivacious French woman in these somewhat dreary surroundings. One evening I opened the wrong door and came on her dancing the can-can, whereupon I discreetly retired; but I often felt tempted to do the same. The Danish suite were all charming and entirely agreed that these evenings were a nightmare, but they said that the old King had gone through this programme for so many years that it was quite impossible to change anything now.

Queen Alexandra was so much pleased with this visit that it seemed churlish to complain, but all the same I was delighted when we returned to London.

There were similar visits to Denmark in 1905, 1906, and 1907, which followed much the same routine, but the tour of 1908 was extended to include Norway and Sweden. Some years earlier Prince Charles, the grandson of King Christian, had married King Edward's third daughter Princess Maud, and in 1905 Princess Margaret of Connaught married Gustavus Adolphus,[5] Duke of Skania, the eldest son of the Crown Prince of Sweden. In that same year Norway and Sweden separated and Prince Charles of Denmark became the new King Haakon of Norway. King Edward and Queen Alexandra, who were accompanied by Princess Victoria, therefore had excellent family reasons for extending their tour.

De Grey called it the Hennessey trip, as everyone came back with three stars. The suite consisted of Charlie Hardinge, who came as Minister in Attendance; Bobby Spencer, who was Lord Chamberlain to the King; Horace Farquhar, then a Lord-in-Waiting; Francis Laking, the King's physician; Stanley Clarke, as Equerry; and myself as Private Secretary. The Queen took Louisa, Countess of Antrim, the Hon. Charlotte Knollys, and George Howe, the Queen's Lord Chamberlain.

We had a rough crossing and it snowed most of the time, but

[5] Later Crown Prince when his father became King Gustav; now King of Sweden.

we found the train most comfortable. After dinner the King didn't play bridge but talked. Bobby Spencer was nervous at the King's chaff, but I told him it was a good omen. He should not have been, but distinctly was, a snob, and resented Hardinge going in front of him as a Minister, but as this could not be altered I begged him to accept the inevitable. We went across in a ferry which took the railway carriages in which we were and therefore we did not have to get out. The Crown Prince of Denmark and suite met us on arrival and travelled with us to Copenhagen, an extremely tiresome European custom, as it meant buttoning ourselves up into tight uniforms and making conversation for two hours.

At Copenhagen the King and Queen of Denmark with the Danish Royal Family in full strength met us at the railway station, and everybody shook hands with everybody else so that there was some confusion when the moment came to get into the carriages. I found it impossible to get through the mob of Princes and Princesses, more especially as they insisted on shaking hands with me as an old friend, having noted the fact that I had been there before when they scrutinized the list of the English suite. So I got blocked and found my carriage had left when I emerged. However, there was a spare carriage, and in this I was put. There was a huge crowd in the streets and the people having cheered themselves hoarse while the procession passed, were having a rest when still another carriage appeared with a single red-coated officer. They thought this overdone and took no notice of me.

I found the Amalienborg Palace very much improved as the new Danish King had made a great many alterations and the rooms were now very comfortable. I had a charming bedroom and sitting-room, but it took me eight minutes to reach King Edward's room, which was in another Palace adjoining the one I was in. When I did so I found him in the breeches and boots of his Danish uniform with a double-breasted English smoking-coat on. It appeared that the heavy luggage had been left behind and there was no alternative but to dine in the uniform which we had worn on arrival. Having let off steam about the luggage he became talkative and told me of amusing incidents that had occurred. He said I ought to draw caricatures of these, but as it entailed caricatures of the Royal Family, I refused, as I had made a rule never to caricature a member of the Royal Family as, however well meant, it would be misunderstood.

While all the rest of the suite ran about like rabbits asking what they should do about dinner, I found that my excellent servant, Shepherd, had put all I wanted for dinner in a dressing-case which he took with him, so that I was the only one who appeared in ordinary evening clothes with decorations at dinner.

There were the usual functions. One day the King inspected the Danish regiment of which he was Colonel, and had luncheon at the officers' mess. His health was proposed and in his reply he spoke briefly in Danish, which seemed to give great pleasure to the officers. Afterwards he told me he could not really speak Danish, but had learnt the speech by heart. These functions necessitated a constant change of clothes as some were in full dress and some in undress uniform, whilst others were in plain clothes. My servant, Shepherd, left everything out on the bed so that I could dash in and change quickly into any dress. At the banquet the King made a most impressive speech in English and the King of Denmark replied. At first, I thought he was speaking Danish as I could not understand a word, but later on I grasped the fact that he was speaking in English. He was a man who was most anxious to please everybody. At first he thought it would be popular to throw in his lot with the extreme Left, but finding that this antagonized the landowners, he veered round and ended by pleasing no one. He seemed to have little personality and few brains.

It was during this visit to Denmark that I was sent on the rather delicate mission of explaining to Countess Hagen, one of the great beauties of Copenhagen, that the reason the King would not be able to visit her was that he would not have time to pay other visits, especially one to Countess Raben, a rival beauty. I got through this fairly well and Countess Hagen said she thought the King was quite right.

Being more or less the pivot of this visit I had quite a tiring time, but Sotheby, my clerk, was invaluable, and was always prepared to sit up at night till any hour. When we left Copenhagen we had a farewell dinner and drove to the station where I subsided in my compartment for a rest, but unfortunately the Swedish officers joined our train at a quarter to one that night, and Stanley Clarke, whose job it was to receive them, asked me to do this for him, and of course I had to, although it meant dressing up in uniform. They were charming, and although I pressed them to have a drink in the restaurant car, they said they preferred to go to bed.

The next morning as we travelled on to Stockholm, I had to be up by eight as the Swedish officers wanted to give information and at the same time receive instructions before breakfast. We went through the programme and they gave details while I only told them what sort of thing Their Majesties liked. At breakfast I found Bobby Spencer, who remarked what strong people the Swedes must be as the breakfast consisted of slices of cold beef, bits of cold sausage, and cheese, none of which he had any stomach for at so early an hour; but these were only extras and he was given an excellent omelette.

We arrived at Stockholm at midday and drove in State carriages to the Palace. The staircase was lined with soldiers wearing the uniform and bear-skin of the old Guard of Napoleon, and we were told that it was Marshal Bernadotte who introduced these costumes when he became King of Sweden. At the top of the stair the soldiers wore the old Swedish Guards uniform with wigs, three-cornered hats, and yellow facings.

The Palace was beautifully furnished with all the art treasures of Europe which Bernadotte had collected. I found I was to stay with the Crown Prince and Crown Princess in an adjoining palace and there I was most comfortable, but again I was miles off the King's room. Even the invaluable Sotheby took an hour to find me.

After tea the first day I got a message that the King wished to see me at once. One of the Crown Princesses' pages, who spoke English perfectly, told me that the quickest way was to go by the servants' underground passage as this would be a short cut. I tried this and of course got hopelessly lost in the labyrinths of passages. After wandering about aimlessly for some time, I saw a housemaid, but as I knew no Swedish I was afraid she would be of no use to me. Luckily I knew the Swedish for King, and shouted at her 'Kongen von England'. She pointed to a spiral staircase in the wall, and up this I went. It was quite dark at the top and finding myself up against a door, I felt for the handle and opened it. To my surprise I found myself in the King's bedroom and there was the King seated at the dressing-table! He was much startled when I bounded into the room, apparently from nowhere. I apologized profusely and explained how I had got there, but he said he didn't even know there was a door in the wall, and when we looked it was so cleverly concealed in the tapestry that no sign of any entrance could be seen from inside the room.

In the evening we had a State banquet of 250 people. It was the largest banquet I had seen. I sat between two Swedish Ministers, who were particularly well-informed about European politics, and had quite an interesting dinner. At the end of dinner the two Kings made speeches and luckily I took down on the back of the menu notes of King Edward's speech. I merely did this to check the shorthand writer who I was told had been specially employed. After dinner I went to my room and found to my consternation that the man had got practically nothing. His notes were quite useless and it was clear he couldn't write shorthand. I was happily able to dictate the whole speech from my copious notes.

I had hardly finished this when I got a message that the King wished me to come at once and play bridge. I was to change from full dress to a blue undress serge coat. I hurried back, going the long way round so as to make certain of getting there, and found the two Kings and Stanley Clarke waiting for me. We started off down the corridor preceded by two footmen walking backwards and carrying candelabra with six candles in each. This may have been very impressive, but I could not help feeling sorry for the housemaids as the wax from the candles seemed to fly in every direction. Behind us came four old pages, presumably to see we didn't get lost. However, we hadn't far to go and we entered a truly lovely room with Gobelin tapestry on the walls and beautiful cabinets and statues, with a bridge table and small tables for our drinks. The two Kings cut together and lost the rubber. It was ordinary bridge in those days. The Swedish King played a hand in hearts and had the English King gone into no trumps they would have won the rubber as they made three tricks. So Sweden found fault with England, but King Edward flattened out his partner by replying that he could easily have won game and rubber had he played properly! We once or twice got rather mixed as to whether we meant the King of Sweden or the King of Clubs, and whether we were alluding to the King of Hearts or the King of England. The second rubber I played with the King of Sweden, who really played very well, but we lost the rubber.

The next morning I got up early so as to get through the work, but as I was having breakfast with the Crown Prince and Crown Princess I did not get anything to eat till 9.30. I was surprised to find quite an English breakfast, and the Crown Prince told me he had taken a great deal of trouble to have the eggs and bacon cooked as in England, but his wife always found fault with them. I feared I might have to adjudicate in a conjugal squabble and so changed the topic. After breakfast the Crown Princess showed me her rooms, which were charming. Then I went to the King, who was anxious that the orders and decorations should be given out that day. Bobby Spencer was to give orders to the biggest swells and was much fussed in consequence. He asked what he should do in the case of men who understood no English, and I wrote him a brief speech in French which he could recite. He rushed off to learn this by heart. However, thanks to the young Duc d'Otrante, who was attached to the King, I managed to get all the orders delivered in a short time.

We found Christiania [6] very different from Copenhagen and Stockholm and so socialistic that a King and Queen seemed out of place. The monarchy was quite new then, and had the Left been in power at the time instead of the Right, the Norwegians would certainly have had a republic. King Haakon was, however, playing his part very well and had secured the love and respect of the majority of the people. The Palace was large and very uncomfortable, but Queen Maud was busy having bathrooms put in and comfortable furniture. We had the usual banquet, which was very indifferently done, as the suite were new to the game and the staff

6 Now Oslo.

had never done a big dinner. One day we went for an expedition up in the mountains and as I was told it might be very cold, I wore a fur coat. This amused King Haakon, who asked me if I thought I was going to the North Pole. As a matter of fact it was quite hot, although there was snow, and I never wanted my coat. On the way back the whole party walked down for half an hour and were much annoyed by an army of photographers who kept snapping them. The King got so cross that he told me to clear them away, and I asked the ubiquitous Mr. Quinn [7] of Scotland Yard to deal with them. It was, however, rather confusing to learn the next day that the King and Queen had bought all the photographs that had been sent them by these photographers.

One night King Haakon told me of his difficulties in face of the republican leanings of the opposition and how careful in consequence he had to be in all he did and said. He intended, he said, to go as much as possible among the people and thought it would be popular if, instead of going in a motor car, he and Queen Maud were to use the tramways.

I told him frankly that I thought this would be a great mistake as familiarity bred contempt. As a naval officer he would know that the captain of a ship never had his meals with the other officers but remained quite aloof. This was, of course, to stop any familiarity with them. I told him that he must get up on a pedestal and remain there. He could then step off occasionally and no harm would be done. The people didn't want a King with whom they could hob-nob but something nebulous like the Delphic oracle. The Monarchy was really the creation of each individual's brain. Every man liked to think what he would do, if he was King. People invested the Monarch with every conceivable virtue and talent. They were bound therefore to be disappointed if they saw him going about like an ordinary man in the street. Whether he took my advice or not I never knew, but I do not recall that he ever tried a tram!

We had barely arrived back in England from the Scandinavian tour when the King and Queen decided to pay a visit to the Em-

---

[7] Later Sir Patrick Quinn. Superintendent of the Special Branch from 1903 until his retirement in 1918.

peror and Empress of Russia at Reval.[8] This visit which took place in June 1908 had entailed a great deal of diplomatic correspondence, and even when we started many details had not definitely been decided. The King took Admiral Sir John Fisher; General Sir John French[9]; Sir Arthur Nicolson,[10] the British Ambassador at St. Petersburg; Charlie Hardinge; Lord Hamilton of Dalzell,[11] Lord-in-Waiting; Sir Archibald Edmonstone, Groom-in-Waiting; Seymour Fortescue, Equerry; and myself as Private Secretary. Hardinge, anticipating much cyphering, had been given permission to bring with him his private secretary, Lord Errington. The Queen took Louisa Countess of Antrim, the Hon. Charlotte Knollys, and General Brocklehurst.

We had a most unpleasant journey. It was fine when we started, but when we got to the North Sea it began to blow. The yacht had a most uncomfortable motion when it pitched, probably because it had been badly designed from the start. I found it bitterly cold and went to my cabin for a greatcoat and found everything on the floor. I determined to remain on deck and then I came across the Queen, who was a first-rate sailor, and didn't seem to mind the rough sea at all, except for the discomfort of everything falling about. I determined to face tea, which I thought might help. I went to the dining-saloon, not feeling very strong. The Queen came in and sat down as if everything was as usual. She had Charlie Hardinge next to her, when suddenly the yacht gave a bad lurch and she was thrown, chair and all, into the corner, while the teapot and kettle came flying after her and only just missed her. All the tea things were smashed and there was a real mess, tea-cake, biscuits, bread and butter, sugar, butter, etc., all collected in a heap. Charlie Hardinge persuaded her to have tea brought to her elsewhere, and she retired still laughing as if it was a good joke.

We arrived at the Kiel Canal at night and the King decided to land for a moment to see Prince Henry of Prussia. We all

[8] Now Tallinn.
[9] Later Field-Marshal; 1st Earl of Ypres. Chief of the Imperial General Staff, 1911–4; Commander-in-Chief of Expeditionary Force in France, 1914–5.
[10] Later 1st Lord Carnock. Permanent Under-Secretary for Foreign Affairs, 1910–16.
[11] 2nd Lord.

trooped off behind the King and as I emerged from the warm yacht into the cold, I was conscious of the presence of troops on the quay. As my eyes got accustomed to the darkness I became aware that there were masses and masses of men drawn up. Prince Henry led the King through a labyrinth of troops and it was a most impressive sight. The King then returned on board bringing Prince Henry with him.

The next day we passed through the canal, being escorted by cavalry on each bank. We seemed to be hardly moving, but the mounted men had to trot out to keep with us. They were relieved half-way, which must have pleased them, as continually trotting for an hour was no doubt tiring.

As we neared Reval there was a fog and we went very slowly and the cruisers and torpedo-destroyers were given orders to keep away from the yacht as far as possible. On arrival at Reval we found the two Russian Royal yachts and a small fleet anchored there.

It was properly the duty of our King to pay the first visit to the Czar, but the Czar, being the nephew, insisted on coming on board the *Victoria & Albert* first. The King gave orders that the ladder and the steam launch were to be got ready as soon as we anchored, but of course we had no chance as the Czar's boat put off and was almost alongside before we could lower the ladder. He came on board and greeted his uncle and aunt most affectionately. After he returned to the *Polar Star* the King returned the visit and we all accompanied him. The Russian yacht was most beautifully fitted up, but there were elaborate military arrangements on board. There was a guard of honour of Russian sailors, and the King, who knew the custom, advanced to them and said in Russian, 'Good morning, my children', and the whole of the Russian sailors replied 'God save the King', also in Russian. We were then given some kirsch, which tasted like boot varnish, and caviare sandwiches. After luncheon we returned on board the Royal yacht. I saw the head of our police who asked me what steps he ought to take to ensure the safety of Their Majesties. I told him to get into a boat and go and see the head of the Russian police, whose name was Azeff and who afterwards became a famous *agent pro-*

vocateur. This he did and they recommended that an officer should be on every gangway on the yacht so as to see who came on board, as uniform was no criterion. It was absolutely necessary that every individual should be scrutinized and passed before allowing him on board the yacht. Instructions were accordingly given by Colin Keppel. In the evening we dined on board the *Polar Star.* It was rather weird, being broad daylight, as the sun apparently does not set till half-past eleven at night, and there was a beautiful red sky. The King as usual made a most impressive speech proposing the health of the Emperor, and this time I did not trust to anybody else to take down the speech, but did it myself. Afterwards we stood about on the deck while the band played. I talked to several Russians and was introduced to Stolypin,[12] a grave, splendid-looking man with a long grey beard. They told me that although the Nihilists had pledged themselves to kill him, he went about as if nothing had happened. It was only two years ago that his daughter was blown up, but he said that if he lived in fear of his life, life would not be worth living. He asked me a good deal about English politics and appeared to be very well up in all that was going on in England.

We were forbidden to go on shore, which was very tiresome, as I should very much have liked to see the town of Reval, which looked most picturesque. That evening the Emperor and Empress dined on board with a large suite. There were so many that a certain number had to dine in the officers' room and I was put in charge of this dinner. After dinner the two monarchs and their suites stood on deck while a steamer full of some choral society came and sang weird Russian songs. I had asked the head of our police whether this was quite safe, since the Emperor had given them permission to come within a few yards of the yacht, and Mr. Quinn went off to consult the head of the Russian police, who told him that there was no danger at all. He had given orders that all the singers were to be stripped and searched before they were allowed to come on board the steamer.

[12] Minister-President of Russia, 1906–11. His confidence in his immunity from attack was misplaced; in 1911 he was shot in a theatre at Kiev, before the eyes of the Imperial family, and died shortly afterwards.

When Mr. Quinn came and told me this I felt there might be a row in England and questions might be asked in the House about it. The greater part of the singers were ladies, and I wondered what would be said if, when the Russian Emperor came to England and some ladies' choral society asked leave to serenade him, our police insisted on stripping them and searching them. I therefore told Mr. Quinn to go back to the head of the Russian police and say that although I hoped every possible precaution would be taken, I felt this was rather too strong a measure. Mr. Quinn came to me and reported later on in the evening that the Russian police had agreed to give up this stringent measure. The Emperor and Empress said good-bye to the King and we all shook hands warmly with the Russian suite, and the next morning we left for England.

CHAPTER XV

*The King's leisure — Racing — Shooting — A private trip
to Ireland — Brighton — Chatsworth — A Mediterranean
cruise — The King in Paris — The Empress Eugénie —
Athens — President Fallières — The Russian and Japanese
Ambassadors*

THE KING'S RESTLESSNESS, which was so remarkable in a man of
sixty and over, rarely resulted in his breaking a single engagement, whether official or private, and the punctuality and regularity of his yearly programme is perhaps the most striking tribute
to that love of order and sense of decorum which was one of his
most marked characteristics. It was the same with sport as with
official functions. With great regularity he attended the great race
meetings in England, the Derby and the Oaks at Epsom early in
June, and the Ascot meeting a fortnight later, being first and fore-
most on the yearly programme.

As Prince of Wales he had won his first Derby in 1896 and his
second in 1900, and always he hoped to win it again. He rarely had
fewer than a dozen horses in training, and on occasion had over
twenty. But his luck or judgement, which had given him such a
remarkable succession of racing victories in his last years as
Prince of Wales, seemed to desert him when he came to the
throne, and from 1901 to 1906 he scarcely won a race. But from
1907 onwards, when he had a record number of horses in training,
there was a crescendo of successes until 1909, when a dozen sparkling victories included the Derby for the third time.

Lord Marcus Beresford was the manager of the King's racing
stable and thoroughbred stud, while Mr. Marsh was the trainer.
They proved a happy combination and the King's racing can have
cost him nothing: in fact after he ascended the throne, it must

have been a very paying proposition to him, for in addition to the races he won he had two stallions, Diamond Jubilee and Persimmon, that brought him in over £30,000 a year.

At most race meetings the King attended as an ordinary sightseer, but Ascot was more formal. During Ascot week it was the custom for the King and Queen on two days to drive to the races in State with six landaus each drawn by four horses with postilions. On the remaining two days the King went privately with the men of the party in carriages driven from the box. But on one occasion the King decided that he would have a wagonette to take him to the races on one of the days he went privately. Queen Victoria had latterly driven about Windsor and Osborne in a carriage with four horses driven from the box, by a very good coachman named Burnham, who looked like the pictures of Jorrocks. Burnham, who had not been wanted since Queen Victoria's death, was delighted to be placed in charge of the wagonette. Stupidly he had got brand new reins for the occasion, and, determined to look smart, he wore white kid gloves. The result was that when he got on the grass rides he was utterly unable to hold the horses, the new reins were cutting into his hands, and his arms gave. He did the only thing possible and that was to pull up. I was in the second wagonette with only a pair of horses and when we suddenly pulled up I bounded out to see what had happened. Burnham in an exhausted condition told me of all his misfortunes and I found that they had decided to take out the leaders and go on with the wheelers only. I explained to the King that Burnham was not in a fit state to go on driving even with only two horses and I suggested that the Duke of Portland [1] should drive instead. Everyone was much amused at my suggestion, but it was finally adopted and Portland got up on the box and drove off with Burnham alongside of him. I thought this was quite obviously the right place for the Master of the Horse.

During all King Edward's reign I rode to Ascot when he went in state, and wore a tall hat, dark blue overalls, and a frock-coat. All the postilions were in old-fashioned liveries and the outriders wore scarlet coats. There was something rather sombre about the

[1] William Cavendish-Bentinck, 6th Duke of Portland.

two Equerries in frock-coats who rode on each side of the carriage, and Rosebery always said they entirely spoilt what otherwise was a pretty piece of pageantry. It was a long and tedious ride of six and a half miles, and we went at a jog-trot all the way. In King George's reign this was all altered and the whole party from Windsor drove in motors to the end of the Park, where they got into the carriages, and the Equerries had only a short ride. After the war, the Equerries were eliminated from the procession.

On one occasion at Ascot it was rather a cold rainy day and King Edward decided to return early to the Castle. The carriages and horses came round after the four o'clock race, but he changed his mind and stayed for the last race. The result was that the horses were kept standing about for over an hour. I was riding a mare that was a beautiful animal to look at, but she had an uncertain temper and had been unreliable on occasions. In her youth she had a bad reputation but had settled down as she grew older. The procession started at a slow walk and she behaved perfectly, but when we got on the grass and the crowd cheered and waved, she suddenly began to buck. I was quite unprepared and it was only by chance that I was not bucked off. A tall hat and frock-coat, however dignified they may look, are obviously unsuited for riding difficult horses, but there I was with the hat at the back of my head and the tails of my frock-coat flying in the wind, nearly unseated and quite unable to control the animal who bucked away until she was level with the leading pair of horses in the carriage. By then, however, I had settled down and had no difficulty in turning her round and bringing her alongside of the carriage, where she became perfectly quiet. Queen Alexandra said something which I did not catch, but Hawkins, the sergeant footman, who was seated behind in the rumble of the carriage, explained: ' 'Er Majesty says you must have got a pin in your saddle, sir'.

Whilst racing was thus the King's favourite outdoor sport, shooting was by no means a poor second. There were four weeks' shooting at Sandringham every year, the principal two coinciding with the King's and the Queen's birthdays on November 9th and December 1st, and always a week or two's shooting at Balmoral in October. At Balmoral the King revived the Gillies' Ball, which had not been given for some years, and a sprinkling of neighbours came. The Prince of Wales brought a party from Abergeldie Castle. The Neumanns brought Wilfred Ashley and his wife, Mrs. George West,[2] George and Alice Keppel, and Cecil Lowther.[3] The Fifes came over from Mar and the Mackenzies from Brackey. Seymour Fortescue and I walked in backwards in front of the King, and the band played the National Anthem. Then there was a silence and at a signal from the King the bagpipes struck up and in marched the Balmoral Highlanders armed with old-fashioned pikes. They made a very striking picture and after marching round the ballroom, drew up in front of the King and saluted. Then the ball began, and about one o'clock the guests followed the King out and had supper. The ball went on, however, till the small hours of the morning.

On October 20, 1903, the King went to Wynyard to stay with the Londonderrys,[4] and the party consisted of the Duke and Duchess of Devonshire, Walter [5] and Lady Doreen Long, the Shaftesburys,[6] Hedworth Williamson, the Ilchesters,[7] George and Alice Keppel, Count Mensdorff, Lord [8] and Lady Crewe, Sir George [9] and Lady Murray, Lord Kintore,[10] Seymour Fortescue, and myself. There were always big rabbit shoots there, and the first day I shot we got 3,000. The Duke of Devonshire got bored with such tame shooting and lit a cigarette, which annoyed Londonderry very much.

The King once told me he always wished he had learnt to smoke a pipe as it was by far the most convenient form of smoking out shooting, especially in a high wind. I therefore determined to give him one to try and took an enormous amount of trouble

[2] Mrs. Cornwallis-West.
[3] Major-General Sir Cecil Lowther.
[4] Charles Vane-Tempest-Stewart, 6th Marquess of Londonderry.
[5] Later 1st Viscount Long of Wraxall.
[6] 9th Earl of Shaftesbury.
[7] 5th Earl of Ilchester.
[8] Robert Crewe-Milnes, 1st Marquess of Crewe. Lord President of the Council, Lord Privy Seal, Colonial Secretary and Secretary for India in successive Liberal Governments. Ambassador in Paris, 1922–8.
[9] Permanent Secretary to Treasury, 1903–11.
[10] Sir Algernon Keith-Falconer, 10th Earl of Kintore.

to get one with a top fitted. I bought some tobacco and a round silver tobacco-holder and all these I shyly presented to His Majesty. One day after luncheon the King produced his new toys and said that he was going to try a pipe for the first time, but he was so long putting the metal top on when he had lit the pipe that it always went out. He had three tries and the more he hurried the more clumsy he became. After the third try proved a failure, he produced a cigar and said 'This is, after all, far simpler', and explained that it was the fault of the tobacco. Personally I never think a cigar-smoker ever cares about a pipe.

On another occasion I gave him a stylographic pen, and although he expressed his gratitude for such a wonderful invention, he always treated it like a conjuring trick. He used it for a short time simply to please me, but really hated it. Then mercifully he lost it and was terrified lest I should give him another, but of course I had seen what a failure it was and never alluded to it again.

The King after dinner held a Council, and it seemed that the last Sovereign to hold a Council outside a Royal palace was Charles II. There was, however, some business which could not wait, and so there was no alternative. Almeric Fitzroy,[11] the Clerk of the Council, came down with the necessary paraphernalia, but seemed rather shocked at the irregularity of the proceedings. There were plenty of Privy Councillors in the house, and so there was no difficulty, but the question arose whether the documents which the King signed in Council should be stated 'given in at Our Court at Wynyard'. Everyone was engaged in the library after the Council looking out historical parallels, but the King decided that the words 'Our Court at Wynyard' should on this occasion be used, but as it might give rise to difficulties later on, the expression 'Our Court at St. James's' should invariably be used in future no matter where the Council might be.

In December I went to Sandringham for the Queen's birthday. On occasions of this sort the guests had to do something or say they were doing something, as the King liked to think all his guests were being amused. It was quite enough to say, 'I am

[11] Later Sir Almeric Fitzroy. Clerk of the Privy Council, 1898–1923.

going to watch the golf'; that passed, but unless some answer was given the King thought out some amusement which really bored the guest stiff.

Always when the King went out partridge-driving it was also the duty of the Equerry to ask each guest at the end of the drive how many birds they had got. On one occasion when the Equerry-in-Waiting was ill I had to perform the duty of informing guests where the King had placed them. I told Lord Rosebery that he had drawn a number between De Grey and Harry Chaplin, and he said he knew what would happen, and that was that De Grey would shoot all his birds and Harry Chaplin would pick them all up. Only birds that had actually been picked up counted. This may have been very amusing for the good shots, but it seemed to hold up the bad shots to ridicule when the totals were read out at luncheon.

Luncheon out shooting was in a large tent and everybody staying in the house had to come no matter what they might have been doing during the morning. Carriages were ordered and we all had to have luncheon in a damp tent. Tea was a full-dress meal with all the women in tea-gowns and the men in short black jackets and black ties. Gottlieb's band played like a bee in a bottle for an hour. Then everyone played games, but those who knew the routine tip-toed off to the library and read or talked. Dinner was magnificent with all the women in tiaras, etc., and all the men with ribands and decorations. Bridge had just become the fashion and the King walked round to see that everyone was engaged. The Queen went to bed soon after midnight and the King between one and one-thirty. I was told that in the old days of baccarat he used to sit up till four or five in the morning and all the men of the party had to remain up whether they were playing or not. The usual practice for those who didn't play was to go to sleep in the billiard-room with a footman specially warned to wake them when the baccarat was over.

When he came to the throne he was always very particular about members of the Household sitting up. No lady could retire before Queen Alexandra went to bed and no man could go to bed before he himself went. Usually Queen Alexandra retired about midnight, and one night early in his reign he walked through the drawing-rooms after she had gone to make sure no man had also left. He counted heads and found there was one short but could not remember who was in waiting. He rang for a page and told him that there should be so many gentlemen in the drawing-rooms but there appeared to be one short: the page was to find out who it was and go and fetch him back. It turned out to be General Sir Dighton Probyn, aged seventy-five, who had not felt well and had gone to bed. The page, however, woke him up and told him the King wanted him. King Edward, who had imagined it was one of the younger guests, was very much amused at this, but Sir Dighton was not.

In February 1904 the King returned to Windsor for the wedding of Prince Algy of Teck [12] and Princess Alice of Albany. His energy was marvellous but at times it seemed to take the form of restlessness. He was never able to stay long in one place, and as for a quiet time with his family it was simply out of the question. The ordinary family life bored him and even when he was at Windsor, Sandringham, or Balmoral he asked as many people as these places would hold. To me, who had become accustomed to very quiet times with practically no guests, it was distinctly amusing, especially as he had the flair of finding interesting and amusing people.

This marriage gave him scope for his powers of organization and everything went without a hitch, but the details were arranged by Clarendon, the Lord Chamberlain, and old Spencer Ponsonby-Fane. A mass of the Royal Family were asked, including the Queen Dowager of the Netherlands and the Queen of the Netherlands. But while all went well within the Castle, the military part outside went wrong: nothing very bad, but enough to upset the King. It happened that Lieutenant-Colonel Bouverie, an amusing, charming, happy-go-lucky soldier of the old type, was commanding a battalion of Coldstream at the time, and having made arrangements to go away and hunt he saw no reason to cancel them. As a matter of fact the military arrangements were very simple

[12] Later Earl of Athlone, after relinquishing German titles. Princess Alice was the only daughter of the Duke of Albany, 4th son of Queen Victoria.

and could have been carried out equally well and probably better by Major Granville-Smith, the Second-in-Command, but unlucky mistakes occurred. In the first place the Officer Commanding the Castle Guard had never been told that King Edward intended to go down to the station to meet the two Queens, but even if his Commanding Officer had forgotten to warn him, he should in any case have gone to the Equerry-in-Waiting and asked for orders. Consequently when the King drove down the hill escorted by the Household Cavalry, the Guard did not turn out. This was not a very serious thing and might possibly have been overlooked had not a second mistake occurred immediately after. The guard of honour was ordered to be at the south-western station, was late, and only reached the station a few minutes before the train arrived. The King exploded with rage at what he called the slipshod arrangements and sent for the Field Officer in Brigade waiting, who should have been Colonel Bouverie. The appearance of Major Granville-Smith with the intimation that Colonel Bouverie was away only added fuel to the fire, but happily the King's wrath was cut short by the arrival of the two Queens. When all the sins of poor Bouverie were embodied in a letter to the General, they looked really formidable and eventually an order was issued ordering the Officers Commanding the Regiment of Household Cavalry and Battalion of Guards always to be on duty when Their Majesties were in residence at Windsor.

At another wedding, a few years later, the necessity for being impeccably dressed was vividly impressed on me. The King was attending, a thing he rarely did, for like most men he was not thrilled by weddings, and was taking with him the Groom-in-Waiting, Sidney Greville, and the Equerry, John Ward. Some ten minutes before the time to start for the wedding he sent for Sidney Greville to ask him to make enquiries about some trifling matter, but hardly had he begun on the subject when he stopped and said, more in sorrow than in anger, 'My dear fellow, where is your white waistcoat? Is it possible you are thinking of going to a *wedding* in a black waistcoat?' Sidney confessed that in the hurry of the moment the importance of the colour of his waistcoat had escaped him. 'You have time to change, if you are quick', said the King. So away Sidney rushed, but as he ran it occurred to him that possibly Johnny Ward might have a spare one, in which case it would obviate the necessity of having to return to his house. So he dashed into Johnny's room, shouting 'Have you two white waistcoats?' Johnny, fearing a sell, replied guardedly 'Why?' Then Sidney explained, and Johnny confessed that it had never occurred to him to wear a white waistcoat. Every drawer in the room was ransacked, and finally two waistcoats were produced, one white, which Johnny insisted on wearing himself so that he might get full marks, and the other of a light-green hue, which seemed the right note for a middle-aged man at a wedding.

So they waited at the garden entrance for the King. His Majesty came down and nodded approval to Sidney, but as he went out to get into the motor, he said to him, 'Johnny Ward knows how to dress; he would never make a mistake like you'.

In October 1906 the King went from Balmoral to stay with the Colebrookes [13] at Abingdon. The house was quite new, the old one having been burnt down some years previously, and everything was beautifully done, the cooking being especially good. I thought at the time that Lady Colebrooke was the genius of the establishment, but I found later that it was entirely Tommy. We went out grouse-shooting every day and the last day M. Poklewski-Koziell, the first Secretary of the Russian Embassy, joined the party. No one knew whether he was safe or not, and as grouse-driving is a particularly dangerous type of shooting, the King was consulted. He at once hit upon a solution and suggested that Poklewski should be placed on the right of the line and I should go next to him to see whether he was safe. I didn't care much about this as, if he was not a safe shot, I should only find this out by being peppered. It reminded me of a Shah of Persia who on a visit to England was shown the gallows, which interested him very much. He asked whether he could see it in use, but the Governor of the gaol said that unfortunately they had no one who was to be hanged. 'That is all right. Take one of my suite!' exclaimed the Shah.

Poklewski, however, turned out to be quite a good shot and not

[13] Edward, 1st Lord Colebrooke. Lord-in-Waiting, 1906-11; later Permanent Lord-in-Waiting to King George V.

the least dangerous. I must say that Tommy Colebrooke, who directed the shoot and therefore did not himself shoot, came with me in my butt to protect me if necessary.

In October 1906 I went with the King to stay at Londesborough, and we had quite an amusing party. There was Mensdorff, the George Keppels, Lady Irene Denison, Harry Chaplin and his daughter, Mrs. Rupert Beckett, Westmorland,[14] and Stanley Clarke (Equerry). Berrand Dawson[15] and Willy (Villiers) Walsh came to stay for one night.

Lady Londesborough was like the White Queen in *Through the Looking Glass* but was very good company. Londesborough[16] was an oddity, but had a great sense of humour. He was heard out shooting to say, 'Oh God, You know how much I like shooting. Why won't You allow me to hit these partridges?' On another occasion in London, when he lived at Hanover Lodge in Regent's Park, he gave a ball and had all the garden lighted with thousands of fairy lights, which in those days were either oil lamps or candles. After dinner he came out and found there had been a thunderstorm; all the lights had gone out and the garden was reduced to a quagmire. He was heard soliloquizing and muttering 'Oh God, how like You!'

In December the King went to stay at Crichel with the Alingtons.[17] The party consisted of Mensdorff, Lady Norreys, Lord and Lady Elcho, Lady Cadogan, Lady E. Sturt, Lord and Lady Crewe, Lady Edith Villiers, Charlie Hardinge, Cassel,[18] Villiers, Lionel Rothschild,[19] Seymour Fortescue, Surgeon Bankart[20], and myself. The house was most comfortable and the evenings amusing, while the shooting was first-rate. One day King Edward sent to say he would not come out till twelve and Humphrey Alington

[14] Anthony Fane, 13th Earl of Westmorland, brother of Lady Londesborough. Later A.D.C. to King George V.
[15] Later Lord Dawson of Penn, Physician-in-Ordinary to the King.
[16] William Denison, 2nd Earl of Londesborough.
[17] Humphrey Sturt, 2nd Lord Alington.
[18] Sir Ernest Cassel.
[19] Later 2nd Lord Rothschild.
[20] Later Surgeon Rear-Admiral Sir Arthur Bankart; Hon. Physician to King Edward.

thought it necessary to stay indoors till then. We, however, all went shooting at 10.30, and Charlie Hardinge was in charge of everything. At a big stand the head keeper came to him and said that he had not put anyone in the place destined for the King (it was marked with a red label on a stick whilst the other places had white ones). As there seemed no prospect of the King coming out in time for this stand, Charlie Hardinge told me to go there and I had a great shoot, birds coming over me from every direction as the beaters were under the impression that the King was there.

In April 1907 the King and Queen paid a private visit to the Dudleys [21] in Ireland, and as far as this kind of visit can be successful, this one was on the whole a success. We spent a week at Viceregal Lodge and there were luncheon and dinner parties. The attitude of the people in the streets was curious as they seemed most loyal but dissociated the King and Queen entirely from the Government. The King, however, was able to make the acquaintance of and talk to a great many interesting persons, but whether this was much use as far as the people were concerned is doubtful.

One day the King reviewed the troops in Phoenix Park, and as he rode, the Queen had to go in a carriage with an escort. I can't remember why, but I had to make the arrangements for the review and I wrote a note to the Queen giving particulars, asking what time she would wish to start and whom she would take with her in her carriage. Receiving no answer of any description, I ordered escort and carriage at a suitable time and told everyone the carriage they were to drive in. I thought it best to issue orders that could be altered than to give none. Everything went perfectly, but the Queen afterwards said to Miss Knollys, 'How did he know what time to start and whom I wished to drive with me?'

Lady Dudley herself was ill and confined to her room and I only saw her once, when we had an interesting conversation on the future of Ireland. She seemed the cleverer of the two and had great imagination, but many of her ideas were unpractical. Later we went to stay with the Duke of Devonshire at Lismore Castle, a medieval-looking place with a courtyard and banqueting hall, but the weather was very bad and almost every day we had torrents

[21] William Ward, 2nd Earl of Dudley. Lord-Lieutenant of Ireland, 1902–6.

of rain. The Duke as a host amused me, as he never took the slightest trouble with his guests and left them severely alone. He never by chance said 'Thank you' to any servant who helped him, and generally ignored anyone who might prove tiresome. At the same time he was one of the most delightful of men to talk to and could, when he chose, be the best of company.

The agent was wonderful and mapped out the programme every day, never making a mistake. King Edward therefore decided to give him the M.V.O. At that time the Victorian Order was comparatively new, and like all new Orders had come in for a certain amount of ridicule in the Press, and amusing stories invented by witty stockbrokers. When I therefore asked the Duke of Devonshire whether he approved of his agent being decorated, he replied in a sleepy way, 'Is that what they call the M.V.O.? If it is I'm sure he wouldn't like to have that.' I convinced him, however, that unless there was some political reason that would make it difficult for the agent to accept an Order from the King, I was quite sure that it would give the greatest pleasure. The Duke gave way, saying he didn't understand anything about Orders, and the agent was quite delighted with the M.V.O.

After the shooting, or indeed after any day's activity, the King loved a game of bridge. Though he played only moderately well, he could criticize his partner's mistakes in no uncertain fashion, and a further disadvantage, from the point of view of the suite, was that one never knew whether one would suddenly be called upon to make up a four or have to wait about as an unwanted fifth or sixth.

One night the King dined at Egypt House with Consuelo, Duchess of Manchester,[22] where we found several good bridge players, including Poklewski-Koziell, who was reputed to be one of the best players in Europe, Mrs. George Keppel, Miss Emily Yznaga and others. The Duchess explained to me after dinner that as two people had thrown her over, there were only two rubbers of bridge and therefore I would have to be left out with her sister Emily Yznaga, but there would be no one in the drawing-room and we

[22] Widow of 8th Duke. Daughter of Antonio Yznaga de Valle, of Ravenswood, Louisiana.

could sit there and talk. It was then a quarter to ten and I knew that the steam pinnace had not been ordered till one. The prospect of talking for three hours and a quarter filled me with dismay, especially with someone I only knew slightly, although she had a reputation of being very good company. There was something so coldblooded in asking anyone to come and talk for three and a quarter hours with no possibility of escape, and I therefore said to her that as we had to sit for so long I proposed we should each choose a book and read. She cordially agreed with me and we went round the drawing-room and selected books that might interest us. We sat down in two armchairs and we never stopped talking till one. It just made all the difference having something to fall back upon, but as a matter of fact we never even opened our books.

The King was also a great theatre-goer, but I remember one occasion when he suspected that my love for the legitimate stage was not quite as strong as I tried to make out.

One evening I was working in my room when Seymour Fortescue dashed in and said he wanted me to do something for him. It was very urgent. I naturally replied that I was ready to do anything he wanted.

He then explained that he had been playing poker at the Atlantic Club and had lost £4,000. As his finances were already in a precarious condition, it was absolutely essential that he should return to the Club and win this money back, but he had to go to the play with King Edward and Queen Alexandra and they were dining at 7.30. I told him that of course I should be delighted to go in his place, but he said it was not quite so easy as that. What he wanted me to do was to go to King Edward and ask whether I might go instead of him as I was anxious to see the play!

This was a more delicate matter, but as time pressed and Seymour Fortescue was in such a dilemma, I agreed to carry out his wishes. So I seized some papers just to give me some excuse for blowing in on the King, raced upstairs, and told the page to ask if I could see His Majesty for a few minutes.

The answer was 'Certainly', and so I went in and showed him some not very important letters which could very well have stood over till the next day. I then said casually, 'I wonder whether Your Majesty would kindly allow me to go to the play tonight instead of Seymour as I am very keen to see this play and I may not have another opportunity. Seymour has most kindly agreed to this.' 'Eh, what?' said the King, who was preparing to settle down to his correspondence. I repeated my request and he said, 'Certainly, certainly'.

Down I went and reported to Seymour that all had gone well and that the King could have no idea of the real reason.

So I dined and went to the play with Their Majesties and Lady Gosford. I got back about 11.30, but remained up in hopes that Seymour would be back, as he had promised that as soon as he had got his money back he would retire from the Club. About 1 a.m. he appeared and told me the joyful news that he had won all the money back and incidentally about £400 to spare. So all was well. When I went to see the King and do the ordinary routine work in the official boxes the next morning, he looked up from the paper he was reading and said quietly, 'Did Seymour get home last night?' I began to stammer and stutter as I was quite unprepared for this, when he continued, 'You see, you don't usually come to me at the last moment and ask if you may go to the play. So it was palpable that Seymour wanted to go somewhere, and as the only thing he could want to do so urgently at night was to gamble, I guessed it was because he had lost money and wanted to get home.' I told him his inference was correct, and he asked for particulars.

When I came downstairs and told Seymour about this he was at first very much put out, but finally roared with laughter. Later he told the King all his adventures.

In September 1907 the King went down to stay with the Sassoons at Brighton. He liked Brighton, finding that the air suited him very well. But at that time of the year Brighton was crowded, and the many visitors having little better to do than stand and stare, eagerly crowded round the Sassoons' residence and threatened to become a nuisance. But the Mayor was equal to the occasion for he caused all the seats and railings in the vicinity to be painted, with the result that nobody could sit down or lean up against the railings outside the house.

Sassoon's house was so small that Holford and I had to live at an hotel, though we had all our meals at Sassoon's. One evening we played bridge till 12.30, and when we tried to get back into our hotel we found it locked up. We rang every bell we could see, but no one came. George Holford had a cold, which made things rather worse, and I foresaw we should be left standing there all night with Holford rapidly developing pneumonia or bronchitis. I went round the hotel and surveyed the windows. I found that with little difficulty I could climb on to one window. I therefore got on George Holford's shoulders and clambered up on the window-sill, and by steadily pushing for a minute or two I opened the window, which to my surprise was not locked. I then jumped into a room, which proved to be the office of the hotel. Unfortunately the door leading out of the office into the hall was locked, so that I was no better off than I was before. Finally I took a run at the door and managed to smash it and its frame out of the surrounding lath and plaster and it fell with a resounding crash into the hall. The noise was terrific, and yet nobody woke up in the hotel. I then went round to the front and let Holford in. Our next task was to find the keys of our rooms. All the hotel keys were hung up on nails, unnumbered, and I thought it quicker to take all the keys with us so that we might try each in turn. I think it was something like thirty-six keys I took up, and as good luck would have it, about the third key we tried fitted the lock, so we were able to go to bed. The next day the landlady of the hotel apologized profusely and wished to send away four servants, but we begged her to overlook it this time, and she let them off with a wigging.

George Holford was quite the most unbusiness-like man I have ever known, and had he not been a shrewd and in some ways a distinctly clever man he must have come to grief. One day I was talking to him and happened to notice piles of unopened letters on his writing-table. He explained that these were all his private letters which he never opened: he sent them as they were to Lindsay, his private secretary. I suggested that he might at least look through them to make certain that there were no letters connected with the King among them. The whole subject seemed to bore him, but he consented to my going through them and of course I found several addressed to him as Equerry-in-Waiting. He suggested my dealing with them, and on opening them I found that they were merely acknowledgements, but there was one from the Lord Provost of Edinburgh calling attention to the fact that he had never received any answer to his communication of the previous week. George was horrified and said that he remembered showing the King a letter from the Lord Provost and that His Majesty had said 'No', but what it was about he could not remember. He begged me to have an answer typed which he could sign, but I pointed out that without knowing what the Lord Provost had asked it was by no means easy to draft a letter. I could hardly wire 'The King says No'. However, he insisted on a letter being written as he said he would otherwise get into trouble. So I dictated a non-committal letter to my shorthand clerk, merely expressing the King's regret at not being able to comply with the request contained in the first letter. Of course this letter was published, and it turned out that the Lord Provost had asked the King to hold a review of the Territorials. Francis Knollys found fault with George, first for dealing with a matter of this kind, and secondly, for writing such a curt refusal and giving no reason, but otherwise there was no harm done.

In January 1907 the King and Queen went to stay with the Duke and Duchess of Devonshire at Chatsworth where an enormous party had been invited to meet them. Everything was managed in a most princely way, and the dinners were a wonderful sight. All the women wore tiaras and jewels, while the men wore Orders and decorations. While everything was beautifully managed, anything that was left to the Duke to decide was invariably forgotten. For instance, with so large a party it was impossible for all the men to shoot, and yet the Duke never selected the guns till very late at night, and so the list was only made known the next morning. Lord Rosebery who was staying there once came down to breakfast in shooting clothes when he happened to meet his valet who said, 'You had better take those clothes off, my lord, as you are not on the shooting list'. Rosebery was furious, and immediately left for London. No one also could discover the principle on which the guns were chosen, but of course there was no principle. If the Duke happened to be sleepy he simply said the same guns as before, so that men who had been left out the first day and imagined they would have their turn, found themselves again omitted on the second day.

One night we had theatricals. Lady Maud Warrender sang, but she seemed too big for the tiny stage and certainly her voice was too powerful for the room. Princess Daisy of Pless [23] sang some songs and looked lovely. After each song she quickly changed her dress, beginning as a geisha and ending in white fur, short skirts, and red-brown boots, while snow fell on her.

One evening we played cards. Lord Rosebery liked playing baccarat for very low stakes and called the game Lotto. Queen Alexandra said she would like to play this game and a long table was produced at which everyone could play. But King Edward and others played bridge. The game began very well with no one staking more than one pound as a maximum, but as is inevitable at baccarat, the stakes got higher and higher. Poklewski, who took the bank, steadily won every coup, although he wanted to lose as it was chicken's feed to him. I had played steadily but lost continually, when Lady Elcho came and asked me to play bridge as they wanted a fourth. I had lost about £30 and did not at all like leaving the game and missing the chance of getting home. De Grey on hearing my objections offered to take my place, but as he never played cards for money, he would only do so if it was understood that he was playing for me, and I gave him *carte blanche* to do what he liked, as I knew that although he rarely played he knew all about the game and was very shrewd. I played very bad bridge with Mrs. Willy Grenfell, Arthur Balfour, and Lady Elcho, and won eight shillings. When the rubber was over I hurried back to the Lotto table to find out what De Grey had done with my money,

[23] Elder daughter of Colonel and Mrs. Cornwallis-West. Married Prince Henry of Pless, and afterwards described herself as 'an English linnet in a German cage'. She obtained a divorce in 1922, published her memoirs in 1928 and died in Germany in 1943.

and found he had won me all back but seven pounds, for which I expressed my deepest gratitude.

Before dinner the third night the King told me that he intended to give the Duke the Grand Cross of the Victorian Order. Knowing how little the Duke knew or cared about such things and nervous lest he should make disparaging remarks about the King's personal Order, I determined to prepare him for the honour. I went to his writing-room where I found him at his writing-table, and after discussing with him some letters he had received I told him of the King's intention to confer the Victorian Order upon him. He asked in a sleepy way what he was expected to do with 'the thing' when he got it. I replied that he must wear it and certainly that night he should wear it instead of the Garter. Anyone less anxious to receive an Order I had never seen, and I had to explain that the King looked upon his personal Order as a high honour, but the Duke seemed to think it would only complicate his dressing. Before dinner the King sent for him and handed him the Order when I believe he suitably expressed his thanks, but he straightway came to my room and asked me to put the Order on properly for him. He said that he presumed that if he wore the Victorian Order, he should not wear any part of the Order of the Garter. I was not prepared for such a difficult conundrum but I told him I had always understood that Knights of the Garter should always wear that Order on all occasions. I therefore suggested that he should wear that night not only the Riband and Star of the Victorian Order but also the Garter Star and diamond Garter on his leg. He said all this seemed complicated and tiresome but he followed my advice and the King seemed to approve as he made no comment.

The last night at dinner I sat next to the Duchess, a very clever and shrewd woman who pretended to be the reverse. She was in a delightful mood, most amusing and witty, and she told many stories of the old days. It was Twelfth Night and we had a sort of Christmas dinner with crackers and paper caps. Queen Alexandra was wonderful at this sort of thing and made everyone play up so that the fun became fast and furious. Arthur Balfour, who had good-naturedly worn a paper cap and helped to play the fool, had

had enough after a short time, and asked me to come and play bridge again with Lady Elcho and Mrs. Grenfell. We went off in high spirits to the bridge room, where we found three silent and serious rubbers of bridge going on. I told Arthur Balfour that we were too sober for the revels but too drunk to play a solemn game of bridge, which amused him very much.

These country-house parties at Chatsworth would be followed by a return to London for the formal opening of Parliament and other official functions at the end of January and early in February, and shortly afterwards the King would leave for Biarritz.

In 1905, however, this procedure was varied by the King and Queen deciding to go on a Mediterranean cruise together. The party consisted of Princess Victoria, Princess Maud and her husband Prince Charles of Denmark, Lady Antrim, Miss Knollys, Lord Salisbury, Sir Francis Laking, Sidney Greville, Harry Stonor, Johnny Ward, and myself. Mr. Fehr, the courier, came to make arrangements on shore, while Mr. Quinn from Scotland Yard took charge of the police arrangements. The latter was a wonderful man, and unless one looked out for him he was never seen, but he was everywhere and always on the spot where he might be wanted. During the cruise we played bridge after dinner, the King, Salisbury, Ward, and myself; any change was impossible as there was no one else who could play. Salisbury was an indifferent, not to say bad player, and was moreover a bad sailor, which made it difficult for him to concentrate his attention on the cards. He continually made bad mistakes and incurred the King's wrath, which made things unpleasant. Johnny Ward and I decided to do all we could to prevent these outbursts of rage. It was all very easy when Salisbury cut with either of us, as we pretended not to notice any mistakes, but when he was the King's partner and made a particularly bad blunder, it was difficult to help him. He really had no wish to play, and only consented to do so because there was no one else. Johnny Ward and I agreed to have a controversy whenever Salisbury played wrong so as to put up a cross-fire which would make it difficult for the King to abuse his partner. Accordingly we often flew at each other with abuse and recriminations demanding reasons why a certain card had been played, and as it was so violent it effectually prevented the King from getting cross. I must say, however, that all the years I played with the King I found him a charming partner. It appeared later that poor Salisbury had been suffering from an abscess on the liver and on reaching London he had to undergo a severe operation and was very ill for some time.

We started from Marseilles and it was quite rough to begin with as a mistral had been blowing, but it became smoother and we had a lovely time. I always had a certain amount of work to do, as we picked up King's Messengers at various ports.

The Queen, Princess Victoria, and Princess Maud, and indeed all the ladies, usually had breakfast in their cabins, but all the men had breakfast in the dining-saloon at 9 a.m. I was always extremely punctual, as if one remained long, one was caught by the King there about half past nine, and this meant remaining with His Majesty for at least three-quarters of an hour. The King was no breakfast-eater, having only a cup of coffee and a bit of toast, but he made up for this by eating an enormous luncheon. The Queen usually came on deck about twelve, and no matter how rough it might be she always looked as if she had stepped out of a bandbox. She was a very good sailor and was unconscious of a rough sea.

Luncheon was at one o'clock, when the Queen sat at the top of the table with the King on her right. When it was smooth the Royal Marine band played outside. At tea the Queen sat at the top of the table and made tea while Miss Knollys presided at the other end. At first all servants were dispensed with, but it sometimes happened that when the conversation became general, some people in the centre of the table never got any tea at all, and so by degrees footmen made their appearance at tea. At dinner the King sat in the centre of the table with the Queen opposite him, while an Equerry sat at each end. Two or three officers of the yacht were usually asked to dinner, and a regular list was kept so that Their Majesties had only to say how many and the next on the list were warned.

We went to Port Mahon in Minorca, but there was nothing much to see: then to Palma in Majorca, where we visited the fine Cathedral. The whole population turned out, and it was interesting to see the King and Queen escorted by a procession of priests walking up the aisle of the Cathedral. The big doors in the west end were thrown open, and at first, on leaving the sunlight, it looked as if they were walking into utter darkness.

One day we went in six motors to Solla up in the mountains, and this necessitated our racing round hairpin bends at top speed to ensure the motors being able to ascend the steep gradients. As there was usually a drop of a thousand feet at least at these corners, one only prayed that the chauffeur would not lose his head. When we were three-quarters of the way up Queen Alexandra had had enough of this and nothing would induce her to continue. She insisted on getting out and walking, and no power on earth could stop her once she had made up her mind to do something. The King, however, flatly refused to leave the motor, and laughed at the danger. I followed the Queen and walked, with the majority of the party, not because we didn't trust the chauffeurs, but because we liked the walk. It was, however, very steep, and I quite understood why the King preferred the motor. He, of course, got to the top half an hour before the walkers, and had to wait, but he took it very philosophically. We had quite a good luncheon at an old inn at Solla, and then returned, but going downhill the motors were able to go quite slowly round the hairpin bends and so there was no danger.

We went on to Algiers, and there the Consul, Mr. Hay Newton, and the Vice-Consul, Mr. Drummond Hay, came on board. They advised the King to send someone on shore to announce his arrival to the Governor-General. As there happened to be no one handy since most of our party had already gone on shore, the King sent for me. When I went to find my uniform I found the tin case, but to my dismay the blue frock-coat which I was told to wear was not there, and my French servant had gone on shore. I had only had him a short time, and thought he might be useful on this voyage, but he turned out to be slovenly, dirty, and very unreliable, nor did he have the remotest idea of what people usually wore. When in London I told him that I was going to play golf he suggested *costume de chasse,* and once when I was living at Buckingham Palace while my house was being painted,

I dressed in my riding-clothes to go out riding before breakfast when I realized I had no hat. So I sent him off to get me a billy-cock hat from my house and he returned with a gibus, with the result that I had to go out without a hat at all.

After searching for my blue frock-coat, I came across one that I had formerly in India. It was correct in pattern as the Vice-roy's A.D.C.s wore the same dress as the King's Equerries, but having been exposed to the sun it had become greenish and faded. However, as we were in Africa, I felt no one would notice, so put it on with aiguillettes, a sword, and cocked hat. I was not over-anxious to be seen by the King, and so asked that the pinnace might be at one of the forward gangways, but as I went there I bumped into the King himself. He nearly shut his eyes with repugnance at the sight of my frock-coat, but pulled himself to-gether and asked why I wore it. I explained briefly what had happened and hurried on, but later I got a message to say I was never to wear it again.

The next day the King and Queen landed and called officially on the Governor-General, General Jonnart, a clever and attractive personality who interested His Majesty. The following day there was an official luncheon and all the leading men in Algiers came: Admiral de Perrin, commanding the Naval Station, General Ser-vières, and General Bailloux, holding the two commands there. The latter was a particularly nice man and knew everyone in Paris. The King talked a great deal to him and roused the jealousy of the others.

Both the King and Queen were much annoyed at Miss Hay Newton, the Consul's daughter, appearing at luncheon in 'flannels' with a squash hat on while all the other ladies were dolled up. I happened to learn that she had only been asked five minutes before luncheon to take the place of some French lady who was taken ill, and therefore had to come as she was. I took some pains to explain this to both the King and the Queen, as I feared the poor girl might be damned for life on account of this.

One afternoon we landed and walked to see a famous garden with tropical plants. The road was narrow and when we heard the hoot of a motor-horn we had to draw up in line almost in the ditch. A beautiful motor swept by covering the King and Queen, and in fact the whole party, with clouds of white dust, and to my astonishment I saw my French servant, Fernand, in the motor with an old man. The King said he didn't know there was such a thing as a motor in Algiers and wondered whose it was. Much to the amusement of everyone I said that it was my servant who was seated inside. Afterwards I asked Fernand, and he told me it was his *oncle à l'héritage,* a merchant in Algiers, whom he had not seen for many years.

On the 23rd we steamed to Alghero in Sardinia and then on to Corsica, where at Ajaccio we saw the house in which Napoleon was born. I was astonished to find how ignorant the party were about Napoleon's early life: with the exception of the King and Queen, no one seemed to have troubled to read about Napoleon before he became great. Laking, the doctor, knew very little about Napoleon at all and asked me whether he had ever married.

After three weeks' cruising it was not to be wondered at that the time had arrived for a practical joke of some sort. Archie Milne,[24] the Commodore of the Royal yacht, had a horror of monkeys on board a ship, and when he heard that there was some idea of someone buying a monkey and taking it home, he gave strict instructions to all the officers that under no consideration were they to allow a monkey on board. Who told him or where he heard the rumour of a monkey being brought I had no idea, but there was, as far as I knew, no foundation for it. Princess Maud happened to be on deck when these orders were being given and came to me to devise some joke that could be played on the Commodore. Not being under naval discipline I consented to think out something, but I realized that jokes played on such a swell as the Commodore might not altogether be a success, more especially as all the officers and the crew would support him. We went on shore that afternoon and when we returned I was amused to see an officer eyeing suspiciously everything that had been bought, but

[24] Sir Archibald Berkeley Milne, 2nd Bart.; Commander-in-Chief, Mediterranean, 1912–14, when, owing to a misunderstanding, the German cruisers *Goeben* and *Breslau* were allowed to escape from the Mediterranean to the Dardanelles.

as none of the parcels were big enough to contain a monkey, nothing was said. I sent for Mr. Hammond, the head steward, and said I wished to have a packing-case made, but instead of a top to it I wanted bars of wood like a cage. He enquired for what purpose I required it, and I replied that I wanted to pack up something valuable I had bought. I knew he would report this to the Commodore, who would naturally suspect the worst. When I went on deck I heard that stricter orders had been given about monkeys and that an officer had been placed on each gangway to inspect anything that came on board. I talked to Princess Maud about a new pet in the hearing of the officers, feeling sure that all I said would be duly reported to the Commodore. Stricter injunctions were given, and soon the whole ship's company was engaged in looking for monkeys. The whole thing was getting out of proportion, and Milne, feeling that he was powerless to prevent Princess Maud bringing a monkey on board, went to the King and asked him to issue a manifesto prohibiting any of the party purchasing monkeys. I happened to see the King and Queen soon after, and heard them discussing Milne's urgent request, which mystified them. I told them it was only a joke and Princess Maud explained the whole thing, at which Their Majesties laughed heartily. At dinner that night poor Milne was teased about it, but he didn't mind and joined in the joke as he was so relieved to hear there had never been any intention of buying a monkey.

On April 28th we returned to Marseilles, where both the King and Queen expected telegrams and letters. The Queen intended to remain on the yacht while the King went to Paris. Mr. Gurney, the Consul, came on board with a large portfolio under his arm and was at once taken down to the King's cabin to deliver the letters and telegrams, but when the unfortunate man opened the portfolio, it was empty. The King was very angry and shouted at the poor man in such a way that he fled from the yacht terrified. The Consulate being some three miles from the landing-stage and only a one-horse cab being available, it took him a full hour to retrieve the letters, during which time His Majesty walked up and down the deck abusing him as a half-wit (he was really a very able man). At last he returned with all the letters, etc., and peace was restored. I can well understand the King's irritation at not receiving his letters and telegrams, as he had sent innumerable letters and telegrams arranging his visit to Paris, and as we were leaving the next morning time was precious. However, we started off and arrived in Paris at ten o'clock at night where His Majesty was received by Sir Francis Bertie, the Ambassador, and M. Delcassé,[25] the Minister for Foreign Affairs.

We went straight to the Hôtel Bristol, where we were very comfortable, but I never remember working so hard as I did during these visits to Paris. Although I had *café au lait* at eight, I never had a minute to spare. Everyone who knew the King came to write their names in the visitors' book, and invariably asked to see me. The result was that practically all the morning was taken up in seeing a stream of visitors. I had Mr. Sotheby, the Privy Purse Clerk, with me, and to him I dictated English letters. I had to write minutes and answers in the official boxes, but as these were only recording the King's decisions, this did not take long. The begging letters and other letters in French I sent to the Embassy with instructions what form the answer should take. There remained private letters in French from friends of the King asking His Majesty to luncheon, dinner, etc. These I had to write in French myself. It didn't take long for the King to hand these letters to me and to murmur 'Say No', 'Say Yes', 'Say I will telephone later', etc., but when late at night I had to write civil answers in French, it took me some time.

I always had difficulties about the police. The King hated any idea of being guarded by police and tried to do everything in his power to dodge any detectives that might be looking after him. M. Lépine, the head of the French police, however, came to see me and explained that he was responsible for the King's safety. If I gave him explicit instructions not to take ordinary precautions, he would of course obey, and wash his hands of the whole thing, but I must realize that if the King was shot at, stabbed, or had a

---

[25] Theophile Delcassé. French Foreign Minister, 1898–1905 (when a disagreement with his colleagues over the Morocco crisis led to his resignation) and 1914–15. Ambassador to Russia, 1913–14. A protagonist of the Triple Entente, and of a strong policy against Germany.

bomb thrown at him, the responsibility would rest with me. There were lunatics in Paris as in every great city, and therefore an attempt to assassinate the King was by no means an impossibility; I must, however, give him instructions on paper not to send plain-clothes police to guard the King. I came to the conclusion that the solution of this problem lay in ensuring the King was properly guarded but doing it in such a way that the King would be quite unconscious of any police protection. I impressed on M. Lépine the importance of sending men whom His Majesty did not know by sight and he was quite satisfied. I agreed to tell him privately where the King was going on condition there was no visible sign of police protection.

I remember on one occasion the King decided to have *déjeuner* at some restaurant at St. Cloud, where there was a garden and parties of people had *déjeuner* in arbours round the garden. We were a mixed party, half English and half French. Reggie Lister, the Secretary at the British Embassy, George and Alice Keppel, were among the English, and the Breteuils and Mme Standish among the French. We met the guests in the hall where we left our hats and coats and walked out in the garden to our arbour. On each side of us were parties having *déjeuner,* and Alice Keppel became nervous as she said one of the men in the party on our right had a villainous face. She argued in a whisper that anyone could come in through the gate at the end of the garden, and wondered whether it was quite safe. I replied that there was ample protection from the police, but she insisted that this could not be so as they would never have allowed an obvious criminal to be so near the King. She was convinced I had given the police the wrong name of the restaurant and that there we were at the mercy of any apache who fancied robbery and any anarchist who loved as-sassination. At last I determined to make sure, and having hidden my handkerchief in my trouser pocket, I went through the panto-mime of a man who has lost one. Finally I got up and said I wanted to get my handkerchief, which I had left in my coat. As I went back through the hall I passed the inside dining-room and there I saw Lépine himself having *déjeuner*. I went in and asked him if he was satisfied with the police arrangements, and he told me the gardener working by the garden gate was a police officer who had orders to admit no one. I said that I was not quite happy about the luncheon parties on either side, particularly the one on the right, and he laughed and said they were all police and their wives. He guessed we were nervous about one, but he said he was a *bon garçon* and one of the best and most trusted detectives in the force. I returned with my handkerchief waving and murmured to Alice Keppel that all was well, and when after luncheon I told her what Lépine had said, she could only express admiration for the methods of the French police.

One day the King went out by himself in the motor and the courier told me confidentially he was going to the Jardin des Plantes to meet a friend who had been a noted beauty in Paris. I telephoned to Lépine and suggested that there should on this occasion be no police in the gardens but possibly they might remain outside. He, however, objected on the grounds that an apache might see His Majesty, recognize him, and attempt to rob him. I therefore agreed to two plain-clothes men being sent there, but stipulated they should be men the King didn't know by sight.

The whole thing, however, came out very unluckily. Lépine had sent two men whom the King had never seen, but unfortunately one of them was taken ill and decided to go off at once to a hospital. On his way he happened to meet one of the detectives who usually went about with the King and who offered to take his place. The King was walking with the lady when he caught sight of the detective he knew and this completely spoilt the romance of the assignation. When he got back to the hotel he asked me how I knew where he was going and why I had warned the police. I replied that it was quite by chance I knew where he was going and that naturally I had warned Lépine, who considered it was dangerous for him to be without any protection and had taken the usual precautions. He contented himself by remarking that he would take good care another time I did not know his movements, and after blowing off steam about the absurdity of the police shadowing him in Paris of all places, he never alluded to the incident again. But after that he not only tried to dodge the police but also to dodge me. He would order the motor at four and then change his mind suddenly and send for it at three, when he would slip out before anyone was ready. But these tricks were useless with the French police, and although they were caught napping the first time, they had motors ready at any time and had no difficulty in following him.

On May 1st the King, accompanied by du Bos, a great man on the turf, Johnny Ward and myself, went to see M. Blanc's racing stable. We arrived at what appeared to be a village but which was only the racing stable in attractive buildings with everything done in the most extravagant way. Afterwards we went on to luncheon at St. Cloud, and du Bos's son joined us, but we said good-bye to Blanc at his stables. Later on at the races the King was surrounded by all the big swells of the French turf and I was amused to see that they never allowed Blanc to come near His Majesty, because he was a *nouveau riche* and therefore not a member of the Jockey Club.

One day the King went to visit the ex-Empress Eugénie at the Grand Hôtel, which seemed a noisy sort of place for her to stay. He took me with him and said he would wait in the motor while I enquired whether it would be convenient for her to receive him, but of course I was to use the incognito titles. I went to the clerk at the desk and said, *'La Comtesse de Pierrefonds, est elle chez elle?'* and he replied, looking at the list, that she was. I asked him to ascertain whether she would receive *'Le Duc de Lancastre'*, but this conveyed nothing to him, and he said, *'Qui ça?'* I wrote it down on a piece of paper and handed it to him, but all he said was *'Bientôt'*. He apparently expected me to sit down and wait while he went on sorting a packet of letters and putting them in pigeon-holes, but I was conscious all the time of the monarch fretting with impatience in a motor in the courtyard. So I told the clerk to hurry up as I was pressed for time, but he only said he must do the letters first. There was nothing for it but to drop the incognito and make him move. *'C'est le Roi d'Angleterre qui demande si l'Impératrice Eugénie veut bien le recevoir.'* This had the desired effect and he went off at once. It appeared later that he was so confused and incoherent that he failed to make the Empress understand who it was. Anyhow, the answer was that the Empress would be pleased to receive him. I went outside and found the King champing his bit at being kept waiting so long. I took him into the hotel and straight to the lift. Of course, he was so accustomed to everyone making way for him that although he was incognito it never occurred to him that anyone would not do so. It happened that as we arrived at the lift a prosperous-looking American with a large cigar in his mouth decided to go up in the lift at the same moment, and conscious that he had more or less bought the whole hotel he walked straight into the lift. The result was that he and the King collided, but weight told, as His Majesty was by far the heavier, and the American cannoned off the King and lost his balance while his cigar shot out of his mouth. He obviously had no idea who the King was and appeared to resent being hustled. As we only went up to the first floor there was hardly time for a row and the American contented himself with regarding the King distastefully. I had to talk to Madame de Arcos, the Empress's lady, while the King stayed nearly an hour.

A few months later I had another curious experience with the ex-Empress Eugénie. Every August the King went to Cowes for the yachting, and in the August of 1905 the Empress Eugénie came too. One day, whilst on the King's yacht, the *Victoria & Albert,* I decided to take the steam pinnace and go over to the Yacht Squadron Garden to meet some friends. The pinnace was steaming closely past one of the yachts when I suddenly saw a parasol waving with a handkerchief tied to it. At first I merely thought it odd but did not imagine it was any business of mine and continued to think of other things, when it struck me that this might be a signal to me. It seemed almost improbable that such a crude method of signalling should be used on such a smart-looking yacht, and I concluded that it was some maid having a joke with the crew. I was, however, not satisfied with this explanation and I told the coxswain to turn round and go to the companion ladder of the yacht. He did so and gave a shout to warn the crew that we were coming, but not a man appeared. So up the ladder I went and to my surprise found not a soul on board, which seemed very weird. The coxswain shouted down the hatchway but no one answered. In the South Sea Islands this sort of thing might easily happen, but at Cowes it was certainly strange that a yacht should be lying there with no one on board. Then I remembered the parasol and therefore unless it was mechanically waved there must be someone about. I walked down the deck and to my surprise found the Empress Eugénie seated quite alone. She greeted me almost affectionately and said I had got her out of an impasse. I thought I was being stupid as I could not for the life of me understand how she came to be quite by herself and apparently under the impression that this was quite a normal state of affairs. She told me, however, that the mate had died suddenly, and as he was a very popular man all the crew wished to attend the funeral. They had decided to draw lots, but she had insisted on their all going as she would be quite able to look after herself for two hours. After they had gone, she had suddenly remembered that she was having tea with the King and Queen at five and there was no possible way of getting to the Royal yacht. As she sat gazing at the sea she noticed my pinnace leave the yacht, but as it came close to her yacht and she would not get to the side quick enough, she tied her handkerchief on her parasol and waved to attract my attention. So of course I told her I would take her in the pinnace; but this was no easy matter as there was a bit of a swell on and the pinnace bobbed up and down. The Empress, who must have been over eighty, got down the ladder, but could not make up her mind to step into the pinnace. Eventually I went first into the pinnace and held out my arms to help her, but even so she hesitated. I then put my hand behind her foot and gave it a pull so that she toppled over, when I caught her in my arms and deposited her on the seat. She said, 'How clever you are, you pulled my leg', but I don't know if she understood the meaning of this slang expression.

Meanwhile the crew returned from the funeral and were horrified when they could find no trace of the Empress. They feared at first she had fallen overboard; but on signalling to the Yacht Squadron they learnt she was safely on board the Royal yacht.

At six I took her back and she wondered whether her crew had even missed her, but there they all were with broad smiles on their faces to welcome her back.

But to return to Paris for a moment. The day before we left I had a real argument with the King, who was very angry. He decided to send a present to du Bos and get Johnny Ward to write and thank him for all the excellent arrangements he had made for visiting Blanc's stables and the races afterwards. Now du Bos, a member of the French Jockey Club and one of the leading men on the French turf, would hardly expect a present, but if one was to be given it should be a good one. As a matter of fact, the King was the most generous of men and gave lovely presents without really appreciating their relative value. Often on State visits he had given gold cigarette-cases and even gold cigarette-cases with his cypher in diamonds. When the King's valet came to me with a plain silver cigarette-case with the King's cypher in enamel on it, I told him to take it back to the King and say that I hardly thought it good enough and that I suggested His Majesty should wait till he returned to London when a better cigarette-case could be sent. The valet explained that the King had given so many presents during the yachting cruise that there was really nothing left. That seemed to be all the more reason for waiting till we returned to London.

Soon afterwards the King came in and I saw at once that he was really very angry and was trying to control himself. Slowly and deliberately he put his hat, gloves, and stick on the table and then said quietly, 'Did you send me a message that the cigarette-case I had chosen was not good enough?' I trembled inwardly but replied in the affirmative. Then he went on in a voice that shook the whole hotel. He asked what I knew about Paris. How could I judge what was a correct present to give to a friend like du Bos? What knowledge had I of the presents he was accustomed to give? Yet I dared to express an opinion on what I obviously had no knowledge. This flood of oratory delivered in a deafening tone swept me off my feet and reduced me to a state of speechless terror, but I recovered as he continued his abuse of me, and when he stopped I replied that I was sorry he didn't take the same view as I had, but as he usually gave such beautiful presents to his friends it was a pity that he should give such a cheap thing to du Bos, who would no doubt show it to everyone in Paris. This so far from

313

pacifying him raised a fresh storm, and when Johnny Ward loyally supported me I thought His Majesty would have a fit, but suddenly he calmed down and dictated a letter to Johnny Ward thanking du Bos for all the excellent arrangements he had made, etc., and asking him to accept a small souvenir from His Majesty. The King rang the bell and handed the note and the cigarette-case, which had been done up in paper, to the waiter and told him to send it off at once. He then triumphantly took up his hat, stick, and gloves, and left the room, slamming the door. After dinner the King came to me waving a letter with triumph, and said, 'This shows what d——d nonsense you talked'. I read the letter couched in extravagant terms expressing the deepest gratitude for the truly beautiful present, etc. etc., but when I handed it back I remarked that du Bos could not well have written anything else. It was usual with the King after he had let himself go and cursed someone to smooth matters by being especially nice to them afterwards, but in this case he resented my being so outspoken and made no attempt to forgive me. It was not till years later that I understood that he had really agreed with me but had been much annoyed at not being able to give something good. During the visit to Berlin when he was ill with a chill and quite unable to attend to anything, he said, 'I must leave the presents entirely to you to do, and I know you will do everything perfectly and not give anything shoddy like I did in Paris'.

At a *déjeuner* in Paris Monsieur and Madame Jean de Reszke were asked to meet the King. De Reszke, in addition to being a great singer, was a charming man with a quaint sense of humour. He had taught his wife to sing and it was said that, like Svengali in Du Maurier's novel, he in a sort of a way hypnotized her when she sang. However that may be, there is no doubt that when he accompanied her she sang divinely.

After *déjeuner* she was asked to sing, but the question arose what *should* she sing? Jean de Reszke asked the King for his favourite song, but His Majesty said he hoped she would sing anything she liked. Songs were suggested but turned down by Jean, and although I ventured to suggest modern songs by Reynaldo Hahn, Debussy, and others, he always, shook his head.

There seemed an impasse, but suddenly he said '*J'y suis*', and suggested *La Traviata,* and this was at once approved of. He explained to me afterwards that he was determined she should sing something the King knew, and that he was quite sure His Majesty, like all that generation, knew this opera well.

One day we went round the Salon with Detaille,[26] who pointed out all the pictures worth seeing. I received instructions to wear a short black London coat and a tall hat. Knowing how particular the King was about dress I hesitated to adopt this sort of Stock Exchange attire, but on my asking the King to make sure I had not got his message wrong, he explained it would be impossible to go in country clothes with a squash hat, and yet a frock-coat would be out of place. He therefore always went to see pictures in a short coat and top-hat. My brain gave way under the strain of grasping these niceties of dress.

Detaille, like de Reszke, in addition to being a great artist, was a delightful human being and very good company. His comments on the pictures were always amusing and he never spared the artist in his criticisms. When we entered one of the rooms we came across a very bad picture and the King began asking why they admitted such daubs, when Detaille coughed loudly and said it was a very fine picture. The King at once tumbled to it that something had happened and remained silent. Details thereupon called up a man who was standing near and presented him to the King. He was the artist of the daub.

We went to luncheon with the Breteuils in their beautiful house in the Avenue du Bois de Boulogne, and I sat between Madame Pourtales and Lépine, the head of the police. I always think the French system of meals may be very good for people who have nothing to do and are only out for amusement, but for busy people they are most inconvenient. I had *café au lait* at 8 a.m. with one roll and butter. Therefore by 12.45, when we had *déjeuner,* I was so hungry that I ate every dish and was quite incapable of doing any work in the afternoon. I wanted either to talk or go to sleep. Of course, the ordinary Frenchman does have a siesta, but that means he does no work till four or five.

[26] Edouard Detaille, the celebrated painter of battle-pictures.

315

The King's position in Paris was really most remarkable. He was credited with enormous powers and the fact that he was a constitutional Sovereign was entirely lost sight of. He was regarded as an autocrat, and in Paris where the people had a craving for hero-worship but had no hero, they placed him on a pedestal and worshipped him. He knew so well how to manage the two entirely distinct worlds in Paris—the Social and the Official world, and never made the mistake of getting them mixed. If it was a State visit or any municipal function, he ignored the Faubourg St. Germain, but on the other hand, when going out to luncheon or dinner, he never expressed any desire to meet the official world.

The King of the Belgians was in Paris at the time and, knowing the King disliked him, he never showed any signs of life. It was therefore very bad luck that he should hit on the same play on the same night as the King. We dined at Voisin's, the King, the Ambassador, Lady Feo Bertie, Reggie Lister, Alice Keppel, Johnny Ward, and myself, and afterwards went to see Granier in *Bonne Intention*. When we entered our box I caught sight of King Leopold, who sank as low as he could in the stalls, like a hare in a field when shooting is going on. However, there was no reason why the two Kings should meet.

The Press was a constant difficulty; every evening I issued a rough statement of what the King had done during the day while I begged reporters to refrain from publishing details of private visits. On that particular night I merely said *'Le Roi dine en ville'*, and the more respectable papers repeated this, but the yellow Press came to the conclusion that as both Kings were at the same theatre they must have dined together. They therefore published fictitious accounts of the two monarchs having dinner together; this annoyed King Edward quite enormously, although I explained how difficult it was to prevent this sort of thing happening and how inadvisable it would be to publish a denial.

This was the last night we spent in Paris and I had to sit up till three in the morning to clean up all the work, as it was impossible to leave anything to stand over.

The following year, 1906, the King and Queen again went for a Mediterranean cruise together, and again I was one of the suite. But this time the main purpose was an official visit to Queen Alexandra's second brother, the King of Greece, at Athens. This was a return visit for the visit that the Greek King had paid to London in the November of 1905. On this earlier occasion the Queen of Greece was unable to come, so King George of Greece brought with him Prince and Princess Nicholas of Greece. The latter was a Russian Grand Duchess and a daughter of the Grand Duke Vladimir. For some reason I was attached to the Greeks instead of one of the Equerries, and a very amusing time I had. First of all King George of Greece was a charming man, very shrewd, with a thorough knowledge of European politics and quite conscious of the slender ties that bound him to the throne of Greece. Danish by birth, he had accepted the throne but at the same time induced the European Powers to guarantee him twenty thousand a year in the event of his being forced to retire. After the banquet King Edward gave in his honour, I happened to talk to Joe Chamberlain, who told me he was in Athens when the King of Greece ascended the throne and he wondered how long His Majesty would remain there. The next day while talking to the King of Greece I repeated what Chamberlain had said, and he replied that at the time he wondered himself how long he would stay. He added, 'I remember Mr. Chamberlain being there: he was at that time full of three cows and an acre'.

I went sightseeing with the Greeks and saw many things in London which I had never taken the trouble to see before. It is only when we take foreigners about that we really see London. On one occasion I got into the carriage and realized that I should be sitting on the right while the King of Greece was on the left. I knew that abroad they regard the position in the carriage of the highest importance and that duels had been fought when a man was low-born and sat on the right instead of the left. So I hesitated to seat myself, but His Grecian Majesty said, 'Sit down. I know you don't have any nonsense of that sort in England.'

Queen Alexandra was very fond and proud of her brother, and King Edward liked him as he was so intelligent and well up in

European politics. King George of Greece seemed to have the lowest opinion not only of the rulers of the Balkan States, but also of the Governments. He attached no importance to anything anyone had said or done in the neighbouring countries to Greece.

The so-called Greek Royal Family were all delightful and so we had a charming time. One day I went out to Tatoi, a private house of the King and Queen of Greece, and we had luncheon out of doors in the most lovely garden. I was very much struck with the truly marvellous way in which Queen Olga of Greece spoke foreign languages. She seemed perfectly at home in any language and spoke English to me, Danish to a Danish architect, Italian to a professor, and when I remembered she was Russian and spoke German and French perfectly, I came to the conclusion that the number of languages she spoke was abnormal.

King Edward plunged into the Cretan problem and was very much taken with the abilities of Esme Howard,[27] who was then in the Consular and not the Diplomatic Service. Mercifully Charlie Hardinge was with him and prevented him behaving like an autocrat.

On April 11th we went to Corfu and saw the Emperor of Germany's villa which was decorated in Pompeian fashion. We went to Sicily and did all the usual trips there. On our return we went to Naples and there the King left for Paris, leaving Queen Alexandra to go on in the yacht. Louisa Antrim, Charlotte Knollys, Sidney Greville, and Harry Stonor remained on the yacht. While we were at Naples the King asked Rosebery to dine, having heard he was at Posillipo. Rosebery turned up in a Yacht Squadron mess-jacket and a white tie. Most people would have never even remarked this, and if they had would never have given it a second thought. But for King Edward this entirely spoilt the whole evening and he eyed Rosebery angrily all through dinner. To make matters worse Rosebery made a joke about his tie and became rather offhand about what was really in the King's mind a serious matter. The King swallowed his wrath, and when Rosebery said immediately we left the dining saloon that he hoped the King would excuse him as he had to get back to Posillipo, His Majesty

[27] Later 1st Lord Howard of Penrith. Ambassador to U.S.A. 1924–30.

begged him to stay on as he had seen nothing of him. This, I think, was to show that in spite of his outrageous conduct in wearing a white tie, he was forgiven. The King went away with me, Seymour Fortescue, and one other and played bridge while Rosebery was drawn into conversation with Queen Alexandra and Princess Victoria. Unfortunately cards are like waves and refuse to obey Royal commands. We had a quite interminable rubber which went on and on. I could see through the door that Queen Alexandra and all the ladies had retired to bed and there seemed no prospect of finishing this tiresome rubber. It was not till a quarter to twelve that we at last finished. The King got up and went out and having said how sorry he was to have been so long, merely bid Rosebery good night. I think that Rosebery had imagined the King wanted to have an interesting conversation with him, and therefore didn't mind waiting, but when it was only to say good night he was very angry, and showed it.

In February 1907, the King and Queen again went on a private visit to Paris, and I was taken as I could talk French; Seymour Fortescue was the other Equerry, and Miss Knollys and Lady Gosford were the two ladies. It was intensely cold, and there was two foot of snow. I had never known Paris so cold before. When we arrived at the station there was a huge crowd of two thousand people although it was supposed to be quite private. Outside the station a large crowd cheered vociferously as we drove to the Embassy, where everybody was cleared out to make way for us. We dined without any visitors at all, and suddenly afterwards the King expressed a wish to go to the play. They told him that it was much too late, and that there would be no possibility of getting a box at so late an hour. (It was past nine o'clock then.) The King, however, having set his mind on going out somewhere, said he would go to the circus, and we all went off and enjoyed it very much. Apparently the performance finished half an hour too soon, for when we came out there were no carriages. The King and Queen were quite delighted at finding themselves in a large crowd; of course, they did not know that most of the people standing near them were detectives. After five minutes we succeeded in getting Reggie Lister's motor, and the rest of us got into cabs.

The following day the King went to call on the President (Fallières). We drove off to the Elysée and the President met us at the door. We had the usual presentations, and then the King and the President went off together and talked for half an hour. I talked to my opposite number, the President's Private Secretary. Then we all said good-bye, and the Chef du Protocole said to me '*A dix minutes*'. He meant that the President was coming back to call on the King. They came in about a quarter of an hour's time and were received by the King and Queen; on this occasion Madame Fallières, in plum-coloured silk, turned up. She was very shy and nervous, but she had been told exactly what to do.

The next day the King and Queen, and all four of us went to luncheon with the President. When we arrived there, we were met by the President and his staff, and were ushered into a room where there were about fifty guests. It is the custom in France for the foreigners to go round first. The King and Queen therefore went round and everybody was presented to them. They both had the most charming way of doing this. The King went first followed by the Queen, and they each had an aide-de-camp calling out the names. The Queen captivated everybody by her charming manner, and the King's method of saying one or two remarks to people to show who were his friends, was very effective. When they had finished, the President and Madame Fallières went round. Anything worse I have rarely seen. The President himself was very awkward and rather nervous, but did his part very well. Poor Madame Fallières, however, had not had much experience of this sort of thing, and floundered hopelessly along, putting her hand out one second and drawing it back the next. The Sous-chef du Protocole was at her elbow and told her what to do and what not to do. It was altogether rather a painful ceremony. A French officer who was next to me said, 'This is really terrible. I cannot look on and see them make a mess of shaking hands after the way in which the King and Queen have done it.' I replied, 'What can you expect? Yours are amateurs, and ours are professionals at this game.'

One evening we went to the play to see Sarah Bernhardt act in a very long poetical play with no plot. Between the acts Sarah

Bernhardt came round to see the King; she remembered seeing me at Cimiez, when I asked her to write her name in Queen Victoria's birthday book.

One night we all went to the play and two boxes had been converted into one to hold us. Strikes were threatened and the stalls were crowded with people waiting for something to happen. During the *entr' acte* I received a message from Lépine, the Head of the police, saying he wished to speak to me. I slipped out and found him in the passage. He said there was rather a serious situation outside as something like five thousand people had assembled outside the theatre with the intention of holding up the Royal motors and inducing the King to get out and make a speech. He added that they had sufficient police ready to prevent this, but as uniformed police generally infuriated mobs and there might in consequence be fighting, he wished to suggest that the King and Queen should leave by the stage door at the back of the theatre. To do this Their Majesties would have to go down a narrow staircase and then go behind the scenes. If I would ascertain whether they would consent to do this he would undertake to have the staircase kept free from people until they had left. I returned to the box and repeated all this to the King, who said that it sounded tiresome and unnecessary, but since Lépine pressed it, he would go through this intricate manœuvre. I went out again and was told that Lépine was in the manager's room, and there I found him and said that Their Majesties were prepared to carry out his advice and leave just before the end of the piece. He said he would come and knock at the door of the box when they should leave. He then summoned the plain-clothes police in the theatre. This interested me very much, as they were all dressed according to the seats they occupied. The man in the gallery was poorly dressed; the one from the upper circle looked just the type of man one would expect to see there, but the man from the balcony stalls was the best, as one would never have connected him in any way with the police. He wore a well-fitting suit of evening clothes, white waistcoat, pearl stud, an opera hat, and white kid gloves, and he carried a cane with a gold top. He came sauntering along like a dandy, but as soon as he saw Lépine he dropped all this and became the police officer giving short snappy answers to the questions asked. All the arrangements were made in two minutes and the men returned to their seats. Towards the end of the last act a knock on the door was heard and the whole party left at once, going through the back of the scenes to the stage door where the motors appeared. Lépine told me afterwards that he circulated quietly the information that the King and Queen had left and that, although there was great disappointment, the crowd slowly dispersed.

It was about this time that efforts were made to bring the Russian and Japanese Ambassadors together, as they had not met since the war of 1904. The King seemed to think that sufficient time had elapsed since the war to enable these two to meet, and asked Lord Lansdowne in a quite private capacity to do what he could. He gave a big dinner and a reception at Lansdowne House to which all the Corps Diplomatique was asked and he included Benckendorff and Hayashi [28] in his dinner.

Everything went well and although the conversation was by no means cordial, the two Ambassadors talked for a short time together. When the moment for leaving arrived, Benckendorff went downstairs to get his hat and coat and found that the hats and coats of those who had attended the dinner had been kept separate from the others and there were no tickets. He found his coat and took the top-hat nearest to it. When however he went outside and put his hat on, he found it came down over his eyes and there was nothing to be done but to change it. Of course, it turned out to be Hayashi's hat, and he had to go up to him and change hats. Benckendorff in telling me about this added, *'Il m'a reçu avec un rire imbecile'*. After this there was no difficulty about their meeting.

---

[28] Count de Benckendorff, Russian Ambassador in London, 1903–17; Count Tadasu Hayashi, Japanese Ambassador, 1900–5. The meeting must have been earlier than the author suggests.

CHAPTER XVI

*Marienbad — The King incognito — Visit to the Austrian
Emperor — Ferdinand of Bulgaria — John Burns — Golf
at Marienbad — Clemenceau — Bosnia and Herzegovina*

POSSIBLY there was no part of the year the King enjoyed more
than his annual cure at Marienbad where, after a few preliminary
difficulties over his incognito, he enjoyed the informality and lack
of restraint of the Continental spa.

In August 1903 the King went to Marienbad attended by Stanley Clarke and myself. Sidney Greville came out with us as he
happened to be taking the waters there, but he went to another
hotel.

At Frankfort we stopped for a short time where the German
Emperor stage-managed a greeting. There was a guard of honour and he was surrounded by innumerable officers and officials
in uniform.

As the King was incognito he travelled under the name of the
Duke of Lancaster, but Mr. Fehr, the courier, had made a mistake and had had the labels printed Lord Lancaster. The King was
furious and said people would think he was an ennobled gun-
maker. One amusing incident occurred with this name; Professor
Ray Lankester [1] came to Marienbad to take the waters, and as the
inhabitants had begun to associate the name Lancaster with the
Royal Family, they came to the conclusion he was a Prince travelling incognito.

The suite of rooms at the Hotel Weimar taken by the King
were very comfortable, and his own bedroom, dining-room, and
sitting-room were specially furnished. All the furniture and pic-

[1] The natural historian and biologist.

323

tures were sold after he left each year for double their value, but I never had the slightest wish to buy any of them.

There were about four thousand people in Marienbad taking the cure, mostly Austrians with a number of bearded and ringleted Polish Jews, who wore a curious old-fashioned top-hat, a long black coat, and high boots. The majority of the water-drinkers were very fat: in fact, I had never seen so many fat people before. We walked down from the hotel at seven o'clock and it was quite disgraceful the way in which they mobbed the King. Wherever we walked we were followed by a dense crowd of several hundreds, and when the King sat down they formed a circle round him and took snapshots. He was very angry and said if this continued it would be impossible for him to stay there. The mistake was that the Burgomaster had put up notices asking people to respect the King's incognito and this really only advertised the fact that he was there.

Walking with the King for two hours before breakfast, having breakfast with him, doing work with him in the morning, luncheon with him, driving out in a motor with him, dinner with him, and bridge after dinner, might have been a very trying experience, but anyone more charming and interesting to talk to I never met. I never attempted to make conversation with him, and we often walked in silence.

The greater part of Marienbad was owned by the monks of Tepl Monastery. They were reputed to be very rich and to have two millions sterling invested in English securities. They wore white cassocks and no hats, but in sunny or cold weather they wore black top-hats, which looked rather incongruous. They remained in seclusion for two years and then went into the world for another two, and so on. Campbell-Bannerman said that their costume was emblematic of their lives, the white cassock standing for their two years' seclusion and the top-hat for the years in the world. The King paid a visit to the Abbot, a very shrewd middle-aged man, and we were shown round the monastery, which seemed very comfortable. The library was magnificent but the chapel was even more ornate with masses of rich gilding. While walking round with Slatin Pasha,[2] who was one of our party, we met an old monk and talked to him. He was much interested at seeing King Edward and said, *'Ich bin auch ein Eduard, aber ein unglücklicher Eduard"* (I am also an Edward, but a miserable Edward).

The crowd behaved better by degrees, but this was owing to the detectives keeping them in order. There were six Austrian detectives under Herr Hans Schober, who seemed a very clever man and who eventually became Chancellor of the Austrian Republic, and two English, Mr. Quinn and a second detective. The second man told me he lived as a cobbler in the East of London and made friends with the anarchists. He never joined them but pretended to be a man smitten with their ideas. I asked him what languages he spoke and he said a little French and German, but mostly Yiddish. When he had to come out with the King he had a sham accident and was carried off to a hospital. There he shaved off his beard and went to Scotland Yard. He reversed this procedure when he returned, and had to wait to allow his beard to grow before he went back. He said that once he found himself in an awkward position because after accompanying the King abroad he returned ostensibly from hospital and went on with his cobbler's work. All the neighbours had subscribed to help him to make a start, and they came to give him two pounds. He didn't dare refuse this but gave it to the clergyman anonymously to be spent on the people in this street.

Harry Chaplin used to come to luncheon, being an old friend of the King's, and very good company he was. He seemed to take the cure very seriously and then have lapses, when he ate forbidden things and drank forbidden drinks. The King was much shocked at this as he was not only being very strict himself, but saw that I followed the doctor's instructions closely.

Madame Waddington, an American and the widow of a French Ambassador in London, amused the King, interlarding her Eng-

---

[2] Baron Rudolph Slatin Pasha, Baron of the Austrian Empire. Governor of Darfur, Sudan, under General Gordon; captured by the Mahdists; Inspector-General of the Sudan, 1900–14. In World War I became head of Aid for Prisoners of War under the Austrian Red Cross.

lish with French and American expressions. Madame de Ganay, a charming Frenchwoman, was also a constant guest, but she sometimes was reduced to silence by Madame Waddington's flow of conversation.

One day the King, Stanley Clarke, and I went to Carlsbad in a motor hired from Vienna, and the visit was to be kept very secret, the courier ordering the luncheon and reserving the table in his own name. Everything seemed perfect as the table was reserved in the garden outside the restaurant where a large number of people were having *déjeuner*. The King's one idea of happiness was to be in the middle of a crowd with no one taking any notice of him. He got very impatient with the waiters, however, who merely treated us as ordinary people who had to take their turn. It was most unlikely that we should remain there long without someone recognizing the King, as his photograph was in every shop window, and soon a crowd began to assemble in the road outside the garden. Then the restaurant filled up and several hundred people accumulated outside. The King was very angry and said some stupid person had given away the secret, but I tried to explain that it was impossible for him not to be recognized. I was not getting on very well with my argument when the town band turned up and played 'God Save the King', and this put the lid on the luncheon. When we got up the whole restaurant rose and an attempt at cheering was made. The King had intended to go for a walk round the town, but as we should have been followed by the town band and several hundred people this was out of the question; we had to take refuge in the motor.

Charlie Hawtrey, the actor, followed the King's example and hired a motor to take him to Carlsbad. He learnt the German for slow and fast, but unfortunately got mixed as to which was which. When the driver began to whisk round dangerous corners at breakneck speed he thought it only prudent to steady him and leant out of the window and shouted '*Schnell, schnell!*' (Fast, fast!), under the impression that he was saying 'Slow, slow!' The chauffeur naturally thought he was not going fast enough and quickened up to sixty miles an hour, with Hawtrey still shouting '*Schnell!*' Mercifully the car was incapable of going any faster.

Occasionally the King picked up curious people and asked them to luncheon. Monsieur and Madame de Varrue came one day. She had been a noted beauty in Paris, and had late in life married a young man who suddenly called himself Baron de Varrue, but as anybody can assume any title in France people wondered why he did not call himself Duke. Mrs. Dale Lace, with an eyeglass, short skirts, and a murky past, also came to luncheon, and some of the habitués were shocked, although she amused the King.

When King George of Greece came, Marienbad thought itself the hub of the universe. Reporters and photographers flocked to the waters while the crowd following the two Kings became greater and greater. Stanley Clarke and I had to walk about with the two Greeks who accompanied the King and talked French all the time.

Madame de Ganay gave a luncheon to the two Kings and their suites, and Princesse Murat and Madame de Chévigné came. There was some feeling when champagne was handed round, as it is strictly forbidden at Marienbad. The King got very angry at temptation being placed in his way, but the Greeks all lapped it up.

When the cure was finished the King went to Vienna to pay a visit to the Austrian Emperor and the suite was increased by the addition of Sidney Pembroke, the Lord Steward, who always looked the part, Seymour Fortescue as a sailor, and Colonel Owen, who commanded the Royals, the regiment of which the Emperor was Colonel. The Emperor sent his own train and so we travelled most comfortably.

I was asleep after luncheon in my compartment when the King sent for me and told me he had received a telegram from Plunkett,[3] the Ambassador, saying that on arrival at Vienna an address from the British residents would be read and His Majesty would be expected to make a reply. The King handed it to me and told me to type a suitable reply, adding that I could easily guess the sort of thing they would say. I unearthed the typewriter from a pile of luggage in one of the vans and found a piece of foolscap paper with the Royal Arms which would at least add dignity to the

[3] Sir Francis Plunkett. Ambassador in Vienna, 1900–5.

reply. I tried to imagine who the British residents in Vienna would be and came to the conclusion that they were probably commercial gents. I therefore made the reply commercial in tone, interspersed with platitudes, and ending in a fine peroration about their helping to strengthen the ties of friendship which so happily existed between the two nations. I can honestly say that the typing was perfect, but whether the reply would fit the address was more than I could say.

When we arrived at Vienna we found the Emperor surrounded by a mass of officers and officials, all of whom were presented to to the King. After inspecting the guard of honour His Majesty received the British residents, who presented an address which was read out by the leading man. The King then read my reply in an impressive way and everything went well. Luckily the address contained nothing but platitudes and so the reply did perfectly.

A procession was then formed and, escorted by cavalry, we all drove through the streets, which were thronged by enthusiastic crowds. The Burg Palace was huge and my room was quite ten minutes' walk from the King's apartments, so that when I came to see His Majesty in a hurry I arrived incoherent and breathless. The tapestried antechamber was exactly like a picture in the Middle Ages. Sentries with pikes guarded each door and in addition there were Viennese, Hungarian, and Bohemian officers arranged in the gorgeous uniforms of previous centuries.

The gala dinner was beautifully done and the King made an impressive speech in German, ending up with an announcement that he had made the Emperor a British Field-Marshal. This seemed to please everyone and we all shouted 'Hoch, hoch!'

It seemed difficult at first to bring the two monarchs together as the Emperor got up at 4 a.m. and worked till breakfast. *Déjeuner* was at twelve and dinner at 5 p.m. The King on the other hand didn't have his coffee till 10 a.m., and although he had of course to conform to the Emperor's time for meals, he was quite unable to go to bed at 7.30 when the Emperor retired; he preferred to go out and see life in Vienna, which resulted in our not getting to bed till 1 a.m. I had so much to do that I had to get up at seven, which the Emperor's people thought was ridiculously late; still, one had to get some sleep.

We had continual functions every day, and I spent a considerable part of the day changing from one uniform into another. I went with the King to the Tombs where he deposited a wreath on the old Emperor's and Archduke Rudolph's [4] tombs. I was interested to see the tombs of Marie Louise and the Duc de Reichstadt,[5] but my lamentable ignorance of Austrian history prevented my appreciating many other historical monuments.

The Viennese Opera was a revelation to me and was far in front of anything I had ever heard. The orchestra was marvellous and the whole entertainment was on a higher musical plane than Covent Garden.

The old Emperor seemed to get on very well with the King, but of course during a State visit there is little or no time for private conversation. Dietrichstein, a brother of Albert Mensdorff, the Austrian Ambassador in London, was attached to us and was kindness itself. He was a tough-looking soldier and quite different in character from his brother. 'Dolly' Teck,[6] the military attaché in Vienna, joined the suite and was also invaluable to us. When Dietrichstein was told to take round Austrian decorations to us before the banquet he found 'Dolly' Teck in his bath and gravely handed him his Order.

We left Vienna in the Emperor's train which came as far as the frontier, and at Gmunden station we stopped half an hour to see the Duke and Duchess of Cumberland.[7] We all got out of our different carriages and formed up in any order but still in uniform. I was astonished to see an old man dressed as a British General but in a uniform of pre-Crimean War pattern, with an antiquated Garter riband. Of course, I grasped that he must be the Duke of Cumberland and I easily recognized the Duchess of

[4] The tragedy of the Crown Prince Rudolph, who is believed to have shot his lover, the Baroness Marie Vetsera, and then to have taken his own life at Mayerling, is familiar to all.

[5] Known to Bonapartists as Napoleon II; son of Emperor Napoleon I and Marie Louise, Archduchess of Austria.

[6] Later 1st Marquess of Cambridge, after relinquishing German titles.

[7] A great-grandson of George III; de jure King of Hanover.

Cumberland and her companion, Queen Christine of Spain.[8] The King presented us: Sidney Pembroke of course came first, then Stanley Clarke, then Colonel Owen. Not unnaturally they did not recognize Queen Christine of Spain and shook her warmly by the hand. I came next and bowed and kissed her hand. Seymour Fortescue, who was behind me, followed my example although he had not the foggiest idea who she was. I always upheld British customs abroad and only kissed the hands of Queens. When the moment arrived to say good-bye the Duke and Duchess of Cumberland came and shook hands with us, but Queen Christine came up only to Seymour Fortescue and me and held out her hand for us to kiss, completely ignoring the others.

In August 1904 I went again with the King to Marienbad and found the same rooms, the same servants, and practically the same people. It was always an advantage to have people to walk with the King as he really had quite enough of us at other times. Arthur and Venetia James, Mark Lockwood [9] and his wife, Lady Romney, Mr. and Mrs. de la Rue, Mrs. Hall Walker,[10] Mrs. Petre, and Gill,[11] the lawyer, were particularly useful in this way. Countess Festetics (*née* Hamilton) always amused and interested the King. She often came to luncheon and dinner, but she never walked in the early morning.

Prince Ferdinand of Bulgaria [12] also came to stay this year and seemed to attract a large crowd whenever he walked out. He amused the King with his witty and cynical conversation and seemed to like being photographed with His Majesty. Once or twice I walked with him, and I must say he was most amusing as he made fun of everybody and everything. He gave an account of his visit to Vienna and ridiculed the life at the Viennese Court. He spoke of the Austrian Emperor as *ce sale vieillard,* and seemed

[8] Widow of King Alfonso XII; mother of Alfonso XIII.

[9] Later 1st Lord Lambourne.

[10] Wife of William Hall Walker, later 1st Lord Wavertree, who bred Minoru, which won the Derby for King Edward VII.

[11] Later Sir Charles Gill. Counsel to, and Honorary Member of, the Jockey Club.

[12] Ferdinand of Bulgaria, Prince since 1886; proclaimed himself Czar, 1908; abdicated in favour of son, Boris, 1918.

to have a very poor opinion of him. I heard later that he had gone to Vienna on purpose to get the Golden Fleece and the Emperor had refused to give it to him. When recounting his early life, he said that when he had ascended the throne of Bulgaria, he determined that if there was any killing to be done, he would be on the side of the killers and not of the killed. This remark later appeared in *Punch,* but I never knew whether they had been told of my conversation with him, or whether it was an aphorism that he frequently repeated.

When the Emperor of Austria came, the crowd in the morning became almost unmanageable, but of course any idea of his walking about in this crowd was out of the question. He took a villa in the town and entertained King Edward at dinner. He also dined with the King, but on both occasions the conversation never turned on European politics as they were both too clever to talk on any difficult subject before others. Whether they got down to the European political situation when they had private talks I have no idea, but I never had to report anything to the Foreign Office.

Sir Henry Campbell-Bannerman was an old habitué of Marienbad and used to come every year, but for some reason or another the King had never taken much notice of him. On this occasion His Majesty asked him to luncheon. Apparently the King thought he would be prosy and heavy, but found to his surprise that he was quite light in hand with a dry sense of humour. He told several amusing stories and was very good company. After this a sort of friendship sprung up between the two and the King seemed to like the straightforward way he had of stating his convictions without fearing that his opinions might be distasteful to His Majesty.

My brother Arthur, who was his Private Secretary, came out with Campbell-Bannerman and the King asked him to luncheon, and drew him out. A few days later he had to manage a luncheon which Campbell-Bannerman gave to the King and Prince Ferdinand of Bulgaria with a few of the regular habitués of Marienbad. It was a magnificent repast and Arthur dropped being a rabid socialist and became the diplomatist with good manners and talking German and French perfectly.

I had now got accustomed to the routine, and as the King allowed one to play golf in the afternoon I got away almost every afternoon. At breakfast I had the local newspaper brought to me and propped a paper up against the coffee-pot. The King did the same, but as Seymour Fortescue couldn't read German, he had to content himself with an English paper two or three days old, but the inevitable result of this was that we talked and rocked with laughter the whole of breakfast. The King was always in good spirits at that time in the morning and liked to recall the old days when he had so many amusing adventures.

The King went to shoot with Prince Trauttmansdorff at Bischof Teinitz and took Harry Chaplin and me with him. It was wonderfully well done and there were about four hundred beaters, men, women, and children, in most picturesque dresses, who formed a circle with a mile radius. The circle was always kept so that when the birds were driven over a valley where the guns were placed, they always settled on the other side and never went outside. It was a very hot day and I eventually got so tired I could hardly put the gun up. One had barely time to cross the valley, a matter of two hundred yards, when the drive was over, before the birds began coming in the opposite direction. We all had men counting the number of birds we shot and I was credited with having got over a hundred brace to my own gun. The other guns were Count Tassilo Festetics and Prince Trauttmansdorff's son-in-law.

Reuter's correspondent was accustomed to send important news as briefly as possible, leaving it to the Press at home to amplify it. He telegraphed, 'King accompanied by Ponsonby Chaplin shot partridges Trauttmansdorff good bag day fine'. In London this was amplified thus: 'The King accompanied by Colonel Ponsonby and the British Chaplain honoured Prince Trauttmansdorff and had a good day's partridge shooting. The birds were plentiful and the day fine'. Everybody thought that the King had found that the British Chaplain was a very good shot and had asked him to come.

In 1906 we found everything in Marienbad much the same as on former visits. We arrived on August 16th, the Emperor of Austria's birthday, and found the town *en fête*. At twelve o'clock the King went down to the church to attend the service in honour of the Emperor's birthday. His Majesty was dressed in the uniform of an Austrian Field-Marshal and we were also all in uniform. The King did not, of course, attend the Mass, but only the Te Deum. The Church was very crowded and the music was lovely.

I had to make it quite clear to the Press that His Majesty did not attend the Mass. One year it was stated in the English papers that the King had been to a Roman Catholic Church and had attended a Roman Catholic service, and this aroused the Protestant element in England to fury. I had found the Press very difficult to deal with, but now everything worked very well. When we first went to Marienbad the newspapers were in the habit of reporting who the King spoke to, what he wore, and all sorts of little petty details, which annoyed His Majesty very much. I therefore sent for all the members of the Press and asked them to come and see me. I imagined there would be about a dozen. To my surprise, however, thirty-seven people turned up. There were English, American, Austrian, French, Russian, German, and Italian. The greater part were men, but there were several women.

I addressed them all and said that the King came to Marienbad entirely for his health, and that he wished his stay there to be entirely private. His Majesty, however, quite realized that the public had some right to know what he was doing, but it often happened that the Press was singularly inaccurate with regard to its statements of His Majesty's movements. I suggested they should depute one of their number to come to me every day, and that I would give the general outline of what the King had been doing; but I could only give it on condition that they would cease to publish small details about His Majesty's apparel and the people to whom he spoke. I then asked them to select somebody and left the room. When I returned ten minutes later they were all talking together at the top of their voices in various languages. It seemed that they were unable to choose anyone. I therefore decided to make the choice myself. I selected Reuter's correspondent. He was not connected with any particular paper and was cosmopolitan. They all agreed to abide by this agreement, with one exception. The lady from the *New York Herald* stayed behind and said that she would not be bound by any such agreement. She said she understood that I wished to muzzle the Press and that she would be no party to it, adding, 'I shall have to report you to Mr. Gordon Bennett,[13] and he will be very angry with you'. I said I was very sorry to hear that she would not come in with the others, but that she was at perfect liberty to do anything she liked. I then sent for Reuter's man and said that any information I gave him with regard to the King's movements was never on any account to be communicated to her. The other correspondents took very good care that she should never be told anything. The result was that, after floundering along for ten days with inaccurate news and little bits of tittle-tattle, she decided to follow the other Press people. She therefore came and humbly apologized and asked that she might be allowed in future to have the advantage of knowing the news of the day.

The Abbot of Tepl, a great dignitary of the Roman Catholic Church, asked the King to shoot and the idea seemed to tickle His Majesty. But the Abbot's idea of shooting was rather primitive; he imagined that you had only to buy a certain number of partridges, put them down in a field, drive them over the guns, and all would go well. The ranger who was to manage the shoot, however, told him that the danger was that the partridges might fly away early in the morning. He therefore recommended that two kites should be flown over the field; the partridges would mistake them for big birds and refuse to fly. Unfortunately they left the kites still flying when the beaters began the drive, with the result that the partridges absolutely refused to get up and fly and either ran or else flew low and constantly alighted. This made the shooting very difficult as the birds remained close in front of the beaters. As a shoot it was a fiasco; but as a day out in the country it was amusing. The King for some obscure reason was placed on the right and hardly got a shot, and I asked the other guns how many birds they had shot and made out we had a total bag of 36 brace, but later I found that the ranger had counted all the birds that had died in the train or been knocked on the head by the beaters, so that eventually a game-card was framed showing that

[13] Proprietor of the *New York Herald*.

the bag had been 150 brace. The guns were the King, Prince Lucinge, Eddy Stonor,[14] Arthur Boyd, Ernest Scott, Seymour Fortescue, and myself. One old monk came out with an old-fashioned gun and a bag of cartridges. This alarmed Eddy Stonor, who asked him where he intended to go. He replied he was going by himself behind the beaters and added, 'It will all be quite safe, but of course if anyone shoots at me, I shall shoot back'.

Before the shoot we had luncheon at the monastery and I imagined that it would consist of bread and water which would have ill suited the King and probably made him cross for the day; but not at all, we had an excellent luncheon, obviously produced by a first-rate cook, with the best wine.

Life at Marienbad was very hard work, as I spent so much time seeing people who were difficult to get rid of. For instance, one day I saw an Austrian Countess who wanted to take her dogs to England and thought I could give her a pass to prevent them going into quarantine. She was followed by an American who had some grievance at the way he had been treated by a British Consul at some place in Austria; while the Abbot of Tepl, who was a great talker, wanted my advice on how to attract English people to Marienbad; other visitors were an officer who had invented a scabbard which telescoped up when the sword was drawn, a sculptor who wanted to do a bust of the King, and last but not least, a beautiful lady from the half-world in Vienna who wanted to have the honour of sleeping with the King. On being told this was out of the question, she said if it came to the worst she would sleep with me, so that she should not waste the money spent on her ticket; but I told her to look elsewhere for a bed.

Having thoroughly learned the inside of a motor in London, I thought I would begin to drive, and therefore hired a motor from a chemist. I explained to him that I wished to drive myself and he charged me accordingly. I took out the German chauffeur and also the King's chauffeur, who both shouted directions at me in English and German. I got on very well for the first hour, but it was an old tin-kettle sort of motor and going up a steep hill I managed to slip a gear. The result was a loud clash inside and the

[14] Brother of Harry Stonor.

motor stopped dead. On examination we found I had smashed one of the gears but I was able to drive back on the other speeds. I sent and asked the chemist how much he would require for the damage done, but received no answer at all, and when I sent a second time he replied that he did not wish to charge anything. Later it transpired that he wished to get a warrant of appointment or the Victorian Order as one of the Town Councillors. Of course it was very necessary for me to be most careful in this respect, and I at once sent down to him and said I must insist on having the account, and suggested paying for the hiring of the motor and giving him £10 as well. I then received a letter from the chemist saying that as I would not accept all this as a present he would be obliged to charge me £175. This was, of course, quite monstrous. He had sent the car to Paris and had practically renewed the inside. When I therefore wrote to him and told him that I refused to pay so much, he became insulting and said that he would go to law about it. From enquiries I made I found that the judge who would try the case was his brother-in-law, and the leading counsel was his nephew. The police, who were most kind, told me that I should have no earthly chance; so I consulted the head Austrian detective, Herr Schober, and asked him whether in his opinion it would be better for me to pay the £175 at once. He replied that the whole thing was a monstrous swindle and that he would suggest my placing the case in the hands of a Viennese lawyer. He begged me, however, to keep what he said private as he did not wish to be quoted in Marienbad.

I took his advice and asked the Ambassador in Vienna to tell me the name of a first-rate lawyer. I wrote out an account of the case and sent it with all the letters which had passed between myself and the chemist. This eminent lawyer wrote back and said the whole thing was absolutely laughable, but that the mistake I had made was in offering to pay anything at all. He said the best thing to do would be to plead extra-territorial rights, and this meant that, as I was a foreigner, the case must be tried in Vienna. He wrote accordingly to the chemist's lawyer and said that the case would be tried in Vienna next month. This had the effect of entirely squashing the whole affair. The chemist knew he had no earthly chance in Vienna and that he would be put to a great deal of expense. The matter was therefore settled by my paying for the hire of the car, and the Mayor came and apologized to me for the impertinence of the chemist. He hoped that the matter would not be mentioned to the King. I had, however, already told the King all about it and His Majesty was very much amused.

About this time Mr. Haldane, then Secretary of State for War, accompanied by Colonel Ellison, came out to stay for two days in order to see the King, but unfortunately on the day he arrived His Majesty was having luncheon out and I was told to take them out to luncheon. I took them to the Rübezahl, a restaurant at the top of a hill overlooking Marienbad, and there we had luncheon outside on the Terrace. Haldane was very light in hand and amusing; but at the end of luncheon we got on the topic of the next war, which he did not believe to be a possibility, but for which he had made every preparation. He sketched out what steps would be taken should England be drawn in, and I remember a seraphic smile lighting up his face when he told me about the Territorial Associations which would deal with a levee *en masse*. Had I suggested that Kitchener as War Minister would scrap them and start an army of his own, he would have proved conclusively that such a thing was not possible.

On August 30th poor Lady Campbell-Bannerman died, and the King went to her funeral service, which was most impressive, part of it being done in English and part in German. The King himself placed a wreath on the coffin, and it was very affecting when His Majesty stepped forward and shook hands with Campbell-Bannerman, who nearly broke down.

When we returned Probyn sent me a message asking me to sign the accounts for the Marienbad visit as Seymour Fortescue had gone abroad. I replied that I should be glad to do this, but I presumed that the word 'signing' them meant being responsible that they were correct, in which case I should like all the details sent to me. No doubt he was accustomed to new brooms, but he told me that it was purely a matter of form, since the accounts were divided between the four departments of the Lord Chamberlain, the Lord Steward, the Master of the Horse, and the Keeper of the

Privy Purse. Each account was audited and carefully looked through by the official's office to whom it was sent, and so there was nothing for me to worry about. However, a voluminous volume was brought to me, and I saw at a glance that the accounts were so presented that it was impossible to say what the cost of anything was. For instance, a special motor was hired for the King's use for three weeks and I was curious to see what exactly it had cost, but as different items were charged to four different accounts any analysis was impossible. I got a chartered accountant to come and asked him to dig out what the food at the King's table had cost per day, what the servants' food had cost, what the hotel charged for the rooms, and what was the cost of the hired chauffeur and his keep. He spent some days in extracting this, and then came to me with startling information. Although the food had necessarily to be quite plain on account of the cure, and although only a little light hock was drunk, the cost of the food was enormous. The charge for the rooms was not excessive, but the hire of the motor for three weeks came to more than a new motor. In addition to the chauffeur's keep (and he appeared to have lived like a prince, drinking the most expensive wines at each meal), the bill for renewing worn-out parts came to over £1,500.

I reported all this to Probyn, who was quite horrified and took the whole thing up most seriously, with the result that the courier got into severe trouble, but he turned out to be a fool and not a knave. There had been no supervision and he had allowed anyone to order what they liked and to let the hotel charge any price.

Owing to the mourning for the King of Denmark (who died on January 29, 1906) the usual dinners were not given, but the King decided to give one to Cabinet Ministers. I sat between Sydney Buxton [15] and John Burns [16] and had quite an interesting dinner. Owing to the current of conversation changing, we had a three-cornered conversation. We began tamely enough, but in order to get on more interesting topics, I asked John Burns what

[15] Later 1st Earl Buxton. Postmaster-General, 1905–10.
[16] Radical M.P. for Battersea, and President of the Local Government Board, 1905–14.

he would do if he were Czar of All the Russias. He replied he would at once go out on a balcony and say he would give the people all they demanded. I remarked, 'Like Louis XVI'. This put him out, but he went on in a grandiose manner, as if he were the Czar, and said he would tell them that the day of suppression was over and that now a new era would begin where liberty of speech, liberty of institutions, would not only be tolerated, but encouraged. I replied that the problem was more complex than it seemed and that the crude idea that all the Czar had to do was to appear on a balcony and promise everything was out of the question. The people in Russia were not ready for self-government and a constitution, as nine-tenths of the population were quite illiterate. Sydney Buxton said that this was so; there was a crust of very highly educated men, while the rest of the population were unable to read or write. There was no middle class to speak of and nothing between the crust of educated men and the peasants. He countered by asking me what I should do, and when I replied that I should despair of the present generation and concentrate on the next by insisting on education of the children at the point of the bayonet, he remarked that I ought to pass on this suggestion to Birrell,[17] the Minister for Education. John Burns went off on the theme that nihilists were really the creation of the Czarist régime. Any man who was merely mildly Liberal was so persecuted that he eventually became an extremist. He said that the reason we had little trouble with communists in this country was that we left them alone. He told a story of how he had gone to see the Diamond Jubilee procession and was wandering about in the crowd when he came across a group of seven well-known anarchists, two Russians, two Italians, and the rest of various nationalities. He asked them what they were doing, and they said they liked to see a fine bit of pageantry. At that moment the procession appeared and to his astonishment they all took off their hats and bowed. He twitted them with being illogical, but they denied it, and said that they admired the way in which Queen Victoria drove about practically unprotected by police, and that if other countries fol-

[17] Augustine Birrell; President of the Board of Education, 1905–7; Chief Secretary to Lord Lieutenant of Ireland, 1907–16; biographer and essayist.

lowed England's example there would be no shooting or bomb-throwing.

John Burns told me he had an intense admiration for the Brigade of Guards, and especially for the Grenadiers. He had in his youth a great contempt for the officers of the Guards and thought they were club loafers, while the men were pampered and unfit to do anything but sentry-go. He had gone on foot to the manœuvres and had completely changed his mind. He had had a gruelling hot time marching with the 1st Battalion of the Grenadiers, and although they had covered twenty miles, not a man fell out; but what had struck him most was that, when the battalion returned to camp, the officer on duty in each company was not allowed to go to the mess tent or even have a drink until he had seen that the men's dinners were brought and until the men had said they had no complaints to make. He had attended the French, German, and Austrian manœuvres and had had an opportunity of comparing the men of the various armies. He was convinced that man for man ours were infinitely superior. I, however, reminded him that comparing a voluntary with a conscript army was not comparing like with like, and that he had better wait until we had swept in the dregs of our town population before making any comparison.

The next year, 1907, we arrived at Marienbad on August 19th. One night the King went to the theatre. The play on the advertisement was called *Die Hölle*.[18] His Majesty thought it was a melodrama, and having nothing else to do thought it would amuse him to go and see it. When we arrived, however, we found it to be a sort of music-hall performance. The actors came from a music-hall away in Vienna called 'Die Hölle'. There were nothing but songs and recitations, and I believe the songs were very improper, but the double meanings were entirely wasted on me. I was intensely bored by the performance. When the second act began very much the same as the first, with a song, the King got up and left.

The next day the papers were full of this incident. They said that the King had gone to an improper performance and had left

[18] "The Underworld."

in disgust to show his disapproval. A day or two afterwards letters came from England thanking the King for making a firm stand in the cause of morality. The people who had not been at the theatre said that the performance must have been pretty hot to make the King and myself leave. It was in vain that I said that all the improper part had been wasted on me; even people in England wrote to me and chaffed me about taking up such a very moral attitude. The Bishop of Ripon (Boyd Carpenter) wrote a letter to the King expressing the satisfaction of the whole Church at the protest the King had publicly made against obscene musical comedy. It was a very flowery letter and one would have thought that the King had made a speech on the subject, so much was made of the incident. I asked the King what reply I should send, and he said, 'Tell the Bishop the exact truth. I have no wish to pose as a protector of morals, especially abroad.'

The King's dog, Caesar, had been ill, and His Majesty wanted to send for Sewell from London. Sewell's charge was £200 for coming out. I expostulated with the King on the extravagance of having out a man who charged so much, but His Majesty said that if his dog was ill he would get the very best man, and he did not care what it cost. Luckily a first-class vet. was found in Vienna who came and cured the dog.

One evening the King dined with Mrs. Hall Walker, and after dinner a new dancer came, by name Maud Allan, who had never danced in London. The King expressed a wish to see her dance, but I was rather doubtful from what I had heard as to whether it would be right for His Majesty to do so. I had been told that she danced more or less naked, and I was afraid that the English Press might get hold of this and make up some wild story. I therefore went to Mrs. Walker and said that I had heard that Miss Maud Allan danced with only two oyster-shells and a five-franc piece, and questioned whether it was quite wise for the King to see her. Mrs. Walker replied that Miss Allan was a great artist and that there was nothing at all offensive in the performance. The question was to get the music, and finally Little, the correspondent of the *Daily Mail*, and the leader of the town band were made to play duets for Miss Maud Allan to dance to. I went at once to Little and explained to him that he was coming in as a friend, and that I trusted that he would not report any of this in the *Daily Mail*. He roared with laughter and said that of course he would treat it quite confidentially. The dance was very exceptional, and I must say that Miss Maud Allan was really wonderful. Her dance as Salome with the head of John the Baptist was really most dramatic, and, although I cannot say she wore many clothes, there was nothing the least indecent about her performance.

The fact of her having danced before the King was used later as an argument with the London County Council to allow her to continue her performance in London.

For three or four years I had been running the golf-course in Marienbad and this year it was necessary to rebuild the Club and to do certain alterations in the way of draining the ground. I had put the Club under a committee composed of Austrians, which was a great improvement. The Abbot, the Burgomaster, two Aldermen, two hotel-keepers, and Prince Trauttmansdorff, as the President, formed the committee. There was also an English committee to decide technical questions of golf. At the last meeting I undertook to raise 6,000 kroner to pay for the various alterations. I was rather nervous afterwards in case I should be landed with a large deficit, but I had no difficulty in raising the money. People came forward most generously and I could have got double the amount if I had wished it. The King himself headed the subscription with a large amount. The committee meetings were rather difficult as the German-speaking portion could not understand English and the English portion could not understand German. Goschen, the Ambassador, and I had to do the interpreting, and when I got up and made any statement I had to make it in both languages, which made it rather hard work.

By 1908 I had become the Manager of the Golf Club, although there was a President, a committee of management, an hon. secretary, and a professional. It was found to be more convenient first to have some person to refer to, and secondly, for the secretary and professional to refuse to solve a problem and insist on its being referred to a higher authority. As the members were of all nationalities, the language question played a great part in these discussions. Once I remember being asked to explain to an old man that he was not a member and was therefore breaking all rules. I tried him in English, French, and German, but he refused to answer. I got someone to try him in Italian, and another to speak Spanish, but it was no use. Eventually he proved to be an Englishman who was stone deaf.

On another occasion I was called out to decide a knotty point that had arisen during a stroke competition. I went out on the links and found a crowd of very excited people all talking various languages. It turned out that a Russian nobleman had invented a mashie with prongs like a hayfork and claimed that anyone could easily play a ball in long grass as the prongs went through the grass like a comb. Apparently he had impaled the ball on one of the prongs and the question arose whether he should drop the ball with the penalty of one stroke or whether he could just shake it off and go on playing. The Tower of Babel was a mere jest to this conversation, which was carried on in Russian, German, French, English, and possibly other languages. I, however, disqualified the Russian for using an illegal club, and refused to argue the point any further: a decision which I may say pleased no one.

During a competition I received an anonymous letter to the effect that one of the competitors, an American, had done seven years' imprisonment for forgery. He was a good-looking, youngish man and extremely popular with everyone. I put the letter in the fire, but a few days later I received another letter, and again a third; but it was clearly no business of mine to enquire into the past history of the members and I therefore paid no attention. My correspondent proved to be a lady whom the American had jilted, and finding I would do nothing she told another lady the story in the strictest confidence. Needless to say it was all over Marienbad in about two hours. It was apparently true that as a youth he had forged and been sent to prison, but he had made good and was in quite a good position somewhere. The wretched man thought it useless to fight the case and bolted by the next train.

As all sorts and conditions of men competed for the Town Prize, the handicapping was often a matter of some difficulty. An

Englishman joined the Club and said his handicap was eighteen, and after seeing him play I thought that this was an optimistic description of his abilities as he seemed to have little idea of the game and usually took up great divots of turf. Before the handicapping was done, Doig, the professional, an astute Scotchman, told me this man was a fraud whose handicap was probably about six and that he could prove it if I would come out on the links. There was a part of the links which could not be seen from any other part, and there we went and sat down in a wood near the tee of one of the holes. After half an hour we saw this man and a friend come along playing infamous golf. When they arrived on the tee, the man told his friend to keep a sharp look-out and then drove six balls, long perfect drives each one, and it was clear that he was quite a good player. Having picked up the balls, they proceeded to play infamous golf again as they came into view of other players. When I did the handicapping I made quite sure of this man not winning by making him plus four. When the handicaps were put up on a notice in the Club, the man was furious and came up to me demanding in a loud voice the reasons for his outrageous handicap when he said he was eighteen. I replied that when he had played two days ago I happened to be in the wood at the fourteenth tee and that I had seen him drive six balls. If he wanted any other evidence he could ask the professional Doig, who was with me. He spluttered at first but suddenly shut up like an umbrella and left the Club. He never played again at Marienbad.

The King was very kind about my golf and usually left me the afternoons free for it, but on one occasion at the last moment when someone failed he asked me to make a fourth at croquet. Croquet is a game the niceties of which I have never mastered, and although I had at various times played, I was a very bad player. To spend hours playing this game did not attract me and I determined to make myself as unpleasant as possible so that I should never be asked again. I drove up with the King to the croquet-ground, which was part of the Golf Club, and found that the game had already been arranged, His Majesty and Madame Letellier against old Harry Chaplin and myself. We played for two and a half hours and whenever I got the chance I sent the King's ball to the other end of the ground. This made him quite furious, and the beautiful Madame Letellier, who was quite a good player, begged me with tears in her eyes not to make him so angry, adding that she understood that courtiers always allowed monarchs to win. I replied that this was out of date and that personally I always made a point of beating the Royal Family at any game if I possibly could. I continued my tactics although it made the game distinctly unpleasant. Harry Chaplin, who had played in his youth, seemed to know all about the game and so we went ahead and looked like winners, but Madame Letellier was too good for us. Just as we were winning she caught us up and made things so awkward that we were held up. Then the King did several hoops and caught us up. We had a very exciting finish and they just won on the post. To my horror the King said that this was by far the best game he had had and that therefore we would have a return match the next day. However, he afterwards relented and said that as he knew I disliked croquet he would get someone else.

During this visit to Marienbad, Clemenceau, then Premier of France, was taking the cure at Karlsbad. He seemed to get on extremely well with the King. It was very tiresome, but I suppose inevitable, that he should be making constant statements to the Press, who gathered round him like flies. Wickham Steed,[19] *The Times* man, told me he had had a special interview and Clemenceau had talked very openly. This, of course, was on a higher plane than the statements to journalists. Marienbad prided itself on being the place where important conversations were held, but hitherto nothing had ever been published.

One day Clemenceau came to luncheon and was brilliantly witty and amusing, talking on every conceivable subject. His views on golf were distinctly original. He said that he knew all about English games and sports. They were only an excuse for bringing the young man and the young woman together and there was nothing in them but that. Did he not often see a *partie de croquet* with young people really engaged in making love? Tennis was very much the same: the young man tried to show how athletic he was, but the real objective was to sit out afterwards with a young lady.

[19] Later Editor of *The Times* and author of *The Hapsburg Monarchy*.

When, however, it came to golf he admitted that his theory didn't apply. He once was at La Boulie golf ground near Paris and he saw a young man and woman starting off for golf. He thought that this was only an excuse for a delightful walk in the woods with infinite possibilities in the way of love-making, but he saw the young man go off to the left and the young girl to the right and they never seemed to get together at all.

At the end of luncheon he became serious and outlined the next big war when Germany would certainly walk straight on Paris and demand a huge indemnity. He said he had asked Edward Grey [20] what the British Empire would do if Germany went through Belgium to Paris, and Grey replied undoubtedly it would create a great stir in England. That, Clemenceau said, would be a lot of use to France. He was warming up to his subject when the King, fearing indiscretions, asked him to come to his room and have a talk.

Prince Danilo of Montenegro [21] was also in Marienbad about this time, and was what the Scotch call 'a puir wratch'. The King asked him to luncheon but beyond that did not take much notice of him in spite of Prince Danilo's efforts. The Prince asked me to tell the King that the dearest wish of his heart was to have a British Order, and that although he had been several days at Marienbad this had not materialized. I replied that the King was incognito and that any idea of giving decorations was out of the question, but he argued that everyone in his own country would consider it a slight if he were not to return with a British Order.

I repeated all this to the King, who said he had never heard such impudence. Did Prince Danilo really imagine that British decorations were chucked about like this? If he did, the sooner he learnt our customs the better.

Prince Danilo had arranged with me that if the answer was favourable I was to come up to him and shake hands when he came to say good-bye to the King, but if unfavourable I was to take no notice of him. When he finally came to take leave of His

[20] Later 1st Viscount Grey of Fallodon. Foreign Secretary, 1905–15.
[21] Crown Prince of Montenegro.

Majesty I remained immovable and looked at the ceiling. I was conscious, however, of his glaring at me the whole time.

On August 17, 1908, the King went to see the Emperor of Austria at Bad Ischl, a small town right up in the mountains where people go for some ailment. After a hot night in the train we arrived at Ischl station about noon and were met by the Emperor and a crowd of Archdukes and Archduchesses. My somewhat superficial studies of the *Almanach de Gotha* unfortunately did not enable me to make out who they all were. The King's suite were Charlie Hardinge, Stanley Clarke, and myself. The Emperor, when we were presented to him by the King, said in French 'An old friend', and shook me warmly by the hand.

At the time I imagined this to be merely good staff work, but I found later there was more in this than I thought. The King had suggested that as this was a purely private visit, no decorations should be given to us, but if the Emperor liked to give us his photograph there would be no objection. The Emperor, however, who thought very little of decorations, thought a signed photograph was the highest thing he could give, and said that he would be glad to give me his photograph as he knew me, but as he didn't know Hardinge or Clarke he would give them decorations. When therefore he greeted me as an old friend, it was to emphasize his decision.

We drove up to our hotel in victorias and I drove with Margutti, who was sort of Chef du Protocole. I did not know him, but many years later he wrote a book of recollections from which it appeared that he invariably accompanied the Emperor. I knew several of the Emperor's suite, notably Count Parr and Prince Dietrichstein, a brother of Count Mensdorff.

On arrival at the hotel the Emperor and his suite drove away and we all had baths. Then Stanley Clarke and I had to do that tiresome business of writing our names in the Visitors' Books of the various Archdukes and Duchesses and leaving cards on their suites. The King was particularly anxious that Prince Liutpold of Bavaria [22] should have the Grand Cross of the Victorian Order in time to wear it at dinner that night. I therefore took advantage

[22] Regent of Bavaria.

of this opportunity of either giving it or leaving it at his house, but when, after writing our names, I asked to see him, I could find no one but a Lady-in-Waiting, who blushingly informed me he was in his bath. So I left it with her.

After luncheon Hardinge went to have a talk with Baron von Aehrenthal,[23] the Austrian Minister for Foreign Affairs. Stanley Clarke and I went for a drive into the country and on the way home we stopped at a village to have some coffee. The innkeeper, seeing an Imperial carriage, charged us a ridiculous sum; when we decided to protest, we found we had forgotten to take any money with us, and had to borrow some from the footman on the carriage and pay what was asked.

Curiously enough there was a small theatre where a burlesque by Oscar Straus was given. We all went in uniform and, as the theatre was like an orchid house with no ventilation of any description, we were all boiled. Afterwards we returned to the Emperor's house for dinner. It was a sort of shooting-box, a wooden hut the walls of which were covered with heads and horns of stags of all descriptions. We dined at a large round table which held about forty.

When talking over the question of decorations with Count Parr, I explained that as it was understood that this was a private visit the King intended to give very few. He said that the Emperor had expressed a hope that the King would confer the Cross of Commander of the Victorian Order on the Hoffourier. I replied that I thought a Hoffourier was a Comptroller of Supplies, but he said that this particular individual had the rank of Colonel in the Army and had the Iron Cross, a high Austrian decoration. As the Emperor had expressly asked me for this there seemed to be no doubt about it, and accordingly I put his name down on the list for the King's approval. As it happened, however, the King had little time to spare, and I never had a chance of explaining the matter to him.

At dinner he was much put out at seeing this official standing behind the Emperor's chair and thought he was one of the servants. Afterwards he told me I had made a frightful blunder and

[23] Count Alois Aehrenthal, Austrian Foreign Minister till death in 1912.

given a high decoration to a footman. He became very angry about this and said I had lowered the standard of British decorations, but when I told him that it was at the Emperor's express wish that I had put his name down, and that the Hoffourier had the rank of Colonel, he agreed that there was no alternative but to give it.

After dinner I had some conversation with the Emperor, who questioned me closely about the words of command given in the Indian Army. I understood that the language question was playing a great part in the Austrian Army. He thought that the Indian Army dialects was a perfect analogy. Afterwards we had a butterfly conversation, touching lightly on one topic after another. I don't remember how we got to the 'Yellow Peril', but I told him the German Emperor thought this was a very real danger. He said, *'Ce pauvre Guillaume. Il ne pense qu'à cela. Il peint des tableaux même pour nous effrayer'*. With the Emperor I found it was the etiquette to talk German when in German Austria, and French when in Hungary or Bohemia.

When the annexation of Bosnia and Herzegovina [24] burst like a thunderclap on Europe a fortnight later and no one knew anything about it, it seemed to me extraordinary that the old Emperor and the King had had long conversations, had gone for a two-hours drive together, and had had luncheon and dinner together, and yet nothing had been said about the annexations. They had discussed European politics and talked openly about the European situation and yet the Emperor had given the King no idea of what the Austrian intentions were. It was perhaps not to be wondered that Aehrenthal said nothing about this to Hardinge, as he was a foxy type and preferred to work underground.

[24] These two provinces, which had long been administered by Austria, were formally annexed as a result of the growing nationalist agitation there (which was brought to a head in 1908 by the Young Turks' declaration that Bosnia and Herzegovina should be represented in the new Parliament at Constantinople) and in order to improve Austria's strategic position in the Balkans. The acute tension between Austria and Servia which culminated at Sarajevo had its origin at this time.

CHAPTER XVII

Prince Henry of the Netherlands — Biarritz — Asquith's visit and its repercussions — The official visit to Berlin, 1909 — Character of William II — Deadlock in Parliament — Malta — Vesuvius — Prince Henry of Prussia

ALTHOUGH my status at this time was that of an Equerry, I rarely had to do an Equerry's duties, apart from having to attend the King in uniform when two Equerries were required. It rarely fell to my lot to have to do odd jobs, as the other Equerries had to do.

I forget what the reason was, but none of the other Equerries was available when the King in 1907 sent a Mission to The Hague to present the Grand Cross of the Bath to Prince Henry of the Netherlands,[1] and I therefore received orders to accompany Prince Alexander of Teck.

We had a delightful time, as all Hague society inundated us with invitations. The presentation ceremony was conducted with the proper ceremonial and we had to dress up in full uniform. One of the Attachés from the Legation was to carry the cushion on which the insignia were placed, and in order to prevent their falling off I stuck the pin at the back of the Star through the velvet cushion. The Attaché, however, was not content with this, but secured the end of the pin by the catch to make doubly sure. The result was that when Prince Alexander, having made a suitable speech, tried to get hold of the Star, he found it firmly fixed to the cushion and spent some time in getting it loose. This rather spoilt the most impressive moment of the ceremony.

Prince Henry was regarded by some members of the Royal Family of Europe as a tiresome man, but it always seemed to me

[1] Consort to Queen Wilhelmina.

351

that he played the difficult part of Prince Consort with some skill, although he was never popular in Holland. Apparently he had learnt to speak English and was very proud of this fact. In the smoking-room after dinner I was brought up to him and the Chamberlain impressed upon me the necessity of speaking English and not German to him. All the Dutch suite spoke French and German, but few could manage English. It was therefore clear that he wished to show them how well he spoke. The conversation was, however, not very easy as he invariably refused any help I offered. I asked him about the wreck of an English vessel where he was said to have shown great gallantry. I said I supposed the waves must have been terrific, and he replied, 'Yes, the sea was very—very—very . . .'

'Rough?'

'No, no, no. The sea was very—very—very . . .'

'Stormy?'

'No, no, no. The sea was very—very—very . . .'

'Violent?'

'No, no, no. But we came in a boat and we threw a—threw a— threw a . . .'

'Rope?'

'No, no, no. We threw a—threw a—threw a . . .'

'Lifebuoy?'

'No, no, no. But we threw a—threw a . . . and we could not, and the sea was very . . .'

The story got about The Hague, with the embellishment that when he said 'the sea was very . . .' I had suggested 'wet'.

There was a banquet at which Prince Alexander made a speech and the Queen responded very well. The following night there was a family dinner and I dined with the Household, when I was surprised to find a dinner of about sixty, composed mostly of people who were to go to a reception afterwards and who had not been included in the banquet. To my horror the Hof Marshall got up and made a beautiful speech in French proposing my health and adding that, as I spoke French, he knew I could reply in that language. There I was with nothing prepared, and even had it been an English speech I should have found some difficulty in replying at a moment's notice, while to speak in French seemed beyond me. However, there was nothing to be done but to get started and I got on very well to begin with; but as I got worked up and tried to put something more than banalities into the speech, it deteriorated very much.

In March 1908, the King went to Biarritz, and took me and Johnny Ward. It was quite delightful there as the hotel was most comfortable and the weather perfect. The King used to ask people to luncheon and occasionally to dinner, and one day decided to ask General Tucker,[2] one of our successful Generals in the South African War, but notorious for his bad language.

Johnny Ward sent out an invitation but received no answer of any kind, and the King came to the conclusion that the letter must have gone astray. A second invitation was sent and was at once accepted by Tucker. When Tucker came to luncheon the King asked him if he had ever received the first one; he replied that he had, but as the invitation was dated April 1st, he feared it was a trap and had therefore taken no notice of it. The King expostulated with him, saying, 'You really did not think I should try and make an April Fool of you?' To which Tucker replied, 'No, sir, but I thought some other damned fool might'.

It was during this visit to Biarritz that one Sunday I had to go to church with the King. Johnny Ward, the Equerry, should have also gone, but having caught a chill, was confined to his bed. The English church was crowded and the King went to the front pew with me alongside of him. When the clergyman announced that there would be an offertory for some purpose I searched my pockets for some money, but only succeeded in finding a louis, having brought no silver with me, unaware that there would be an offertory. I debated in my mind whether I should put this or nothing in the plate, but it seemed impossible for me to put in nothing while I was in such a conspicuous position.

When the hymn at the end of the service began a beautiful man came round with a plate over which was a red velvet cloth, and went first to the King, who put in a louis: then to me, and I put

[2] Lieutenant-General Sir Charles Tucker.

in a louis alongside of the King's. This looked like poker, 'I'll see that louis', but there seemed no alternative.

After church the King was rather vexed and asked if I always put a louis or a sovereign in the bag. I hastily explained that I had nothing else, but he seemed to think I had spoilt his donation. He considered it only right to put in a gold piece, but when I did the same, people thought nothing of his generosity.

Soon the work became very heavy as Campbell-Bannerman intended to resign and Asquith was to be Prime Minister. This necessitated a great deal of cyphering and decyphering, but mercifully I had Lindsay [3] from the Embassy in Paris to help me. I was besieged by the Press, who wanted to know all sorts of details, but of course I always referred them to Downing Street. The question arose as to whether the King should return to London to be present while the new Cabinet was being formed, but he said that all this could be quite well done by cypher telegrams. The larger question whether he should not return to see Asquith instead of Asquith coming out to see him was more difficult. At first there seemed some insuperable objection to Asquith's coming out to Biarritz early in April, as his presence in the House of Commons was essential while the Licensing Bill was being debated. Haldane cyphered out to me and explained this at some length, but the King, who did not like this argument, merely told me to reply that they must postpone the Bill till the following week. Having got rid of this point, the King told me to sound Asquith and ask him privately whether he had any objection to coming out to Biarritz as it was so inconvenient for the King to return to London. Asquith replied that he would be glad to come out as it would be an advantage to be abroad during the difficult time of forming a Cabinet. Meanwhile the Press in England clamoured for the King's return.

The secret was well kept and none of the Press had any idea that Asquith was coming to Biarritz, and when he arrived there was no one about. I went to the station in the King's car to meet him but timed it so that I should arrive a few minutes after the

[3] Later Sir Ronald Lindsay, Ambassador in Constantinople, Berlin and Washington.

train was due. I took him back to the hotel and he went to his room to have a wash and brush up, but he had hardly set foot in the hotel before it was all over Biarritz that he had arrived, and the Press soon swarmed round. Asquith seemed rather nervous about the ceremony of kissing hands in case he should make a mess of it, but I told him that first of all the King would do everything, and secondly, that as there would only be His Majesty and himself it didn't really matter what happened. Everything went well and the King and Asquith remained closeted for an hour. At luncheon Asquith was in great form and told us a lot of amusing political stories. When he was not sure how the point of the story would be received by the King he invariably addressed me, but the King was delighted with his *racontage*.

In the afternoon I asked him whether he would care for a walk, but unfortunately it started to rain and he declined. He told me that talking over the different posts to be filled in the Cabinet with a perfectly disinterested person like the King, had been of great use to him. They had apparently discussed every single member of the old Cabinet and the reasons for a change. The next morning Asquith left early; he had train fever so that the moment the motor appeared, and it always came round much too early, we got in and drove to the station. Of course we arrived a quarter of an hour too soon and had to walk up and down talking politics. He was very sanguine and foresaw no difficulty in passing all the Liberal programme.

A day or two later a venomous leading article appeared in *The Times* on Asquith having to come out to Biarritz to form a Government. No mention was made of his having offered to do so or of his preferring to get away from Downing Street, where he never had a moment's peace. Instead, the article ran as follows:

That this high constitutional function intimately bound up with the most delicate adjustments of our political system has taken place at Biarritz, a modern day's journey beyond the confines of the Kingdom, is a very wide departure from hitherto unbroken precedent. It may perhaps be regarded as a picturesque and graceful tribute to the reality of the Entente with our French friends that the King and the Prime Minister should find themselves so much at home in their beautiful country as to be able to transact the most important constitutional business on French soil. Still the precedent is not one to be followed and everyone with a sound knowledge of our political system must hope that nothing of the kind will ever happen again. Circumstances are doubtless conceivable in which it might be necessary to resort to this mode of transacting constitutional business, but in this case we are glad to believe that His Majesty is in excellent health. No other plea but that of necessity can be regarded as entirely adequate at a time when the importance of keeping the constitutional function of the Crown fully in evidence cannot be exaggerated. There are other inconveniences. A week has been unnecessarily lost at a critical period of the session, and if any hitch should occur in Mr. Asquith's arrangements—a thing by no means rare on such occasions—it will not be immediately possible for the King or his Minister to have those further personal conversations which would become desirable and perhaps indispensable.

As this was a direct attack on the King, I wrote to enquire privately why *The Times* had produced such a violent article without taking the trouble to ascertain the facts, and I was informed that Colonel Repington,[4] the Military Correspondent of *The Times*, had written it. This explained everything. Repington had been made to leave the Army because of some indiscretion. He approached Lord Roberts and asked to be reinstated in the Army, with apparent success. He therefore supported Lord Roberts in all his articles but when the reinstatement was submitted to the King His Majesty refused to allow it. So Repington, finding Lord Roberts useless, turned to Haldane, who seems to have thought a clever man like Repington should certainly be allowed back in the Army. A second time, however, the King refused and so the proposal was abandoned. Repington, finding that each time it was the King who prevented his going back to the Army determined

[4] Lieutenant-Colonel C. A'C. Repington, whose *Diary*, published in 1920, caused great scandal.

to take the first opportunity of attacking His Majesty in the Press. When there was criticism in London for the King's sending for Asquith to come to Biarritz he begged to be allowed to write the leading article, and put in as much venom as he dared.

The Christmas of 1908 was spent at Sandringham, and as usual the whole Royal Family was practically united. This Christmas the King's second daughter, the Queen of Norway, spent it at the adjoining estate at Appleton, and there were frequent comings and goings between the two. It was just before Christmas that Tosti came to stay at Sandringham. He was excellent company, besides being a good singer and pianist. Queen Alexandra used to like him to accompany her in duets, usually in the evening, but one day she thought she would like to play after tea but no Tosti was to be found. Pages and footmen hunted for him everywhere, but in vain. I happened to be in the hall and wondered why people seemed to be running about. I stopped one of the pages, who explained that the Queen wanted Tosti and that he was nowhere to be found.

I said 'I will get him at once', and the pages seemed much amused, explaining that the library, billiard-room, every drawing-room and even the bachelors' bedrooms had been searched. I sat down at the piano and with the loud pedal on I thumped 'Good-bye', so that it could be heard everywhere. There was a gallery running round the top of the hall and a sort of window in this gallery looking down into the hall. Tosti's head suddenly appeared in this window wondering who on earth was murdering his most famous melody. I merely said to the page, 'There he is', and shut the piano.

The next day Princess Victoria asked me to go out riding. I came down to the door, and found King Haakon of Norway also going as we were bound for Appleton to see Queen Maud. We went across the fields through a lot of gates, but Princess Victoria knew every inch of the country, and when we got half-way there we met Queen Maud in a wagonette, which she was driving herself.

Queen Maud was full of chaff and invited Princess Victoria to jump a small hedge. Princess Victoria's horse, however, would not have anything to do with it, and refused every time. So Queen Maud shouted to me to jump it. I replied that the horse did not jump, and she said: 'That's rot. It's because you funk.' After this I had no other alternative but to put the horse at the hedge. The first time the animal stopped dead, having never been taught how to jump, and began eating the hedge, so I turned it round, gave it a crack with the whip, dug in both spurs and set it at the hedge. The animal quivered with excitement, and bounded in the air, and got over to the other side, much to the amusement of Queen Maud. When I returned the Queen came out and recognized the horse as one of her favourite hacks. Princess Victoria said to me in a whisper it was best not to mention the incident about jumping as the Queen would not like it.

It was about this time that the King suggested to the German Emperor that he (King Edward) should pay a State visit to Berlin. The Emperor had always had the grievance that although King Edward had visited Paris, Brussels, Vienna, Copenhagen, Stockholm, Christiania, and Rome, his own particular capital city remained unvisited by his 'Dear Uncle'. There had, of course, been frequent previous meetings, including the official visit to Kiel, but Kiel was not Berlin. The King's decision to visit Berlin was, however, caused by a desire not only to please the German Emperor, but also to improve the strained relations between the two countries. The Emperor was enthusiastic, and being eager to make adequate arrangements in good time, suggested the second week in February. The programme was thoroughly discussed early in January, and was soon agreed upon.

On February 8, 1909, therefore we left London for Berlin. The suite consisted of Lady Antrim, Miss Knollys, Lord Crew, Secretary of State for the Colonies (Minister in Attendance), Lord Althorp[5] (Lord Chamberlain), Lord Howe (Lord Chamberlain to the Queen), Sir Charles Hardinge (representing the Foreign Office), Field-Marshall Lord Grenfell,[6] Admiral Sir Day Bosan-

[5] Later 6th Earl Spencer.
[6] Francis Wallace Grenfell, 1st Lord Grenfell of Kilvey.

quet, Cunninghame-Graham [7] (Groom-in-Waiting), Sir James Reid (Physician), Streatfeild [8] (Equerry), and myself (acting Private Secretary).

We crossed over in the *Alexandra,* the smaller of the two royal yachts, because it could get into Calais. On arrival we were met by a host of French officials and I had to land as quickly as I could to ensure that only the really important men should be presented to Their Majesties. It was nearly two before we got any luncheon on the train, but a restaurant car had been specially fitted up with a table down the centre and, of course, the food was excellent.

At dinner that night Queen Alexandra was in great form and kept the conversation going in an amusing strain. When the train lurched and a footman upset some quails on her, actually leaving a quail hanging on her hair, she kept us in roars of laughter describing how she would arrive in Berlin *coiffée de cailles.*

I had been asked by the editor of the *Guards Magazine* to write something to interest the private soldiers, and I wrote a thrilling tale of a sentry at Windsor Castle who unwittingly became one of the chief actors in a drama connected with the visit of foreign princes. Queen Alexandra had put books to read in the train in a bag which she would require only on reaching Calais. She had therefore nothing to read going down to Dover. When she discovered this she went into the King's room and of all curious periodicals to choose, she took the *Guards Magazine.* She was so much amused at my story that at dinner she proceeded to tell it, which made me very uncomfortable; but mercifully when she was in the middle of it another lurch upset the claret on the table, and as this necessitated servants wiping up the mess, there was no opportunity of finishing it.

The next morning we reached Rathenow, which is on the Brandenburg frontier. Here an unfortunate thing happened: the King was not ready. Afterwards I ascertained that his valet had mistaken the time, which had been changed at the frontier. All the suite were, however, in full uniform and got out of their carriages.

[7] Commander C. E. F. Cunninghame-Graham.
[8] Later Colonel Sir Henry Streatfeild.

There was a guard of honour and a band and the bandmaster had been given orders to continue playing 'God Save the King' until His Majesty appeared. The result was that the British National Anthem was played by the band for ten solid minutes till we all nearly screamed. At length the King appeared dressed as a German Field-Marshall, and inspected the guard of honour and regiment of hussars. It was rather a long walk, and in order to make up lost time the King went at a brisk pace and was very much blown in consequence.

When we arrived at the Lehrter Bahnhof in Berlin, the spot marked for the train to stop was arranged on the assumption that the King would get out of his own carriage, but he decided to change into the Queen's carriage, which was quite a hundred yards down the train. The result was that the Emperor, Empress, and all the Princes and Princesses were in the wrong place and had to come running down the platform in the most undignified way.

A long procession of carriages was formed, and escorted by cavalry we drove through the streets, which were lined with masses of troops. Suddenly the carriages stopped for some time, and Lord Grenfell appeared and said he had to get into our carriage. It turned out that the horses in the Queen's and Empress's carriage had jibbed and refused to move, with the result that the occupants had to get into another carriage and this necessitated a re-shuffle throughout the procession. The Emperor was furious when his carriage was the only one to reach the *Schloss* and he heard of this. He told Reischach, the Master of the Horse, that he wouldn't have had it happen for the world before the English, who were all good horse-masters. There was, however, no one who could be dignified by the name of Horsemaster in the suite, and I comforted Reischach by the reflection that we at least knew enough about horses to understand how unreliable the most perfectly trained animals are when frightened by the cheering and waving of flags.

On arrival at the *Schloss* we found the stairs lined with men dressed in uniforms of the time of Frederick the Great. Very picturesque, but trying for officers to wear fancy dress and wigs with pigtails. There began a series of functions all very well done.

The King, however, was not well, as he was suffering from a bronchial chill, with the result that he was always tired and anxious to get everything over as quickly as possible. Even the question of decorations and presents to be given didn't seem to interest him, and I saw I should have to do this without any help from him. I drew up a list on exactly the same lines as the other State visits that he had paid, but it was no easy matter to satisfy the Germans, as the Kings of Spain, Sweden, and Italy had recently visited Berlin and had scattered decorations broadcast. A somewhat overbearing Prussian General, who was head of the decorations department, was introduced to me and said, 'I will show you the list of decorations given by the King of Sweden and King of Spain'.

I thanked him, but explained that the King of England had his own rules, and did not follow either the procedure of the King of Sweden or the King of Spain. Having to talk German all the time rather cramped me, and perhaps gave him the impression that I was rude, as my utterances were necessarily short and to the point. He quietly folded up the paper, got up, clicked his heels and bowed. He then asked me whether it would be convenient for me to come and see him at his office. I assented, and went the next day down to the Behrenstrasse, where he offered to help me by showing me the list of decorations given by the Emperor in England. I again thanked him, but pointed out that it might be quicker if he were to take down the list of decorations the King proposed to give. When I gave him a list of some thirty he gasped for breath and said that there must be some mistake. I firmly pointed out that this was the English custom. He then asked whether His Majesty intended to give the Garter to General von Plessen. I saw at once that he knew nothing about our Orders, and explained at some length that the Garter was given only to crowned heads or Crown Princes. He said that the Black Eagle was the German equivalent, and as that decoration had been given to Lord Roberts, he thought some very high decoration should undoubtedly be given to General von Plessen. We had on the whole an unpleasant interview.

I was exceptionally busy, and had to sit up till two in the morning to get through the work. I had a clerk, Mr. Punshon, who talked German. He proved invaluable, but found it very hard work. On these occasions the Acting Private Secretary becomes the pivot of everything, and in addition to having to write all letters and telegrams, I had constantly to see and advise the other members of the suite. There was also a mass of Germans to be seen, and naturally this took up a good deal of my time.

The programme for the three days' State visit was a heavy one. In addition to the family luncheons and dinners, there was a civic reception at the Brandenburg Gate, luncheons with the 1st Prussian Dragoon Guards and the British Ambassador, a Court ball, a motor drive to Potsdam, a gala performance at the Opera, and a visit to the Rathaus.

The visit to the Rathaus was very interesting. The whole building was crammed with people, and the Burgomaster made a long speech and presented an album in a case. The King replied in German, and there was breathless silence. At the conclusion of his speech he received enthusiastic applause.

That evening there was a gala dinner which was magnificently done, and the King and the Emperor spoke. I think that the King, fearing what the Emperor might say, insisted on both speeches being seen by the other beforehand, and read instead of spoken. We then retired into a long gallery where I spoke to all sorts of people I knew. The ball then began, and we returned to the Weisser Saal and witnessed all sorts of extraordinary old-fashioned dances. There was something ludicrous about German officers in modern uniform dancing minuets, but as the Emperor explained to me afterwards, people did not come to a Court ball to amuse themselves but to learn deportment. After the ball we went to supper, which was served at a large number of small tables in various rooms. All of us were placed among the Princes and Princesses. At my table were two of the Emperor's sons, and various Princesses, who explained to me that they had tried to introduce the two-step, and while the Emperor was at supper they had instructed the band to play some well-known tune. The Emperor heard it and there was a proper row.

On February 11th we drove down to Potsdam and returned

for luncheon with Queen Victoria's Dragoon Guards. The King and Queen dined with the Crown Prince, and afterwards we went to the Opera, where we saw *Sardanapalus,* a ballet by the Emperor. It was beautifully done, and the last act, where the monarch sits on all his treasures and sets fire to them, was most realistic. There was an *entr'acte,* and the custom was for the visiting Sovereigns to go round and say a few words to everyone. The King, however, was suffering from a bronchial cold with fever, and having bravely undertaken to sit out the ballet, decided to give up this part of the evening's entertainment. Thereupon the Queen undertook to do it by herself. She went round, not hearing a word that was said in reply, and charmed everyone by her manner. I have never seen anything better done.

To my mind the effect of this visit was nil. One felt that a few charming men really liked us, but with the majority I derived the impression that they hated us. The Germans never forgave the King for having, as they imagined, isolated them from the rest of Europe. They attributed to him the fact that Germany practically stood alone in the councils of Europe. The Emperor for his part seemed to do all he could to make the visit a success, but he was never at his ease with the King. There were always forced jokes, and the whole atmosphere when the two were together seemed charged with dangerous electricity. I really saw very little of the suite, being so busy, but what struck me particularly was the King's wonderful power of directing everything. Ill as he was, the whole of the suite waited to hear his orders.

The day before we left Berlin I received a letter from Princess Daisy of Pless begging me to tell the King of a wonderful throat doctor in Berlin and adding that if His Majesty would see him she would arrange matters. This was a medical question and I gave it to Sir James Reid, who naturally consulted the Emperor's physician. The man in question proved to be a doctor employed by operatic singers to clear their throats before they sang. The Emperor was apparently told about this letter and said if the man came to the Castle he would have him forcibly ejected. I therefore wrote and told Princess Daisy the King did not wish to see him. My letter crossed another from her saying that if the train could stop at a station just outside Berlin she would have the man there ready. When, however, she received my letter she wrote to Charlie Hardinge and invoked his assistance. He was under the impression that this was quite a new request and asked the King whether he would see the man, but the request was refused. So the train never stopped, and I saw Princess Daisy of Pless and a man standing disconsolately on the platform at the station she had named as we glided past.

After being with the German Emperor some time one began to see that his brilliance was most superficial and all his conversation studied beforehand. It seemed to me that he anticipated what subjects of conversation would crop up and then got his staff to look out statistics, which he afterwards brought out in conversation, with the result that people were astounded at his knowledge. He was particularly good at committing statistics to memory. When he was in London he asked some Admiral what the tonnage of the new Dreadnoughts was, and when the answer was not absolutely correct he corrected it, and incidentally brought in the statistics of all the latest ships in the British Navy. Everyone said how wonderful, and what profound knowledge his conversation implied, but, of course, he had just learnt these statistics up before dinner.

I must say that he caught me out properly when one day at Friedrichshof he asked me across the table how many there were on the London County Council, who were qualified to vote, and how many years elapsed between the elections. I had very vague ideas on all these questions, but I bravely answered all of them, making shots at the numbers. 'I don't think you're right,' replied the Emperor, and then he proceeded to give chapter and verse. I must say it was very effective and everyone present marvelled at his knowledge.

Quite apart from this superficial acting, the Emperor had great fascination as a conversationalist, as he was always so keen and interested. He practically stood on one's feet, glaring into one's eyes and giving grunts of approval, which acted as a spur. As a Sovereign he had learnt his work thoroughly, and I imagine that if he had to talk with an officer in charge of submarines he worked

up the subject; and equally with a judge, an architect or a finan-
cier, he would prepare his subject beforehand. His sense of humour was of the blatant type and he was unable to appreciate any
subtle witticism, but I have heard him tell stories which were
quite funny. He was the creation of the Germans themselves.
They wanted a sabre-rattling autocrat with theatrical ways, attempting to dominate Europe sending telegrams and making bom-
bastic speeches, and he did his best to supply them with the superman they required. He liked to be thought a superman and painted
pictures, wrote sermons, arranged ballets and criticized architec-
ture with equal dexterity, and in fact prided himself on directing
every form of activity in Germany.

We returned to England on February 14th, the King's cold
and fatigue scarcely improving during the return journey. Two
days later he opened the stormiest session that Parliament had
known for many years. The King's Speech from the throne made
an emphatic reference to the cordiality of our relations with Germany, but the naval estimates a month later brought into fresh
prominence the rivalry between England and Germany, and the
Cabinet differences on the same subject. All this was comparatively smooth water compared with the turbulence that attended
Lloyd George's Budget of 1909 and the stubborn attitude of the
House of Lords.

The deadlock between the two Houses of Parliament began to
assume great importance in October and all sorts of wild rumours
went round London. It was said that Asquith intended to go to
the King and demand the creation of a large number of peers,
but nothing definite was known. Asquith came up to Balmoral and
had conversations with the King about the political situation, but
apparently never got down to the root of the matter. When he left
he gave His Majesty a memorandum he had drawn up on the subject, but even in this there were only general considerations and
nothing really definite.

The King seemed to think the attitude of the House of Lords
suicidal, and although it was most distasteful to him to have to
take any part in this dispute, he always thought he would be able
to arrange the matter privately in conversations. Esher spent his

time in looking up precedents, and wrote a very able memorandum pointing out that Lord Lansdowne had said that if the General Election proved that the country wished the Budget passed, the House of Lords would withdraw their opposition, and there would then be no necessity to create any peers.

The King was determined to try private conversations and asked Asquith if there was any objection from a constitutional point of view to his seeing Lansdowne and Balfour. Whether Asquith quite liked the idea is not clear, but he replied there would be nothing incorrect in His Majesty seeing them. Accordingly they both came to Buckingham Palace and had a long talk with the King, but it was all very disappointing as they assumed a *nonpossumus* attitude and refused to discuss any compromise.

The King and Queen went for a cruise in the Mediterranean in May 1909 and the Empress Marie [9] and Princess Victoria accompanied them. The King started from Biarritz and met the others at Marseilles. Louisa Antrim and Charlotte Knollys were with the Queen, while Seymour Fortescue and I came with the King.

We were just settling down to enjoy ourselves when an unfortunate incident nearly marred the whole success of the cruise. The King had decided to pay a visit to the Duke of Connaught at Malta, and was just looking through the programme that had been drawn up for his reception when a telegram arrived from the Commander-in-Chief of the Mediterranean Fleet to say that all ships had been ordered off to make a demonstration. King Edward was perfectly furious and in his rage became most unreasonable. Colin Keppel, who was in command of the Royal yacht, could do nothing with him and suggested my being sent for. When I entered the King's cabin I at once grasped that there was thunder in the air. 'What do you think of that?' the King shouted at me as he tossed me a telegram, and before I had time to answer he stormed away at the disgraceful way he was treated. He ended a very violent peroration by saying he had a good mind to order the Fleet back to Malta. I then perceived that a serious position might be reached and that it was up to me to stem the

[9] Of Russia.

tide. I said that probably a situation must suddenly have arisen which necessitated prompt action on the part of the Government, and that it would have been difficult for them to take into consideration His Majesty's presence in the Mediterranean. I had intended to pursue the theme and point out how disastrous it would have been had it been said that, owing to his intended visit to Malta, the demonstration had to be abandoned, but I saw there was no need to pursue the argument. The King nodded thoughtfully, but did not say anything. I then added that what struck me as being inconceivable was that neither the Prime Minister nor the First Lord of the Admiralty had the ordinary courtesy to keep him informed of what was being done. Here the King saw a perfectly logical grievance, and after breaking into a storm of abuse of the Government, told me to send messages in cypher to both Ministers which, had they been sent as he dictated them, would certainly have startled the recipients and would probably have entailed their resignation.

I went to my cabin and softened down the messages, merely pointing out that the King was surprised to find that the Fleet had been ordered off just as he was going to Malta. His Majesty presumed that an acute situation had arisen which necessitated instant measures being taken, but was surprised that no one had the common courtesy to inform him of the fact. Asquith in his reply sent ample apologies, but McKenna showed fight. He expressed great regret at the omission to keep the King informed, but pointed out that as His Majesty was cruising about the Mediterranean and no one knew where exactly he was, it was by no means easy with the best intentions to acquaint him of the Cabinet's decision. The King was mollified by Asquith's reply, but on seeing McKenna's cypher telegram to me again got very cross, and told me to fire a second barrel pointing out that as the Royal yacht's exact whereabouts were telegraphed every day to the Admiralty, the excuse could hardly hold water.

This unfortunate incident rather spoilt the visit to Malta, where the Duke of Connaught was living in the capacity of High Commissioner and Commander-in-Chief of the Mediterranean. He was very bitter at being made the fifth wheel to the coach and complained he had been put in an impossible position with ill-defined duties.

After cruising about we went to Baiae, where the King and Queen of Italy were on board their yacht. The meeting of the monarchs was very cordial and the Italians generally charming. One of the Italian A.D.C.s told me he was only staying on in the Army because he longed to have a chance of fighting the Austrians. I remarked that I thought there was such a thing as the Triple Alliance, but he said that this was drawn up by Kings, Emperors and Governments, whereas the whole of the Italian people were mad keen to fight the Austrians.

The King of Italy was an expert photographer and even had a cinematograph which constantly worked. It was the custom for an ordinary mortal like myself, when taking a photograph of a monarch, to salute before pressing the catch and again after doing so, but no one had told me what the etiquette was when the monarch was the photographer and oneself was the victim. When the King of Italy expressed a wish to photograph me in uniform I sprang to attention and saluted. When I heard his camera click I again saluted. I consulted Seymour Fortescue as to whether this was not overdoing it, but he said with foreign monarchs you could never do too much saluting.

We went on to Naples where a picnic party was arranged and a whole train engaged to take us up to look at Mount Vesuvius. We slowly toiled up this mountain as far as the railway went and there we found donkeys, which apparently the Queen had ordered unbeknown to the King. His Majesty said that nothing on earth would induce him to mount a small donkey, and there I think he was right, as he weighed sixteen stone; but neither had he the smallest intention of walking up to the crater. He would therefore go for a short walk with Seymour Fortescue and the remainder could go up on the donkeys. Princess Victoria, however, decided to stay with her father, and then Louisa Antrim and Charlotte Knollys preferred to walk. This left the Queen, the Empress Marie and myself to undertake the ascent, but at the last moment we decided to take the courier Mr. Fehr. We started off and the Empress's donkey was by far the fastest and romped away from the others. The next fastest was ridden by the Queen, and the courier had to ride hard to keep up. After half an hour I suddenly heard a shrill whistle from the engine of our train, and I could visualize the King getting impatient. So with difficulty I induced my donkey to amble along and came up to the Queen. I shouted at her that the King was having the whistle blown to tell us to return, but she merely said that if we wanted to see the crater it was no use coming up only half way. The Empress's donkey was by then quite a quarter of a mile ahead. Having, as I thought, done my duty I relapsed into silence and fell back, but soon I heard the whistle again, this time repeated again and again, and I feared the King had got hold of the string and was pulling it himself. A second time I urged my donkey on and tried to convey to the Queen what the continual whistling meant. She had by that time had enough, and since we seemed to have made no appreciable advance up the mountain she agreed to turn back, and begged me to tell the Empress, who was a speck in the distance. Obviously, I had to make my donkey trot and this I did with difficulty. Fehr the courier was a long distance behind—whether this was because he foresaw trouble or because his donkey was unable to go faster I don't know. Trotting over indented lava on a donkey of uncertain habits was not amusing, but eventually I succeeded in catching up the Empress and explained matters to her. She was much disappointed at not going on, but consented to return. We went back, and although Queen Alexandra had started back already and was therefore some distance ahead, the Empress's donkey being the fastest was the first to reach the train. The King, who was boiling with rage, was quite unable to let off steam on the Empress or even on Queen Alexandra. The courier mysteriously disappeared, and I was left coming in a bad third on a weary donkey. The vials of the monarch's wrath were therefore emptied on my innocent head. As I knew that his remarks were intended for the others I didn't remonstrate.

On our return to England in May many people commented on the King's pallor and the fact that he appeared to be ageing fast. With the summer, however, he improved, and for the Czar's visit to England in the August of 1909 he was at the top of his form.

Towards the end of the year his listlessness began to increase, and shortly after Christmas he had a touch of influenza.

In February, therefore, he went down to Mr. and Mrs. Arthur Sassoon's to recuperate. We had very difficult dinners at first because the King sat silent, and this rather chilled the conversation. Mrs. Sassoon was quite wonderful and, realizing that the King didn't want to talk, kept the ball rolling with me and Seymour Fortescue.

Asquith came down to see the King, and I met him at the station and brought him to the house. He remained closeted with the King for a long time and when he emerged he said he would like to go for a walk. So out we went, although there was quite a crowd outside. It was raining and blowing a gale, which made conversation almost impossible, and I therefore learnt little or nothing about the object of his visit.

When I saw the King later in the afternoon I said I supposed that Asquith had come to arrange about the guarantees,[10] but he said: 'Oh dear, no!' He discussed the political situation with me and said the position was very difficult. It seemed to me incomprehensible that Asquith should take the trouble to come down to Brighton from London to tell the King that the political position was very difficult.

We returned to London in the middle of February, with the King apparently improved in health, but the doctors were anxious to get him away from the English winter. It was arranged that he should leave for Biarritz on March 6th or 7th and stay a little longer than usual. There were many public functions to be carried out before then, including the reception of Prince Henry of Prussia. On February 18th, after a long day's work at Buckingham Palace, I came by chance into the Equerries' room about 11:30 p.m. and found Prince Henry of Prussia, his Equerry, Commander von Usedom, and Cunninghame-Graham, who was attached to His Royal Highness. They were talking about charities

---

[10] It was generally assumed that Asquith had obtained 'guarantees' from the King that he would create sufficient peers to coerce the House of Lords. In fact, in December 1909, the King had refused to give any such guarantees till after a second General Election.

when I came in and their talk continued for some time, when Prince Henry suddenly turned on me and said: 'Fritz, why is it we cannot get on?' I was first rather taken aback, and began generalities about the Press being responsible for the bad feeling and about commercial rivalry. Prince Henry shook his head and said: 'No, Fritz, that won't do.' So of course I was put on my mettle. I told him that it was not surprising that a feeling of distrust and suspicion had arisen when Germany insisted on building a fleet. Germany did not want a fleet to fight France or Russia or any other Power. We were therefore justified in assuming that this fleet was intended to fight England.

Prince Henry got very keen and excited and said that nothing was further from their thoughts than a war with England. They had now forty years' peace and had been able to form themselves into a nation. For the one hundred years before that they had been constantly fighting and had never had a chance. Most of the battles in the Napoleonic Wars had taken place in Germany itself. Now they were prospering, what possible object could they have in going to war with us? They had nothing to gain, and in any case it would cripple them and they would probably lose their trade. He wished people here would understand that Germany only wished to defend her commerce and that any idea of invasion was out of the question. He said that they had no plan of invasion; if such a thing was possible he wished we would explain how it could be done, but to any thinking man it must be evident that it would be impossible to send off transports full of men as long as there was even one submarine afloat.

I pointed out that, although this might be the case, he must see that a strong German Fleet threatened our national existence. We practically had no Army, and were we to lose command of the sea we should lose not only all our colonies but our independence. I said that as long as Germany continued to build we were bound to do the same, and I asked him where it was going to end. Naturally the increased taxation was being felt by all classes in both countries, and the middle class, who felt it most, were told it was on account of the German naval programme. He replied that this feeling of suspicion and distrust did not exist in Germany, and that two years ago, in order to show his confidence, he had taken the whole Fleet away to Maderia and Gibraltar and had remained away two months. Yet in spite of this we insisted on massing the whole Fleet at Dover. Why did we do this? He had asked McKenna, the First Lord of the Admiralty, who had replied that it was done for motives of economy! He repeated the question to me: Why did we mass the Fleet at Dover?

I replied that a Fleet was not kept for pleasure-boats or for digging potatoes. It was kept for one purpose, i.e. war, and therefore it was only common sense that we should keep the Fleet at a point where we should be mostly likely to want it .

He laughed and said, 'You are the first that has dared to tell me that.' I pointed out that the fact that Germany had made all arrangements for fighting on the Russian frontier in no way implied that she had any intention of going to war with Russia. It was only common sense after all to make the best possible disposition in peace-time of forces that were intended for war.

Prince Henry agreed with this, but said that in Germany this was construed into a direct preparation for war. A large number of people in Germany had a fixed idea that England would on the slightest excuse come and smash the German Fleet, and at present they were at our mercy. All they wanted was to be able to say 'Hands off'. In any difference of opinion on European questions they had to take what we dictated 'lying down'. They had studied European history and they knew that whenever any European Power rose to any predominance, we smashed them. He instanced, the Dutch, Spaniards, and later the French. They did not in Germany mean to follow the example of the others.

They had no wish for war, but they did not mean to remain defenceless and at our mercy. It was absurd to think that they wished in any way to compete with us. All they did want was to be strong enough to hold their own in the event of our attacking them.

I saw Mr. Asquith the next day and he told me that Prince Henry had asked to see him and discuss relations between the two countries. I told him of my conversation and he begged me to let him have a précis of it. He added that he hoped Prince Henry would not be so outspoken, as he might have to tell him some home truths.

I therefore sent him a typed copy describing the conversation, and two days after I saw him at the State Ball. He came up and thanked me. He said it had been of the greatest use to him, although Prince Henry had been much more guarded in his conversation. He had sent it to the Foreign Office and the Admiralty, and had asked for facts and figures so that he might make no mistake.

Years later, when the War broke out, I reminded Asquith of this conversation and asked him whether he thought Prince Henry a fool or a knave: that is to say, had he been made a fool of by Admiral Tirpitz, who had told him that he must go to England to allay all suspicion, or did he know the true facts and was he merely posing as a candid friend to conceal Germany's warlike intentions? Asquith replied he thought the latter. Prince Henry was no fool, and Tirpitz must have told him all his plans. It was clear, therefore, that he had agreed to go to England and through me to get the German view conveyed to the King. Personally I came to the conclusion that Prince Henry's visit had in no way been instigated by Tirpitz, and that, being a genuine friend of England, he had tried his best to smooth matters. He was a perfectly straightforward man and never gave one the impression of having any Machiavellian cunning.

CHAPTER XVIII

The King's illness and death — Character of King Edward VII — A lovable, wayward and human Monarch — Generosity — Interest in foreign affairs

THE YEAR 1910 opened with the King at Sandringham as usual, and the old routine of visits to various country houses followed. Parliament was opened in State on February 22nd—three weeks later than usual owing to the preceding general election—and for several weeks the King remained in London with the political temperature still at boiling point. But in March he left for Biarritz, spending a few days at Paris *en route*. I did not accompany the King on this journey, and read with some concern the guarded statements in the Press that the King had been 'indisposed' while at Biarritz. A fortnight later, early in April, I went out to Biarritz to relieve Arthur Davidson, and I found to my surprise that the King had been very much worse than the Press said. While it was known that he had been confined to his room with a cold, the Press, guided by Mr. Grey of the *Daily Mail,* had decided that it would not be right to frighten people with the details of the illness. They agreed to suppress all references to his illness on the condition that they were kept fully informed of the true state of affairs so that they might judge if it was serious enough to tell the British public. I had therefore to see Mr. Grey every day and tell him the true facts, but by the time I arrived at Biarritz the King was very much better. The curious part of all this was that none of the visitors in the hotel had given away the true facts. They knew he never went out and kept to his own room, but they never bothered their heads about his illness. Apparently he had nearly had pneumonia, but as he had not had it there seemed no reason why the public should be frightened. Personally I have always been

375

in favour of telling the true facts to the public. Once you conceal the truth the public have no more faith in official bulletins.

The King got so much better that we returned to England, and during the crossing I had quite an interesting conversation with him as to how far the Sovereign could rightly go in settling the differences between the two Houses of Parliament. Three days later, April 30th, we went down to Sandringham, but instructions were sent down not to open any of the drawing-rooms as Queen Alexandra was abroad. The King, Johnny Ward and I went off to Liverpool Street Station, where we found Sir Dighton Probyn, Gavin Hamilton,[1] Archie Edmonstone and Stanley Clarke. We had breakfast in the train and arrived at Wolferton at noon, where there was only one motor to meet us. Johnny Ward and I had to walk; we didn't get far as the King's motor returned to pick us up.

We found the King in the garden with Probyn, Beck the agent, and Cook the gardener, looking at the alterations which had been carried out. It came on to rain and we all went in. After luncheon I played golf with Johnny Ward and returned to tea. At dinner the King seemed in his usual form and told stories of amusing incidents of former years. After dinner he played bridge with Hamilton, Ward and Clarke, while I went off to do some pressing work. The next day, Sunday, we all walked across the garden and park to church, but the King drove in a clarence, although it was only a short distance. After church the King walked round the garden before luncheon. He then insisted on sitting in Knollys's work-room and doing the routine work there. There was no fire in this room and it struck me as chilly, but after tea, or rather coffee, in the Equerries' room, he discussed with me the proposal to have a referendum instead of another General Election. It was a proposal that was advocated by some newspapers as a possible solution to the deadlock between the Houses, but of course there were several objections to it. He then discussed an article in the *Spectator* which I had given him to read and said it was excellent. Before dinner I went again to his room and talked about Haldane and new proposals for the Territorial Army, which seemed to interest him. It poured with rain during the morning of May 2nd

[1] Lord Hamilton of Dalzell.

and in the afternoon we went up to London. Although the King was not in a talkative mood, it never occurred to me or anyone else that he was beginning a serious illness. In fact, he went to the theatre that night as if he was quite well. The next day Laking, the doctor, told me he had definitely got bronchitis, and that it would be necessary for him to be very careful. I saw him during the day and showed him some letters, and although he coughed occasionally he seemed quite himself. That evening Streatfeild, Walter Campbell [2] and I dined with the King in the Chinese Room. He complained that he could not eat anything, although he did not cough much. After dinner he smoked a huge cigar; anything worse for a man with a cough I could not imagine, but curiously enough it seemed to soothe him. Streatfeild and Campbell then disappeared and the King and I went into the Japanese Room next door, where we remained silent. Presently in came Alice Keppel and Venetia James. We talked for a short time and then we played bridge, as he explained this prevented his talking. After a short talk the King went off to bed. I still never had the impression that he was seriously ill and thought it was merely the remains of the illness he had had at Biarritz.

On May 4th Jimmy Reid told me the King had definitely got bronchitis badly and was very far from well. I remained in all day in case I should be wanted, and in the evening the King sent for me about seven. He said he had had a wretched night and that he could neither eat nor sleep, but still he took the greatest interest in everything and made notes as usual on the despatches. I tried to be cheerful, but it was clear he was a sick man. The extraordinary thing was that he insisted on having interviews with Admirals, etc., which must have been a great effort. I had dinner with Probyn and Streatfeild, but I had hardly begun when the King sent for me. I went up and found him looking wretched. He said he didn't feel inclined for bridge and had cancelled it. Who the other two were he didn't say, and as it was obviously wrong for him to talk I retired.

The next morning, May 5th, I rode in Rotten Row from seven-

[2] Captain Sir Walter Campbell, Groom-in-Waiting and Deputy Ranger of Windsor Park.

377

thirty to eight-thirty, as I felt sure I should not be wanted so early. Jimmy Reid told me that although in some ways the King was not so bad as he had been at Biarritz, there was the complication of the heart which might fail at any moment through being unduly strained. I remained in for the rest of the day and in the afternoon the news came that the King was worse, and that Sir Douglas Powell, who had arrived, did not like the turn things were taking.

It was so difficult to continue working as if everything was normal, but a meeting had been summoned to discuss the inspection of the Boy Scouts at Windsor. Sir R. Baden-Powell, Colonel Stanley Maude [3] from the War Office, Sir Walter Campbell and Mr. Forrest, Deputy Surveyor, arrived, and we sat round and fixed up the details. I tried to behave as if nothing was the matter, but all the time I was wondering whether this inspection would ever take place. Suddenly I got a message from the King saying I was to go to the station to meet the Queen, who had returned hurriedly from Corfu. I drove with Streatfeild to Victoria Station and there saw the Prince and Princess of Wales, Prince David [4] and Prince Bertie.[5] I introduced to them the Greek Chargé d'Affaires, and had some conversation with Cosmo Bonsor and Sir Edward Henry, the head of the police. The train came in, and after I had shaken hands with the Queen and Princess Victoria, I again brought up the Greek Chargé d'Affaires to be presented to the Queen.

It had been decided that the Queen should drive round to the garden entrance of Buckingham Palace while the great Officers of State and all the Household should remain in the Grand Entrance Hall. This arrangement had been carefully planned to comply with two distinct and contrary orders: first, from the King, that everyone was to meet the Queen, and second, from the Prince of Wales, that no one should be present when the Queen arrived. As a matter of fact, what happened was that when all the Household found

[3] Later Lieutenant-General Sir Stanley Maude. Commander-in-Chief, Mesopotamia, 1916.
[4] Later King Edward VIII.
[5] Later King George VI.

that the Queen did not come to the Grand Entrance they all started off running to the garden entrance, but that had been anticipated, and Sir Charles Frederick, the Master of the Household, was at the end of the passage to stop them.

I then remained talking to the Prince of Wales, Francis Knollys and Arthur Davidson for some time, when a message arrived that the King wished to speak to me. I was very nervous, but rushed upstairs. I was told he was in the audience-room where he saw Ambassadors, etc., a room with red brocade on the walls and many well-known pictures by old masters. As I was accustomed to see him in his work-room, which was next door, this made me more nervous than ever, and when I entered I found no one there. I grasped that I had arrived too soon, and when I heard the King's voice in his bedroom saying, 'That will do, I must go now,' I thought it best to retire and wait outside. After two or three minutes more the nurse came out to see if I was there, and I entered the room trying to look as if everything was as usual. I found the King sitting at his writing-table with a rug round his legs, and I was rather shocked with his appearance. His colour was grey and he appeared to be unable to sit upright and to be sunken. At first he had difficulty with his breathing and was like a man out of breath, but this gradually got better. He said he would sign what there was in the boxes, and I proceeded to open them and handed him documents for his signature. They were merely routine submissions, and he signed these one after the other and seemed to like the work. Even the Foreign Office telegrams he read, but I kept back some documents that would have necessitated a discussion and therefore conversation. I then tried to leave the room, but he wanted to know what had happened at my meeting about the inspection of the Boy Scouts. I again tried to go, but he said in a gasping voice, 'You managed so well at Biarritz. I hope everyone was thanked.' Then, after a painful pause, 'Especially the Press.' I told him I had thanked them all. I said in as cheerful voice as I could command that I hoped he would soon be better. He replied, 'I feel wretchedly ill. I can't sleep, I can't eat. They really must do something for me.'

I was to be relieved the next day by Arthur Davidson, and the extraordinary thing was that, ill as he was, he remembered this. He turned to me and said, 'In case I don't see you again, good-bye.' I shook him by the hand, but I do not think that he meant anything more than what he usually said when I went out of waiting.

I never saw him again, for he died the next day. Meanwhile, I went down to Tangley, my house in the country, where I had hoped to spend a few weeks with my family. Late that night I received a telephone message telling me that Queen Alexandra wished me to come up to London. I motored up at once and went upstairs at Buckingham Palace, where I met the nurse, who told me the Queen was in the King's room and that I had better wait downstairs. I had hardly descended the stairs when a page came and explained to me that the Queen was waiting for me. I went into the King's room and there I found the Queen. I attempted to kiss her hand, not from ceremony but in sympathy, but she would not allow me to do so. She thanked me for the letter I had written her, and then led me into the next room. The blinds were down and there was a screen round the bed, so that at first I could see nothing, but when we came round it I saw the poor King lying apparently asleep. His face looked natural and peaceful and there was no sign of suffering. I was very much awed and hardly liked to speak except in a whisper, but the Queen spoke quite naturally and said how peaceful he looked and that it was a comfort to think he had suffered no pain. She added that it was not Sandringham but that 'horrid Biarritz' that had killed him, although no doubt the political crisis had had something to do with it. I couldn't argue, but I knew this was not true. She said she felt as if she had been turned into stone, unable to cry, unable to grasp the meaning of it all, and incapable of doing anything. She added she would like to go and hide in the country, but there was this terrible State Funeral and all the dreadful arrangements that had to be made.

I was with her about ten minutes and when I came out I met the new King and Queen. I debated in my mind what I should do, and although kissing their hands seemed a tiresome formality so out of keeping with the simplicity of Queen Alexandra's grief, and although I knew that both King George and Queen Mary disliked anything at all theatrical in private, I came to the conclusion that as everyone else had probably gone through this formality I had better go through it, too. I sank down on one knee and kissed their hands in turn.

In accordance with precedent the King's Company kept watch over the body of King Edward, and it was a most impressive sight to see them relieving guard, but there was a certain amount of jealousy in the Army at their claiming the exclusive right of this privilege. The first part of the funeral consisted in taking the body to Westminister Hall where the lying-in-state would take place. This was an innovation which proved very popular, and thousands of people formed long queues stretching far down the riverside in order to witness the sight. In addition to the King's Company, the Gentlemen-at-Arms, the Sovereign's Bodyguard, also took turns at keeping watch. The final funeral procession through London was well managed and the crowd was the largest I have ever seen. King Edward's Equerries were the pall-bearers, but as the extra Equerries were afterwards added and all sorts of officials thought they had the right to walk at the side of the gun-carriage, there was a crowd-jostling effect which was undignified. The final ceremony at Windsor was entrusted to me, and with memories of Queen Victoria's funeral only nine years earlier I found no difficulty in organisation.

The gathering of Kings at Windsor was truly remarkable, and there is no record of so large a number having ever met before. In addition to the German Emperor there were the Kings of Spain,[6] Portugal, Denmark, Belgium,[7] Norway and Bulgaria. Of these by far the greatest personalities were the German Emperor and the King of Bulgaria. The latter had a strong but evil personality, and gave one the impression that he could be capable of any crime; and history bore this out. The fact that he had remained so long on the throne of Bulgaria proved that he was a man who would stick at nothing. The King of Spain was perhaps

[6] Alfonso XIII.

[7] King Albert, who had succeeded Leopold II in the previous year.

the cleverest of them, but the nicest to meet was the King of Norway.

With King Edward's passing we lost a lovable, wayward and human monarch. He was one who came to decisions by instinct and not by logic, and rarely made a mistake in his judgment of men. On the whole, he preferred the society of the female sex and was never happier than in the company of pretty women. He always thought a men's dinner party was tiresome and dull. I remember one Ascot week, after the death of the King of Denmark, it was decided to have a men's party as Queen Alexandra was in mourning, and I happened to be with him when the list of guests was sent into him on his arrival at Windsor. He looked at it and said with a sigh, 'What tiresome evenings we shall have!'

It was on this occasion that he and Lord Rosebery had some difference of opinion the first night. I never discovered what it was all about, but the result was that while apparently it made no impression on the King, Lord Rosebery sulked and became impossible during practically the whole week. If anyone tried to draw him into conversation he turned an eye like a fish on them and withered them with biting sarcasm. So everyone avoided him. After dinner he would get a book and read, but he never joined in any of the jokes such parties produce.

The last night I happened to be at a loose end for something to do after dinner, when to my surprise he called out to me to come and talk. He suggested that as it was a fine warm night we should sit out on the Terrace. I rang the bell and asked for two easy-chairs to be put out on the East Terrace, and there we went. All the pent-up mirth that had been firmly suppressed during the week came bubbling out and I cried with laughter at his witticisms. Unfortunately I laughed so loud that it attracted the attention of several of the guests, who came out on to the Terrace to see what it was that had amused me so much. Soon there were a dozen or more standing round our basket arm-chairs, and Rosebery, liking an audience, became wittier and wittier. Soon the Castle walls were echoing with roars of laughter. King Edward, who was playing bridge, heard these sounds of merriment and when he was dummy walked about to see the cause. To his surprise he found the other drawing-rooms practically empty and, guided by the sounds, he came out on the Terrace and joined the crowd in the dark.

I suddenly recognised his laughter and jumped up and offered him my chair, but he refused it. Rosebery also got up, but remained silent. There was an awkward pause, and King Edward remarked that he must go back to his bridge. Rosebery then quietly followed and went back to his book.

The King's great attraction was that he was a very good listener. During the interviews and audiences, no matter on what subject, he was always able to fix his attention on his visitor. Men who came from Central Africa or from some other remote place were delighted at being asked questions, and came away with a great admiration for the King, who really had only listened intently; I have seen the King apparently deeply interested in something which I knew bored him.

In society it was often the King's custom to pretend to know nothing about a subject, and even to refused to understand some obvious point connected with that subject, when all the time he knew much more than the people who were trying to explain it. I never quite understood why he assumed this attitude, but it probably was the outcome of his wish to become discreet. As Prince of Wales he was always reputed to be most indiscreet, and several instances could be quoted of his giving away secrets. The truth was that he was only occasionally told secrets, and while it is easy to be discreet when one knows everything, it is much more difficult to keep occasional bits of news secret, more especially when going about in society as King Edward did. When he became King and knew all the inner workings of all State affairs there was no one more discreet. It occurred to me, therefore, that this peculiar trait he had of professing ignorance on some comparatively trivial subject may have come from his determination to become discreet.

The King had an unholy passion for decorations; not only did he revolutionize the wearing of medals and decorations in England, but his great wish was to see men wearing as many as possible. In Queen Victoria's reign foreign decorations were unknown, for she had all the old-fashioned prejudice against her subjects wearing foreign decorations; during the seven years I was with her I never received one, yet during King Edward's reign I received eighteen. Although possibly Queen Victoria's attitude was the right one, if any monarch travelled as King Edward did it was impossible to ignore the customs of other nations and not to give a certain number of decorations when monarchs meet; for if nothing is given there are apt to be difficulties and misunderstandings. Foreign decorations were originally given to save the expense of giving snuff-boxes, etc. A man who received a Grand Cross of some Order, value £25, was happier than a man who received a snuff-box worth £200, so monarchs saved their purses and pandered to the unwholesome craving of human beings to wear decorations which they had in no way earned.

Of course, very adverse comments were made when the King commenced to distribute the Victorian Order in a lavish way. People who had been brought up to venerate decorations were rather shocked at first when the papers published a long list of decorations given by the King on one of his State visits abroad, yet His Majesty gave only a fraction of what other foreign monarchs did. The King's original idea was that since the Victorian Order had been so little given during Queen Victoria's reign, it was practically unknown. He therefore determined to remedy this; but whether he originally intended to go so far as he eventually did I really do not know. The more he gave, the more people wanted it, and often it became a most difficult problem to know where to stop.

Once, when going to Portsmouth, he said after luncheon that he intended to give several Victorian Orders, and I pointed out that this would be a mistake, as on former visits he had not done so, and it might lead naval officers to expect decorations whenever he went to one of the naval bases. He was furious and shouted at me that I knew nothing about such things and that, being a soldier, I was, of course, jealous of the Navy. I, however, stuck to it, and said that the Victoria Order would be laughed at if it were given on such occasions. He was still more angry and crushed me with the remark that he didn't know that the Victorian Order was mine to give. After this explosion I at once retired, but I was interested to see that when he did visit Portsmouth he gave no decorations.

The pleasure of giving never seemed to diminish with King Edward. Most very rich men are so imposed upon and meet with so little gratitude that they derive no pleasure after a time from being generous, and develop into stingy men, but King Edward up to the end took great pleasure in giving presents or in doing someone a kind action. He was by nature the most generous of men, and it was this trait in his character that induced him to give so many decorations. He liked the obvious pleasure it gave the recipient. At any game of cards he disliked losing intensely, but loved paying his losses and did so as if he were making his opponent a present.

He had a most curious brain and at one time one would find him a big, strong, far-seeing man, grasping the situation at a glance and taking a broadminded view of it; at another one would be almost surprised at the smallness of his mind. He would be almost childish in his views, and would obstinately refuse to understand the question at issue. It was with matters that did not interest him that he was at his worst, and he would never make the slightest effort to go into the details of anything that bored him; but with questions that interested him no detail would be too small for his attention.

I found that Foreign Affairs, the Army and the Navy interested him most, while internal politics and the Colonies bored him. He would rush through any question relating to the latter, but would read thoroughly through even insignificant letters relating to the former. He read through every dispatch from abroad, often when the subject was very dull. Any inaccuracy annoyed him: even a slip of the pen put him out.

I remember once being with him on board the yacht, and after he had carefully perused some (to my mind) very uninteresting dispatches from abroad, I handed him the basis for discussion at the Imperial Conference with a long and interesting covering letter from Alfred Lyttelton.[8] He ticked it off and handed it back to me saying, 'I will take that as read.' I protested, however, that as the

[8] Colonial Secretary, 1903-5.

Colonial Premiers would be in London when he returned, and as he would meet them at dinner, it was absolutely necessary that he should master the details of their discussions. He hastily said that he had not time then, but would do so later. Feeling sure he would never take the trouble to read through all this printed matter, I made a précis of it and had it typed. This I sent to him by a page, and when I next saw him he said that it was 'no doubt very interesting' but he did not appear to have read much of it. I therefore went over the ground again, and to my amusement he turned round in his chair with a determined face: 'Yes, you are quite right. I must get hold of this.' He then gave his whole mind to it and in a short time had mastered it. I think that he was grateful to me when he went to London: he talked to several of the Premiers and drew them out.

In foreign affairs he was, however, always interested. He read carefully all the blue-prints and never failed to put his finger on any weak spot there may have been. With the Army and Navy he was equally good except in the matter of uniform, where he appeared petty and small-minded; but so great was his influence in matters of dress that he revolutionized the appearance of the officers of both Services. Formerly a certain slovenliness had been the fashion, but after the King ascended the throne this was all changed and smartness and uniformity of dress became the order of the day.

I never quite understood why he made people so frightened of him, but there can be no doubt that even his most intimate friends were all terrified of him. Abroad this was more noticeable, and on the many journeys I took with him I had only to mention his name and at once all resistance vanished. Whenever he expressed any wish there was never any opposition for he was by far the biggest man and the most striking personality in Europe.

I have seen Cabinet Ministers, Ambassadors, Generals and Admirals absolutely curl up in his presence when trying to maintain their point. As regards myself, I varied. If I was quite certain of my facts I never minded standing up to him. In fact, I always noticed that he invariably respected people who stood up to him, and he carried this so far that he was always taken in by dictatorial and cocksure people. At times, however, I was perfectly terrified of him, more especially if I was in unusual surroundings. In his business-room, standing by his chair, I was quite at home, so to speak, and found no difficulty in arguing with him, but when at luncheon or staying at a country house he got cross over a matter I knew little about, he fairly scared me.

Yet in spite of all this King Edward had that indefinable quality of making all his staff devoted to him. All his personal House-hold loved him and his friends were deeply attached to him. The reason was that he was intensely human and that he was a great enough man to show his friends his true self with all the weak-nesses of a human being. He never posed and never pretended to be any better than he was. The upper and lower classes loved him, although the middle class were often shocked at his actions.

BOOK III

BOOK III

CHAPTER XIX

York Cottage — The King's stamps — The constitutional
crisis — Death of Mrs Ramsay MacDonald — Riding at
Windsor — The Irish crisis

[*Although King George V, who was crowned amid great
splendour at Westminister Abbey in June* 1911, *had admired
and respected his father little short of idolatry, their tastes were
in many ways sharply contrasted. The new King's domestic life
was simple and homely, and most of his friends were not drawn
from the brilliant and worldly circle in which his father had
moved with such ease.*

The author now Sir Frederick Ponsonby (K.C.V.O., 1910),
*continued to act as Assistant Private Secretary and Equerry to
the new King.*]

WHEN THE KING DECIDED to let his mother, Queen Alexandra,
continue to live at the big house at Sandringham, while he and the
Queen lived at York Cottage, everyone was surprised; but all the
King's Household determined to make this arrangement work.
Not only did the King allow his mother to live in Sandringham
House, but even paid a few thousands every year to enable her
to do so.

Charles Cust [1] got into severe trouble through speaking his
mind too freely; but really what he said was quite common sense.
It was reported to Princess Victoria that he had said that he
thought it quite absurd that a large house like Sandringham
should be inhabited by an old lady and her daughter, while tiny
York Cottage should have to accommodate a married man with

[1] Captain Sir Charles Cust, R.N., 3rd Bart. Equerry to King George V since
1892. Died 1931.

a family of six, more especially when that man happened to be the King. Princess Victoria said she would never forgive him for saying such unkind things and would never speak to him again. The King intervened and smoothed the ruffled waters; he told Charles Cust that he could not see what the devil it had got to do with him and, of course, there was a great deal in this.

King George V hated all insincerity and flattery, but after a time he got so accustomed to people agreeing with him that he resented the candid friend business. At one time he took a dislike to me as he thought I invariably disagreed with any views he happened to express, but after a time he regarded me as an unavoidable critic.

Anyhow, as I was doing the work of Private Secretary, I found it all very uncomfortable. I wanted very little—merely a small room with a writing table and a telephone, and enough room for official boxes and files. This would not appear difficult; but as, in addition to the King, Queen and six children, there were a lady-in-waiting, an equerry, a governess, a tutor and myself, every available room was occupied. The servants were mostly billeted in neighboring cottages, so that taking a servant's room was no solution.

When I first went to York Cottage the Queen asked me to use the schoolroom for my writing-room and also for seeing people; but after a few days I found that it was the one place where all the young princes and Princess Mary[2] were accustomed to meet and talk. I thought then of the billiard-room which was very little used, and gathered up my boxes and retired there. I had hardly been there for a quarter of an hour when Prince Harry looked in and asked if he and Prince George[3] could play billiards. I said of course they could and, again gathering up my papers, I retired to my bedroom and sent a footman for the boxes. I had quite a nice bedroom, although it had a very small writing-table, but there I felt safe from interruption. The Chief Constable of Norfolk came to see me and was rather surprised at being ushered into my bedroom; while he was with me, Rowland Grant, the Rector, and

[2] The Princess Royal.
[3] Later Duke of Gloucester and Duke of Kent.

Beck, the agent, also came and had to sit in the passage and wait. Everything went well; but when the Chief Constable asked if he could telephone to King's Lynn, I told him he could not, as there was only a telephone in the schoolroom where the young princes were and one in the passage where everyone in the house listened to what was said.

The Queen heard of this and told me she hoped I would go back to the schoolroom but I pointed out that it was wrong for one person to evict six selfishly and that really I was quite happy writing in my bedroom.

The King began collecting stamps when he was Duke of York, and eventually became an ardent philatelist with the best collection of British stamps in the world.

When he was Prince of Wales an old lady wrote him a long letter and at the same time sent an album full of stamps. She explained that her late husband had begun as early as 1855 to collect stamps and had continued until the day of his death. She had found the album amongst his effects, but was not sufficiently knowledgeable about stamps to estimate whether the collection was of any value. She had therefore written to a stamp dealer in a neighbouring town and asked him to come out and look at it. The dealer on looking through it had offered her £50 for it, but she told him she would think it over. She then consulted her doctor and asked his advice as to whether she should accept £50. He unhesitatingly replied certainly not, and advised her to write to a relation or friend and ascertain what the best way of selling the collection would be. After going through a list of her relations and friends she came to the conclusion that there was no one who had even a rudimentary knowledge of stamp-collecting to whom she could apply for advice. She therefore determined to write to the Prince of Wales, of whose collection she had read in the newspapers.

The Prince of Wales glanced through the album and at once saw it was a very valuable collection. In it he saw a 2½d. Bahama stamp for which he had been looking for years. He told Derek

393

Keppel [4] to reply that the collection was a valuable one and that she should send it to Puttick and Simpson, the auctioneers in London, and pay £10 in advertising the sale.

The old lady carefully followed his advice and the collection was put into a good sale. Meanwhile, the Prince of Wales gave instructions to his curator of stamps to buy this particular Bahama stamp at any price. The whole collection fetched over £7,000 and the Bahama stamp alone realized as much as £1,400.

A week later Sir Arthur Davidson, Equerry to King Edward, had occasion to telephone to the Prince of Wales about something, and having finished he added: 'I know how interested Your Royal Highness is in stamps. Did you happen to see in the newspapers that some damned fool had given as much as £1,400 for one stamp?' A quiet and restrained voice answered: 'I was the damned fool.'

[*King George V came to the throne in the middle of a constitutional crisis, which had originally been caused by the rejection of the Budget of* 1909 *by the House of Lords. A General Election had followed in January* 1910, *with the result that Conservatives and Liberals emerged with equal numbers, the balance of power being held by* 40 *Socialists and* 81 *Irish Nationalists. For a moment the Cabinet hesitated, and then decided to remain in office. To bind the Socialists and Irish Nationalists to him Asquith introduced a Parliament Bill limiting the power of the House of Lords, and this was duly passed by the Commons. The dominant issue of the day thus became the Parliament Bill, and the question arose whether the King would guarantee to create a sufficient number of peers to ensure its passage through the House of Lords. An inter-party conference failed, and the King gave the required assurance, but this was not made public until another General Election in December* 1910 *had resulted in no real change in the position of parties in the House of Commons. In face of this threatened use of the prerogative the Lords passed the Parliament Bill in August* 1911.]

[4] The Hon. Sir Derek Keppel, Equerry to King George V as Prince of Wales and later as King; Master of His Majesty's Household, 1912-36.

When I first learnt that the King had given the guarantees asked for by the Government I was horrified, and it seemed as if His Majesty had sacrificed the House of Lords to save his own skin. The whole business appeared to be underhand and quite alien to the King's nature and instincts. Of course it was a dead secret, but I never mentioned the matter to a soul, but rumours began to grow in London and I was constantly asked what the truth was. I invariably said that I knew nothing about it.

It was not till I was on the Royal yacht, in August 1911, that the King told me the whole story. He said that Asquith and Crewe had come to him and asked him to give the necessary guarantees. He had formally refused to do so, and thereupon Asquith had said that if this was so he had no alternative but to resign at once, and give as his reason that the King had refused to follow his advice. There would be a General Election, and everyone would know that the King had taken sides in a political controversy and had supported the Conservatives. As there was no chance of the Conservatives being returned to power, the same Government (the Liberals) would return, and what then would be the King's position? He would be accused of thwarting the will of the people, and to no purpose. Had there been an alternative government the King might very properly have sent for Balfour and accepted Asquith's resignation; but it was well known that Balfour could not form a ministry, and if the election was fought on the issue of the King against the people, Balfour would certainly not be returned with a majority.

Asquith urged His Majesty to act constitutionally and give way. It was his duty as Prime Minister to give advice to the Sovereign, and he had no hesitation in advising the King to give the guarantees that were asked for.

The King told Asquith that it seemed to him that whatever he did would be wrong, and that he would be advised by the party whose views he did not support. He asked for time to think the whole thing over, but Asquith replied that unfortunately he must have an immediate answer, since the action of the Government depended entirely on what His Majesty said. I think it was Knollys who really was responsible for persuading the King to give the guarantees. Although all his life Knollys had been a mild Liberal, he had latterly become an ardent partisan of the Government; this, to my mind, was wrong, as the Private Secretary to the Sovereign should really be neutral, and he had become, so the Conservatives said, a tool of the Cabinet. There is, however, no doubt that when he joined Asquith and Crewe in advising His Majesty to give the guarantees it had a great effect on the King, who all his life had been accustomed to regard his father's adviser as the wisest authority he could follow.

It appears that after a long discussion the King said he was, of course, prepared to act constitutionally, but would the Conservatives agree that he was doing so? Asquith replied that they were not in a position to give advice, and that in following the advice of himself as Prime Minister and of the Cabinet, he would always be defended by all parties in the House. The King accordingly said that there did not appear to be any alternative, but what he disliked was the underhand way it was done. If there had been no secrecy, and if the Prime Minister had come forward in a straightforward way and asked for the guarantees, he would not have minded; but to give them privately like this seemed like betraying the Conservatives.

I also had some talk with Knollys on the subject, and he argued that to have refused would have been to imperil the monarchy. He said that with a constitutional monarchy, the King, being merely a figurehead, had no power whatever in the matter, and that if he attempted to interfere it would alienate all moderate men. He made out a conclusive case for giving the guarantees, but his defence of the secret way in which it was done was distinctly weak. Stamfordham, on the other hand, was furious with Knollys and thought he had let the King down badly.

The whole incident seemed to me to have been mishandled. I entirely agreed that the King must act constitutionally, but coming to a secret agreement with the Liberal Party was quite a different matter. I always thought it should have been done in a straightforward way.[5]

[5] The author's meaning is perhaps not perfectly clear at this point. What the King really objected to was being asked to give the guarantees secretly to the

In October 1912 I happened to see in the newspapers that there appeared to be some difficulty in finding a suitable person for the Governorship of Bombay; I thought that as I had been so long in the Royal Household I should like to try something quite new. There was no risk of my being accused of leaving the King in the lurch, as at that time he had two Private Secretaries, Knollys and Stamfordham. The latter was young for his age and would be prepared to remain on for many years. In any case, there was Wigram,[6] who was shaping well, to fill any vacancy. Carington, as Privy Purse, was by no means old. Therefore the King had plenty of people to fall back upon.

I wrote to Crewe, who was Secretary of State for India, and asked him whether I might be considered for Bombay. He merely acknowledged my letter, but ten days later asked me to come and see him. He then asked if I was prepared to stay out four years, how much of my own money I was prepared to spend, whether the climate would suit me. He then asked me to ask the King's permission to accept the appointment, and wished me to make it clear that he would not think of offering it to me if the King had the slightest objection. I went down to Sandringham and had a long talk with the King, who said he didn't want to lose me, but he wouldn't stand in my way. I was, therefore, at liberty to accept. I wrote accordingly to Crewe, who replied that the Prime Minister (Asquith) was so busy that he had not had any opportunity of talking to him about the appointment. In the meantime the King told Stamfordham about it, but never said that it was for the moment a secret. Stamfordham dined with Farquhar and sat next to Mrs. Rupert Beckett. He told her about my appointment without thinking there was anything confidential, and she at once re-

Government *before they were required*. Lord Stamfordham, in a letter written to a friend at the time, said: 'Had the Prime Minister and the Cabinet known His Majesty as well as I do they could have trusted him to act rightly and constitutionally whenever the circumstances might make it necessary for him to do so. They would thus have saved him from being obliged to enter into a secret understanding as to his course of action in what was at that time a mere hypothetical contingency.'

[6] Clive Wigram, later 1st Lord Wigram of Clewer. Assistant Private Secretary and Equerry, 1910–31; then Private Secretary and later Keeper of the Privy Purse.

peated it to all the dinner party. The result was that it was all over London the following day, and the newspapers gave it out as having been definitely settled.

I received so many letters of congratulation, to say nothing of applications to go in my staff and offers from firms to supply me with every sort of thing, that I had to employ a special shorthand writer to reply to them. I also told the Press Association that nothing had been settled, but they refused to believe me as the news had come from Stamfordham. I was therefore placed in a very difficult position and hardly knew what to reply to the shower of letters I received. The newspapers received the appointment very well and published flattering notes on my career.

Meanwhile, Asquith came down to Windsor, and saw the King. When he learnt that the King was by no means anxious I should leave him, he determined to stop the appointment. Crewe found himself in rather a difficult situation, but agreed to knock the whole thing on the head in order to please the King. Mrs. Asquith told me all this later. He therefore wrote to me and said he regretted he could not put forward my name to the Prime Minister. He added that he had never actually offered me the appointment. I replied with some warmth that it seemed incredible that he should ask me all those questions and then tell me to go and see the King to ask for his permission, if he had never intended to appoint me. He replied that although the appointment was made by him, the Prime Minister had the last word and had refused to consider me. I went to see Asquith, but did no good as he had definitely decided, in accordance with the King's wishes, not to sanction my appointment. I asked that this should be conveyed to the Press, but he said it was not necessary for him to say whom he did not intend to appoint.

When the Press heard that I was not to go to Bombay they rushed to the conclusion that Asquith intended to appoint one of his relations,[7] and selected Glenconner [8] as the most likely.

[7] This conclusion was not correct; in the end it was decided to extend the term of office of Sir George Clarke, who had been Governor since 1907.

[8] Edward Tennant, 1st Lord Glenconner; brother of Mr. Asquith's second wife.

I was not unnaturally very much disappointed, as I looked upon it as a certainty. Crewe, of course, was in a difficult position, but showed considerable skill in extricating himself, although it required letters of four pages to put up a smoke screen and hide the fact that it was really the King, and not the Prime Minister, who had put a spoke in my wheel.

While I was at Bolton Abbey in 1911, where the King was staying with the Duke of Devonshire,[9] I saw in the newspapers that Mrs. Ramsay MacDonald was dangerously ill. I therefore suggested to the King that I should send a telegram to Ramsay MacDonald. At that time there was no official Labour Party, but there were a certain number of Members of Parliament who were known as Labour Members and Ramsay MacDonald was at their head.

The King hesitated, as Labour Members were known as extremists and confused with Communists. However, eventually His Majesty approved of a telegram being sent. I sent a very guarded telegram merely saying how sorry the King was to hear of Mrs. MacDonald's illness and expressing a hope that she would soon recover. This was published by Ramsay MacDonald and all the Conservatives were upset at the King toying with anarchism, as they put it. I, however, argued that although the number of Labour Members might be small, Ramsay MacDonald was their leader, and on an occasion of this sort the King was justified in sending him a message.

Eddy Derby [10] remonstrated with me and said that such a telegram would be misunderstood by the public. Charles Cust openly said it was a great mistake and even Stamfordham wrote very strongly objecting to this message. The King, I think, was influenced by all these protests, and consequently when Mrs. Ramsay MacDonald died a month later he sent no message of sympathy. I was very much annoyed at this because, even supposing the original telegram was a mistake, it looked so meaningless for the

[9] 9th Duke of Devonshire; succeeded uncle, 1908.
[10] Later King Edward VIII.

King to send a message when she was ill and then ignore the tragedy of her death.

The most ignominious experience I had riding was at Windsor. The King rode a very slow horse and the Prince of Wales,[11] Princess Mary and Prince Bertie [12] loved galloping about as hard as they could go. The result was that the horse I rode at first invariably tried to join them and I had a restless uncomfortable ride, always afraid of bumping into the King. I therefore asked for a very quiet horse which would go with the King's.

But I was never told that the animal that was selected for me had bucked off Lord Stamfordham and also a groom. There was one thing he could not stand, and that was anything coming past his head from the back. Lord Stamfordham had been bucked off when attempting to open a gate with his crop, and the groom had been sent flying when he took his hat off.

The animal behaved perfectly with me, and I trotted and cantered alongside the King in the most sedate manner. When the children galloped about and returned at full speed he never took the slightest notice, and I thought to myself that it was obviously the very horse for riding with the King.

We were coming down from the Copper Horse on to the road down a grassy slope when the Queen drove by in a carriage drawn by two grey horses with an outrider in front. Quite unconscious of any danger I took off my hat with a graceful sweep of the hand; the next moment I was upside down in the ferns. The King roared with laughter and Godfrey-Faussett [13] on his horse went off to catch my animal which, having bucked me off, was quietly grazing. I mounted again and lamely explained that I had been completely taken unawares. As we rode back down the long walk I told the King I thought it must have been my hat that upset the horse; in order to prove my point I took my hat off again with a sweep, taking care to sit very tight this time. The horse at once

[11] 17th Earl of Derby.
[12] Later King George VI.
[13] Captain (later Sir) Bryan Godfrey-Faussett, R.N.; Equerry to King George V.

put his head down and bucked and bucked; having put my hat on again, I laid into him with my riding whip with such effect that he nearly knocked the King out of the saddle, whereupon His Majesty said that the sooner the horse was got rid of the better. The story was repeated to everyone and I came in for a good deal of chaff. Lord Rosebery took the matter rather seriously and asked me what I intended to do about it, as it seemed to be a disgrace to be kicked off before both the King and the Queen, but I told him my reputation would stand it. When he heard I had ridden steeplechases and innumerable point-to-points and that I had been Whip of the drag, he agreed there was nothing to worry about.

[*The Irish crisis of* 1914 *tested the King's powers of conciliation to the full. Mr. Asquith's Bill for Irish Home Rule had passed the House of Commons, but the House of Lords attempted to exclude Ulster from its provisions. Meanwhile, the Ulster Volunteers, led by Sir Edward Carson, prepared to resist Home Rule by force, and announced their intention of setting up a separate Government in Belfast. They were supported by a great deal of British public opinion, and a so-called mutiny of British troops at the Curragh showed on which side their sympathies lay. This grave situation led the King to summon a conference, whose origins the author describes below; it met in July* 1914 *and, as Rosebery had predicted, achieved nothing. Only the outbreak of war settled the difficulties for the time being.*]

As Assistant Private Secretary I found that political questions are rather delicate matters; although care had constantly to be exercised with them, Stamfordham seemed to object (and probably quite rightly) to anyone but himself touching them.

I had already come to the conclusion some time before that the King's position would inevitably be very difficult when the Royal Assent had to be given to the Home Rule Bill.

If His Majesty gave it he would be branded as the betrayer of Ulster and execrated by the Unionist Party; yet it seemed out of the question for him to refuse it. As a constitutional monarch he really had no alternative but to follow the advice of his ministers; but if there had been a General Election after the Home Rule Bill had been passed, what would his position have been if the Conservatives came in? He might conceivably have had to give the Royal Assent to the repeal of a Bill which had received his approval.

The whole situation from the King's point of view was an 'impasse'. There was the Liberal Party committed to the South of Ireland, the Conservative to the North. It was all very well for the Conservatives to say they were delighted with the situation as it meant the then Government was in great difficulties; but if they ever had had to repeal the Home Rule Bill, they would have been faced with Civil War in the South of Ireland, in the same way as the Liberal Government had to contemplate a rising in the North. I read a pamphlet by a Mr. Murray Macdonald, a somewhat prosy writer who tried to state the problem dispassionately, but he got into difficulties when he attempted a solution.

I suggested a conference to Stamfordham, but he said the whole problem required further discussion before any solution could be decided upon.

I saw Rosebery at Windsor when he came down for the Chapter of the Order of the Garter, but the moment was not propitious for serious discussion and we only had a hurried conversation. He merely said he saw no advantage to be gained by a conference nor did he consider that any conference would ever come to a decision. I saw him at a garden party at Marlborough House and said I had never had an opportunity of stating the case fairly. He asked me down to Mentmore, and said we could discuss it easier over a bottle of claret.

I went and stayed at Mentmore and found there was no one else. It was a *tête-à-tête* between Lord Rosebery and myself. The house was like the British Museum, full of art treasures: every picture was priceless, every piece of furniture had a history. We dined in a dining-room of the *rococo* style with heavy gilt carvings and looking-glasses, and were waited on by a butler and three ponderous footmen.

Remembering that I was very fond of claret, he had a magnum

of Lafitte '75 specially selected from his cellar. I thought I ought to begin at once with the political problem, but he told me to wait until we were alone, and so we talked of cabbages and kings. He was in a delightful, irresponsible mood, very witty and amusing; but after the coffee and cigars had been handed round he suddenly became serious and said: 'Now, let me hear what you have to say.'

I found some difficulty in getting started on a serious conversation after so much joking and I was afraid of being tedious. However, once I started I warmed to the work and explained the political situation as it appeared to me, and then the King's position. He listened most attentively and then said: 'Will you come out for a drive with me and we can then continue our talk without interruption?'

Having donned our coats we went to the front door where a nice old-fashioned, c-springed carriage, with a postilion and two horses, awaited us. No orders of any description were given to the postilion and we drove off into the dark. I found it a most delightful atmosphere for a discussion, and for one and a half hours we drove round the country.

I pointed out the political dilemma into which both parties were drifting. At present the Home Rule Bill would be automatically passed and the Government would then go out. The Conservatives would then come in and would be forced to repeal the Home Rule Bill; all the rifles would then be transferred from the North to the South and, even if an armed resistance to the law was not organized, there would be general lawlessness in the South. So far from settling the Irish difficulty, the situation would be made even more acute than it was. Nothing would be settled and in two years' time we should be in precisely the same position. But what role should the King play in all this? If the Home Rule Bill was brought up for the Royal Assent the King, constitutionally, would have to give it; he would be execrated by all Ulster and accused of having betrayed the Unionist Party. Ulster would be in rebellion and there would be rioting, all of which would be attributed to His Majesty's action. Then the Conservatives would come in and repeal the Bill, again asking for the Royal Assent, which constitutionally would have to be given, and anarchy would break out in the South.

On the other hand, if the King refused to give his assent to the Home Rule Bill, as some wild Conservatives in the Press had suggested, he would make himself the catspaw of the Conservatives and rouse the anger not only of the Liberal Party and Irish Nationalists, but also of all moderate men throughout the country. Whatever he did would be wrong, and the only solution of the difficulty from the King's point of view was a conference.

Lord Rosebery argued that no conference could ever succeed, as they must inevitably split on the fundamental difference between Home Rule and extended local government; he pointed out that the opposition would have little to gain by bringing the conference to a successful issue, because the Government would gain all the credit. Although he adhered to his original opinion that the whole thing was impracticable, he went on to say that whether a conference succeeded or not it would be quite a good card for the King to play; it would at least show that he was doing what he could to arrive at a settlement. I maintained that whatever party endeavoured to settle this vexed question would do so on party lines, and therefore it would only be a temporary settlement.

I explained that my idea was that the King should not dot the i's and cross the t's and that he should not mention Home Rule at all. He should simply summon a conference to suggest a solution for the congestion of business at Westminster, an evil that was generally admitted on both sides of the House; there would thus be no divergence of opinion about the agenda of the conference. His Majesty would then ask it to evolve a scheme of devolution which would be applicable to the whole United Kingdom, and this they could discuss without mentioning Ireland; but, of course, if any practical scheme resulted from their deliberations, Ireland would come in automatically.

Possibly this conference might decide the constitution and powers of a second chamber, and might even tackle the problem of Imperial representation. Rosebery laughed and said, 'Anything else?'

He pointed out that it was impossible to reproduce in any way the circumstances under which the first conference had met—on King Edward's death—and even that conference had failed. He gave me the impression that he had lost touch with the political world and that he was unwilling to rouse himself to take any serious view of the problem.

We returned to the house about eleven o'clock, and at once Lord Rosebery went to bed, as he said if he began talking he would lose that sleepy feeling one gets from driving.

I reported my conversation with Lord Rosebery to Stamford-ham in a letter, but I don't imagine he was pleased at my endeavours to find a solution. I had a long talk with the King and discussed the idea of a conference, but he said he was not clear how far a constitutional monarch might go. He told me the *Daily Express* had published a scatter-brained article on his position, and had called upon all Unionists to write to him and beg him to refuse the Royal Assent to the Bill until it had been referred to the country. This had apparently annoyed the King, as it implied that the veto was a real thing and that it could be used in the present difficulty.

The King told me that he had asked Asquith whether it was seriously thought by the people of this country that the veto could be used constitutionally. From the mass of letters he had received, to say nothing of the articles in the Press, the impression seemed to have gained ground that now the veto of the Lords had been so restricted, the Royal Assent had become a real thing, and that it was therefore up to him to give it or withhold it.

Asquith laughed at the whole idea; he described it as fantastic, and pointed out that the Royal veto had not been used since the reign of Queen Anne. It was merely a nominal prerogative which successive ministers had not considered worth while removing. The King agreed, but this was not properly understood by the man in the street, who would accuse him of having betrayed Ulster and caused civil war. He asked Asquith whether he had read an article on the subject in the *Spectator,* and Asquith replied that he rarely read and never agreed with the *Spectator,* but in this case he had read the article and thought it excellent.

The King then asked him whether he considered Ulster's opposition serious, and what would be the outcome of the passing of the Bill.

Asquith took an optimistic view of the situation, although he admitted that there might be trouble in Ulster. He thought Ulster would soon settle down, and added that all opposition would have died away by then had it not been for Carson.[14]

The King, however, stuck to his point, which was that he was to be asked to give his assent to a Bill which inevitably would result in civil war, and that the Army would look to him to prevent their being placed in the unenviable position of having to shoot down their fellow countrymen. Asquith quite took the point and said he would be willing to accept a compromise: if the Conservatives would suggest some feasible scheme by which Ulster would stand out for, say, five years, he would gladly consider it.

The King then asked what he thought of a conference, and Asquith replied that he saw no necessity for one at present, nor did he consider that a conference would be able to do any good in the present situation. The King argued that it was a possible solution of the present deadlock, and said he intended to send for Lord Lansdowne and ask him what he thought of the proposal from the Conservative point of view. Any mention of the Opposition always put up the backs of Cabinet Ministers, and Asquith said that although he, of course, had no objection, whatever Lansdowne said or thought would not affect him in any way. He promised to write a memorandum on the whole subject and send it to His Majesty.

The Irish problem seemed more hopeless than ever and soon the King was involved in a great difficulty; the military 'coup' in Ulster created a very awkward situation. Asquith surpassed himself in the House and explained away all the doubtful points. Every time Bonar Law [15] seemed to have an overwhelming case against the Government Asquith deftly turned the tables and won the approval of the House.

[14] Sir Edward, later Lord Carson; later a member of the War Cabinet.
[15] Andrew Bonar Law, Leader of Opposition in the House of Commons, 1911–15. Later Prime Minister, 1922–3.

The difficulty was this: Sir Charles Fergusson [16] distinctly stated to his troops that the orders had come from the King himself and that therefore they must obey. His Majesty investigated this thoroughly, and sent for all the copies of the orders issued to the troops.

Many Generals wrote long letters, so that the King had more or less got the complete story. It seemed useless to demand an explanation of the Prime Minister, as he answered with perfect truth that he knew nothing about it.

Things had got so serious that the King decided to make a move. The South of Ireland had begun to arm seriously, with the tacit approval of the Government, and Ireland drifted slowly but inevitably to civil war.

His Majesty thought that eventually the decision would be left in his hands and that the Home Rule Bill would be laid before him; the Liberals would not dare to have it amended for fear of losing it altogether. If he gave his approval there would be civil war, and if he refused the Nationalists would rise and the whole of Ireland would be in a blaze. He therefore decided to try a conference as a last resort. He proposed to summon the following: Asquith and Lloyd George from the Liberal Party, Lord Lansdowne and Bonar Law from the Conservatives, Carson and Craig [17] from Ulster, and Redmond [18] and Devlin [19] from the Nationalists. [20]

[16] General Sir Charles Fergusson, 7th Bart., of Kilkerran.

[17] James Craig, later 1st Viscount Craigavon. Became first Prime Minister of Northern Ireland in 1921.

[18] John Redmond, Chairman of Irish Parliamentary (Nationalist) Party.

[19] Joseph Devlin, at that time Nationalist M.P. for Belfast West.

[20] Such was the composition of the conference when it finally met.

CHAPTER XX

A German royal wedding — The King's visit to Paris, 1914

[Despite the simplicity of the King's home life, it was soon evident that he intended to continue the ceremonial traditions of the Edwardian era in public affairs. His coronation was splendid with pageantry; it was followed by impressive State visits to Ireland, Wales and Scotland and by the coronation durbar in India.]

THE QUESTION whether the King should pay State visits to foreign monarchs had been for some time under discussion, and Sir Edward Grey, who was given to understand he would have to accompany His Majesty, seemed, in consequence, rather averse to any idea of State visits at all. I, however, argued that it would cause endless and continual difficulties if the King didn't visit the Great Powers. It would be impossible for the King to pass through France or Italy, if ever His Majesty went yachting, without raising the question, and, after all, it would not take long for Their Majesties to spend a week at the capitals of the Great Powers.

Nothing had been decided when the German Emperor sent the King a formal invitation to attend the wedding of his daughter, Princess Victoria, to the Duke of Brunswick,[1] in May 1913.

The King determined to accept the invitation; Sir Edward Grey was directed to explain to the French Ambassador that this was a family visit, and should in no way be regarded as one of the State visits.

The French Government were clearly suspicious, as they feared

[1] Son of the Duke of Cumberland.

they were going to be left in the lurch while we made friends with Germany.

I had to make all the arrangements as usual, but it was quite easy as I knew Goschen, the British Ambassador in Berlin, so intimately.

The King's suite consisted of Annaly[2] (Lord-in-Waiting), Stamfordham (Private Secretary), Colin Keppel and myself (Equerries-in-Waiting), and Harry Verney[3] (Groom-in-Waiting). The Queen's suite: the Duchess of Devonshire[4] (Mistress of the Robes), Lady Minto (Lady-in-Waiting), Shaftesbury (Lord Chamberlain to the Queen), and Sir James Reid (the King's Doctor).

As the King did not take a Minister in attendance, the visit was not to be regarded as a State one, this being the criterion between a State and a private visit.

We crossed over by day to Flushing in the *Victoria & Albert* and had a wonderfully good crossing. We were all able to sit about on deck and enjoy ourselves.

There was little ceremony at Flushing and we got into the train about eleven at night. The next morning we had coffee in the train and then dressed up in full uniform. At Rathenow (about forty minutes from Berlin) the Ambassador (Goschen) and his staff joined us, also the German officers attached to the King and Queen.

There was General von Loewenfeldt, a charming man, who talked English perfectly, having often been in England. He had a delightful sense of humour and was much lighter in hand than most Germans.

The King inspected the Guard of Honour and the German suite were presented to both the King and the Queen. All the suites then got into the restaurant car and had some coffee and beer, but we all found it rather hard work talking to the German suite for an hour.

[2] Luke White, 3rd Lord Annaly.
[3] Sir Harry Lloyd Verney; Groom-in-Waiting, 1911–31.
[4] Wife of 9th Duke.

We arrived in Berlin at 11.30 a.m. and there we found the Emperor, the Empress and a large number of Princes and Princesses.

The Guard of Honour was quite magnificent, and after the King and the Emperor had walked down and inspected it, the band struck up and they marched past with the 'parade march', stepping up to their noses.

This visit differed from a State visit because we were not the central figures, so to speak. In a State visit everything turns on the visiting sovereigns. Every hour is mapped out. But on this occasion we were only a portion of the marriage guests and therefore we were left a good deal to ourselves.

We were all given magnificent suites of rooms. There were, however, three of us at an hotel, and when I arrived I found that I was to be one of these. The King, however, would not hear of my going to an hotel, as he said it would be difficult to get at me, so Shaftesbury most kindly offered to change with me, and I took his rooms in the Castle.

We began quietly by a Household dinner, which was very nice as we were all able to retire early.

On the 22nd, the following day, the Czar arrived, and the King insisted on going to the station to meet him. I believe the Emperor was rather put out at first, but when the King explained he had no wish to join the procession, but would go in a motor by back streets, the Emperor withdrew all his objections.

The Czar brought with him over a hundred policemen, which complicated matters very much. As it was the whole of Berlin was full of police, and this addition made the regulations stricter than ever.

When the Russian suite came to luncheon it was, of course, our business to make their acquaintance, but very few of our suite understood the foreign customs. Annaly was quite hopeless in these matters. I therefore went off, and finding I knew Prince Orloff and General Mossoloff I asked them to introduce me to the others. I then got hold of Annaly and took him round as our head man. Having done this, I got Shaftesbury and Colin Keppel and the others to go round.

Of course, the Englishman is bad at this sort of thing and usually thinks it does not matter, but abroad these sort of things count enormously.

On the 23rd we went after breakfast to see the King's regiment at drill. We motored down to the edge of the common and then got on horses. Reischach, who ran the show, asked me whether the King understood how to make a horse canter. I replied that certainly he did, but when we started I found that it was no easy matter to make my own horse canter. The animal was so well broken that nothing would induce it to break into a canter until it was forced to do so by its rider. I jammed in both spurs and gave it a jab in the mouth, which made it bound forward.

I rode alongside of the King and told him this, but he thought it wisest not to try tricks; so we arrived at a trot, which did not look well. We witnessed some somewhat antiquated parade movements which were, however, well carried out.

The King went to luncheon at the Embassy with Sir William Goschen. I did not go, but I heard it was all very well done, and the King made a capital speech to the British community.

In the evening we went to see *Kerkyra,* a piece inspired by the Emperor, giving scenes of Corfu. Between the acts the King and the Czar went round and talked to various celebrities. The cordon round the Royal Box and *foyer* was so strictly kept that once a person got outside nothing on earth would enable him to return. Sir James Reid, the King's doctor, happened to take the wrong turn in the opera when leaving his box, and so got outside the cordon. When he tried to retrace his steps he was at once stopped by the police. He explained who he was; he showed them the Grand Cross of the Red Eagle which the Emperor had bestowed on him, but all to no purpose. They would not hear of his returning, and finally he was pushed out in the crowd in the street. There he struggled manfully, and begged to be allowed through to return to the Castle, but in vain. Finally, he was rescued by Mr. Quinn, the head of the police with us, and put into a cab and sent home. Mr. Quinn explained that even he could not get him back into the Opera House.

On the 24th the wedding took place, and certainly it was a most

RECOLLECTIONS OF THREE REIGNS

tiring function as, of course, we had to stand all the time. The whole thing was wonderfully well arranged and copious instructions were issued to everyone, so there was really no excuse for anyone to go wrong. Every conceivable detail was thought out, and in addition to the instructions chamberlains were posted in each room to see that the less intelligent guests did not wander about and block up the passage where the procession would pass.

At 4.30 p.m. we all assembled in various rooms, and there was really very little difficulty about finding our places. A certain amount of polite pushing is, however, essential on such occasions, as if one gives way one is apt to find oneself at the tail of the procession. The bride led the way with her ladies. Then came the bridegroom with his suite. The Emperor with the Duchess of Cumberland, and the Empress with the Duke of Cumberland followed. After a large suite the wedding guests came, headed by the Czar and the Queen, who were followed by the King and the Crown Princess.

When we came to the Chapel we found there were no seats. Everybody stood, and there seemed a very large number of people. The wedding ceremony was simple, and was followed by an address from the Court Chaplain which seemed quite good, and the whole thing only lasted about half an hour. Then we all processed out again, the suites dashing in when their masters or mistresses passed.

We went to the *Weisser Saal* where there was a *Defiliercour.*[5] It so happened that we were crushed into the back where we could see nothing. General Loewenfeldt, who throughout was wonderful in looking after us, went off at once to Count Eulenburg and got his permission to put us in the forefront, so we saw all this part very well. All the *Corps Diplomatique* and the principal officials came past the bride and bridegroom. There were no names read out and a large string band played. Both men and women came past. In order to keep the women closed up, each woman carried the train of the woman in front and dropped it on entering the room. It was wonderfully well done.

We then all trooped off to dinner and I found my place with-

[5] Levee.

413

out the least difficulty. I had to talk German to both ladies on each side, as they had no English. We were 1,200 at dinner at small tables in various rooms, and the food was excellent. It was really a wonderful performance to seat so many, and I very much doubt whether we in England have ever attempted such a thing.

Count Eulenburg was a genius at organization and directed the whole ceremony himself.

We were then told to get into our places again, and off we rushed in various directions. I made straight for General Loewenfeldt and never left him. We returned to the *Weisser Saal* to witness the *Fackeltanz*.[6] This quaint old dance was only performed at Royal weddings in Germany, and only members of the Royal family (that is, Royal Highnesses) might take part in it. Highnesses and Serene Highnesses were excluded. On this occasion an exception was made in the case of Prince Albert of Schleswig Holstein,[7] who, in honour of the King's visit, was admitted.

The bride began by making a low curtsey to the Emperor and then to the Duke of Cumberland, and preceded by pages bearing candles in silver candelabra, these three made a tour of the ballroom. The bridegroom followed with the Emperor and the Duchess of Cumberland. When they returned to the dais the bride again curtsied right and left and took on two more, the King and the Czar; and so on until she had danced with all the Royal Princes.

This dance began at eight o'clock and lasted an hour. We were all dead beat by then, standing so long. Except for dinner we had been standing about since four o'clock. We retired to our rooms to a well-earned smoke.

On the 25th the King had luncheon with his regiment, the Queen Victoria Cuirassiers. They were charming, and really it was very like an English regiment in customs and manners. The Emperor insisted on coming, which put the King out very much. His Majesty feared that the Emepror might take advantage of the occasion to make an indiscreet speech. He therefore asked that there should be no speeches, and the Colonel was simply to pro-

[6] Torch-dance.
[7] Son of Prince and Princess Christian.

pose the King's health and the King would propose the health of the regiment.

It all went off very well; the Emperor was in great spirits, and talked incessantly to Stamfordham, telling stories and cracking jokes. After luncheon we were all photographed.

On the 26th we all went down by train to pay a visit to the old Grand Duchess of Mecklenburg-Strelitz.[8] We arrived at Strelitz and found the Grand Duchess on the platform. She was 90, and quite wonderful. We drove up through crowded streets. Strelitz seemed to be a sleepy sort of place, but all the inhabitants turned out and the streets were decorated with flags.

On arrival at the Castle we were all shown round and then stood about talking. Shaftesbury said to me in a whisper: 'There is a tiresome German General who has fastened on to me and won't leave me alone.' I replied: 'That happens to be our host, the Grand Duke!' I was brought up to be presented to the old Grand Duchess. She said: 'Sir Frederick? What does that mean? You always used to be Fritz.'

Then she talked to me of my father and old days at Windsor. Like all old people she remembered distinctly what happened years ago, but was rather hazy about recent events. She was very proud of being an English Princess.

We had a large luncheon and then the King told me to make out a list of decorations and presents. I did this as quickly as possible, and when the King approved I gave the decorations out. It was a great rush and naturally I had to rely on information supplied to me. It turned out afterwards that the *Hofmarschall*,[9] having quarrelled with the Master of the Horse, never put the latter's name down on the list. When we got home this error was rectified.

We returned to Berlin in the afternoon, the Grand Duchess coming to the station to see Their Majesties off.

On the 27th the Emperor and the King motored down to Potsdam to review the garrison. The Queen and Empress followed with the suites. General Loewenfeldt and I were the only two to

[8] Daughter of 1st Duke of Cambridge.
[9] Court-Marshal; in England, his equivalent is the Lord Chamberlain.

ride. The parade ground is very small and will not admit of a large staff. On arrival at the old Castle at Potsdam we got on our horses. I was given a magnificent animal, more like a motor-car than a horse. It was so perfectly trained that by touching the rein you could make it do anything. I believe in Germany they are apt to overtrain horses. The animals appeared to become automata, and are almost tiresome to ride.

The only two wearing British uniforms on the parade were the Emperor (who wore an English Field Marshal's uniform) and myself.

I had some talk with the Emperor on the subject of aeroplanes and dirigibles, which, he said, would undoubtedly play a great part in future warfare. The King and the Emperor then rode out, followed by Loewenfeldt and myself. We came straight to the parade ground outside the Castle. It was a magnificent sight, and, of course, we saw the pick of the German Army.

The Emperor left his place with the King and went past the head of the Guards. The way he managed his horse was certainly wonderful. His left arm was a deformity and absolutely powerless. Usually when he rode he held the reins in his right hand; when he rode past, however, it was necessary for him to hold a sword in his right hand and the reins in his left. The horse was therefore practically left to itself. No one looking on would have thought so, but the Emperor seemed quite at his ease. He saluted with a magnificent sweep of the sword and then cantered slowly round to join the King. Reischach, the Master of the Horse, told me that the horse had practised this manœuvre every morning for months.

When the Emperor passed down the ranks he shouted at each regiment, 'Guten Morgen, Garde Cuirassier', or whatever regiment he passed, and the men all shouted, 'Guten Morgen, Majestaet'. This is, of course, copied from the Russians.

We had a large luncheon party at the Castle and afterwards we returned to Berlin in the afternoon.

Whether the visit was a success, I really don't know. On these occasions everyone goes out of their way to be civil, and one hardly has an opportunity of judging the real feeling. On the whole, I am inclined to think that the visit helped towards establishing good feeling between the two countries, but, of course, one can never get over the fact that we were practically rivals, and that the German navy league had done all it could to poison the minds of the people against us. Of our suite I saw very little. I must say, however, that both the Duchess of Devonshire and Mary Minto were wonderful. They were never wrong the whole time, always punctual, always at the right door. This may not sound difficult, but there were quite eight possible doors, and often the orders were so contradictory that it required a certain amount of initiative to make certain of both time and place.

Annaly was much looked up to by German officers as he was a master of foxhounds. He rarely had the right dress on and never went to the right door. He was very sketchy about all the arrangements and usually got lost at critical moments. Still, he was so much *persona grata* with everyone that it did not matter. I asked him, as head of the suite, to give some presents and orders to the principal swells. He left the Grand Cross of the Victorian Order (destined for some high official) in a cab, and quite forgot to give a snuff-box in diamonds to Count Eulenburg, who should have been the first to receive a present from the King.

Stamfordham was, as usual, excellent. Being Private Secretary, and therefore strictly speaking in charge of all the arrangements, he never minded leaving everything in my hands, and never interfered. Shaftesbury was delightful, but a little inclined to leave the Queen to go about unattended, when, of course, he should be constantly about in case he should be wanted. Colin Keppel was admirable, always there, and taking infinite trouble to keep the suite informed of all the arrangements. Harry Verney, who did the cards, never made a mistake. It is a tiresome business and takes up some time, but he was most punctilious about writing our names on Royalties and showering cards about. We had two clerks with us: Mayne, who talked German perfectly and who was therefore invaluable; and Talland, who worked with Stamfordham when no knowledge of German was required.

We had a comparatively quiet time about decorations. The

Germans had begun to grasp our methods and so they gave up applying for decorations. The only difficulty was that the Czar insisted on showering decorations about. This naturally provoked comparisons. The Czar gave over six hundred decorations and about one hundred presents, while the King gave thirty-five decorations and about fifty presents.

The curious part was that in consequence the Germans tumbled over each other to get an English Order, but hardly took the trouble to apply for a Russian one. In fact, they laughed at them.

A story went round Berlin about a General whose house was burgled. Everything of value was abstracted by the thief, and even all the General's decorations, with the exception of one, the Stanislaus. This the burglar left behind, and when the detectives tried to unravel the mystery why the burglar had left this particular decoration behind they came to the conclusion that the reason was that he already had it.

When the King decided to go to Paris in April 1914, he invited Cambon, the French Ambassador, to come and decide the main functions during the visit. Cambon took away the impression that the King would not go to a gala performance of the opera or attend a review.

Later I saw Frank Bertie, our Ambassador in Paris, and he told me that if the King did not go to a review it would be most unpopular. I told him he should make this point clear when he saw the King, and that I would back him up. The King, when he heard this, said he would certainly go to a review if he could ride, but the idea of sitting in a carriage was repugnant to him. Bertie replied that unfortunately that was the only way in which he could attend a review in Paris. It would be obviously impossible for His Majesty to ride while the President [10] sat in a carriage. The King said: 'Then let the President ride with me in evening clothes!' Finally, however, the King saw that he must conform to the French custom and agreed to drive with the French President.

At first a performance at the Théâtre Français was proposed,

[10] Raymond Poincaré, President of the Republic, 1913–20; Premier of France, 1911–13, 1922–4 and 1926–9.

but happening to meet Douglas Dawson,[11] he told me that Cambon had deprecated there being no Gala Opera. This was entirely my opinion. During the many State visits I had attended I had seen how popular Gala Operas were. People liked dressing up in fine clothes and looking at each other, and many more people also had an opportunity of seeing the King and Queen and President together than in a theatre.

I therefore tackled Bertie on this point and explained that the French idea of the Théâtre Français originated from Cambon, who had gathered Their Majesties disliked the opera. Bertie reluctantly gave way and agreed to discuss the matter with the King. During an interview with the King and Queen this point was brought forward, and Their Majesties, on hearing the various arguments, agreed to go to a Gala Opera. So all was well.

Then we had considerable difficulties with the Protocol about small points. They insisted on the French suite coming to Calais, but as the Queen disliked the idea of having to talk to strangers at *déjeuner* in the train, more especially as it might be a rough crossing, I asked Bertie to arrange for them to join the Royal train outside Paris. The Protocol, however, kicked against such an arrangement, and quoted precedents of the visits of French Presidents to England, where the Prince of Wales and English suite had gone down to Dover. I, however, remained firm on this point, and insisted on the King's wishes being carried out.

One curious point the Protocol laid great stress on, and that was that the French Naval Attaché should accompany Their Majesties from London. It was inconceivable that they should make such a fuss about so small a point. Yet they almost refused pointblank to give way. I wrote to Bertie and pointed out that the Protocol were like the middle class who wished to be thought gentlemen. They were always on the look-out for slights and frightened of making concessions for fear of losing their dignity. They should be made to understand that it was their duty to comply with any wish Their Majesties expressed, so long as the President was not concerned. What would be thought in Russia, for in-

[11] Brigadier-General Sir Douglas Dawson; Comptroller in the Lord Chamberlain's Department, 1907–20.

419

stance, if the King insisted on the English Naval Attaché accompanying the Emperor and Empress of Russia from St. Petersburg? It was an impossible request to put forward officially. Finally, at the last moment, they gave way.

The King and Queen, more especially the latter, were much pleased at the way in which all their wishes had been carried out. When I saw Bertie on our arrival in Paris I told him how pleased Their Majesties had been. He made a face, and said it had not been easy, adding: 'Do you often write so forcibly to His Majesty's Ambassadors?' I replied that when the King or Queen wanted something done I usually put the point perfectly clear. He laughed and said: 'You certainly did so this time.'

The King and Queen drove in State with a travelling escort to Victoria Station. Lady Desborough, Lord Charles Nairne [12] and I attended Their Majesties. The whole suite were as follows: The Duchess of Devonshire (Mistress of the Robes), Lady Desborough (Lady-in-Waiting), Edward Grey (Minister-in-Attendance), Annaly (Lord-in-Waiting), Shaftesbury (Lord Chamberlain to the Queen), Stamfordham (Private Secretary), Jimmy Reid [13] (Groom-in-Waiting), myself and Charlie Fitzmaurice (Equerries-in-Waiting), Tyrrell [14] (Private Secretary to Minister in Attendance).

We had a lovely crossing and half-way across we were met by the French escort, consisting of two cruisers and six destroyers. A naval hydroplane flew round us and an ordinary aeroplane, carrying a photographer with a cinematograph, took views of the yacht and cruisers.

At Calais I fetched the Prefect-General and Mayor and brought them on board the yacht. Then the King landed and inspected the naval and military Guards of Honour. I was amused to see that

[12] Lord Charles Mercer Nairne, 2nd son of 5th Marquess of Lansdowne (assumed surnames Mercer Nairne when the Lansdowne Scottish estates were made over to him in 1914); Equerry to King George V, 1910–14; killed in action, October 1914.

[13] Later Major-General the Hon. Sir William Lambton.

[14] Later 1st Lord Tyrrell of Avon. Permanent Under-Secretary at Foreign Office, 1925–8; then Ambassador in Paris.

although the Guards of Honour did not actually present arms, they carried their right hands across to the rifle. It was explained that this was the intermediate motion to the slope arms, and that therefore no time was wasted in teaching it to the men.

In the train we had *déjeuner,* and although I had asked especially to have small tables, there was only one long one in the restaurant car. It happened that we were thirteen, and Their Majesties both had a rooted objection to sitting down thirteen. I determined to stand out myself, but Sir James Reid insisted on being left out as he explained that he did not eat any luncheon. I was most grateful to him.

At Chantilly the French suite got in, and there was also a Guard of Honour. The restaurant car was really most unsuited for presentations, and we all got huddled away somehow. Before arriving in Paris the King sent for me and talked about some arrangement. The Queen was there and laughingly told me that she had tried to get a gown of the latest fashion. She slowly turned round in front of me to show me the beauties of her toilet and I said how charming I thought it; but even to my untutored eye it was clearly of a fashion of years before.

When we arrived in Paris there seemed to be a great many people on the platform. The President presented every one and then the King inspected the Guard of Honour. As soon as Their Majesties and the President walked away, the crowd seemed to rush in and several of the suite had the greatest difficulty in getting through.

We drove in open carriages and were enthusiastically received by a huge crowd. On arrival at the Ministry for Foreign Affairs the President left, and we had tea. Then Their Majesties paid a visit to the President at the Elysée and incidentally gave him a gold cup. The King was furious the next day to see in the newspapers that it was described as silver gilt.

The King decided to present that night six medallions from Windsor. They had formerly formed part of the statue of Louis XVI and had been bought by George IV. They were in bronze and modelled by Desjardins. His Majesty told me to arrange to have them ready at the Elysée. So I got hold of Colonel Aldebert, one of the Military Staff of the President, and arranged that I should send them to him. I then got hold of a reliable man to take them, and asked the King's second valet to show them to him. He pointed out two large wooden packing-cases, and so having made sure that my instructions were quite clear, I went off to dress for dinner. I found a large number of Pressmen, photographers and various officials waiting to see me and had a very brisk time. Just as I was dressing the telephone in my bedroom rang, and I found it was Colonel Aldebert asking me whether he should have the boxes unpacked. I replied certainly he should, and proceeded to dress. Again the telephone went, and again it was Colonel Aldebert, who said he had found six busts of the King and Queen.

He added: '*Je me demande pourquoi six?*' I then realized that the King's valet had sent the wrong box. I hastily explained the whole thing to Colonel Aldebert and, having tumbled into my full dress uniform, I flew off and got hold of Howlett the valet. I was told by the footman that he was busy with the King's uniform. I replied that the matter was so serious that if he did not come at once there would be serious trouble. He soon after appeared with an aggrieved expression. He was usually so wonderful and businesslike that I was surprised at his making such a mistake, but I explained that I must have the right box at once. I got hold of the trusty Frenchman and explained that he was to take them at once to the Elysée and bring back the other two boxes. I just managed to give these instructions before the King and Queen appeared ready to drive off to dinner at the Elysée.

It would have become a huge joke in Paris if the King had by mistake presented six busts of himself and the Queen to the President. Luckily, however, all went well, and after the dinner the King in a short speech presented the medallions to the President. The dinner was bad at the Elysée, as they apparently had no idea of catering for two hundred; I sat between Madame Marcel Prévost and Madame de Lannay, the wife of the President du Conseil Municipal. The King read his speech remarkably well in French, but with a true British accent. After dinner we smoked, and then there was an entertainment which was charming.

Although I had *café-au-lait* the next morning at 8.30, at 8.45
M. du Bos came to make the final arrangements for the races on
the following day. Then followed a series of visitors, and a great
many I did not see. At 11:15 we started for the Embassy, where
the British deputations presented addresses and the King made a
reply. I was not invited to luncheon, so went to the Hotel Crillon
where I had an excellent luncheon with the other members of the
suite. We then dressed in uniform and drove to the Embassy to
join the King. There we were all told off to carriages and the
whole procession started for Vincennes. They do not understand
how to marshal a procession in France. It is really quite easy, but
it is necessary either to fill up all the carriages before the procession starts, or to arrange for the first carriage to go at a walk
until the others are in their places. In this case the King and the
President went off at once, and the remaining carriages did not
catch them up until they had gone quite a mile. The escort, some
trotting, some cantering, had to do as best they could to get into
proper formation.

The Review was well managed from a spectacular point of
view, but, of course, there is something incongruous in the King
and President seated in a carriage and looking on from seats in a
stand. At the conclusion the King gave the General a message to
the troops, which was afterwards published. We drove back in the
same procession as before. The streets were packed with a dense
crowd, and they gave the King and Queen a great ovation. I have
never seen anywhere such enthusiasm, which shows how popular
the *Entente Cordiale* was. All the way there was much cheering
and waving of handkerchiefs.

At the Hôtel de Ville the King stopped to receive addresses of
welcome. I had the King's reply in my hand and I realized how
important it was that I should be near the King when the ceremony began. I remembered, however, that when King Edward
went to the Hôtel de Ville the Deputies and Senators were allowed
to chip in and the suite got detached from the King; so when the
procession stopped I bounded out of the fifth carriage, a long way
back, and ran down the street. I never attempted to go near the
crowd. This was well, for Charles Nairne, who tried a short cut

through the crowd, got blocked and never turned up until quite late. I bounded along and managed to get in just behind Their Majesties. Then, just as I remembered, the Deputies all closed in and walked in procession, with the result that the rest of the suite were left behind, struggling in a dense mass of humanity.

When the King arrived in the room where the addresses were to be presented, there were only Deputies, etc., slowly filtering into the room. I, however, whispered to him that I was there and had his speech, which quite reassured him. During the recital of the two somewhat long addresses the remainder of the suite arrived and took their places. The King read his reply very well, taking plenty of time, and pausing. Then a tour of the Hôtel de Ville was made and healths were proposed. The King, however, had a short sentence ready in which he proposed the toast of the President of the Municipal Council.

We returned to the Quai d'Orsay, and the scene in the Avenue de L'Opera and the Rue de la Paix was truly marvellous. There must have been thousands of people in the streets and in the windows. Annally, who wore a bearskin cap, had quite an ovation, but he was not sure that the cheers were not jeers.

The King and Queen entertained the President and Madame Poincaré at the Embassy, and I must say it was beautifully done. The dinner was excellent and the old plate and candelabra looked very well. Frank Bertie had taken much trouble about this and nothing could have been better; Lady Feo,[15] on the other hand, looked intensely bored and hardly took any part at all.

Afterwards we went to the Opera: the streets were again packed with a dense crowd and the police had some difficulty in keeping the people back. The staircase of the Opera was a fine sight, and troops with cuirasses lined the steps, which looked remarkably well at night. The house itself did not look like much, as most of the smart ladies were away from Paris. The pieces chosen were most unsuitable, being short selected scenes from modern operas. There was something rather dismal about the performance. Instead of some spectacular opera with a crowded stage there were two or three singers, and so it fell rather flat.

[15] Bertie.

I again had a rush the next morning, owing to the large number of people who wished to see me. We started in motors at eleven and went to the Hospital. Owing to Bertie refusing to go in the motor told off for him, the King and Queen got away by themselves and arrived practically alone. The police, seeing no motor following, let the crowd of carriages in, and so the other motors got blocked. However, it did not matter as Granville [16] and the others from the Embassy were there to receive them. Then a visit to the Musée des Beaux Arts, where there was an exhibition of English things, quite good in its way. The King and Queen returned to the Quai d'Orsay for a short time and then went to luncheon with Breteuil. Those of us who were not asked had luncheon again at the Crillon. We then went to the races, and I took with me two presents, one for Prince Murat [17] and the other for du Bos. The King and Queen arrived soon after the President and sat in the Tribune. I knew this Tribune and how deadly dull it was, so I slipped out and went off to the Jockey Club Stand, where I found a great many amusing people.

Their Majesties went to tea with the directors, and the suite had some difficulty in getting through. Annaly and Shaftesbury never succeeded in doing so. I found many friends: Madame de Ganay, Mrs. Standish, Lady Granard, Lady Craven, Mrs. Lulu Harcourt and several others.

In the evening we dined with the Minister for Foreign Affairs. We were again about two hundred, and the food was most indifferent. Afterwards we smoked, and I talked to Villa-Urrutia, the Spanish Ambassador, who told me that the King of Spain had given 750 decorations in Paris, and he could not understand how the King only managed to give forty. I said: 'At any rate you satisfied everybody.' He replied: 'Not at all. We gave seven hundred and fifty decorations, and we had seven hundred and fifty dissatisfied people; you gave forty, and you only have forty dissatisfied people.'

I then spoke to M. Hennion, the head of the police, and told him

---

[16] Granville Leveson Gower, 3rd Earl Granville; Councillor of Embassy, Paris, 1913–17; Ambassador in Brussels, 1928–33.
[17] A descendant of Joachim Murat, Napoleonic King of Naples.

the King had wished me to inquire how a man was who had been hurt by the crowd. He took advantage of this to ask for more decorations, but I turned a deaf ear. He again repeated his remarks the next morning, but I pointed out to him that the King had gone by the list submitted by the Protocol, and no more could be given. He insisted that his men were more worthy of decorations than the police specially attached to Their Majesties, but I said that this was a point which he must argue out with the Protocol.

We then had a dramatic performance which was excellent, except for the dancing. In a restricted space dancing is never quite a success.

I proposed to take all the suite out to supper, but they all refused, being too tired. There was not a kick left in any of them.

How delightful the French are individually and how unsatisfactory and even odious they are collectively. This is just the reverse with the Germans, whom I never like individually but whom I admire collectively.

CHAPTER XXI

*The outbreak of war — Prince Lichnowsky — The Greek
royal family — A court martial — The Duc d'Orleans —
Kitchener and the Military Cross*

ON AUGUST 4th 1914 I rode as usual in the Park and met there
Lord Lansdowne, John Revelstoke,[1] Dunmore[2] and Billy Lambton. I passed the time of day with them, but conversation was
difficult as none of us knew what exactly the position was with
regard to Germany. Lord Lansdowne said he assumed that Germany would do everything possible to avoid our being brought
into the war and this seemed the general impression, but no one
dared prophesy what would happen. As I rode home I passed
Frank Mildmay[3] and asked him what he was doing in a motor
at so early an hour. He said he was going down to the House of
Commons to retain a seat for the debate.

At Buckingham Palace, where I went after breakfast, I found
it very difficult to get through the routine work. It seemed to me
that nothing mattered. However, I found a box of telegrams from
the Foreign Office deeply interesting, and the news that we had
given Germany up to midnight was thrilling. Telegrams from all
parts of Europe came to the King during the day, and the situation
seemed to get more and more hopeless.

Soon after tea the King sent for me and told me he wished me
to go and see the German Ambassador,[4] Prince Lichnowsky. His
Majesty gave me an outline of what I was to say and did this
surprisingly well. I telephoned to the German Embassy and asked
what time it would be convenient for the German Ambassador to

[1] John Baring, 2nd Lord Revelstoke.
[2] Alexander Murray, 8th Earl of Dunmore; V.C., Afghanistan, 1897.
[3] Later 1st Lord Mildmay of Flete; then Unionist M.P. for Totnes.
[4] 1912–4. Princess Lichnowsky was a novelist and playwright.

receive me. I was told His Excellency suggested five o'clock and I agreed to come at that time.

I walked off to the German Embassy and the footman said the Ambassador was still engaged; would I wait for a few moments? Under the impression that I was being conducted to a waiting-room, I walked gaily in and found to my surprise Princess Lichnowsky having tea with some artistic friends. She was very cordial and offered me some tea, which I declined. She then introduced me to Roger Fry[5] and two other Englishmen whose names I didn't catch. Feeling that the situation demanded delicate handling, I started the conversation by saying I presumed that she had been talking to Mr. Fry about house decoration. She replied that she had intended to do all sorts of things, but now it was too late. I pretended not to understand what she meant and asked about an exhibition that Fry had had. So we all discussed modern house decoration in the abstract. Nero fiddling while Rome burnt seemed more intelligible than my talking about art while the streets were thronged with excited people and the ultimatum to Germany expired at midnight. However, Fry played up and we had an animated conversation in which Princess Lichnowsky joined as if there was no idea of war. I felt all the time that once we allowed this artificial conversation to drop we should find some difficulty in starting it again.

After ten minutes Prince Lichnowsky came in and apologized for keeping me waiting. He asked me to come to his room, and when we got there he sat at his writing-table with his head sunk on his breast. I sat facing him in an arm-chair. I had imagined it would be a conversation, but as he remained silent I grasped I should have to make a sort of speech. I said that the King had sent me privately to say how very deeply he deplored the turn events had taken. No one had done more to preserve the friendly relations between the two countries than the King, and His Majesty would always remember the manner in which the Ambassador had seconded those efforts. His Majesty felt that the Ambassador, who knew England so well, had done all in his power to represent the British point of view in the most favourable way to the German

[5] Artist and critic; a champion of the post-impressionists.

Government. Unfortunately, their efforts had failed and the King had wished me to tell him how much he personally regretted the Ambassador's departure. I added that the Queen had asked me at the same time to express her regret to Princess Lichnowsky at not being able to receive her before her departure.

Lichnowsky listened attentively and didn't attempt to interrupt until I had finished. He then said he was deeply touched at the King's kind thought in sending me with such a message. He would like to assure the King that it was with the deepest regret that he was leaving London. When he had first come it had been his intention to do everything in his power to improve the relations between the two countries, and he had even imagined that he was being successful. It had all seemed so simple to begin with, as there was really no reason why Germany and England should not work together. The commercial rivalry between the two countries merely acted as a stimulant to both. The German Fleet was really not intended as a menace to England and, with a little goodwill, some arrangement might have been arrived at. The Press in both countries, he thought, was responsible for any ill-feeling that existed. It was with a sense of bitter disappointment at his failure that he was now leaving. Never would he forget the kindness that had been shown him by everyone in London, but he was particularly sensible of the invariable courtesy shown by Their Majesties. He begged me to convey to the King his profound thanks for this last attention, and assured me that nothing had moved him more than the King's kind thought of him at such a time. He added that he would not fail to give the Queen's kind message to his wife. He spoke most dramatically and nearly broke down at the end. I ended this rather painful interview by silently shaking hands with him.

I had rather delicate work arranging the journey of the children of the Queen of Greece.[6] The King showed me a telegram from the Queen of Greece imploring him to look after her children, who were in an hotel at Eastbourne under the charge of a nurse, and asking him to have them sent to Flushing as soon as possible. He had replied that every care would be taken of them, and had

6 Queen Sophia.

added 'Fritz Ponsonby will undertake this'. This addition to his telegram seemed superfluous, but he said that it would give her confidence. He appeared to think this was quite an easy matter and that all that was necessary was to give instructions to the nurse. I ventured to point out that it would by no means be an easy matter. In the first place no steamers were running, and in the second place the Channel was said to be swarming with submarines and bristling with mines; it would be necessary to take infinite precautions to ensure the children's safe passage.

I got on the telephone to the hotel and eventually succeeded in talking to the nurse; mercifully she turned out to be an eminently practical Englishwoman, full of common sense. I told her to have everything packed up and to be ready to start at a moment's notice, but warned her not to move until she had definite instructions from me. Then I went to the Admiralty, where I was conscious of being a nuisance, but the Naval Secretary (Dudley de Chair)[7] at once got to work and chartered a boat, giving orders at the same time to a destroyer to escort it. Then to the Foreign Office, where I obtained the necessary permits and passports. I sent a telegram to the Greek Consul at Amsterdam instructing him to meet the boat, and another to the Queen of Greece outlining all these arrangements, but beyond a telegram from the Admiralty to say the children had arrived safely I never heard any more.

When war broke out I joined up, but was told that they had no room for me in the Grenadiers as a Lieutenant-Colonel or even a Major. I therefore became a Captain, and was told to report myself to the officer commanding the Reserve Battalion at the School of Music at Kensington. I could get no proper khaki uniform and had to wear the khaki I had in the South African War; it was the object of much criticism because it was too light in colour.

The arrival of the reservists from all parts of England was most interesting to watch. Men in every walk of life arrived and it seemed to me that it would take some time to get this mob of men into shape, but the next day there they were all smartly

[7] Later Admiral Sir Dudley de Chair. Commanded 3rd Battle Squadron, 1917–18.

dressed and sergeants barking words of command at them as if they had never been away. I was given a company of 200 splendid men and many, too many, officers, and was told to begin training them. It was the blind leading the blind, but I worked away every night and acquired a certain smattering of military knowledge. One day, when I came back from training, I found Frankie Lloyd,[8] the General commanding the London district, with a brilliant Staff on the Barrack Square at Chelsea. He sent for me and told me I was to be specially promoted to my former rank of Lieutenant-Colonel. Having done nothing to deserve this promotion I scented a trap, and a trap it certainly was. It appeared that there were a great many difficult cases to be tried by Court Martial, and I was to be appointed President of all Courts Martial in London, Windsor and Sandown, where troops were temporarily encamped.

At first I was rather at sea, not having been on a Court Martial for nearly twenty years, but by degrees I became an expert. I remember particularly one Court Martial—on a serious case in the Irish Guards—as it had a dramatic setting. There were twenty young officers under instruction and, although they only had to look on, they had to be sworn in. Then there was a thunderstorm, and the whole room became so dark that candles in bottles were produced and placed on the table. The man who was being tried for insubordination and striking a superior officer, etc., had been cross-examining every witness and asking all sorts of irrelevant questions. So I determined to put things clearly before him. I addressed him and explained the charges, pointing out that he had to disprove them, but it was useless asking all these questions which in no way refuted the charges. As I spoke the storm broke over the hut we were in. Peals of thunder, flashes of lightning and a deluge of rain made the whole scene most dramatic. When the man suddenly cried, 'I plead guilty and throw myself on the mercy of the Court', I wondered whether I had not influenced him too much; but although I explained again that I had only wished him to understand the position, he refused to alter his plea of guilty.

The King, meanwhile, was having a very hard time inspecting

8 Lieutenant-General Sir Francis Lloyd.

troops and going round munition factories, and was under the impression I was kicking my heels and doing nothing. He therefore sent for me and explained that he had given me leave to go under the impression I would be wanted in France, but it was hardly right I should throw all the work on Stamfordham and Wigram and still be in London.

[*In October* 1914, *however, the author went to France with the* 7*th Division, and was there long enough to be mentioned in dispatches. He was recalled at the end of the month and was appointed Keeper of the Privy Purse in succession to Sir William Carington, who had just died. He thus became responsible for all personal payments made by the King out of his private property.*]

In 1915 the Duc d'Orleans [9] wrote to the King and placed his services at His Majesty's disposal. It was a theatrical sort of letter, obviously intended for eventual publication, but the King, who knew the Duke, was not inclined to take it seriously; still, an answer of some sort had to be sent. His Majesty told me to see Lord Kitchener about it, but it seemed difficult to bother a busy man like Lord Kitchener about a silly thing like this. I therefore spoke to Fitzgerald,[10] who suggested my writing a letter explaining the matter.

In his letter the Duke said that he had naturally at once placed his services at the disposal of the French Government; but, although he had had a very civil reply thanking him for his offer, the Minister for War pointed out that according to French law he was not allowed to land in France, and therefore the French Government was unable to take advantage of his offer.

I sent the letter as it was to Kitchener and then I went to the

[9] Then Head of the Bourbon-Orleans House; son of Comte de Paris and nephew of Duc de Chartres. Successive waves of tolerance and intolerance buffeted him to and fro between England, Belgium and France, from which he was twice expelled.

[10] Lieutenant-Colonel Oswald Fitzgerald, Personal Military Secretary to Secretary of State for War, 1914–16. He lost his life, with Kitchener, in H.M.S. *Hampshire,* 1916.

Savoy Hotel to see the Duke. He had been at Sandhurst with me and was at that time very puerile and brainless. He received me with effusive cordiality and kissed me on both cheeks, which I disliked intensely; he then delivered what seemed a carefully pre-pared oration, telling me that his soldier's heart beat to be in the trenches alongside of his fellow countrymen. All he asked was to be allowed to serve in Belgium with the British Army. I pointed out to him that he could not get there without going through France, as all the ports were in the hands of the Germans; but he maintained that if he were to be made an officer in the British Army the French Government would raise no objection. The in-terview ended awkwardly, as I could hold out no hopes of his ever getting to the front.

The next day I got a letter from Kitchener saying that any idea of the Duke's going to Belgium was quite out of the question, and he would tell him so; but possibly some billet could be offered to him at home.

I had now taken over entirely the tiresome question of decora-tions, as the King and Stamfordham were busy with more im-portant matters. Naturally, I consulted the King on all important matters. It had been for some time abundantly clear that our existing decorations were inadequate for a war of this magnitude, and that some decoration other than the V.C. and D.S.O. would be necessary for officers. There appeared to be some dissatisfac-tion at the front, and while, of course, the whole standard had been raised, there seemed no rewards for junior officers whose bravery did not entitle them to the V.C. The D.S.O. was originally designed for this purpose, but eventually it was restricted to senior officers; during the South African War, too, it had been prosti-tuted, as several officers who had never left the base received it.

I spoke to the King on the subject, and His Majesty said that he thought that the Distinguished Service Cross, which was given in the Navy, should be made applicable to the Army. This seemed the obvious remedy, but when I came to discuss the question with Kitchener and Churchill I found there were many difficulties in the way. Kitchener at first agreed to the proposal on the under-

433

standing that the statutes should be altered to suit the Army, but when I saw Churchill at the Admiralty he flatly refused to allow the statutes to be altered. Kitchener thereupon flatly refused to have anything more to do with this cross, and said the Army must start a new decoration of its own.

The King at first was very much opposed to the idea of the two Services having different decorations; but when I pointed out to him that in the matter of medals they already differed entirely, he said he saw no alternative to a new cross for the Army being instituted. The Navy is more logical than the Army because they have the Distinguished Service Order, the Distinguished Service Cross and the Distinguished Service Medal. Kitchener was in a great hurry to get this new cross out and summoned a committee to work out the details; but before the committee met I saw him and asked whether he intended to copy the Naval Distinguished Service Cross. He glared at me and said: 'Most certainly not!' I expressed a hope that the new cross would be reserved for fighting officers and would not be given to staff officers; but he said that a staff officer in charge of intricate operations during an offensive deserved greater recognition than a man who performed an individual act of gallantry. One man was merely responsible for his life, whereas the other might be responsible for thousands of lives. He added that if a decoration was held to imply that the recipient had never been engaged in actual fighting no one would care to have it.

The whole thing was done in such a hurry that I was surprised that more mistakes were not made.

I attended the meeting of the committee appointed to institute the new cross and found that it consisted of the Adjutant-General, the Military Secretary, the Secretary of the War Office, Douglas Dawson and myself, with Kitchener in the chair.

The word 'autocrat' can only give a feeble idea of what Kitchener was at that time. The War Office blindly carried out his orders, and no one ever thought of questioning his proposals or of attempting to argue with him. The committee was therefore a farce, as the officials of the War Office were like a Greek Chorus echoing his opinions. The only two who asked awkward questions and tried to get the subject thoroughly thrashed out were Douglas Dawson and myself. When we came to the design I suggested we should have something really good, but Kitchener said it would take too long and there was no necessity to have anything damned artistic. However, it was agreed to have as many designs as possible to choose from, or rather from which Kitchener might make the selection. I longed to say that not one of the committee had the slightest knowledge of silver work and therefore we were as a body totally incapable of selecting the best work; but I felt it would not do to say so, more especially as Kitchener seemed to fancy himself as an artist, and was constantly engaged in drawing pathetic designs on the blotting-paper.

The second meeting of the committee took place soon afterwards, and in the short time available I was not able to do more than get one or two artists to draw rough sketches. Douglas Dawson, however, had asked Farnham Burke,[11] one of the leading Heralds, to draw designs. To my mind they were very second rate, but considerable trouble had been taken with them and silver paint had been used which I was afraid would captivate Kitchener. Sure enough, as soon as he saw Farnham Burke's efforts he refused even to look at the rough sketches, and at once selected the design with the silver paint. This was a triumph for Douglas Dawson, who from the first had been very strongly opposed to any artist being employed, and he remarked to me that he was glad to think that the design he had put forward was the best; I retorted that so far from being the best it was probably the worst, as Kitchener knew as much about silver work as a Hindoo did about skates.

The choosing of the ribbon was not without humour, as everyone seemed to think it was such an easy thing to do. Kitchener began by describing a ribbon which he thought would be attractive, but I told him this was the Emperor of Austria's Jubilee Medal and, although this was not a serious objection, it was a pity to have a ribbon that was worn by nearly everyone in Austria. His second attempt produced the ribbon of the Conspicuous Gal-

[11] Later Sir Henry Farnham Burke.

lantry Medal of the Navy, and a third proved to be the Black
Eagle of Germany. I had a book giving all the ribbons of Europe,
and as soon as anything was produced I was able to see whether
it was the ribbon of any existing medal or decoration. Kitchener
became quite exasperated and said: 'This damned fellow contra-
dicts me whenever I say anything. We'll have no nonsense; I've
got it, plain black and white, simple and dignified,' to which I
remarked that that happened to be the Iron Cross. That broke up
the meeting, and Kitchener said he would choose the ribbon with
the King.

The King and Kitchener spent half an hour choosing medal ribbons. I left a book containing all British ribbons and one with all
foreign ones on the table, with a basket containing all the different
coloured ribbons which my wife got for me. I put in a prominent
place the card with my wife's suggestions, so that they might see
what possibilities there were. Eventually I was sent for and shown
with triumph a ribbon they had selected which was not in any
book; I found they had chosen the one my wife had made out,
mauve on a white ground. Certainly this was very distinctive, and
not likely to be mistaken for any existing decoration.

It was decided to call the new medal the Military Cross, but
there was no guarantee that it would not be given for services at
the base or on the line of communication, which was a great pity.
The King then proposed to start a Military Medal.

CHAPTER XXII

The King visits the Western Front, 1915 — The General's dissatisfaction — The King's accident

[*During the war the King paid several visits to the Western Front. The first was in November* 1914, *the second, described below, in October* 1915; *in* 1917 *Queen Mary accompanied him.*]

I WAS convinced that the more the King went to France the better, as it was only natural that people should expect the Sovereign to be with his Army; but I quite admitted that any interference, or even the appearance of wishing to interfere, in any way with the authorities at the front would be a grave mistake. I urged Bigge to advise the King to go in the spring and again in the summer, but he took the view that His Majesty was doing far better work at home. Naturally, I agreed to be silent on the question, as it was quite outside my scope as Keeper of the Privy Purse, and so nothing was done.

Now it appeared that the King himself had expressed his determination to go to France; but the moment seemed inopportune, as a general move was in contemplation. It was not considered wise for the King to be present, for fear the offensive should prove unsuccessful and ill-conditioned people should accuse His Majesty of having interfered. I think there was something in this, as when the King had gone to France the year before all the Generals had left their commands to come and pay their respects to him.

Eventually October was definitely fixed for the visit to the front, and the question arose who should accompany the King. The King decided to take me and put me in charge of all the arrangements, but was faced by the problem of which Equerry should come with us. Godfrey-Faussett was actually in waiting in October and so by all rules he should have been chosen; but, on the other hand, he had been away with the mine-sweepers for over six months, while Cust had not been away at all. I came to the conclusion on the whole it would be only fair for His Majesty to take Cust.

The King at first did not bother much about this and acquiesced in all my proposals, but a storm arose as Godfrey-Faussett resented not being taken. He argued that to take Cust would be to inflict an undeserved snub on him, more especially as Cust was a sailor like himself; it could not therefore be said that a sailor was unsuitable.

The King, to whom he poured out his lamentations, found himself in a very difficult situation since he was equally a friend of both; he therefore said he had left these details to me. Godfrey-Faussett at once attacked me on the subject, but I maintained I was right and that as he had quite rightly gone off to the war and done his bit, it was only right to give this trip to Cust, who had stayed and borne the burden and heat of the day.

The arrangements were not difficult, as Meat Lowther [1] was Military Secretary at G.H.Q., and he was a past master at this sort of thing. I foresaw there would be trouble ahead when the President wished to meet the King, and I suggested that the King should take the initiative and propose a meeting, rather than wait for Poincaré to put forward proposals; but His Majesty thought this unnecessary.

One night I received a telegram in cypher from Lowther saying that the Protocol had suggested that the King should inspect one of the French armies in the South of France and adding that the President hoped His Majesty would dine and sleep in the presidential train. I instinctively felt that this would be distasteful to the King, as it would mean a long journey there and back and also many hours spent with the President. I gave the King the telegram and he told me to suggest a French Army Corps somewhere near the British lines, so that he could motor over, carry out his inspection and return to his house the same evening. I sent Lowther a long telegram amplifying the King's suggestions.

[1] Later Major-General Sir Cecil Lowther.

I suggested to the King that he should have two houses instead of one. In the biggest house there would only be the King, Cust and myself, and in the smallest he should have two Indian Rajahs and a General A.D.C. from each Dominion. These would attend him on all official occasions, but only dine or have luncheon with him when he wanted them. He, however, refused to consider any scheme of this description and preferred not to have such a large staff as I had suggested.

Everything was arranged as the King wished, and a French Army Corps within motorable distance was selected.

On the last occasion the King had gone to France much disappointment had been expressed at His Majesty's always being either on foot or in a motor-car where no one could see him. I therefore suggested that at all inspections of troops His Majesty should ride; but there was the difficulty that the distances between the places where the inspections were to be held were so great that one horse or even two would not be enough. The King approved of the idea and told me to make arrangements for a fresh horse at each inspection. In writing to Lowther I emphasized the fact that animals specially selected on account of their being quiet should be chosen, and that their appearance was quite immaterial as no one would be likely to look at a horse when they could look at a King.

The arrangements for the journey presented no difficulty, but Lowther had to come over from France twice to settle small details. Elaborate precautions were taken by the authorities to prevent anyone knowing that the King was going to France; the luggage was sent to the station in hired vans, and there was no red carpet or any preparations at the station that would convey to the public the impression that the King was travelling.

The King and myself in khaki, with Charles Cust in a monkey jacket, left Buckingham Palace quietly in a motor-car at 9.20 one morning and drove to Victoria Station where Mr. Dent, the General Manager, had a special train discreetly waiting. On arrival at Dover we at once went on board the ordinary steamboat *Victoria,* which was kept exclusively for His Majesty's use. Amongst others who crossed with us was Admiral Bacon, who had been Fisher's right-hand man, and as such had incurred such unpopularity in naval circles that he had been forced to retire; now he was in command of the Dover patrol. It was interesting to see how the war had extinguished all these personal animosities.

The King, who had been particularly down on him in old days, greeted him with warmth and talked to him most of the way over to France. Even Charles Cust, who had been a very bitter opponent of Fisher's policy, was most affable and talked to him as an old friend. We were escorted by four destroyers and two small airships, the latter finding some difficulty in going slowly enough to keep with us.

On arrival at Boulogne we found a large array of distinguished officers, including the Commander-in-Chief, Sir John French, and Lowther.

French seemed rather shy and did not melt much, but the King plied him with questions and told him he should on no account have come so far from G.H.Q.

A mass of French's officials were drawn up on the quay, but it was all well arranged and only the big swells were presented. The King and French drove off in the first car and we followed. At the town station the King dropped French, who returned by train to St. Omer and then got into his own train. Derek Keppel, who had gone on ahead to make arrangements, and Cédard, the King's cook (a most important addition to the retinue) met us at the station.

In the afternoon the King went to see the Bassin Loubet, where all ammunition was landed. We walked through shed after shed all packed with ammunition and were told bewildering statistics. For instance, the reserve of small arms ammunition was over sixty-seven million rounds.

Then to No. 14 General Hospital at Wimereux, where we were received by General Sloggett,[2] Head of the Army Medical Service in France. Sir Bertrand Dawson was also there, having thrown his enormous practice in London to the winds.

2 Lieutenant-General Sir Arthur Sloggett.

After we had gone round the whole Hospital the King said that if there was time I was to arrange a visit to the Australian Hospital, as Lady Dudley (Rachel) had particularly asked him to go there. I consulted General Sloggett and Surgeon-General R. H. S. Sawyer, and they both approved, although they admitted they had nothing to do with the arrangements. Anxious not to upset a programme arranged by someone else, I waited till Lowther came along and consulted him. He saw no objection, but as the time was necessarily limited it might be necessary to drop out some other hospital.

I therefore told the King that it could be arranged and arrangements were made accordingly. I subsequently heard that there had been much tribulation at another hospital, where the doctors and nurses waited in vain for the King to come, and that General Clayton [3] was not at all pleased at this change of programme. Lady Dudley, however, was delighted, and showed the King round the whole place.

We left there for the Indian Convalescent Depot, where all the Indian soldiers of every sort and description were drawn up.

After the King had walked round, a burly Gurkha stepped out and shouted three cheers for . . . for . . . His knowledge of English failed him and he could not remember the English for King Emperor. An officer prompted, however, and all the men cheered heartily.

We dined in the restaurant car where, of course, everything was excellent; but nothing to drink. Only plain water was allowed, which made it rather dull.

We arrived at Havre very early and had breakfast in the train. At 10.30 Sir Frederick Clayton and General Asser [4] came with the French officials, all of whom were presented to the King; then we went in motors to the Central Training Ground. Afterwards the King inspected the remount depots, and it was wonderful to see what care was being taken of the horses. The Canadian Base Depot was then inspected with quite unnecessary minuteness. I always think that it is a waste of time asking the King to walk

[3] Lieutenant-General Sir Frederick Clayton.
[4] General Sir John Asser, G.O.C. Lines of Communication.

through wash-houses and kitchens, which are much the same everywhere. In the afternoon the King visited the hospital on the Quai d'Escale, and it was curious to see a gaudily painted room in what had obviously been a casino converted into a hospital. Some of the men there had been gassed and it was painful to watch them, blue in the face and gasping for breath. I found one was a German and regretted the pity I had wasted on him; but the King rebuked me and said that after all he was only a poor dying human being, in no way responsible for the German horrors.

We then went through sheds of stores for the Army, and the figures we were told were bewildering. I remember being shown ninety days' rum rations for 500,000 men and being told that there was enough rum to float a battleship. The ordnance workshops were interesting: we saw old rifles, accoutrements, boots and even guns being renovated and turned out as good as new; in fact, the boots produced were preferred by the men to new ones. The salvage corps instituted by Kitchener collected all the damaged articles covered with mud, and sent them to these shops, where they were sorted and, unless past repair, returned to the front.

The King started off early the next morning with Sir Frederick Clayton and Brigadier-General Marrable (the base commandant) and continued his inspections.

We were lodged in the Château de la Jusnelle, Aire, that had been taken for the King. It was what we should call in England a small country house of the villa type; but it took us all in at a pinch, and was quite comfortable as French houses go.

Charles Cust and I shared a room, which I always dislike; but he was as good a companion as one could want. He didn't snore and was a very early riser, so that when I got up in the morning he was well out of the way. This house suited the King very well, as there were no spare rooms and consequently it was impossible to have anyone to stay. The dining-room was small and large dinner parties were out of the question.

One night the Prince of Wales and Lord Claud Hamilton[5]

---

[5] Captain Lord Claud Hamilton; later Equerry to Prince of Wales, 1919, and Equerry to King George V. Now Comptroller and Treasurer in Queen Mary's Household.

turned up and stayed for dinner. It always seemed to me that the Prince was at that time very nervous before his father; he remained singularly silent, only opening his mouth when he was addressed and then weighing carefully each word he uttered. The King talked away and was in great spirits, so that there was really no need for any of us to do more than keep the ball rolling.

The next day the King attended Church Parade at Aire, a little old-fashioned town with a market-place of the French description covered with cobblestones. Some 800 men were drawn up in the square and a band contributed to the solemnity of the occasion. There was a large attendance of Generals and staff officers; in fact, there was quite an epidemic of religious fervour on the part of the staff. The sermon was preached by the Rev. Jacob Blackbourne, who did not rise to the occasion; he preached a very commonplace sermon.

When we got back we found the King and Queen of the Belgians, who came for luncheon, accompanied by Prince Alexander of Teck.[6] I sat between Prince Alexander and General Biberg, A.D.C. to the King of the Belgians, a fine soldier who had been badly wounded in the early part of the war and who had lost his two sons. The luncheon was very good, but as the King had pledged himself to abstain from all alcoholic drink, nothing but water was handed round. I have always thought that alcohol in some form is a necessity during luncheons of this description, where conversation is necessarily an effort and when anyone who speaks invariably finds himself addressing the whole table. As a matter of fact neither the King nor Queen of the Belgians was much given to small-talk and, although they might have had much to discuss privately with our King, they could not well embark on private matters before all of us. I did my best with General Biberg in French, but after half an hour my brain, unassisted by alcohol, refused to supply me with new topics.

By an unfortunate oversight the King forgot to wear his Belgian Order. Of course, he hated wearing stars in khaki, and intended to forbid the practice which was creeping in amongst the Generals.

[6] Later Earl of Athlone, after relinquishing German titles.

French was the chief offender, as he always covered himself with foreign baubles. Henry Wilson [7] said about him: 'He is a nice little man in his bath, but when he puts his clothes on you can't trust him, and you never know what he will wear.'

There was, however, no reason why the King should not have worn a bit of ribbon of the Order of Leopold among his ribbons; Prince Algie told me the King of the Belgians, who had taken the trouble to wear the Star of the Garter, was rather surprised.

The King of the Belgians spoke slowly in a deep bass voice. He asked me about the political situation in England and then said: 'In peace-time the democratic idea is very good, but in war-time it is a failure; one should change one's Parliaments as one changes one's Generals.' I ventured to remark that changing Parliaments in England was not so easy.

In the evening General Hubert Gough [8] and General Haking [9] came to see the King, and in the course of conversation said that some change at G.H.Q. was imperatively necessary. They both maintained that unless a new Chief of Staff in England and a new Commander-in-Chief in France were appointed there would be serious trouble. When, later, Robertson [10] came, the King asked him what he thought, and apparently he was in entire agreement with the others.

Douglas Haig [11] dined and was not very communicative, but he never shone much in conversation, although when he did speak it was sound stuff. He certainly did not give the impression of being the great soldier he undoubtedly was. After dinner he had a long talk to the King alone, but I don't know what he said. I gathered from His Majesty that he spoke strongly about there

[7] Later Field-Marshal Sir Henry Wilson. Before 1914 advocated close military cooperation with France; during War acted as liaison with French Army and advised Lloyd George; as C.I.G.S., 1918–22, urged strong policy in Ireland; assassinated by Irish revolutionaries, 1922.

[8] General (later Sir) Hubert Gough; commanded ill-fated Fifth Army, 1916–18.

[9] General (later Sir) R. C. B. Haking; commanded XI Corps, 1915–18.

[10] Later Field-Marshal Sir William Robertson. Succeeded Sir Archibald Murray as Chief of the Imperial General Staff in December 1915.

[11] Then commanding First Army, Succeeded French as Commander-in-Chief, 1915–19; Field-Marshal, 1917; created 1st Earl Haig, 1919.

being no proper plan of campaign. The King said he would repeat all he heard to Asquith, who intended discussing whether some change would not be advisable.

We went on October 27th to see the President near Ribemont. Allenby,[12] who had just been appointed to command the Third Army, met the King; with him was General Morland.[13] A telegram arrived saying that the President would be an hour late, and so there was nothing to be done but to wait. As it was bitterly cold the King entered a cottage where the woman, having no idea who he was, prattled away and told him about the German soldiers who had been there. She said that at first they had behaved very well and that there had been no trouble; but after a few days they had received orders to frighten the inhabitants. Then even the most good-natured of them broke out and smashed something. She showed the King and Allenby the cupboards in her room, which had been smashed in with a rifle-butt although they were not locked.

Finally, the President arrived dressed in a long blue cloak, with a yachting cap and yellow gaiters and boots. The King presented all of us and the President greeted me like an old friend. This denoted good staff work, as he could not well have remembered me.

The President then presented his suite, and we drove off in motors, the King and the President in the first car, the Prince of Wales and a French politician in the second, and General Duparge and I in the third. As there was only room for one car on the parade ground a rather undignified procession of French and English had to run across a field to catch up with the King's car. The troops we were to see consisted of the 10th Corps under Maxse;[14] after the usual march past three cheers were given, first for the King and secondly for the President, one Brigadier adding rather tamely: 'Vive la France!' The King took exception to this and told Maxse he should have known better; the President should have come first.

[12] Later 1st Viscount Allenby, Field-Marshal; commanded Palestine Campaign, 1917–18.
[13] Later General Sir Thomas Morland.
[14] Later General Sir Ivor Maxse. At this time in command of 18th Division; later commanded 18th Army Corps.

We walked to our cars and inspected some second-line trenches. Then to Chateau Marieux, the headquarters of Major-General Sir T. Snow,[15] where His Majesty gave a luncheon to the President. The luncheon should by rights have been at General Allenby's, but he had only just been appointed and therefore had no cook.

I had written beforehand to say there would be no speeches; this was a wise precaution, as the President was much addicted to speaking. The King sat between the President and M. Millerand,[16] while the Prince of Wales, who sat opposite, had two French officers on each side. The fact that none of the French could talk English and Generals Allenby and Snow knew practically no French made the luncheon a silent meal—more especially as water alone was drunk. The luncheon itself was very well done and quite worthy of the occasion. Frank Mildmay was responsible for it and had even obtained fruit from his country place in England for the occasion.

After luncheon we motored to Acheux, where five battalions of the 7th Corps, under the command of Major-General Count Gleichen,[17] were drawn up.

By way of pageantry the parade cannot be said to have been a success: the men looked blue with cold and the President and M. Millerand looked rather ridiculous walking through the mud. After going down the line we stopped under a sort of tent, and here the President presented the Prince of Wales with the Croix de Guerre. Much to our disappointment he did not embrace His Royal Highness. It was the one thing the Prince hated, and we warned him he would have to submit to it. The Prince had very strange views on foreign decorations, and we had the greatest difficulty in getting him to wear the ribbon of the Croix de Guerre. At first he flatly refused, as he said he had not earned it; but I pointed out to him that his refusal to wear it would hurt the feelings of the French, so reluctantly he pinned it on.

[15] Later Lieutenant-General Sir Thomas Snow. Commanded VII Corps, 1915–18.

[16] Alexandre Millerand, then French War Minister; President of the French Republic, 1920–4.

[17] Then in command of 37th Division.

The President then decorated a certain number of Generals who were drawn up in front of him. Those who were given the Commandership of the Legion of Honour looked rather ridiculous when it was put round their necks.

We then drove off to see more troops and the King insisted on getting into an open car for this. The President disliked this intensely as it was a bitterly cold day, but, of course, he had no option in the matter.

Then the King took leave of the President and he motored home (two and a half hours' drive).

On the next day we left Aire at 7 a.m. and motored to Amiens, where we arrived about 10 a.m.

We arrived at a small station and found the President and General Joffre[18] with their respective suites. The King shook them warmly by the hand and went through the form of presenting us. The President gave us little shakes of the hand and never said a word. I thought how different it was to a monarchy. The Sovereign of any other country after having been with us all the day before would have said something just to take the stiffness off the presentation, but presumably the President is never allowed to talk. I found my friend of yesterday, General Duparge, and greeted him warmly.

The whole party motored off to the review ground at Blincourt, where 36,000 men who had been fighting in Champagne were drawn up. They received the King with the Royal Salute and then, after much bugling and drumming, the President decorated some officers and men, pinning the decoration himself on their coats and then kissing them on both cheeks; after which more bugling and drumming.

The King and President with their suites then walked to the saluting point and here I got an opportunity of talking to Joffre. I told him that the King was anxious to give a message to the whole French Army, and not merely to the troops on parade. His Majesty felt that if he spoke to the General-in-Command it would

[18] Commander-in-Chief of French Armies on the Western Front, 1914–16; later Marshal.

seem as if his remarks were only intended for the troops under his command. I was therefore told by the King to suggest that his message should be published in the Orders of the French Army.

Joffre said it was a very good idea, and thought such a message would have an excellent effect on the French troops.

The troopers marched past, and it was a very fine sight to see these bearded warriors go in line of battalions. The Algerian troops were interesting to see and the King expressed a wish to see some Spahis later.

At the conclusion of the parade General Blondart rode up and saluted the King. The King, who was no French scholar, told him how much he admired the troops and how wonderful he thought it was—just a short speech which did very well.

Three Spahis were brought up for the King to see and the peculiarities of their dress were explained. One of these men on galloping away fell with his horse, and it was feared he had broken his neck; but it turned out eventually he had only been stunned. It was amusing to see the difference between the behaviour of the King and the President. The King, on seeing the man fall, at once went to see what had happened. This was the natural impulse; the President, on the other hand, who had been trained to control his natural impulses, remained where he was, uncertain whether it was the right thing for a President to get mixed up with an accident of this sort. However, when it came to the President and his staff remaining behind while everyone else went forward, he determined to follow the King and joined in with the others.

We then entered motors and went through Compiègne to the Headquarters of the 35th Corps.

It was a large country house with a beautiful park, and the luncheon was wonderfully well done. The King sat between General Joffre and General Dubois; while the President sat opposite, with the Prince of Wales on his right and General Lowther on his left. I sat next to General Dubois and found him most amusing and interesting to talk to. I had written previously to ask that there should be no speeches and so none were made, but I imagine that President Poincaré was disappointed as he liked making speeches.

We motored after luncheon to Belleu, where we were received by General Franchet d'Esperey.[19] We walked in file up a communication trench and as we went three shells burst over our heads, the nearest one about four hundred yards off. I at first thought it was a bit of stage management, but on talking to my neighbour, one of the Generals, I ascertained that the Germans were actually shelling the place. The General, whom I asked, said he was not sure it was not overdone. If, by a fluke, a shell had burst in the trench, what a bag the Germans would have had!

We went into underground caves and emerged to look out on shelters. It was interesting to see the German lines, but there was little activity while we were there.

We then motored to Longpoint, where the King took leave of the President. He travelled back to Aire by train, arriving the next morning at 7 a.m.

On the 28th of October the King left as usual in a motor-car with the Prince of Wales and Lowther, while Charles Cust and I followed in another. We met Sir Douglas Haig and his staff at a cross-roads and the King and I mounted horses. The animal provided for the King was a beautiful specimen of a charger; Haig had insisted on mounting the King on his own horse. The worst of Generals' horses is that they get little or no exercise and, although this particular animal had been trained to troops cheering, it had been imperfectly done. The cheering that greets the King is a totally different thing from a few men cheering simply to train a horse. I rode Sir Richard Sutton's [20] horse and it seemed a very perfectly trained charger, but then it did not belong to a General.

There were three parades, under the command of Sir Henry Rawlinson.[21] The wet weather made the ground impossible for any march past. It was therefore decided to simply ride down the line. The Generals in command of each parade had been warned not to call for three cheers until the King was a certain distance

[19] Later Marshal Franchet d'Esperey. Commanded French Army Group on Western Front; Commander-in-Chief, Salonika, 1918.
[20] 6th Bart.
[21] Later 1st Lord Rawlinson of Trent. Commanded 4th Corps 4th Army.

449

off; it all seemed admirably managed. The King, accompanied by Rawlinson, with Douglas Haig and myself immediately behind, rode down the troops drawn up in mass of quarter columns; then, on the King's riding away, the troops were to give three cheers.

The King's horse behaved admirably and never took any notice of the cheering. His Majesty got so at home on the animal that on one parade he dropped the reins on the horse's neck and decorated Captain Foss [22] with the V.C., an operation which required both hands.

We then cantered off some little way and the King inspected the Flying Corps. There were not more than about fifty men in all. Having ridden down the line, the King spoke to the Commanding Officer and asked him about the new machines. Seeing his superior engaged in conversation with the King, it occurred to the second-in-command, who apparently was ignorant of the instructions issued on the subject, that it devolved on him to call for three cheers; he promptly did so while the King's horse was not more than a few yards off. The animal quivered with terror and crouched down on its haunches. Then suddenly springing up it reared straight up in the air and, its hind legs slipping, it fell back right on top of the King. Now the whole point of my riding immediately behind the King was that I might be of some use if anything of the sort happened; but all this took place so quickly that I never had time to reach His Majesty.

I at once jumped off and flung the reins to the nearest man. I ran up and knelt down by the King, who had had all the wind knocked out of him. For two or three minutes he lay quite still, and then opened his eyes.

My first thought was that he had probably broken his pelvis, but he suddenly expressed a wish to stand up and we supported him on each side. I then came to the conclusion that nothing could be broken—a conclusion which I afterwards learned was absolutely wrong. He asked for his cap and told me to look after his riding cane.

[22] Captain C. C. Foss, of the Bedfordshire and Hertfordshire Regiment, was awarded the Victoria Cross for most conspicuous bravery at Neuve Chapelle, 12 March, 1915.

Sir Douglas Haig then inquired what was to be done, and I at once replied that it would be best to get him to bed at his château at Aire. I asked Douglas Haig to send for the motors and also to telegraph for a good doctor. We carried him about fifty yards to his motor, and I asked the Prince of Wales to get in with him while Lowther got on the box. It seemed an interminable journey to Charles Cust and me, who followed in the second motor. As we went along we met regiments marching to the ground where the inspection of the Guards Division was to have taken place. At a railway crossing we were kept waiting quite five minutes, and Cust, who went to see how things were going on, returned to say that the King was in great pain. He found Derek Keppel and Claud Hamilton in an open motor and asked them to go to Bailleul to fetch Sir Anthony Bowlby, the King's surgeon.

At last we arrived at the villa at Aire, and of course everyone was out. I hammered at the kitchen window and finally got one of the cooks to fetch the sergeant footman. In the meantime the Prince of Wales, Lowther and Cust had lifted the King and carried him from the motor up the stone stairs to the door which, luckily, by that time was open. They decided to carry him at once to his bedroom and lay him on a sofa. He still seemed in great pain and explained to me that he had no intention of allowing himself to be examined by every doctor that came. He would wait until Bertrand Dawson or Bowlby arrived. Cust remembered that the nurse who had attended the King when he had typhus some twenty years ago was on a barge in a canal near at hand, so we sent a car for her.

Surgeon-General Macpherson,[23] the D.M.S., arrived to see what he could do, and Colonel Wallace [24]—a most eminent man, I believe, and even a specialist in such cases—had been sent by Sir Douglas Haig, but the King refused to see him. I explained matters to him and he said he quite appreciated the King's point; he thought there would be no harm in waiting for Bowlby. After luncheon Sir Bertrand Dawson and Sir Anthony Bowlby arrived from Bailleul. All these eminent surgeons had a consultation, and

[23] Later Major-General Sir William Macpherson. D.M.S., 1st Army.
[24] Later Sir Cuthbert Wallace, Consulting Surgeon to 1st Army.

finally produced a bulletin which they all wanted to sign. Sir Arthur Sloggett was allowed to sign first, the remainder following in order of rank.

I telephoned to Buckingham Palace and managed to make Stamfordham hear, which was truly wonderful at so great a distance. I asked him to tell the Queen, but to beg Her Majesty not to think of coming out. Such was the King's express wish. Later in the evening the King sent for me and said he wished the Prince of Wales to go to London and tell the Queen all about the accident.

His Majesty appeared more comfortable and said that when he was still he was in no pain, but the slightest movement gave him untold agonies.

Sir John French came to see the King a day or two later and remained about ten minutes. When he came out he said to me that it would not be long before the whole incident reached the Germans through spies, and that the enemy's aeroplanes would buzz round and drop bombs on the villa. He said it was therefore necessary to move the King shortly, and argued that if the doctors were agreed there would be less risk in moving him than in bombs.

In the afternoon I repeated all this to the King, but all he said was: 'You can tell French from me to go to hell and stay there. I don't intend to move for any bombs.'

Dawson, who happened to be at the door, heard these gracious words and repeated them to French, who was hugely amused.

The journey home at the beginning of November was arranged by Sloggett and very well it was done, too. A hospital train was at the station and conveyed the King to Boulogne.

At Aire station the King decorated Sergeant Brooks [25] with the V.C.—rather a pretty little ceremony as the man had to kneel down by the King's bed while Charles Cust read out a statement of his services.

I remained in the background and, with the help of Mr. Quinn

[25] Lance-Sergeant Brooks, Coldstream Guards; awarded Victoria Cross for most conspicuous bravery near Loos, October 1915.

of Scotland Yard, kept all stations, etc., free of people. I thought the King would hate a crowd.

At Boulogne we had to decide whether the ship could start, and this I left to Cust and Admiral Bacon. This was perhaps a mistake, as no sailor ever thinks the sea rough. As it turned out, however, it was distinctly rough when we got half-way across and the King suffered very much.

Treves met us at Folkestone and came up in the train with us.

I think on the whole the issue of the bulletins at once was right. It is always best on such occasions to take the public into one's confidence. There was, however, much criticism: people said that the signatures of five doctors gave a totally wrong impression, making out the injuries to be much worse than they were. However, on the whole I am convinced that we did right.

The King told me that Treves had explained to him that I did absolutely the wrong thing in putting him at once into a motor. I should have left him lying down until a doctor arrived. My assumption that nothing was broken because he stood up was perfectly false. Cases had been known of men standing up with their pelvis broken.

CHAPTER XXIII

A strange request — 'The luckiest man in the world' — Lady Colebrooke — When to work — Rations in the royal household — Sir William Robertson and the Armistice — The King's visit to Paris, 1918 — Lloyd George, Asquith and the war medals

ONE DAY IN 1915 Jim Athlumney,[1] the Provost Marshal in London, came into my room at Buckingham Palace, clicked his heels and saluted. Then in dramatic tones he said, 'I want the King's permission to shoot a German spy, named Captain Lodi, in the ditch of the Tower of London.' I was considerably startled by such a curious request, but merely asked why the King's permission was necessary. He said that as the Tower of London was a Royal Palace, the King's Coroner would have to sign the death certificate and he could not do this without the King's permission.

It was quite obvious to me that the King's name should not be used in connection with the unpleasant but necessary shooting of spies. I therefore told him to come back in the afternoon as it was impossible for me to give him an answer at once. As soon as he had left I got on the telephone to the Lord Chancellor's Secretary, Sir Claud Schuster,[2] and explained the whole thing to him. I asked him to repeat all I said to the Lord Chancellor, and to add that it would be well if the law officers of the Crown could think of some way of preventing the King's name being used in connection with this execution. After two hours I received a message to the effect that as the Tower ditch was outside the Tower of London, and therefore not in a Royal Palace, there was no necessity to obtain the King's approval.

[1] James Somerville, 6th (and last) Lord Athlumney.
[2] Later 1st Lord Schuster.

455

During the war I heard in one week the expressions: 'I am the unluckiest man in the world' and 'I am the luckiest man in the world'; the contrast between the speakers and their standards of luck and ill-luck was so complete that the occasions have always remained fresh in my mind.

Staying in a country house I met an old sportsman of over 60 who looked upon the war as a tiresome episode that interfered with his shooting, hunting and fishing. In spite of the war, however, he seemed to indulge these sports as often as possible. He was a particularly fine fisherman and liked dry-fly fishing. He related his experiences to me and said that when he came down to a fishing he had taken the wind was in the wrong quarter; this prevented him going out the first few days. When the weather changed and the wind got round to the right corner he suddenly was crippled by an attack of gout which laid him prostrate. He added: 'I am the unluckiest man in the world!'

A few days later I accompanied the King and Queen when they visited a hospital of wounded soldiers. I was talking to one of the doctors in the tail of the procession going round the wards, when I heard an officer say to the King: 'I am the luckiest man in the world!' I pushed through the others to see the speaker and I saw an officer who had lost an eye, an arm and a leg: in fact, all his left side. He went on to say that during a raid in the German trenches his party had suddenly come under heavy machine-gun fire and they had all been killed except him. The only reason his life had been saved was that he was last and had only exposed a portion of his left side round the corner.

In June 1916 I went with the King round some ammunition works and we found all sorts of people we knew engaged on what was obviously unskilled labour. We also came across Lady Colebrooke, whose well-known cleverness with her fingers had gained her a post requiring great skill. If London society was divided up into skilled and unskilled categories, I wonder how many would get into the former.

From my point of view the great strength of absolute ignorance seemed to entitle me to great respect. If I had been able to say I knew something about this as I had once made ammunition, I should have been looked upon as an amateur and possibly a failure; but when I said I knew nothing about such things I took up a detached and apparently impregnable position. It was all very wonderful and the statistics as usual were quite bewildering.

I was at one time rather puzzled as to how to find time to do anything beyond my ordinary work and the usual private letters and accounts. Although my duties with the King were not really heavy, they were exacting, and by the end of the day I invariably found that the time had slipped away and I had not had time to read anything beyond the newspapers, or write anything besides my official and private correspondence. I found that working late at night I had no difficulty in using my brain, whereas in the early morning before breakfast I was quite unable to do anything at all.

It seems, however, that men are all different in this respect and that while some are at their best at night others prefer the early morning. I asked Sir John Fisher when he did his best work, and he told me that he invariably got up at 5.30 a.m. when he was First Sea Lord and worked uninterruptedly from 6 to 9 a.m. He had a large breakfast and nothing in the middle of the day but a glass of lemonade and a biscuit.

Sir Rufus Isaacs [3] told me that when he was busily engaged in the Law Courts and also in the House of Commons, he invariably got up at 5 a.m. and worked on his brief from 5.30 to 9 a.m. He went to the Law Courts all day and then to the House of Commons in the afternoon, where he might be kept till late at night. I asked him how long he could keep this up and he said for about two months. I repeated this to Lord Kitchener, who said that his experience was that when he wished to study anything and acquire information, the early morning was best; but that when he had to write anything founded on the knowledge he had acquired, the night was the proper time.

[3] Later 1st Marquess of Reading. Attorney-General, 1910-13 (first to sit in Cabinet); later Viceroy of India.

The King and Queen had decided to take the rations very seriously and at breakfast those who were late got nothing. When I say late, the ordinary meaning of the word hardly conveyed the wonderful punctuality of the King and Queen. One was late if the clock sounded when one was on the stairs, even in a small house like York Cottage. In order to make sure of getting something to eat one had to be before time. Lord Marcus Beresford, who came to stay, quickly got the hang of this and dogged the Queen's footsteps into the dining-room. The point was that there was just enough and no more for everyone; but as most people helped themselves too generously, there was nothing left for the person who came last.

Godfrey-Faussett was kept on the telephone one day and came into the dining-room after everyone else had sat down. He found nothing to eat and immediately rang the bell and asked for a boiled egg. If he had ordered a dozen turkeys he could not have made a bigger stir. The King accused him of being a slave to his inside, of unpatriotic behaviour, and even went so far as to hint that we should lose the war on account of his gluttony.

When Sir William Robertson was Chief of the General Staff in London the King lent him York House at St. James's Palace. He had always been *persona grata* with His Majesty, who liked his plain speaking and blunt manner.

I used to ride with him at eight o'clock in the morning, but at that early hour he was never very communicative and sometimes we rode without speaking to each other. When the Armistice was declared I was riding with him when we met Judge Kavath, who was head of the financial blockade, an American with a shrewd sense of humour and a fine speaker. He came up to Robertson and said: 'I cannot let this opportunity pass, General, without conveying to you my own and I am sure also the congratulations of my countrymen on the successful termination of hostilities.' He went on as if he was addressing a mass meeting, and ended up with a magnificent peroration.

Robertson merely replied: 'Ugh, thanks', and cantered off. Kavath said this was truly English.

On one occasion the Queen at dinner turned to him and told him of some absurd order that had been issued from the War Office. He replied: 'It sounds so idiotic that I am sure there must be some very good reason for it.'

[*After the Armistice the King decided to visit Paris again, taking the two elder Princes with him. The author went on ahead to arrange the details. The visit was a great success, and the King afterwards went on a protracted tour of the battle-fields.*]

The details of the King's visit were not difficult to arrange, and I really came to the conclusion that it was farcical to have gone on ahead to Paris. Eddy Derby was particularly good at this sort of thing, and Monsieur Martin, the Chef du Protocole, never made a mistake, so there was really nothing for me to do.

On Thursday morning it was arranged that the Ambassador, myself and the staff officers attached should meet the Royal train at Chantilly. This seemed quite a simple manœuvre, but we made a mistake here: we should have insisted on a special train. As it turned out the officers attached were given military motors and they offered us a lift. All the chauffeurs of any age had just been demobilized and their places had been taken by all sorts of men who could not drive at all. We started in three cars: Eddy Derby in No. 1 with a French General, myself in No. 2 with a French Colonel and a Major, and the remainder in No. 3.

The moment we started I grasped that the driver was a novice. He missed two nasty accidents by going at racing speed suddenly. It was car No. 3 that first came to grief, colliding with a taxi and knocking down a china-stall at the side of the road. We, of course, pulled up, and the occupants of car No. 3 were placed in the other two cars. We went quite well for some time as the road was straight, when suddenly our car tilted over at a dangerous angle, caught the pavement, and with a crash came to a standstill. It appeared that the driver had not known the turning was so sharp and had turned too late. We were all mixed up on the top of each other inside the car, so there was nothing for it but to get into the first car, six inside and three on the box! We eventually arrived at Chantilly just in time, as the King's train covered with flags

drew up. We all got in, and so did the Prefect of the Arrondisse-
ment and the Mayor of Chantilly. This rather complicated matters, as the King had arranged to have everyone presented after
the train left, but I explained that we had to get rid of the Prefect
and the Mayor before moving, so the King came in and shook
hands all round; then we all had *déjeuner*.

At the Bois de Boulogne there was a Guard of Honour, with
the President and all the celebrities of France. The King inspected
the Guard of Honour, and then we all filed out of the station
while the band crashed 'La Marseillaise' and 'Le God Save' alternately.

Although it was drizzling with rain the crowd in the Avenue
du Bois de Boulogne was the most wonderful I have ever seen.
Of course, the absence of men from the crowd made the note of
the cheering much higher in tone than usual, and occasionally,
when we came across a bunch of British soldiers, it seemed quite
a different thing. But there is no doubt that the tremendous emotion of the crowd was something quite out of the ordinary. Monsieur Pichon, who was with me in a carriage, was so overcome
that he broke down and cried like a child. We came soon after the
Prince of Wales and Prince Bertie and saw the enthusiasm before
it had expended itself. On arrival at the Ministry for Foreign
Affairs we found there was three-quarters of an hour to wait before paying a visit to the President, so the King told me to telephone and make it a quarter of an hour earlier. This seemed to
suit Poincaré, and so off we went again in open carriages to the
Elysée. The King paid quite a long visit there and the brilliant
suite in damp khaki stood about and talked to the President's people. Personally, I had had quite enough of my opposite member
after five minutes, but all Frenchmen only require starting off and
they can talk for hours.

On our return a closed carriage with glass all round had been
provided for the King, as the rain was coming down rather heavily, but the King refused to go in it and insisted on having an open
carriage. So we all drove back and there were still quite a number
of people in the streets. The King went to tea at the Embassy and
the Prince of Wales and Prince Bertie went to the Leave Club. I

was told by Sir D. Henderson [4] that this was a remarkably successful visit, and the Prince's manner with the men was admirable.

Dinner at the Elysée, where the President came to the door and all the guests filed past the King, the Princes and the Poincarés; we were about 160 at dinner, and this was called *'un dîner intime'*. It was a very brilliant sight, with silver plate and much electric light in very highly ornamented rooms. The President recited his speech by heart as if he were making it for the first time—a dangerous proceeding unless he had someone to prompt him. He delivered it very well and with great oratory. The King read his through admirably and everybody in the room heard. There was, as usual, no applause for either speech, which always makes it fall rather flat. Afterwards we smoked and talked to various people. I asked the Protocol whether we could have an opportunity of thanking the President for our *Légions d'Honneur,* and also whether we could be presented to Madame Poincaré. He said both were unnecessary, but when we asked the General looking after us he thought we should at least thank the President. So we all got together when Poincaré rushed round. He, however, shook us warmly by the hand without giving us a chance of uttering the beautiful speeches of thanks we had hastily prepared in our minds; Greig [5] was the one who stuck to it longest, and he got out quite a sentence before he had to let go the President's hand.

On Friday morning an extremely well-managed, although somewhat unnecessary, show at the Embassy took place: all the men on leave in Paris marched past. They came by in groups so as to prevent sudden overcrowding, and marked time with the Scots Guards' band playing in the corner.

The knighting of George Grahame [6] was a dismal affair. Eddy Derby was anxious that this should be done as publicly as possible, and had even suggested it taking place at the same time as the investiture of Foch, but the King would not hear of this, and as

[4] Lieutenant-General Sir David Henderson; Director of Military Aeronautics, 1913–18; Director of Red Cross Societies.

[5] Group-Captain Sir Louis Greig; Gentleman-Usher to King George V, 1924–36.

[6] Minister Plenipotentiary, Paris 1918–20; later British Ambassador in Belgium and Spain.

a compromise it was to be done in the morning. Eddy went out and drove some people into the room to witness the show; why they were being forced indoors they knew not. When about fourteen people had been rounded up, Charles Cust, with his glasses at the end of his nose, undertook the ceremony; forcing Grahame on to his knee with one hand and handing the sword to the King with the other, he announced the honour. Personally, I always think that these half-cock ceremonies are a mistake. Either have the full investiture properly done or else quite a private show. However, Eddy was delighted and that was the great point.

Luncheon at the Ministry of Foreign Affairs with Pichon; very beautifully done and very rich food. There were no toasts or speeches. I sat between two South American diplomats who bored me stiff. Then we drove off to the Hôtel de Ville, and that was very much the same as usual in the way of cheering. The midinettes at the windows and on the balconies made a great deal of noise, but there was not the same emotion as the first day in the Champs Elysées. The usual crowd was there, quite unruly. The two addresses from the town were beautifully read, although the second one showed the Prefet de la Seine was very nervous. The King read his reply very well, and invoked a great deal of applause quite unexpectedly by his last sentence in which he said he would always look upon the people of Paris as his friends.

Then began that chaotic procession to drink the toasts; all the crowd joined in, and we found ourselves right down the course with no chance of getting anywhere near the King. I was lucky and followed Greig who, being an international football player, understood how to deal with the crowd. I was joined by Joffre, who was being swept along in the stream, and finally we ended up somewhere near the *table d'honneur*. Orders had been given for all the King's suite to come through, and this nearly ended in a free fight. The King and President went out on the balcony, which I think was an innovation. Walking back the same way always seems such a mistake, and it was with the greatest difficulty that some of us got through to the carriages. Derek Keppel stayed behind to decorate the municipal swells, and I drove back alone with Monsieur Saint-Seuve, the President's Private Secretary.

He had a grey moustache and was mistaken constantly for Clemenceau; at times he had quite an ovation with *'Vive Clemenceau!'* from the house-tops.

We all got back rather damp, and the King again went to tea at the Embassy. The King of Montenegro [7] wished to see the King, but this was firmly knocked on the head. Then the Comte d'Eu wished to come, but suddenly there came the news of the accident to his son and he went to England. Prince George of Greece [8] came and I had some difficulty with him. I told him to ask for me and he thought this unnecessary, but of course we had to keep it out of the Press.

The dinner and reception at the Embassy was beautifully done, although it was no very easy matter to decide who should be asked. There seemed to be a lot of people there. The decoration of Foch was, I believe, a success, but the crowd pressed round so much that no one could see what was happening. Then the band began too soon, which rather spoilt the effect. The King and President came away at 10.30 p.m., but the Prince of Wales and Prince Albert stayed till 12.30 a.m.

I had been wondering whether on a special occasion of this sort the King should not be attended by celebrities, or Generals and Admirals. It must be very damping to the enthusiasm of the crowd to have to cheer Charles Cust or Wigram or myself. Yet it is difficult to know whether on such occasions he should take with him soldiers, sailors or politicians. Perhaps a sprinkling of all three. The French suite were just the same as we were, and so the mob had not much to look at. When the King next came to Paris in the spring for the Victory Review I hoped he would take Haig and Beatty with him, and the War Cabinet could go in the last carriage!

One day in May 1919 I went to see Henry Wilson at the War Office, in response to a message that he would like to have a talk with me. He usually made such fun of everything that a serious

[7] King Nicholas of Montenegro, whose equivocal attitude towards the Central Powers had made him mistrusted by the Allies during the war.
[8] Eldest son of King Constantine, and later (January 1923) King of Greece.

talk was never easy. I found him having an office cup of tea and, as I expected, in a cynical mood, laughing at everything and everybody.

However, he soon developed his theme, which was that the King should offer the war medals to Lloyd George as the Prime Minister who had 'won the war'. He said: 'I can't bear to think of that dear little man sobbing himself to sleep, his pillow wet with tears every night, saying, "I won the war and nobody gave me anything".'

I told him that while I agreed that no honour would be too great for Lloyd George, I thought the war medals inappropriate, as they would imply that he had actually fought in the war. He replied that as Lloyd George would not take anything which carried a knighthood with it, all the higher Orders were out of the question. The only thing the King could offer was the war medals.

I promised after further argument to repeat all he said to His Majesty. When I did so later I was surprised to find that the King rather liked the idea, but said it would be difficult to leave out Asquith.

In the evening I knocked up against Walter Long, to whom Henry Wilson had confided the idea. Walter Long was strongly opposed to it and said that the whole thing was absurd. It would merely make Lloyd George and Asquith the laughing-stock of the Army.[9]

[9] Nevertheless, the medals were awarded. Asquith and Lloyd George were the only civilians to get them.

CHAPTER XXIV

The Empress Marie's valuables

[*The outbreak of the Russian Revolution in 1917 found the
Dowager Empress Marie at Kiev. She met her son Nicholas II
for the last time at Mohilev later in the year. Though she was
given several opportunities of leaving Russia, she lived quietly
for a time in the Crimea with other members of the Imperial
family. She finally left for England in April 1919, and later
settled at Hvidöre, in Denmark, her native land. She died at
Copenhagen in October 1928.*]

I HAPPENED TO BE in London in November 1919 when the
Dowager Empress of Russia's things arrived from Russia. The
King, therefore, asked me to receive them from the captain of a
British cruiser and store them at Buckingham Palace.

The Bolshevik Government was such a mixture of comic opera
and tragedy that anything might happen. I don't know exactly
why, but it occurred to me that it would be well to take precautions and to have everything I did witnessed. There was, of
course, the British naval officer who had brought the goods from
Russia, and there was also the Inspector of Buckingham Palace
(Mr. Sands) who could give evidence; but I felt this was not
enough. So I wrote to Monsieur Nabokoff,[1] the Chargé d'Affaires
at the so-called Russian Embassy, and asked him to come and
help me as my knowledge of Russian was nil. I made very little
of it and merely asked for his advice. I also asked Harry Stonor
to come and help, and as he was in London, doing nothing in
particular, he kindly came along at once.

I left word at the different doors that all these were to be

[1] An official of the Imperial Russian Embassy who had survived the Revolution.

shown up to the Throne Room, and I sent word to the Inspector that the packing-cases were to be brought up just as they were and the cords and seals were to be left intact.

It was a curious scene. The Throne Room, all gold and red damask, with chandeliers; the throne at the end of the room with canopy above and curtains at the side; dust sheets laid over the carpet and fifteen huge packing-cases corded and sealed; myself, Harry Stonor, Nabokoff and Sands, with innumerable workmen who had brought up the packing-cases. I first of all asked the naval officer to examine the cases and tell me if he was prepared to swear they were the same as those handed over to him by the Bolshevik Government, and whether he could say if the cords and seals had been changed. While he was examining them I noticed that Nabokoff was getting very uncomfortable and was edging towards the door, no doubt with a view to hurrying off. I called him back and made him sit down, explaining that it was the Russian documents I had to fill in that worried me. As soon as the naval officer finished his inspection and told me he was prepared to swear that nothing had been touched, I asked Nabokoff to verify the seals as those of the Soviet Government and then gave orders that the packing-cases were to be opened. The first one, about four feet high and eight feet long, contained nothing but pokers, shovels and tongs of the commonest description. The second contained harness and saddlery, most of which had perished. The third, labelled 'Books from the Empress's Library', was full of trash, old Russian railway guides, and children's books and novels. So one by one the packing-cases were opened and nothing but absolutely worthless trash was found. Nabokoff became more and more uncomfortable and made several attempts to escape, but I held him in conversation.

When the farce was finished I sent for paper, pens and ink, and first of all asked the naval officer to write a statement that the cases were untouched. I then asked Nabokoff to witness the contents, but he said this was impossible. So I drew up a rough list of the contents of each case and, having signed it myself, handed it to him. He signed it, feeling he had no alternative. Then I got Sands to sign it, and told him to remove all the rubbish. I kept the original, but sent a copy of these statements to the Foreign Office, together with the Russian papers which I was asked to sign. Of course, the obvious idea of the Bolsheviks was to say I had made away with the valuable pictures, books and bibelots of the Empress, or else that the naval officer had done so; but, of course, now they would never dare make any such charge. It seemed inconceivable that the Bolsheviks should have taken so much trouble with the farce, but no doubt they made great capital over their goodness in letting the Empress Marie have all her valuable things. The Foreign Office duly reported this to the Soviet Government, who took no notice; from their point of view it was simply a *coup manqué*.

When the Grand Duchess Xenia [2] was left stranded, the King, with his usual kindness, determined to give her sufficient allowance to live on; but as she understood nothing about money, having had unlimited wealth all her life, it was by no means easy to grapple with her finances. Monsieur Bark,[3] who had been the last Finance Minister under the Czarist régime, offered his services, and these were at once accepted. He found that the Grand Duchess was really penniless. She had sold all her jewels to a scoundrel she had happened to meet and he went off without paying her. The first thing to do was to get rid of her house in Paris, and this Bark succeeded in doing. Then he tried to find out what other liabilities there were, but she was so delightfully unbusinesslike that he was never sure that he had cut her off from all her entanglements. Finally, the King lent her Frogmore Cottage and gave her £2,400 a year. I engaged the clerk who did the accounts for the park to look after her accounts also, and hand over the balance to her after salaries and wages, etc., had been deducted. But I found she practically starved herself, and never spent a penny on her clothes, in order to give more to her sons.

When the Empress Marie of Russia eventually settled down in Denmark, the King and Queen, Queen Alexandra and Princess Victoria all subscribed to give her £10,000 a year. Eventually the

[2] Elder daughter of Empress Marie, and sister of Nicholas II.
[3] Later Sir Peter Bark; Russian Finance Minister, 1914–7.

King paid her the whole amount. The difficulty was that as she formerly had unlimited wealth, she had absolutely no idea of the value of money. It seemed generally agreed that a cheque book in the hands of one whose generosity was proverbial, but who knew nothing about money, would be a fatal mistake; but for me to attempt to run her finances from London would be practically impossible. Prince Axel [4] of Denmark was called into consultation and after much discussion it was arranged that Captain Andrup of the Danish Navy should undertake to run her finances: that is to say that he should pay the salaries of the suite and the servants' wages and keep the Household books, and then every month hand over to the Empress any balance there might be. I was to arrange for so much ready money to be paid to him monthly and this arrangement worked very well. The Empress grasped that the more she entertained the less money she would have at the end of the month, and cut down her invitations accordingly.

There was some difficulty about jewels. When the Empress Marie escaped from Russia she managed to take away with her two boxes of jewels. As was only to be expected in Russia, one box disappeared on the journey; but there still remained the second box, said to contain valuable jewels. The King was afraid that unless steps were taken to preserve these jewels intact, the Empress would give them away. I was therefore asked to see that this did not happen. After some correspondence I arranged with Captain Andrup that he was to have a safe and that there were to be two keys to open it. One key was to be kept by him and one by the Empress's dresser. Whenever she expressed a wish to see the jewels the dresser was to telephone to Andrup and get his key. Afterwards he was to make sure that none of the jewels had disappeared. Apparently this worked smoothly, and when the Empress died in October 1928 the jewels were still in the safe.

I was told confidentially in October 1928 that after the Empress Marie's funeral all sorts of people would try and get hold of the

[4] 2nd son of Prince Waldemar, youngest son of King Christian IX of Denmark.

jewels, and the husband of the Grand Duchess Olga [5] would naturally ask to see her share. There were also several other Russians who would hope to get something, and therefore I told the King something ought to be done to protect the Grand Duchesses. His Majesty at first proposed to send Derek Keppel to Copenhagen, but of course he would not be in a position to deal with the Russians. I suggested the wonderful Monsieur Bark, whose advice would have great weight with them, and the King agreed. I telegraphed to Bark and told him to come and see me, and I then said he was to get hold of the jewels and send them to the King. There were stories about international crooks waiting to steal the jewels as soon as they were moved from Copenhagen, so it was not an altogether easy job I was giving him. I had anticipated trouble, either with the Russians or with the crooks, and I had therefore told the British Minister in Copenhagen,[6] Sir Thomas Hohler, to have a messenger he could implicitly trust at the Legation: as soon as Bark brought the jewels to him, this messenger was to start at once for London. The parcel was to be addressed to me. Bark agreed that this was the best way of bringing them to London, because he might be shadowed if he left taking the jewels with him.

I received a cypher telegram from Bark asking me to insure the jewels for half a million, but I was convinced that this was an exaggerated idea of their value; I replied that I would insure them for £200,000.

I had given him a letter from me to the two Grand Duchesses asking them to hand over the jewels to him, and telling them that the King would undertake their sale.

On October 28th I was told that the messenger from Copenhagen would arrive at 6 p.m., and so I went to Buckingham Palace and waited. I waited till 7.45 p.m. and then telephoned to the Foreign Office, but they had heard nothing. So I went to dinner at the Turf and was back at 8.30 p.m., but still no messenger. At 9.30 p.m. I again telephoned the Foreign Office, but they could throw no light on the matter. I was beginning to fear that the

[5] Younger sister of Czar Nicholas II.
[6] 1928–33.

469

messenger had fallen into the clutches of some crooks, when at 11 p.m. the Foreign Office telephoned to say that he had merely had a very bad passage and that he would be with me at 11.30 p.m. He arrived in due course, and I thanked him profusely and put the jewels in my safe.

Bark had telegraphed agreeing to my insuring the jewels for £200,000, and this I managed to do, but not without difficulty. The insurance people did not fancy the job and seemed to fear that there were so many people after the jewels that it was very problematical their ever arriving in London. Anyhow, I was able to telegraph the King that the 'parcel' from Copenhagen had arrived safely.

When Bark turned up in London a day or two later he told me that when he arrived in Copenhagen he soon understood that no one would do anything to get hold of the jewels until after the funeral; he then determined to get hold of them before the funeral so that he could get a start. He went to the Palace and asked to see the Grand Duchesses Xenia and Olga. He gave them my letters and explained he had come from the King, who thought it would be wise for them to send the jewels to him at once. His Majesty would keep them until Their Imperial Highnesses decided what they wished done with them and, if necessary, would be responsible for their sale. The two Grand Duchesses were at first rather startled at such precipitate haste being shown; but remembering the fiasco of the Grand Duchess Xenia's jewels they finally acquiesced. The jewels were taken from the safe, sealed up in a box and handed to Bark. He did not lose a minute and dashed off at once to the British Legation. Unfortunately, Hohler was laid up in hospital, but one of the Secretaries was ready for him, and the messenger went straight off by the next train to London with the jewels. Bark himself hurried back and attended the funeral so that everyone should see he was still there. He told me he did not trouble to stay and hear what happened after the funeral and whether there was a howl of disappointment from the Russian relations; but he supposes that those who had made any plans for the jewels must have been furious to hear that they had already gone to London.

An amusing incident, showing how one's imagination can run away with one, occurred when I had received the jewels from the messenger and deposited them in the safe at Buckingham Palace. It was nearly midnight when I got into my motor and returned to my house in Surrey. I was driving myself and was quite alone. Filled with stories about international crooks and Grand Dukes, I went down the Ripley road and when I got down to the woods and heathland I was suddenly conscious of a powerful motor behind me. I quickened up, but in the old car I was in could not manage to do more than forty-five; the car behind had no difficulty in keeping up with me. I therefore slowed down to twenty miles an hour in order to let it pass, but to my surprise it slowed down, too, and remained close behind me. It was a pitch-dark night and the powerful headlights of this car were really of great assistance to me; but there was something very strange in the way it followed me so closely. I imagined that it carried people who wanted to get hold of me in a quiet, unfrequented part of the road. I determined therefore to go about thirty miles an hour, which would give me a margin of fifteen miles an hour in case I wanted to get away quickly. Nothing happened except that whatever pace I went there was the car immediately behind me. It followed me closely into Guildford and when I turned off to go to Great Tangley Manor there it was again, still behind me. But when I turned across the common to get to my house it went straight on.

I learnt quite by chance from the local garage the next day that the car had belonged to an old lady who lived in the neighbourhood. Being nervous about driving at night, she had given instructions to her chauffeur that he might go any pace he liked, but that he was never to pass another car going the same way.

When the King returned from Sandringham I imagined that all I should have to do would be to hand over the jewels to him; but he was at once taken ill and remained in a critical condition for months. As the two Grand Duchesses were naturally anxious to have some money to go on with, I consulted the Queen, who said that she would undertake to give them an allowance to go on with until the jewels were sold. It was nearly four months before the King recovered sufficiently to attend to this question. When he did so, I reminded him that there was no inventory of the jewels and that the Grand Duchess Xenia might possibly think that we did things here like they formerly did in Russia; that is to say, that many jewels would disappear. I suggested she should be present when her box was opened before they were handed over for sale. It was perhaps a needless precaution, but as her own jewels had been taken by a swindler I felt one could not be too careful.

Mr. Hardy from Hennell & Sons came down from London, and I brought him into the rooms where the box of jewels were and told him he would be asked to make an inventory and then take them away and sell them. The Queen came in with the Grand Duchess, who saw the box tied up with tape as she had sent it. Ropes of the most wonderful pearls were taken out, all graduated, the largest being the size of a big cherry. Cabochon emeralds and large rubies and sapphires were laid out. I then retired discreetly from the room. Afterwards I saw Mr. Hardy who said that if the Grand Duchess were pressed for money he would be willing to advance a hundred thousand pounds on the jewels. But he hoped that he might be given plenty of time to sell them as undoubtedly they were wonderful stones. I told him to wait until I had found out what the King and Queen wished and I luckily found Their Majesties disengaged. They told me to give instructions to Hardy that he was to price them all, and that he could certainly have a year and even longer to sell them.

Eventually these jewels fetched £350,000, so that Monsieur Bark was not so far out as I thought when he put their value at half a million. The King had this large sum put in trust for the Grand Duchesses.

CHAPTER XXV

The State visit to Brussels, 1922 — The King visits the war graves

[*Early in May* 1922 *the King and Queen paid a State visit to Belgium, the first made by any British sovereign for seventy years.*]

I WAS KEPT very busy making all the arrangements for the State visit to Brussels and the subsequent tour round the graveyards in France and Belgium.

George Grahame the Ambassador in Brussels, was most businesslike and excellent, but we had had a certain amount of trouble because the King wished to do what the King of the Belgians liked and the King of the Belgians wanted to do what the King liked. The result was that no decision was ever arrived at; but I took to answering that the King only wished to do what the King of the Belgians liked, but assuming that His Belgian Majesty had no particular wishes on the subject the King proposed to do so and so. This at least had the advantage of putting up some proposal which could be knocked out if necessary.

The only real trouble we had was with the Corps Diplomatique in Brussels. The Belgians had lately been raised to the dignity of Ambassadors instead of Ministers and the whole Corps Diplomatique was on the lookout to see that this fact was not lost sight of.

According to the universal European custom I telegraphed to say that the Queen would receive only Ambassadresses and not the wives of Ministers and Chargés d'Affaires, but this had hardly been announced before trouble arose.

The Papal Nuncio, the doyen of the Corps Diplomatique, took up the case of the wives of Ministers and told Grahame that he

473

must insist on their being received by the Queen. Grahame had no alternative but to pass the message on to me and when I showed it to the King and Queen they were furious; they said they would not be dictated to by people who did not know the ABC of the business. I therefore sent a civilly worded telegram which Grahame could show to the Papal Nuncio and expressed regret that Their Majesties did not see their way to depart from the usual procedure.

This by no means satisfied the diplomats in Brussels and I received an answer to the effect that they in no way admitted that this was the usual procedure, and that they still pressed for the wives of Ministers and Chargés d'Affaires to be received. This time I laid them out with facts and quoted the precedents of Paris and Berlin before the War, to say nothing of innumerable instances in King Edward's reign. This silenced them and no more was heard of the contention.

I also had some slight trouble in cutting down the number of addresses; Grahame was most helpful in this and saw that unless we restricted the number to certain well-known institutions there would be no end.

Sir Fabian Ware,[1] who was running the whole tour round the graveyards, was quite admirable and thought of every possible contingency.

I had, however, to sit heavily on a proposal which he put forward for a French political Minister to accompany us all the time on the train; this would have been insufferable, and it would have meant the King and Haig talking French at luncheon and dinner every day.

One precaution I took was to ask Hardinge (the Ambassador in Paris) to tell the President that the King was making a private pilgrimage to the graveyards, and that His Majesty begged the President would not take the trouble to come up to the North to meet His Majesty, and merely say '*Bon jour*'.

President Millerand replied that this suited him perfectly, and that he would certainly respect the privacy of the King's visit. The

[1] A former editor of *The Morning Post;* Permanent Vice-Chairman, Imperial War Graves Commission, 1917–48.

King, I think, fancied that all this was unnecessary, but I am sure that if we had not squared the President he would have been forced to propose a meeting.

May 10th 1922 found me installed in Brussels. The suite of rooms given to me were large and luxurious apartments, which could in no case be called comfortable. I had a bedroom, a large drawing-room with seventeen upright chairs placed round the room and a tiny writing-table in the middle, and a bathroom about the size of Paddington Station with very elaborate washing appliances at different ends. The Belgians certainly do not understand the meaning of the word 'comfort'.

On the previous day I reached Victoria Station in plenty of time and talked to Beatty and Haig when I found them; then the Duke of Connaught came up and at once found mistakes in Haig's uniform, but this did not seem to worry the Field Marshal very much.

The King and Queen arrived with Princess Alice and Prince Algie,[2] and all the suite managed to get into their right carriages.

At Dover we found a crowd of bigwigs on the platform and a Guard of Honour of the Royal Irish (which, of course, was soon to be disbanded); Beauchamp,[3] the Lord Warden of the Cinque Ports, jealously watching Camden,[4] the Lord Lieutenant, to make sure that he did not go first; Lord Horne,[5] commanding the Eastern Command, and the Admiral from the Nore. There was another Guard of Honour of the Marines on the quay, and the King had to inspect both these before going on board.

The sea was like a mill pond and even the Queen, who is a very bad sailor, could find no fault with it. When we got outside the harbour the escort of destroyers joined us, three on each side and one astern, so that we looked like a miniature fleet. The Queen, who had had great experience of combating sea-sickness, took up a position amidships, which, of course, was perfectly sound tac-

2 The Earl and Countess of Athlone.
3 William Lygon, 7th Earl Beauchamp.
4 John Pratt, 4th Marquess Camden.
5 Henry Sinclair Horne, 1st Lord Horne; had commanded 1st Army in France.

tics; but as it was not only opposite the ventilator to the engine room from which a smell of oil emanated, but also just below the funnel which was emitting black smuts, I begged her to move and got some bluejackets to bring the chairs. I then walked about and found a quite ideal place for chairs in the stern, quite protected from wind, smell and smuts; but when I begged the Queen to come there she flatly refused to budge, and said that if it became rough the stern was the worst place.

So I got Haig to come there and we were joined later by Athlone. We had a deeply interesting talk, as Haig told us a great deal that was not generally known about the War. He said that of all the curiosities in the way of letters that he had had, the most curious was one from Pétain saying that Paris must be saved at all risks, and that there was nothing for it but to order the French Army to break away from the British Army and form up round Paris. This was in 1917. The situation was saved by Antoine, who finally induced Pétain to cancel the order. Haig asked what the effect would now be if this correspondence were to be published, as it would show that the French at one time seriously contemplated leaving us in the lurch.

He told us a great many interesting things, and when I asked him if these would one day be made public he merely said not by him.

As we neared Calais the King went round the yacht with Beatty and tried to decide what was to be done with all the things when it was dismantled; but, as Beatty shrewdly remarked, offering a vessel for sale and selling it are two totally different things, especially when practically no one would be able to afford to keep so large a yacht.

At Calais there was a mob of people and Ramsay (Lady Patricia's husband) came on board and helped to straighten things out; the Prefect, the Mayor, the General and the Admiral all wanted to make speeches, and in fact the Prefect began what looked like a long harangue, but the others were so keen to have a chance that the poor man was interrupted after a few minutes. Finally, the King and Queen landed and pushed their way through an army of photographers and others. There was a Guard of Honour

476

on the platform and they remained at the salute, which consisted only of putting their right arms across their bodies, as the present arms is not allowed in the French Army. The King told Reggie Seymour [6] to tell the officer in command to order arms, but he didn't know what this was in French and had to consult someone before this could be carried out.

We found the train boiling hot, and in spite of all the arrangements I had made giving a compartment to each person the suite got mixed up. Douglas Haig took someone else's compartment and Princess Alice took Mary Minto's. The luncheon was excellent, and as the train went through the devastated area Haig told us of incidents. I had taken the precaution of sending not only the King and Queen but all the suite a map of the country through which we were to pass, but of course when the King asked for one, no one had one. Reggie Seymour, who seemed to think I could produce anything at any moment, appealed to me, and I told him to ask my clerk, the incomparable Mr. Marten, who at once produced a spare one.

There was some difficulty about a Frenchman accompanying the King, and it was eventually decided that a sort of liaison officer should come from the French Army. A Colonel Oudrey was selected for this duty and turned out to be a charming man who never got in the light. He came in at the end of luncheon and was prepared to answer any question, but we had practically passed through the devastated area by then and so we didn't want any information.

At Enghien we all got out and found the Duc de Brabant,[7] Sir George Grahame (the British Ambassador) and the Belgian suite to be attached to the King. Their Majesties shook hands with all there and we returned to the train where we had tea.

Moncheur was in a terrible state about the decoration question, which always looms very large on these occasions. The King had decided to give nothing to the Minister of Foreign Affairs, M. Jaspar,[8] because he was at Genoa, and the G.C.V.O. to the Prime

---

[6] Later Sir Reginald Seymour; Equerry to King George V.
[7] Prince Leopold, later King Leopold III.
[8] Later Prime Minister.

Minister,[9] M. Theunis, because that was the usual procedure, but it appeared that this had created an awkward situation. Theunis said that he would not accept the Order as it was not high enough and Jaspar insisted on getting something. I told Moncheur that I would talk this over with the King later, and then I asked Grahame what he thought. He said that it was all a matter of jealousy, as Theunis said he was as good as Carton de Wiart [10] who, when Prime Minister, had received a G.C.M.G. We had, he thought, got into difficulties through following the foreign custom of giving decorations and yet not giving our highest ones. During the War we had given the G.C.B to Prime Ministers, and it was difficult to explain to foreigners why we now refused to do so. Jaspar had thought so much of receiving an English Order that he had already written three letters on the subject.

On arrival at Brussels we found a large concourse of people and a Guard of Honour. The King of the Belgians, who towered above everybody, being six feet four inches (although he is a good deal shorter than Grahame the Ambassador), did everything very well; he came up and shook hands with me as if I was an old friend, though he can hardly have known me by sight.

There were three carriages with postilions, and the two Kings and Beatty went in the first, the two Queens and Haig in the second. I went in the third carriage with the Grande Maîtresse de la Cour and Mary Minto, and the rest of the suite went in motors, but owing to a mistake Wigram had been left out. This was, however, easily rectified.

The crowd in the streets gave the King a very good reception, which was really remarkable considering all the trouble there had been at Genoa.[11] I was told that this was due to the tone of the Press, which had taken the line that however much the politicians

[9] 1921-5.
[10] Comte Henri Carton de Wiart, Belgian Prime Minister, 1920 and '21.
[11] The Conference held at Genoa (April-May, 1922) was the first real attempt to establish relations between the Western European Governments and the Soviet Union. It broke down partly owing to the separate treaty concluded by Germany and the Soviet Union at Rapallo, and partly owing to Belgium's demand, put forward despite British disapproval, that the Soviet Union should fully restore all foreign-owned property in Russia.

478

of both countries might squabble the two peoples, headed by their respective Kings, would always be friends.

On arrival at the Palace there were all the Government Ministers and a host of officers to be presented to the King and Queen, and then we dispersed to our rooms. It was unfortunate that my rooms should be at one end of the Palace—which was quite a quarter of a mile long—and the King's room at the other end, as it took me quite a quarter of an hour to get to His Majesty through corridors and up and down staircases.

On the night of May 9th we had a banquet which was really very well done. I found out from an official (who really did the whole thing) that we should not sit down much before 8.15, and I therefore told the King that I did not propose to be ready much before 8, but His Majesty said that he had it from the King of the Belgians that 7.30 was the proper time. The worst of a military education is that one is taught to obey blindly instructions given to one even if one has reason to suppose they are wrong. Accordingly, I appeared at 7.30 sharp and found the two Kings and Queens had already been ready for ten minutes. Cardinal Mercier [12] was allowed to join the Royal party and there we waited for three-quarters of an hour. I resisted the temptation of telling the King I was right, as he seemed in no humour for even the lightest of jests, and the King of the Belgians was even more put out. Poor man, he was suffering from acute neuritis, and the heavy shoulder cords and aiguilettes pressing on the nerves in his shoulders gave him untold pain.

Finally, we were all let loose in the banqueting hall, where 400 guests were already seated. All the arrangements were admirable and the food was good and well served.

The King of the Belgians made an impressive speech and our King replied in French. Of course, he had to read the speech, but he did very well and took plenty of time about it. Afterwards all the guests went into a long gallery and the King and Queen had notable Belgians brought up before them. I was very much impressed by Cardinal Mercier with whom I talked for some time

[12] Archbishop of Malines and formerly Professor of Philosophy at Louvain.

after dinner, and I found him quite a human being. Being so tall, he made a remarkable figure in his cardinal's robe, but the effect was a little marred by his having a red nose. I talked to politicians and civic authorities, but it is not easy on such occasions to get into anything really interesting.

When the whole thing was over I went off with Beatty and Haig to our wing, and as I was uncertain of the way I gladly accepted Beatty's offer to lead me by the shortest way to my room. Beatty said he was accustomed to use the compass and would therefore never get lost in the labyrinth of passages and staircases through which we had to pass. Haig and I therefore followed while Beatty led the way, but after we had walked ten minutes we did not seem to be getting to any familiar passages and it turned out that we had gone absolutely in the wrong direction. So we called a halt and Haig then said he would lead us and that by far the quickest way would be to go outside and walk down the front instead of threading our way again through the passages. Beatty and I agreed and we started off outside but when we got to the last big door Haig went on under the impression that even the side doors would be open. I thought this impossible and suggested to Beatty that we should wait at the big door until Haig had made certain the side door was open. Beatty who was still nettled at his failure thought he would get a bit back if Haig failed and sure enough the side door was locked and we saw Haig retracing his steps. Beatty jeered, and I then took the lead and succeeded in reaching our apartments. As I told the King next day, quite a simple thing like getting back to one's room becomes a matter of great difficulty when one is led first by a man who has commanded the British Fleet and secondly by a man who has led the biggest Army we have ever had in the field.

The next morning we went to the Tir National, which is a rifle range actually in Brussels so arranged as to prevent any bullet going astray; there the King and Queen laid a wreath on Nurse Cavell's tomb. It was quite a simple ceremony, but it aroused a great deal of feeling not only in Belgium, but also in England.

The wreath was, however, very heavy, and Colonel Lyon[13]

[13] Later Brigadier-General Francis Lyon.

(the military attaché) and I had to help Their Majesties with it. We then went to a panorama, but it was only rather good. The King and Queen went to see Prince [14] and Princess Napoleon, and those of us who were not wanted went back to the Palace.

The luncheon at the Embassy was very well done in spite of the fact that there was no Ambassadress. I sat next to M. Vander-velde,[15] the leader of the Labour Party, who was both amusing and interesting. He told me he was going to Russia to see for himself the state of the country, as he did not believe half the accounts that were issued in the Press. I told him that as far as I knew when anyone went to Russia they were invariably shown what they wanted to see: those who wanted to depict horrors were shown horrors, whereas those who maintained the country was settling down were shown a happy and contented peasantry. He said the statistics were invariably wrong, but that was not con-fined to Russia; he gave as an instance a panic that had occurred in Brussels when it was reported that 10,000 Communists, all armed and provided with big guns, were marching on the city. The police took precautions and the troops were strengthened. He, however, doubted the accuracy of the report and walked out alone to see what was happening. He found 150 men with flags and a few rifles, but no guns of any description, and after talking for an hour to the leaders the whole lot dispersed.

In the afternoon we drove escorted by cavalry to the Hôtel de Ville, and a vast crowd of people thronged the streets. It was all very well done and first we had an address read by the Burgo-master Max,[16] who seemed a great personality. The King read a reply and then we settled down to a performance which was ad-mirable—not too long—dancing at various epochs, in which nine actresses took part. The King and Queen had to give to each of

[14] Then head of Napoleon family; lived in Brussels after expulsion from France in 1886.

[15] Professor Emile Vandervelde; Belgian Foreign Minister, 1925-7 and au-thor of *Le Parti Ouvrier Belge*.

[16] Adolphe Max, Burgomaster of Brussels in 1914. The German authorities took exception to his spirited resistance and imprisoned him first at Namur and later in Germany. He was welcomed back in 1918 with unprecedented en-thusiasm.

them a brooch, and at first I was told to do it for them. But I argued that the whole point of the brooch would be lost if I gave it, and finally induced the Queen to give them as the King flatly refused to. We then went out on the balcony, where Their Majesties had a great ovation. Trumpeters were on the roof and it was most effective when one lot answered another like an echo, while the massed bands played British regimental marches.

We drove back amidst great enthusiasm to the Palace.

On the night of May 10th we had a private dinner: the two Kings and Queens, the Duc de Brabant and his sister, the highest officials of the Belgian Court, Mary Minto, Beatty and myself. The remainder of the two suites dined somewhere else. The dinner was very good and well served. Afterwards we smoked and talked till near eleven and then to bed.

The next morning there was the reception of the Foreign Ambassadors and Ministers. The practice in King Edward's reign was for all the Corps Diplomatique to be drawn up in a circle and for His Majesty to go round talking. The King, however, disliked this as he said, with a great deal of truth, that the next Ambassador or Minister would always be listening to what he was saying to the first. I therefore told Grahame to arrange the whole thing differently and to have the Corps Diplomatique in one room in their right order, so that they could be let in one by one to the room in which the King was. This apparently worked very well, and Beatty and Haig played up and talked to various Ambassadors in the ante-room.

Then we had the presentation of addresses, which is always a most tiresome business. When the deputations were ready I went to join the King. This was on paper quite easy, but in practice I found it extremely difficult, as it meant going from room to room, about five or six in all, and then making shots at the right door; some of the rooms had innumerable doors and I tried all the wrong doors first, but eventually I opened a door and found myself in the King's bedroom, where the King and Queen were waiting. They came along at once, and I was then able to direct them through the proper doors.

The presentation of addresses with replies read by the King took about half an hour. I had had some trouble in keeping the deputations small, as everyone wished to come, but when the Belgians found that we knew the game better than they did they gave no more trouble.

In the afternoon we drove in six motors to the Congo Museum, and on the way there the two Kings and Queens were subjected to a new experience in the way of photography. Although they were going at a good pace, a motor containing two photographers and a cinematograph came racing along and when level with the Royal car took snapshots and worked the cinematograph almost pointblank at them. This seemed a dangerous proceeding as the two cars, side by side, went racing down the road, and had anything been coming in the opposite direction there would certainly have been an accident.

There was a large crowd at the Museum, and the Minister of the Colonies took the King round, while the Governor of the Congo, who happened to be at home, went with the Queen. To people who are interested in Central African curiosities the Museum was no doubt interesting, but we had to rush through, followed by Press and photographers, and it was therefore difficult to stop and look at anything.

We all dined on May 11th with the Kings and Queens at a more or less private dinner, and afterwards I had a long talk with the Queen of the Belgians, who was full of life and go. I drew her out about the War, and she said that being married to a man who was quite unconscious of shell fire was no great catch. She frankly admitted that she herself hated the whole thing, but the King of the Belgians, although most considerate, could never understand her point of view. Several incidents she related were full of humour. Then the King of the Belgians came up to me, but he seemed to have exhausted his stock of small-talk, and as a general move was made I had no time to start something interesting.

Beatty, Haig, Verney and I were asked to remain behind when the others went to bed, and as we already had decorations we were given presents. These were not of a very high standard or anything near as good as the ones our King gave. I had asked for photographs and I received a signed one of the King and Queen in a special frame.

This morning we started off early on the tour round the grave-yards, and according to custom there was no ceremony, but the King of the Belgians insisted on coming to the station.

I put Reggie Seymour in charge of the train and became a passenger, merely answering conundrums and keeping my eye on the arrangements.

Sir Fabian Ware and the French officer, Colonel Oudrey, joined us. First, we went to Zeebrugge, which the King thought unnecessary as he had already been there. There were only small grave-yards, but when we got down near Ypres the number of graves became bewildering.

In order to please the Belgians, and at the same time not go out of our way to visit any Belgian cemeteries, the King gave a wreath to a Belgian General and asked him to place it on the tombs of the brave Belgian soldiers.

This all went very well in spite of the fact that the crowd was under no control and pressed forward round the King. The architect showed a plan of the new Messines Gate it was proposed to erect in memory of the dead whose bodies had never been found.

We were hard at it during the last two days, motoring miles and miles through the devastated districts and stopping at various cemeteries. The procedure when we stopped was for the officers in charge of the district and the gardeners from the surrounding cemeteries to be drawn up. The King then shook hands with all of them and then went round the cemetery accompanied only by the officer under whose charge the particular cemetery was, and the gardner or gardeners in charge. The difficulty was the Prefects and Mayors, who always wanted to make long speeches. This is where Colonel Oudrey, our French officer, came in; when a man looked like making a speech we whispered *'Discours!'* to Oudrey, who at once tackled the man and tactfully stopped it.

The visit to the French cemetery was most impressive, principally because the King, on the spur of the moment, hit upon the idea of having a two-minute silence after he had placed the wreath.

Marshal Foch came with Weygand,[17] and it was most interesting to see Foch and Haig sharing a map and pointing out places of interest to the King.

We were most comfortable in the train but, of course, the presence of the French officer prevented the conversation being quite as outspoken as it would have been. He was a charming man with a keen sense of humour, but he did not talk English and this often necessitated the whole conversation being in French, which neither Haig nor the King was very good at.

[17] Later General (Maxime) Weygand. Chef d'État-Major du Maréchal Foch, 1914–23; Commander-in-Chief French Army, 1940; Vichy Governor of Algeria, 1941; then imprisoned by Germans.

CHAPTER XXVI

Some opinions on secret treaties, Strachey's 'Queen Victoria', the Lansdowne letter and post-war France — Lord Milner, Lord Curzon and the Garter — Bonar Law's game of chess — Charles Cust's death — The King's shooting — The King at Eastbourne

SOME TIME IN 1921 I had an interesting talk at Balmoral with Soveral, the Archbishop of York,[1] Esher, Sir Walter Lawrence[2] and John Revelstoke.

Soveral told me that when the publication of the Treaty with Germany[3] relating to the Portuguese Colonies was contemplated by Sir E. Grey at the beginning of 1914, he protested in vain. Finding that his efforts were useless, he took steps to ensure that the French were informed of the proposed publication, and Poincaré, who was then President, took such a serious view of the matter that the idea of publication was abandoned. It was only Grey's dislike of secret treaties that made him ever contemplate the publication.

This interested me, as I remembered that when the King was going to Paris in the spring of 1914, Wickham Steed, then foreign editor of *The Times,* got wind of this and asked me whether there was any truth in the report, as any understanding with Germany would certainly upset the French.

Talking of Strachey's *Queen Victoria,*[4] the Archbishop of York said that it had rehabilitated her in the eyes of the present genera-

[1] The Most Reverend Cosmo Lang; later (1928) Archbishop of Canterbury.
[2] 1st Bart.; a distinguished Indian Civil Servant.
[3] In August 1898, a secret treaty was concluded between Britain and Germany, providing for the partition of Portuguese Colonies in Africa if Portugal were forced to alienate them owing to financial difficulties.
[4] Lytton Strachey's *Queen Victoria* was published in 1921.

tion. They had begun to sneer at that period and criticize adversely the big people of that time. They welcomed, therefore, the ironical methods of Strachey's pen and were ready to abide by his version of the Queen. They were surprised to find that in spite of all his irony, so far from belittling the Queen, he brought into strong relief her great personality.

Esher said that Lloyd George had stated that in his opinion a cheap edition of this book would have a derogatory effect on the monarchy. The Archbishop agreed, as he said 'Demos' had never quite understood the criticism of the Victorian age in any case.

Talking of Lansdowne's notorious letter to the *Daily Telegraph,* the Archbishop said that there was now a great deal to be said in favour of it; Lansdowne's great knowledge of European politics had warned him that a fight to a finish would entail the dismemberment of the Austrian Empire and the bankruptcy of Central Europe. He had foreseen that this would eventually mean the German part of Austria joining Germany. Had peace been made at that time Europe would have been far more capable of recuperation than it actually was. Lansdowne had told the Archbishop that history would judge, and in years to come it would be found that he was right.

Esher said it was a high-minded, disinterested action on Lansdowne's part; but it was badly stage-managed, ill timed and not well explained.

In reply to our contention that France was now being unreasonable, Esher said we must remember that France lived in constant terror of a resuscitated Germany. She had originally asked that the Rhine might be made the frontier, but the other Powers would not agree to this; then she had agreed to give up this scheme on the understanding that America and England would stand by her in a defensive alliance. As this had now fallen through she saw herself left to the tender mercies of Germany. Speaking of Germany's recuperative powers, Esher said that not only were they all working like niggers, but that as we had relieved them of the great expense of an army and navy they were far better off than France and ourselves.

Sir Walter Lawrence thought the French Press unreasonable,

and Esher pointed out that it in no way reflected the opinions of the French people. He said that the whole system was different in France and people who wrote articles paid to have them inserted. Almost any policy would be advocated in the Press if sufficient money was paid.

John Revelstoke told us that in 1911 he was the British representative on some international loan conference, on which all the European Powers were represented. It was agreed that the Press of each country should be asked to boom the loan. This he succeeded in doing in England for £1,500; in France the cost was £60,000.

When Lord Milner was given the Order of the Garter it never occurred to him that there was any difficulty about how it should be worn. He had to attend a Levee, and when he dressed he was faced by the problem over which shoulder should the riband go. As there was no time to ask anyone's advice he decided to wear it like the Order of the Bath, over the right shoulder; but the Garter, the Thistle and the St. Patrick differ from all other Orders, as they are worn over the left shoulder. Quite unconscious that he was wearing his riband over the wrong shoulder he appeared in the antechamber at St. James's Palace, where everyone assembles. There, unfortunately, he met George Curzon, who was scandalized at his ignorance; so strongly, in fact, did Curzon feel that after the Levee he wrote Milner a letter saying that it was almost inconceivable that anyone who had been given this ancient Order, the highest Order in the land, should not even take the trouble to ascertain how it was worn.

It happened some months later that one of the Levees at St. James's Palace happened to come on a collar day. Collar days are certain Saints' days and festivals on which, according to the ancient statutes, the knights of the various orders of chivalry wear the collar of their Orders, but on such occasions the riband is not worn because the badge is attached to the collar. This is a constant source of trouble to eminent men, who are inclined to be vague about their dress. George Curzon, who was very busy at the time, came rather late to the Levee and only arrived in the Throne

Room just before the King arrived; so it was not noticed that he was committing the most heinous offence of wearing a riband *as well as* a collar. Of course, the King observed this at once but made little of it, only chaffing Curzon about the mistake; Milner, who was also present, heard these remarks and afterwards wrote to Curzon, repeating nearly word for word that it was almost inconceivable that anyone who had been given this ancient Order, etc. etc.

In April 1921 Bonar Law and his daughter came to stay at Windsor Castle from Saturday to Monday. I knew him slightly and had once or twice played bridge with him. Although reserved and difficult to know, he became quite human when he thawed and had a great sense of humour. After his son was killed in the war he gave up going out into society and never went anywhere except to the House of Commons.

It was four years after his son's death when he came to Windsor and so he had more or less recovered from his grief.

On Sunday the King said to me that he and the Queen were motoring to see somebody, and I was therefore to find out what Bonar Law would like to do and make the necessary arrangements. I asked Bonar Law to say frankly what he would like most to do. Would he like to go round the pictures and furniture? But he said this would bore him. I then suggested the library, but he said that he would want a week at least to see this even superficially. He would rather go out. I suggested the farms, but he said this would be worse than the pictures. After I had exhausted all the usual sights with no success, I said he had better propose something himself. He said he would like to go for a drive in the park with his daughter, and I replied that nothing would be easier.

I asked whether he would care to play bridge when he returned, but he said he had quite given up cards, and added that what he would really like was a game of chess. He warned me, however, that it was no use asking him to play 'bumble-puppy' chess, as that was tiresome. He had of late years studied chess very thoroughly and now invariably played with professionals, but of course he could not expect anything of this sort at Windsor; all he asked was someone who could play a first-class game. I said I quite understood and would arrange all this.

I went away and ordered the carriage, but scratched my head over the chess. My own chess was infantile and therefore out of the question, and although I knew that some of the Household played chess, I was quite sure that their games came under the head of 'bumble-puppy' and that it was waste of time to ask them to take on Bonar Law. It suddenly occurred to me that Sir Walter Parratt had in his day been a first-rate player, and that I remembered his telling me that he found all the chess problems in the newspapers never took him more than ten minutes to solve.

So I wrote a note to him asking him to come and play Bonar Law at chess soon after six; that is, after the evening service at St. George's Chapel. Then a short scribble to Bonar Law explaining who Parratt was. When I thought I had arranged everything I found there was some difficulty about the board and chessmen. There were innumerable and valuable sets under glass cases, but a common or garden board seemed impossible to find. I consulted Derek Keppel, the Master of the Household, and he at once started his myrmidons on the scent of one. Eventually, an ordinary set was found in the cupboard of the room that was formerly where Princess Mary worked with her governess.

Keppel arranged a charming setting for the game with a small table, two comfortable arm-chairs and shaded electric light lamps.

I went to the room soon after six and talked to Bonar Law. When Parratt came in I introduced them and while a footman handed cigars and offered tea or coffee Bonar Law whispered in my ear: 'Isn't my opponent a bit old?' I merely replied that he knew the game; as a matter of fact, Parratt was 80 or more. So I left them.

I heard afterwards that they played in dead silence for an hour and that Parratt then said: *'That* is checkmate.' Bonar Law replied: 'Not at all, I have seven different moves.' 'Precisely,' said Parratt, 'but if you move one, I do so and so. Checkmate. If you move two, I do so and so; again checkmate.' He went through the whole seven moves and described what would happen in each case.

Bonar Law studied this for twenty minutes and then said:

'That is right.' I told the King and, not very tactfully, when His Majesty came to dinner he said to Bonar Law: 'I hear old Parratt beat your head off at chess.' Bonar Law merely said he had had a very interesting game.

Poor Charles Cust's death in 1931 was a great blow to the King and all the Household felt the loss. His great charm was that he was so offensively rude to people he didn't like, and when therefore his face lit up and his blue eyes sparkled when he met one, there was no doubt at all that he was pleased. The impostor, the swaggerer, were his particular 'bêtes noires' and he never made any attempt to conceal his dislike. Curiously, the rabbit type he was always kind to, and he generally found in such men unexpected qualities quite alien to their rodent nature. Little children delighted him and flocked to him naturally, while many grown-ups approached him with utmost caution. To the King he was invaluable; he never hesitated to speak his mind bluntly and even brutally, but His Majesty knew him so well that he never minded even being flatly contradicted by him. I remember soon after the King had ascended the throne, Cust was seated in the billiards-room at Balmoral looking at books from the London and Times Libraries, which he had piled on the floor in front of him. The King came in and said: 'I say, Charles, is that the way you treat my books?'

Cust replied: '*Your* books! Why, you haven't in the whole of this house got a book that's worth reading. Your so-called library is nothing but beautifully bound piffle.'

Later, the King repeated this to me and asked me whether it was true. I told him that this was an accurate description of the library; it had been the practice during both Queen Victoria's and King Edward's reigns to put there presentation books which were usually quite unreadable, the best ones having been sent to the library at Windsor. His Majesty said he had not had time to look at the books in the library, but if this was the case a certain sum every year should be devoted to the purchase of interesting Scottish books and the worthless ones should be weeded out.

[*In November* 1928 *the King fell seriously ill with a lung complaint which affected his heart. His recovery was slow and incomplete*]

After his illness the King was told not to overtire himself out shooting, and therefore rode on a shooting pony from covert to covert. Sometimes, when we were walking up ground covered with bracken and gorse, it was impossible for him to take part. He used to go ahead on his pony and station himself where he might possibly get a woodcock.

On one of these occasions I was walking down a grass ride. I had been warned that His Majesty was on ahead and told that it was quite safe to shoot on the left of the ride but on no account on the right, as his exact position was uncertain.

A woodcock got up in front of me and I waited until it had got clearly to the left of the ride and then shot it. Prince George,[5] who was the gun on my left, shouted something at me, but as I did not quite catch what he said I asked one of the keepers who was walking with me what it was. The keeper replied: 'I understood His Royal Highness to say "Regicide".'

[*In December* 1934 *the King caught a bad cold and cough at Sandringham. He recovered, but was now very easily tired.*]

The King, on the advice of Lord Dawson, determined to go to Eastbourne for three weeks, so as to get away from fogs in London during February. Sandringham was impossible owing to the cold east winds. The Duke of Devonshire offered to lend His Majesty Compton Place, which would ensure privacy. We came to the conclusion that both the King and the Queen would be intensely bored there, and arrangements were made for a cinema to be installed. This could be made ready at short notice, and the King had only to say when he wanted to see a film.

I went down there to talk over with the King various problems relating to the Silver Jubilee. Before I left London I received a curious message that I was to come in time for tea, as the film

[5] Later Duke of Kent.

493

Lives of a Bengal Lancer was to be shown at six; also, did I like oysters? I duly arrived in time for tea, but was mystified by the query about oysters. It turned out that the King strongly objected to plates of oysters being wasted and that on the first night three of the Household had refused to eat them. Therefore it was necessary to ascertain beforehand whether everyone ate them.

The King had explained to me that he had brought very few servants, but when the cinema took place and the servants were allowed to come I found there were forty-five. I wondered how many there would have been if the King had not expressed the wish to have a few. There were no pages and we were waited on by six red-coated footmen, but whether this made any difference to the total number I do not know. The King had not quite thrown off the effects of his chill, which may have been a form of influenza, and was not inclined to talk at dinner; but the Queen was excellent and kept the ball rolling well.

[*The author was created* 1st *Lord Sysonby in the Birthday Honours of* 1935, *and died suddenly on October* 20th, 1935, *exactly three months before King George V.*]

The End

INDEX

INDEX